THE REACTIONARY REVOLUTION

The Catholic Revival in French Literature, 1870–1914

THE REACTIONARY REVOLUTION

THE CATHOLIC REVIVAL
IN FRENCH LITERATURE
1870–1914

by

RICHARD GRIFFITHS

*Fellow of Selwyn College
Cambridge*

CONSTABLE
LONDON

Published by
Constable and Company Ltd.
10–12 Orange Street, London W.C.2

Copyright © 1966 Richard Griffiths

First published 1966

PQ295.N279 G8 1966

Subjects:
1. French literature—history and criticism.
2. French literature—Catholic authors—
   history and criticism.

Printed in England by
C. Tinling & Co. Ltd.,
Liverpool, London and Prescot.

To the memory of

Louis Massignon
Donald Beves
Humphry Trevelyan

Masters and Friends

Contents

vii

Preface

THOUGH this book is a study primarily concerned with literature, it naturally includes much which impinges on the field of the historian, particularly of the ecclesiastical historian. For it is, above all, an attempt to explain certain elements in the literature of the period 1870–1914, elements which may all too easily remain incomprehensible until placed in the context of contemporary events and trends of thought.

It is dangerous to think in generalities; the great authors of the Catholic literary revival, Huysmans, Bloy, Péguy, Jammes, Claudel, are in many respects completely unlike each other and their contemporaries. Nevertheless, even in these authors there are many things in common which remain difficult for the modern reader to understand, until they are placed in the context of their time. It has been the author's task, therefore, to trace certain of the common characteristics of the Catholic thought of the period, particularly as they were reflected in literature. In the process, no attempt has been made to cover the major authors in their entirety, but only in so far as they are affected by these trends; little purpose would be served by a series of individual studies, particularly of the major authors, on whom the critical literature is already so immense. The minor Catholic authors of the period have, on the other hand, occasionally been studied rather more than their literary merit would justify, usually because they illustrate admirably a trend which might remain puzzling in the form in which it appears in Péguy, Claudel, or any other major writer. Adolphe Retté is a good example of a writer whose literary merit is almost nil, but who illustrated at their most extreme certain tendencies of contemporary Catholic thought.

The primary function of this book, then, is the placing of certain Catholic authors of the period is relation one to another, and the explanation of certain characteristics of their work. Individual studies of these authors have often neglected this more general aspect, and the general literary histories of the period have fallen into two traps; firstly, that of proceeding author by author, producing thumbnail sketches with little coherence, and secondly, that of presuming that the word Catholic can be taken as a synonym of literary excellence. (An exception to this is Miss Elizabeth Fraser's *Le Renouveau Religieux d'après le Roman Français de 1886 à 1914*, an interesting and useful work which, however, uses the term 'religious' in a very broad sense, and treats of all the reactions against nineteenth century materialism, with little differentiation of the effects of the various religious doctrines.)

I am not a Roman Catholic, though I am extremely sympathetic to that religion; I hope that I have erred neither on one side nor the other, but that a balanced view of the literature of the period may have emerged from my work.

I would like, above all, to thank Monsieur Pierre Lambert, both for placing his magnificent collection of books and manuscripts at my disposal, and for the great stores of advice and information which he was always so ready to provide.

I would also like to pay tribute to the late Professor Louis Massignon, who originally inspired the writing of this book, and whose recent death left a gap in the world of international scholarship which can never fully be refilled.

Many other people have most generously given help and advice. I wish particularly to thank Mme. Catherine Backès, M. Jean-Louis Backès, Mr. Renford Bambrough, Mr. Alan Bell, Father Maurice Belval, S.J., Father André Blanchet, S.J., Dr. Robert Bolgar, M. Pierre Claudel, Mr. John Coombes, Mr. Maurice Cowling, M. Gilbert Gadoffre, Maître Maurice Garçon, M. Henri Gouhier, Father Raymond Halter, M. Gabriel-Ursin Langé, M. Henry Lefai, M. Henri Massis, Dr. Edward Norman, M. Émile Poulat, the late M. Jean Tremblot de la Croix, Dr. Alec Vidler and Dr. Michael Wood.

Many thanks are due to the Master and Fellows of Selwyn College for the opportunities which they so generously provided for the research from which the present volume has sprung.

R.M.G.

PART ONE

Introduction and Some General Characteristics

CHAPTER ONE

General Introduction

CATHOLIC literature is not necessarily the same thing as literature written by Catholics[1]. For a great many Catholics (as for a great many Anglicans, Jews, deists, positivists) the writing of a literary work has not automatically involved a deep concern with matters of faith. Compendia of Catholic literature, compiled by pious and well-meaning critics, have too often jumbled together writers whose sole point of contact is the fact that they are Catholics. The Catholic literary revival which took place in France at the end of the nineteenth century has suffered much not only from becoming intermingled with non-religious literature written by Catholics, and with literature written against a backcloth of religious beliefs, but with no specifically religious preoccupations in subject or treatment; it has also been stuffed willy-nilly into the same pigeon-hole as pious literature of a very different type, representative of a far older tradition.

What was the Catholic literary revival? If we strip away other elements we find a hard core of writers in whom, for the first time in two centuries, a deep involvement in religious matters was associated with works of literary value. The novel, poetry, and later the theatre, began in the 1880's to turn to religious subjects. In the novel it was a reaction against positivism, materialism and naturalism which contributed towards this trend. In poetry the same reaction led to the consuming interest, on the part of so many poets of the nineteenth century, in the question of an *au-delà* which, in different manners, it was poetry's duty to seek out and portray. This culminated in certain cases in a religious involvement. Religious symbolism became one particularly evocative, if over-stylised, form of poetic symbolism. God took the place of the Idea. In the plays of Claudel this religious form of symbolism achieved a success which had never been reached by the symbolist theatre itself.

On the literary front the movement is important for this very injection of new values, new preoccupations and even new stylistic

3

qualities; and it was by a strong religious involvement that such *literary* changes took place. A writer like Bazin might continue to write in an essentially Balzacian medium, despite a tinge of sentimentality absent from that master; Paul Féval might continue the tradition of Dumas; but such writers continue in these older modes mainly because, in their works, their religion is an accepted background rather than a burning actuality. Where Bazin portrays an ordinary action in a Christian setting, writers like Huysmans and Bloy depict an extraordinary action in which certain Christian super-realities have their part. The mystical and the miraculous are the elements which make up the literary and the religious originality of the works of the Revival proper.

If the movement is important on the literary front, it is extremely interesting in the political and religious fields too, for its reflection of certain unexpected trends among the Catholic *élite* of the time. The novels, the poetry and the theatre of this era, even when written by Catholics not of the Revival, were almost unanimous in taking an intransigent, reactionary attitude in relation to matters of both faith and politics. In almost every field the attempts at compromise made by certain of their Catholic predecessors and contemporaries were dismissed out of hand, as the writers entrenched themselves more and more firmly in the most extreme positions. The great revival of Catholic literature, therefore, and the immense spate of conversions among the literary *élite* from the 1880's right up to the First World War, were in fact a form of literary and social revolution. But in the intransigent tenacity with which these writers held to views which had seemed to many out-of-date even at the beginning of the century, the revolution showed itself to be in this sense a reaction of the Right.

In the earlier part of the nineteenth century there had been manifestations, in various Catholic fields, of a common concern to bring the Church and the Catholic faith into line with the modern world and with modern man. Chateaubriand, faced with the unbelief produced by the eighteenth century, had attempted to persuade people of the value of the Christian faith by an appeal to their emotions, and by calling on them to feel rather than to understand. The important thing, for him, was to show the beauty of the Catholic religion, rather than to demonstrate its truth. Bonald, and to a certain extent de Maistre, despite their reactionary views upon other matters, had attempted to use reason as the main support towards putting forward Christian ideas; Bonald claimed the truth of Christian conclusions by the fact that they coincided with those produced by purely human and pragmatic reasoning. In the political field, Lamennais saw the future of the Church as lying in an understanding with the moving political forces of the nineteenth century, democracy and the people (though he did not realise that they do not always mean the same thing). Social problems were approached by Lacordaire and Ozanam in the same spirit.

Towards the end of the century this desire to bring the Church into line with the modern world extended itself to other fields as well. A compromise with the forces of science, which had been advocated by such men as Vogüé and the abbé de Broglie, led to the experiments in biblical exegesis made by Loisy, and the new approach to Church history exemplified by the abbé Duchesne. Similarly, in the field of philosophy, men such as Blondel, Le Roy and Laberthonnière tried to bring Catholic belief more into line with what they considered to be acceptable to the mind of modern man; they glossed over the idea of transcendental revelation, and attempted to show that the proofs of transcendental truth were immanent in man himself. Thus did Catholicism, for these men, become identified with the individualism so necessary to nineteenth-century rationalist philosophy.

But the men of the Revival of the end of the century would have none of this. They avoided the sentimentalism of Chateaubriand and the Romantic Catholics, the rationalism of Bonald and de Maistre, the liberalism of Lamennais, and the modernism of their contemporaries. Their ideal was a return to what they considered to be the traditional values of the Church, and their practical method was a renunciation of any form of compromise with any of the forces which were opposed to this aim.

To a certain extent they reflect a continuation, in the literary field, of one of the sides in the controversy which had racked the Church in the time of the Second Empire. Just as Veuillot, in the political field, had summoned all his forces of intransigence to bear on the enemies of the Church, and had scorned any form of moderation such as was preached by liberal Catholics of the type of Dupanloup and Falloux, so these writers continued this tradition, but not merely in the sphere of the Church's political action.

It would be a mistake to wish to make use of the terms Ultra-

montane and Gallican extensively in reference to this period. After
1870 there was little left in the way of Gallicanism; indeed, the
nearest approach to it, and that a distant one, would seem to have
been Pope Leo XIII's own attempts at understanding with the
secular power; and this is Gallican only in its Erastian concept of
the Church in France. The Council of 1870 was the final blow to
Gallicanism, which had already been severely weakened by
events earlier in the century, and by the very different sorts of
allegiance which it had commanded. Lamennais, for example,
had been ultramontane because of his desire to serve the best
interests of the Church, and to detach it from an Erastian link with
a reactionary State, in order to forge a new one with the people;
but later in the century, with a more reactionary pope and with a
more liberal régime in France, the intransigent Catholics were far
more connected with the cause of Ultramontanism, and the liberal
Catholics were identified with what remained of Gallicanism. The
triumph of Pius IX's policies at the 1870 Council meant the
temporary success of intransigent policies, but the permanent
success of Ultramontanism.

The Catholic literary revival, however, began at the very time
when the policies of Pius IX were, in many spheres, being
amended, if not reversed, in the more liberal pontificate of Leo
XIII. It was a time, too, when the main reactionary Church figures
of the Second Empire had died, or faded from power. Louis
Veuillot had resigned from his newspaper *L'Univers* in 1879, and
died in 1883; Monseigneur Pie had died in 1881; and the Comte
de Chambord, the legitimist heir to the French throne, died in
1883. Added to this Leo XIII had already, in the 1880's, begun the
series of encyclicals promulgating moderate policies, some of them
directed at France itself—*Nobilissima Gallorum Gens* (1884),
Immortale Dei (1885), *Libertas* (1888), *Rerum Novarum* (1891), *Au
milieu des sollicitudes* (1892). The message of these encyclicals was
followed by a small but significant part of the French Church. But,
while one might not expect the vast majority of ignorant peasant
laymen or country priests to follow quickly or easily these new
doctrines against which they had been inoculated so effectively by
the interpretation which many of their superiors had put upon
Pius IX's encyclical *Quanta Cura* and its *Syllabus of Errors* (1864),
it is extremely interesting to see, among the artistic and literary
élite of the country, not merely a slowness in accepting the new

ideas, but a positive rejection of them, a rejection which was to continue as one of the main elements in Catholic literature right up to the First World War.

This reaction was not confined merely to the political plane. The mistrust of science, and the fear of the positivist ideas which appeared to stem from it, led in most of the Catholic writers of the time to a rejection not merely of intellectualism but of the use of the intellect itself in religious matters. This anti-rationalism, as it became, manifested itself as a belief based entirely upon divine revelation, and to a great extent upon miraculous revelation. The mystical element in the Catholic religion became elevated to an even more important position than it normally holds, and in the early stages of the Revival the rather extreme eschatological concepts of certain sects, such as that of Vintras, and of certain writers, such as Hello, had a great effect upon the more unbalanced of the authors of the time.

Rationalism in religion was suspect to all but a few, of whom Bourget is the only truly important creative writer; and Leo XIII's call for a renewal of Christian philosophy on the model of St. Thomas Aquinas, while it affected certain priests, theologians and philosophers, culminating just before the Great War with Maritain, nevertheless had little effect on creative literature.[2]

Their reaction against rationalism, however, did not prevent these writers from accepting with joy the results reached by certain philosophers of the earlier part of the century, results which did much to back up their own emotionally arrived at reactionary views. It is thus that Bonald and de Maistre's political views, together with those of the philosopher Blanc de Saint-Bonnet (1815–80) and the Spanish exile Donoso-Cortès (1809–53), had immense influence in this period, as did also the economic and political views of the sociologist Le Play (1808–82). Though their methods of reaching their opinions were not copied, the opinions themselves are quoted with approval by such diverse people as Huysmans, Bloy, Baumann, Bourget, Barrès and Maurras.

The Revival itself was a movement of immense enthusiasm, in which most of the prominent figures were recent converts. As such, these authors often went to extremes not only in the political field, but also in that of Catholic doctrine. They stressed many of those aspects of the Catholic faith which are most difficult for an unbeliever to stomach, and, in a reaction against the sentimentalism

B   7

of so much nineteenth-century Catholicism, they stressed the harsh nature of Christianity as they saw it. Seeing themselves as a minority group, not only in the country as a whole, but also among their fellow-Catholics, they laid greater weight upon these differences than upon any common ground by which they might influence others towards their own views.

In the 1880's a Catholic Revival, though it would not have appeared so to the average man of the time, was only to be expected. Two centuries of unbelief (or, at best, deism) in intellectual circles, culminating in the positivist excesses of the Second Empire, could not but produce, eventually, a strong reaction; and that this reaction should take place primarily in the world of literature, where imagination and sensibility have so great a part to play, is not surprising. The vast claims of positivism were the last straw of a load which had been building up since the days of the *philosophes*; and in the space of a few years the complete refusal to accept the fact that a man could be intelligent *and* a Catholic—a prejudice which had grown up in the positivist reign at the Sorbonne—had been reversed in popular opinion, thanks mainly to the new literature they had been reading, and to the examples, continually before their eyes, of the conversions of great men.

Before the 1880's there had been little Catholic writing of value in the realm of pure literature, or, as the French call it, 'la grande littérature'. Chateaubriand's *Le Génie du Christianisme* (1802) and *Les Martyrs* (1809) had been a magnificent start to the century, but from then onwards the more important of those writings which were specifically Catholic (for though some of the Romantics leaned at one time or another towards some form of religious feeling, this tended on the whole to be a vague form of deism) were theological or political works, in the form of pamphlets or philosophical treatises. Bonald, de Maistre, Ballanche, Lamennais, Frayssinous, Nettement, Ozanam, Montalembert, all wrote, from their differing points of view, works of great importance in this form; but the interest of these works is not primarily literary. By the 1840's, too, examples are already appearing of that violent polemical journalism which was such a feature of Catholic writing in mid-century, with Louis Veuillot in *L'Univers*, and a whole array of liberal Catholics, of whom stylistically one of the most remarkable was Falloux, in *Le Correspondant*. But though Veuillot wrote a couple of novels, these were negligible from the point of view of literary value, and had little success; they are of interest to us only in relation to his later view that it was impossible to write such a thing as a Catholic novel.

Other elements of interest in Catholic expression were the sermons preached by various eminent priests, and above all those preached by Lacordaire in Notre-Dame de Paris in the years 1835–7. In these sermons Lacordaire broke loose from much of what was bad in Catholic oratorical expression, and indirectly paved the way for a new approach to the spoken and written word in Catholic circles. Beside him, however, there were not only the ornate, stylised and dead expression of the traditional Catholic orator, but also, in a multitude of minor works of Catholic piety, the over-sentimentality which is a perpetual danger in less educated religious literature. These works of piety can claim no place in a history of literature, but are of keen interest to the social historian. They, and a tradition of pious poetry which has little in the way of literary aspiration, remain present in Catholic circles right up to our own time.

The only Catholic literary works of importance in this first half of the century[3] were the very small literary output of Maurice de Guérin, and the letters and journal of his sister, Eugénie. These continued the tradition of religious sentimentalism which we found in Chateaubriand, and one wonders what literary attention either Maurice or Eugénie would have received had there been any other Catholic authors of any weight writing at the same time.

During the Second Empire there was little in the way of opposition to the overwhelming influence of the realist novel, except the sentimental, idealistic novels of Octave Feuillet, a writer of little literary value who nevertheless gained quite a large reading public. Feuillet was a Catholic, but his Catholicism had little to do with the sentiments portrayed in these novels, the most famous of which is the *Roman d'un jeune homme pauvre* (1858). Feuillet's brand of sickly sentiment was nevertheless one of the few exceptions to the new type of novel-writing, together with the historical novels of Paul Féval (1817–87), whose late conversion had little more effect than to make him attempt to withdraw un-Catholic remarks and situations from what are essentially Romantic historical novels in the Dumas tradition. Neither the works of Feuillet nor those of Féval come under the term 'Catholic literature' as it was defined at the beginning of this chapter.

With Barbey d'Aurevilly (1808–89), however, we come to something which can more easily be classed under that heading. This author had been writing novels of a wild, Romantic nature since 1834; in him there was much that was typical both of the early Romanticism of the 1830's, and of its more violent continuation towards the end of the century which Signor Mario Praz has studied in his book *The Romantic Agony*. Suddenly, in the mid-60's, Barbey turned his attention to the Catholic religion; he wrote a novel, *Un Prêtre Marié* (1865), which revolved around a specifically religious subject, and he wrote a new Preface (1866) to one of his former works, *Une Vieille Maîtresse* (1851), claiming it to be a work of Christian inspiration and of Christian morality. This is unconvincing when one looks at the work itself, but the fact remains that from then on Barbey's intentions were supposedly Catholic. It is only when one looks more closely at the works written from these years onward, and particularly at *Un Prêtre Marié* and *Les Diaboliques* (1874), that one sees Barbey's Catholicism to be essentially one more consciously Romantic trait, used almost entirely for purposes of literary effect, rather than for a balanced sharing of literary and religious effects strengthened by religious conviction, such as we shall find in what we have agreed to call the Catholic Revival proper. Barbey uses Catholicism; but he remains essentially the same author as before his conversion.

Among those whom we shall find, a few years later, following this same line of Romantic Catholicism, or rather Catholic Romanticism, are authors such as Villiers de l'Isle Adam (1840–89), and 'Sâr' Joséphin Péladan (1858–1918).

Apart from Barbey d'Aurevilly, the Second Empire is remarkable for the first emergence of the writer Ernest Hello (1828–85), whose *M. Renan: L'Allemagne et l'Athéisme au XIXe siècle* (1858), struck a blow both at the German philosophy which was invading France, and also at the positivist ideas of Comte, Taine and Renan which were already beginning to rule French thought. This early work by Hello is somewhat different from his later works— *Le Jour du Seigneur* (1870), *L'Homme* (1872), *Paroles de Dieu* (1878), *Contes Extraordinaires* (1879),—in which the defence of religion against the attacks of science is intermingled with various mystical ideas of somewhat doubtful value. And in his own personal influence on certain writers, such as Bloy, Hello (who often dared not put into print his wilder fantasies) was one of the

people most instrumental in introducing, in the first years of the
Revival, those elements of a somewhat false mysticism which all
but turned it into the wrong path.

Veuillot, Hello and Blanc de Saint-Bonnet are perhaps the three
writers of the Second Empire who most influenced, in very different ways, the Revival of Catholic literature which began to show
its first glimmering of light in the late 1870's and early 1880's.
Veuillot's intransigence, violence, and cutting polemical style,
Hello's rejection of the 'Reign of Science' and his preoccupation
with the more extreme forms of mysticism, and Blanc de Saint-
Bonnet's partisanship of legitimism, infallibility, and a hierarchical
society based on work, the family, and a Christian acceptance of
suffering—all these things were reflected to a greater or lesser
extent in the Catholic authors who followed them. Barbey
d'Aurevilly's literary influence was less lasting, though the writers
of the Revival admired him greatly, ignoring, or feigning to ignore,
the dilettantism of his religious belief. Such widely differing people
as Léon Bloy, Bourget and Péladan were among his group of
youthful admirers, and the praise accorded to him by Huysmans
(albeit in his pre-conversion work '*À Rebours*) reflects the adulation
of a generation.

It was Barbey d'Aurevilly who fired the admiration of this
younger generation for Blanc de Saint-Bonnet, whom he saw as
one of the true 'prophets of the past' in the line of de Maistre,
Bonald, etc. It was Barbey, too, who was the cause of the conversion of the young Léon Bloy in 1869, a conversion which was to
have immense consequences.

For about ten years after his conversion Léon Bloy (1846–1917)
produced nothing in the way of important literary works; two
minor books and a mass of articles were his main output in this
period. It was in the 1880's, after what he considered to be a major
mystical crisis in the years 1878–82, that Bloy produced the first
of the works which one associates most readily with his name—
Le Révélateur du Globe (1884), a mystical study of Christopher
Columbus, and his great autobiographical novel *Le Désespéré*
(1886). This book was a milestone in the history of the French
Catholic novel, and was the first of a series of autobiographical
religious novels which were to include those of Huysmans, as well
as Bloy's own later *La Femme Pauvre* (1897).

Bloy was a man of violence, in every sphere of his life, and this violence is reflected in his works. In the mystical sphere, above all, many of his exaggerations were to bring the Revival dangerously near to heresy. But his violence is that of his age, and his intransigence a reflection of the religious intensity of many of his contemporaries, who were converts like himself.

The explosion of Catholic literature in the 1880's extended to all *genres*. In 1880 the poet Paul Verlaine (1844–96) produced a volume of Catholic poetry, *Sagesse*, which was followed in 1888 by a new collection, *Amour*. While a great deal of this poetry does not match the excellence of his secular poetry, it is certainly a great advance on previous Catholic poetry of the century, and has its moments of genius. It paved the way, also, for the Catholic poetry of Germain Nouveau (1852–1920) and eventually for the writings of Francis Jammes (1868–1938), which, though so very different in their calm simplicity from the rather self-conscious gestures of Verlaine, nevertheless owe much to the freeing of Catholic poetry by that author from the insipidity of pious musings.

In 1886, the same year as *Le Désespéré*, Vicomte Eugène-Melchior de Vogüé had produced his study of the Russian novel, *Le Roman Russe*, in which he had made his famous plea for a novel free from the shackles of naturalism, a mystical novel which would deal with things of the spirit as well as the flesh. The young naturalist author Huysmans (1848–1907), who had already begun to rebel against the theories of his master Zola in the novel *À Rebours* (1884), seeking release from naturalist technique by escape into the realm of aesthetic experience, echoed the sentiments of Vogüé in the first pages of his next novel *Là-bas* (1891), in which he attempted to combine two plots on different planes into a 'spiritualisme naturaliste'. The researches into occultism and satanism which formed so great a part of this book were the first steps on the path which led Huysmans to that conversion which he was to describe in *En Route* (1895).

In these same years another great religious literary event was the publication of Paul Bourget's novel *Le Disciple* (1889). Bourget (1852–1934) had already carved out a successful career as a novelist; his novels of romantic situations in high society had been saved by a psychological insight which he turned to more serious purpose in his *Essais de psychologie contemporaine* (1883). He was a disciple of Taine, and his novel *Le Disciple* was all the more remarkable for this reason. For in this book Bourget proclaimed

the emptiness of positivist doctrines, the dangers of life un-
supported by fixed moral values, and the appalling responsibility of
the teacher who ignores these values. *Le Disciple* was the precursor
of a series of novels—*L'Étape* (1902), *Un Divorce* (1904), *L'Émigré*
(1907), *Le Démon de Midi* (1914), *Le Sens de la Mort* (1915)—in
which Bourget sought the solution to various problems of this
world in the traditional values of the Church. His method remained
to a large extent that of the positivists, but he turned it to proving
the opposite of their doctrines.

It was in the 1880's also that an author who was to revolutionise
the French stage experienced his conversion to the Catholic faith.
Paul Claudel (1868–1955), converted on Christmas Day, 1886, was
received into the Church in 1890. His first play, *Tête d'Or* (1889),
contains reflections of his spiritual struggle at the time, a struggle
which was to be resolved, in his later plays, into a confident
certainty. The plays Claudel wrote before the turn of the century,[4]
in which the symbolism is remote and detached from life and the
characters often act more as symbols than people, lack the perfect
unity achieved in the later plays, particularly *Partage de Midi*
(1905) and *L'Annonce faite à Marie* (1910). It was perhaps that
personal and religious crisis that Claudel underwent in these years
at the turn of the century which made him centre his whole
dramatic conception in so much more unified a way round a central
Christian theme, and to make his symbolism therefore a good deal
more meaningful and effective; or it may have been a more perfect
understanding of certain aspects of Christian doctrine. Be that as
it may, it is in these later plays, culminating in *Le Soulier de Satin*
(1924), that the symbolist theatre truly began to live. The unity
provided by the religious basis for the action prevents that dispersal
of attention and disunity of detail which one finds, for example,
in the plays of Maeterlinck. Claudel's plays are the climax of the
French symbolist theatre; in fact they are its only really successful
expression. And his Christian belief was a significant element in
his success.

We must not forget some of the other literary and religious
events which accompanied this first explosion of the 1880's.
Barbey d'Aurevilly was continuing to write his Romantic-cum-
religious novels, and Villiers de l'Isle Adam was producing his
Contes Cruels (1883), *Axel* (1885), *Nouveaux Contes Cruels*
(1886) and *L'Ève Future* (1886). Péladan, too, was indulging in

13

novels in which occultism and Catholicism mingle with all the bric-à-brac of the Decadence; *Le Vice Suprême* (1884) is probably the most famous of them. This decade was the final fling of the type of Catholic literature represented, in varying degrees, by these three men. Barbey and Villiers both died in 1889, and Péladan, who was at any rate a far lesser man, brought nothing new to literature in the years that followed.

This was the era, too, of the great fashion for occultism in which so many authors so freely dabbled and which left its mark even on the more serious Catholic literature of the epoch. Wagnerism, theosophy, spiritualism—these and many other aspects of the literature of the Decadence have been associated perhaps rather too freely with the Revival by many critics. There is no denying that they entered to a certain extent into the formation of many writers, as they did for so many people in the Paris of that era; but those for whom they were to have an overriding importance were not so much the serious Catholic authors whom we wish to study as the fringe Decadents, such as Stanislas de Guaïta or Péladan. Those elements of occultism which seriously influenced some of the authors of the Catholic Revival were not those pursued by the *cénacles* of *fin de siècle* Paris, but rather those which enter into the more esoteric doctrines of the Church.

The literary upheaval produced by the infusion of Catholicism coincided, strangely enough, with the first years of Leo XIII's pontificate; but it also coincided with the first great period of Republican action against the Church. The Decrees on the Congregations and on education, which were passed in the years 1879–86, first brought home fully to Catholics the danger which the Church ran in a secular Republic. Compared with the later actions of the Combes administration (1902–5), these earlier decisions appear moderate in scope, and often inefficient in operation; but Combes is no real yardstick to judge by, and one must realise that these first anti-clerical actions of the nascent Republic generated in the average Catholic of the time a spirit of violent opposition, and a mistrust of all compromise with a government which from now on was to be considered as the natural enemy of the Church. This is possibly one of the reasons for the intransigent attitudes taken by the authors of the Revival, of this and of subsequent generations, in their relations with the Republic.

This reaction on the part of the Catholic authors was partly responsible for the failure of the directives of Leo XIII to influence them. The great call to *Ralliement* sounded in 1892 fell on deaf ears in literary circles, except for one or two minor exceptions. The actions which the Republic had taken in the 1880's had strengthened many Catholics' natural hatred of democracy, and removed any possibility of their rallying to the Republic. Throughout this period various Catholic journals continued, in their various ways, the tradition of Veuillot; for example, the Assumptionists' paper *La Croix*, founded as a daily in 1883, and edited by Father Bailly, Drumont's *Libre Parole*, founded 1892, and Élise Veuillot's *La Vérité française*, founded in 1893 to continue her father's tradition, when Eugène Veuillot, his brother, had 'rallied' with *L'Univers* to the Republic, according to Leo's commands.

After its first great effect the Revival continued in much the same way until the end of the century. Bloy continued his progress, with his great work *Le Salut par les Juifs* (1892), his second novel *La Femme Pauvre* (1897) and various other writings, including his *Journal*. Huysmans, after *En Route*, continued his religious autobiography with *La Cathédrale* (1898). Claudel was writing the plays of his 'first period'. Various minor novelists entered the field of the religious novel, and a few more literary figures, such as François Coppée, became converted. But the main impression is one of consolidation of a position taken. This was the period of the first flowering of modernism in France, both exegetical and philosophical; but its influence on literature is almost non-existent at this time, and, indeed, that of the *Ralliement* is only reflected in the novels of a minor author called George Fonsegrive, editor of *La Quinzaine*, who signed his books with the pseudonym Yves le Querdec.

The Dreyfus Affair, which came to its highest point of anguish in 1898, was instrumental in entrenching Catholics and Republicans even more deeply into the most extreme convictions; it not only produced a new flowering of extremist political movements, but also brought into great prominence two authors who, though neither of them were Catholics, were to influence this and several succeeding generations of Catholic thought. These men were Maurice Barrès (1862–1923) and Charles Maurras (1868–1952).

Barrès, whose literary career had started as early as 1888 with *Sous l'Oeil des Barbares*, which was to be the first of three volumes devoted to the 'Culte du Moi',[5] soon moved from an aggressive individualism to a concern with order and patriotism. He became a fervent Boulangist, and was elected a *député*. His views on the Boulanger crisis and on the subsequent Panama scandal were expressed in the trilogy of novels entitled *Le Roman de l'Energie Nationale*.[6] These novels were devoted, also, to the question of national and provincial roots, of 'la terre et les morts', and of the danger of uprooting young people from their native province and instilling into them ideas alien to their ancestry. Barrès was a founder member of the *Ligue de la Patrie Française* (1898), and, with his vigorous statements on the Dreyfus Case, was one of the strongest voices in the revival of extreme nationalism at that time. This revival was continued by his novels on the Alsace-Lorraine question, *Au Service de l'Allemagne* (1905) and *Colette Baudoche* (1909), which, together with a certain number of novels and articles by Catholic authors, did much to keep alive the spirit of *revanche* in the French nation. Barrès, though not a Catholic, was attached to that religion by national and hereditary ties. His vast influence on his own and the following generation reached many different areas of society, but one of the greatest of these areas of influence was that of the young Catholics.

In 1898, the same year that the *Ligue de la Patrie Française* was founded, Charles Maurras joined a movement founded by Henri Vaugeois which was to have an incalculable effect for half a century —the *Action Française*. This movement had many of the same objects as Barrès, but posited, under Maurras's influence, one means alone of achieving them: the restoration of the monarchy. Maurras, like Barrès, was to become the idol not only of his own generation but of the next as well. His pronouncements on literary, political and religious problems, which were at times expressed in separate works, but more often in articles, first for the weekly *Revue de l'Action Française*, and then after 1908 in the daily *Action Française* newspaper, were avidly followed by a whole generation. Maurras stood for order, anti-individualism, tradition, patriotism; he saw in the Catholic Church one of the main means of achieving these ends. Around him and his newspaper some of the finest political and historical writers of his time were to gather, men of all types of belief, many of them Catholics. Léon Daudet, possibly the most remarkable of his collaborators, was of this last group, and many of the young converts of the new century moved swiftly towards the political convictions of the *Action Française*.

For the new century, which started with the violent anti-clerical actions of the Combes administration, was also the scene of another large wave of conversions such as had been seen in the 1880's. Of the new generation of converts many were under the wing, as it were, of writers of that older group. Léon Bloy, for example, could count among those whose conversion he had helped the young philosopher Jacques Maritain and his wife Raïssa; Huysmans, whose novel *En Route* had sparked off so many conversions, was one of the first to welcome into the Church the critic and novelist Adolphe Retté.

These years at the beginning of the century contain so much in the way of Catholic literature that one hardly knows which way to turn. Huysmans, Bloy, Bourget and Claudel were all continuing their extensive output, though in the case of Huysmans this was cut short by his premature death in 1907. New stars of great importance were arising, such as Péguy, Jammes and Baumann; and around them scores of new writers, minor novelists and poets, were to be found. Of these lesser writers, however, some are admittedly of that category described at the beginning of this chapter, whose Catholicism is more of a natural backcloth than a burning necessity of their works. Even novelists who were extremely famous in their own day, such as René Bazin and Henry Bordeaux, have often very tenuous links with the main stream of Catholic literature of their time. Their involvement occasionally comes out on certain points—the importance of family life, for example, or, in Bazin's case, the revanchist attitude to Alsace-Lorraine—but their novels lie, structurally, in the realist line stemming back to Balzac, with a dash of conventional *pieusard* sentimentality, and they have little in common with the Catholic novel as it was developing in their time.

A writer who, as a middle-aged man, planted himself firmly in that mainstream with his first novel is Émile Baumann (1868–1941). His novels strike us nowadays as badly constructed, over-complicated and often hysterical in tone; they are very poor from the literary point of view. But in their excess they present us very clearly with many of the main characteristics of the Catholic novel at this stage of its development, and explain much of what had gone before and what was to come after; and, indeed, their popularity at the time of their publication shows us some of the chief preoccupations of contemporary Catholic readers, who would hardly have raved merely about their literary merits. Baumann's main novels before the war were *L'Immolé* (1908), *La Fosse aux Lions* (1911) and *Le Baptême de Pauline Ardel* (1914), and his career was to continue throughout the inter-war period.

The two most important authors to emerge in this pre-war decade were Francis Jammes (1868–1938) and Charles Péguy (1873–1914). Both of them are figures who stand very much on their own, though they also have, in certain respects, very close links with the Catholic thought of their age. Jammes's conversion, in 1905, was no *coup de foudre*, and few of his ideas were changed by what was essentially a reinforcement of attitudes which already existed within him. His poetry, in its simplicity and its concentration on the simple virtues of the land, the innocence of the child and the peasant, is a high point of Catholic poetry of this period. He has stripped away the conventional imagery and the elaborate sentimentalism of so much Catholic poetry, and has produced a taut simplicity in which ever word counts, and in which even the most apparently banal of scenes is transformed by a dynamic and original use of imagery. He is cut off from many of the main trends of thought of the Revival as a whole, and particularly from the violent aspects we have been describing.

Charles Péguy was a man who came to Catholicism from a very different direction from most of the other converts of this time. He was at first a socialist, and an atheist. His paper *Les Cahiers de la Quinzaine* took a violently pro-Dreyfus view in the years of the crisis, and included among its early contributors people of all points of view, but particularly of the Left. Péguy's conversion, which is supposed to have taken place in 1908, strangely enough made little impression on his basic views, which were traditionalistic, patriotic, and surprisingly unsocialist. His views on social reform became perhaps more paternalistic in these later years, but his 'socialism' and his Catholicism seem to have had many of the same features, in fact far more than is usually supposed. He died at the front in 1914, in the first weeks of the war. Péguy's main output, both in prose and verse, appeared in his paper *Les Cahiers de la Quinzaine*. The verse mainly took the form of vast Christian mysteries, and culminated in the immense, repetitive poem *Ève* (1913). His prose is some of the most effective in the French language, and his verse contains many of the same oratorical characteristics.

There is no need to mention here every one of the mass of

Catholic writers who surrounded these main figures. It is enough, perhaps to mention such diverse novelists as Adolphe Retté (1863–1930), and Jean Nesmy (b. 1876), or such poets as Louis Le Cardonnel (1862–1936) and Charles Grolleau (1857–1940). These writers would on the whole hardly be worth prolonged literary study; but many such minor writers will be of use to us in so far as they represent certain trends of thought common to Catholic literature of the time.

Among those whom it is imperative to mention here, however, is that group of writers, centering round Péguy, who were among the first to be affected by the philosophy of Bergson: the young novelist Ernest Psichari (1883–1914), whose later conversion, intimately bound up with army life and the experience he had had in a colonial regiment, was to inspire the war generation with patriotic and religious fervour; the witty, intelligent young Henri Massis (b. 1886), whose views on the Sorbonne and the younger generation were to be expressed in two studies produced in collaboration with Alfred de Tarde, *L'Esprit de la Nouvelle Sorbonne* (1911) and *Les Jeunes Gens d'Aujourd'hui* (1913); and the philosophers Jacques (b. 1882) and Raïssa (1883–1960) Maritain, who were soon to move from Bergsonism to the study of Thomist philosophy. The Maritains were converted by Léon Bloy in 1906; Psichari and Massis took the plunge in 1913; but their writings, even before their conversion, show them to have been very close to such a step for a long time.

Another young group, of slightly less importance, was that which formed around the magazine *Les Cahiers de l'Amitié de France* (1912–14). The most important of these writers, whom the abbé Maugendre has studied in his book *La Renaissance Catholique en France au XXe siècle*, were Robert Valléry-Radot, novelist and poet, André Lafon, novelist and poet, Eusèbe de Brémond d'Ars and Martial Piéchaud, poets, and the young François Mauriac. These writers were on the whole neither as original nor as excellent as they and their biographers have claimed. Even Mauriac's first novel, *L'Enfant chargé de chaînes*, is very uneven; Valléry-Radot's *Un Homme de Désir* is fairly conventional stuff; and André Lafon's novels reflect the sentimentality that was one of the failings of the poetry of the group.

This younger generation leaned, on the whole, towards the political Right. Retté, Massis, Psichari, Jacques Maritain and

Valléry-Radot were among those who sooner or later came strongly under the influence of Maurras and *Action Française*. They are typical of that generation of youth described by Massis and Tarde in *Les Jeunes Gens d'Aujourd'hui* (1913) and by the novelist Roger Martin du Gard in the last section of his novel *Jean Barois* (1913): young people obsessed with tradition, solidity and order, and strongly Catholic in this traditional manner. Some, indeed, such as Mauriac, dabbled in the social Catholicism which grouped around *Le Sillon*, but these were the exception rather than the rule. This generation of authors continued, on the whole, the tradition of opposition both to modernism and to liberal Catholicism set by their elders. Indeed, in the more reactionary pontificate of Pius X (1903–14), and particularly after the condemnation of modernism in 1907, and of *Le Sillon* in 1910, the intransigence of Catholic authors became stronger even than that of the Pope. It was only after the 1914–18 war that a novel fully supporting the modernist experiment was to appear—Albert Autin's *L'Anathème*.

The war was to do much to heal many of the wounds of this period, and in particular the opposition between Church and Republic. It is a fitting close to our period, for after it Catholic literature was to become something quite different; but it is impossible to understand many later events, whether literary, religious or political, without reference to the period 1870–1914, that time of upheaval which left its mark upon so many who later became famous.

NOTES

¹ Throughout this work the term 'Catholic' will be taken to mean 'Roman Catholic'.

² Except for Claudel, who all the same makes little *philosophical* use of St. Thomas.

³ Here, I think, we must discount Baudelaire, whose Catholicism, even if it exists in the form some critics ascribe to it, is nevertheless of doubtful importance in relation to the serious problems which his poetry places before us.

⁴ *La Ville* (first version, 1891), *La Jeune Fille Violaine* (first version, 1892), *L'Échange* (1894), and to a certain extent *Le Repos du Septième Jour* (1896), *La Ville* (second version, 1897) and *La Jeune Fille Violaine* (second version, 1898).

⁵ The others being *Un Homme Libre* (1889) and *Le Jardin de Bérénice* (1891).

⁶ *Les Déracinés* (1897), *L'Appel au Soldat* (1900) and *Leurs Figures* (1902).

CHAPTER TWO

Non-intellectualism in Religious Matters

THE Catholic literary revival was not, in the main, a movement of intellectuals. This fact may at first sight appear surprising, for it appears to be a period of the most intensive and original religious thought. With the various forms of modernism and liberal Catholicism on the one hand, and the revival of Thomist studies on the other, the impression one would receive when reading the theologians and religious philosophers of the period would be one of intellectual vitality and change; yet the creative writers of the same period, the poets, novelists and playwrights, reflect little or nothing of all this. Modernism and social and liberal Catholicism are either ignored or violently attacked in their works; Thomism and the revival of scholastic studies are admired but on the whole rejected as being of little use in the present situation. The movement is one of a traditional Christianity relying on revelation rather than the intellect, tradition rather than novelty, simplicity rather than complication.

What are the reasons for this? For many authors the materialism of the nineteenth century against which they were reacting was intimately connected with the intellectual methods of its exponents. From the mistrust of these particular methods to a mistrust of intellectualism in general was but a short step. Science had claimed too much, and was thus refused too much. From a rejection of science we move almost naturally to a rejection of the use of reason and the intellect. Revelation and tradition must be the basis for religion.

In their attitude towards the intellect these Catholic authors were making the same sort of mistake that Raïssa Maritain was later to ascribe to Bergson; they did not understand that the intellect is something more than the false use that had been made of it in the nineteenth century. Bergson, she says, was wrong in opposing intuition and intellect, to the detriment of the latter: 'S'il refuse au concept tout pouvoir authentique d'appréhender le réel, c'est qu'il dénie a l'intelligence ses bases et ses sommets qui sont justement l'intuition.'[1]

Intuition, in these terms, does not necessarily mean an entirely personal faculty, resolving man's problems from within, but rather an intuitive faculty of receiving divine inspiration. The idea of a personal approach to religion was abhorrent to most of the Catholic writers of the time. Not only would such individualism be, at its extreme, heretical; it was also contrary to the prejudices instilled in these writers by the world around them.

For these Catholic writers were also reacting against the belief, so powerful in the eighteenth and nineteenth centuries, in man's ability to reach perfection by his own personal efforts and by his own knowledge. This, together with the 'danger' of Protestantism, combined to give the average Catholic a healthy fear of anything which smacked of an individual approach to religion. It is hardly surprising, therefore, that they did not make the mistake, in their anti-intellectualism, of turning to the 'immanentism' of philosophical modernists such as Laberthonnière, Le Roy and Blondel (the most logical followers of Bergson), in which the denial of the possibility of reaching truth through purely intellectual processes leads to the conclusion that this search should be an activity of our whole being. Such a conclusion, contemporary Catholics believed, forced man into the Kantian position: that he must at all times make an analysis of his own inner life in order to reach a general truth. This form of individualism seemed too near to the dangers our writers were trying to avoid.

So the reaction against nineteenth-century Positivism was violent, and led to a complete mistrust of the use of the intellect in religious matters. On the other hand, the equally strong reaction against individualism prevented too great a trust in personal intuition, and made of the Catholic literary revival a movement of revelation and tradition, whose approach to God was transcendental rather than immanent. Nothing, however, can prevent the heretical implications of a complete dismissal of reason in relation to religious matters.

Science and Religion

It was the pretension of 'science'[2] that it could explain everything. Its adherents had been convinced that it was the only way to truth, and that eventually, as the scientific method became more nearly perfect, all would become clear. 'Je suis convaincu qu'il y a une science des origines de l'humanité qui sera construite un jour non par la spéculation abstraite, mais par la recherche scientifique,' wrote Renan;[3] and it was the eventual apparent collapse of this claim which sowed the seeds of doubt in the efficacy of science in many minds. In *Du Diable à Dieu* Adolphe Retté describes how, as a militant anti-clerical, he was making a speech to some workers about the great powers of science, when one of them trustingly asked what it explained about man's origins. Retté tried in vain to continue; the workers, with their simple minds, were no longer impressed, and he found his own faith in science leaving him.[4] Similarly Brunetière in *La Science et la Religion* denies the claims of science, saying that its methods are incapable, not just of re-solving, but even of stating the only important questions, those which deal with the origins of man, his rules for conduct, and his future destiny: 'L'inconnaissable nous entoure, il nous enveloppe, il nous étreint, et nous ne pouvons tirer des lois de la physique ou des résultats de la physiologie aucun moyen d'en rien connaître.'[5]

But science had not only claimed all knowledge; it had also had aspirations towards being the basis of morality. Positivism became, for many people, a kind of religion, with its own morality and its own beliefs. Auguste Comte himself states the principles of this religion of Humanity; but they are most clearly expressed in Littré's book *Conservation, Révolution et Positivisme*,[6] where Comte's ideas appear in a much more easily readable form. This work was immensely influential. In it we find positivism put for-ward as a replacement for Christianity, which does not correspond to the scientific approach to life. As something is needed to recon-struct the good side of Christianity (which is the moral system embodied in it), so a new kind of religion must be formed. The new religion formed by positivism is the worship of Humanity, which Charles Maurras, in his study of Comte, describes as 'l'ensemble des hommes qui ont coopéré au grand ouvrage humain, ceux qui se prolongent en nous, que nous continuons, ceux dont nous sommes les débiteurs véritables. . . .'[7]

This worship of Humanity is brilliantly satirised by Villiers de l'Isle Adam in his short story *Le Traitement du Docteur Tristan*, where the doctor's way of curing those who 'hear voices' (whether they speak of patriotism, faith or whatever) is to speak in their ear the one word 'Humanité'. 'Les yeux sur son chronomètre, il en

C

arrive, aprés vingt minutes, à le prononcer dix-sept fois par seconde, sans en confondre les syllabes. . . .'[8]

Villiers's attack is typical of many, though much more amusing. It is typical, above all, in its excess. He will not accept the basically good intentions of the positivist religion; for him, it is essentially destructive, and he stresses this by such phrases as: '. . . les désinences de certains termes, aujourd'hui démodés et dont il est presque impossible de retrouver la signification—par exemple, de mots tels que: Générosité! Foi! Désintéressement! Ame immortelle! etc., et autres expressions fantastiques.' He refuses to understand that man can strive for an ideal *via* positivism.

Such a reaction was common to most Catholic writers of the time. Having been asked for everything, these violent souls were now prepared to concede nothing. Science was regarded as having absolutely no value in relation to religious matters, and, as a corollary to this, the value of reason was also denied. Verlaine's implacable opposition to knowledge, his faith in the traditional beliefs of his fathers, is typical of the whole generation:

> Frères, lâchez la science gourmande
>
> Qui veut voler sur les ceps défendus
> Le fruit sanglant qu'il ne faut pas connaître.
> Lâchez son bras qui vous tient attendus
> Pour des enfers que Dieu n'a pas fait naître,
>
> Mais qui sont l'oeuvre affreuse du péché,
> Car Nous, les fils attentifs de l'histoire,
> Nous tenons pour l'honneur, jamais taché,
> De la Tradition, supplice et gloire!
>
> Nous sommes sûrs des Aïeux nous disant
> Qu'ils ont vu Dieu sous telle ou telle forme . . .
>
> Ils ont tout dit. Savoir le reste est bien;
> Que deux et deux font quatre, à merveille! . . .
>
> Gardez que trop chercher ne vous séduise
> Loin d'une sage et forte humilité . . .
> Le seul savant, c'est encore Moïse![9]

Brunetière, though he violently attacked the ridiculous claims of science, did not go to the opposite extreme. He demarcated the limits of science and religion, as he saw them, and even suggested that the one could help the other:

A défaut d'une certitude entière, mathématique et raisonnée, si nous avons besoin de nous former une idée de ce que nous sommes, et si le lien social ne peut subsister qu'à cette condition, les sciences peuvent nous y aider, mais il ne leur appartient pas de déterminer, et encore bien moins de juger cette idée.[10]

He even accepts the work of scientific biblical exegesis, but defines its limits. We must admit, he says, that its conclusions have definitely been established. We can even admit that, from the third or fourth century onwards, Christianity has been propagated, developed and upheld by purely human means. Let us even suppose that Christian dogma, metaphysics and ethics are purely adaptations of Greek philosophy to the needs of the biblical text. Let us admit that the Gospels were written neither by the authors who give them their name, nor at the time traditionally assigned to them. What is the result of all this?

En serait-il moins vrai qu'à une époque déterminée, sur les bords du lac de Génésareth, un homme a paru qui s'est dit, qui s'est cru, et que l'on a cru fils de Dieu? Le caractère général de son enseignement ou de sa prédication en est-il changé dans son fond ou modifié dans sa teneur essentielle? Son oeuvre en est-elle moins ce qu'elle est? Et si non, qui ne voit que la question subsiste tout entière et qu'elle est, comme nous disions, la seule: Était-il ou n'était-il pas Dieu?[11]

But the attitude of the Catholic novelists and poets of the time towards such attempts at moderation and compromise with science as are expressed in the biblical work of such modernists as Loisy is summed up brutally by Léon Bloy in his *Journal*:

Elle est jolie, la nouvelle école exégétique, en ce qui regarde l'interprétation ou seulement la lecture des Textes Saints. Il y a des prêtres qui pensent, au mépris du Concile de Trente, qu'il y a mieux que la Vulgate. J'en connais un que la queue du chien de Tobie empêche de dormir.[12]

He regards this form of exegesis (his own, as we shall see later, rests on no such rational or intellectual bases) as a negation of Holy Writ, and as one of the greatest dangers to faith: 'Négation pure et simple du Texte Sacré. Jamais la foi n'a couru un plus grand danger.'[13]

The same reaction to scientific exegetical study is to be found in Claudel, whose own biblical exegesis is strongly influenced, as is that of Bloy, by the ideas of the abbé Tardif de Moidrey. Claudel refers, in his letter to Rivière, to 'ces pauvres gens qui étaient terrifiés par le fier équipage de la science moderne et qui s'efforçaient de mettre la Genèse en accord avec les "découvertes" de l'évolution ou de la théorie de Laplace.' Now that the work of modern science has been ruined to its foundations, where, he asks, are all these 'apologistes tremblotants'?[14]

Similarly Péguy, even before his conversion, refers with scorn to the exegetical modernists:

> Les catholiques sont à battre, avec un gros bâton, quand ils se mettent à parler sur un certain ton scientifique de leurs admirables légendes, afin de se mettre, de se hisser, à la hauteur de deux philologues traitant de trois versions d'un même épisode homérique.[15]

There is a curious silence upon the subject of modernism in the Catholic novels of the period. Though the translation from the Italian of Foggazzaro's novel *Il Santo* had a good deal of popular success in France, the French Catholic novelists had no interest in the revolutionary ideas, both exegetical and liturgical, of such men as Loisy and Tyrrell, even before their condemnation by the Church; and after the condemnation one could hardly expect a literary movement so grounded in the concept of authority to do anything but condemn them in its turn, together with the liberal Catholicism which seemed to them to be so closely connected with the modernist movement.[16] The novel's attitude was shared by poetry and the theatre; 'la grande littérature' was largely indifferent or hostile; it was in the ranks of the philosophers and the historians (e.g. Bremond) that the modernist theologians found their few articulate allies, and the most sympathetic picture we get, before the 1914–18 war, of the modernist movement is given to us in a novel by a non-Catholic, Roger Martin du Gard's *Jean Barois*.

An 'Intellectual': Paul Bourget

Bourget is the great exception, among Catholic novelists, to the anti-intellectual movement we have been describing. The son of a university professor, he had gone through a thorough training in philosophy at university himself, and he was never to lose his appreciation of the importance of the human intellect. Taine was to remain throughout his life one of his masters. In fact, he refused to refer to his 'conversion', saying that there had never been a decisive change in his thought, but that he had gradually, by a process of reasoning and by the scientific study of life, come to believe in the necessity of God; in this way he describes the psychological studies of love contained in the novels of his 'first' period as part of this preliminary search.

In the novels of his 'second period', the 'romans à thèse' which start with *Le Disciple* (1889), we find that those characters who come to Catholicism do so via their reason; Jean Monneron, for example, in *L'Étape* (1902). Similarly the religious and political ideas expressed are based, in the main, on Bourget's heroes Bonald and Le Play, both of whom stress the use of reason in reaching their opinions. An extremely clear example of this is the speech against divorce made by the priest, Father Euvrard, in Chapter One of *Un Divorce* (1904), which echoes, idea by idea, the philosophy expressed by Bonald in his tract *Du Divorce*.[17] The priest is a scholar, a former member of the Académie des Sciences, and stresses the use of scientific observation and of reason; he refers to 'l'identité entre la loi de l'Église et la loi de la réalite, entre l'enseignement de l'expérience et celui de la Révélation,' and his speech is filled with such remarks as this: 'Que répond la raison? Que la société se compose de familles et que, tant valent ces familles, tant vaut cette société.' Bourget even stresses the point by a footnote, quoting an Italian positivist as holding exactly the same ideas as the priest with regard to divorce.[18] Similarly Bonald had based his whole argument on the human reason: 'Si je cite la religion chrétienne à l'appui de mes raisonnemens, c'est pour en faire voir la conformité à la raison la plus éclairée, et nullement pour y chercher des motifs capables de subjuguer la raison.'[19]

So Bourget's opposition to modernism does not come from a mistrust of science and of the use of intelligence, but rather from a fundamental disagreement with the results of this use in this specific case. Bourget's reading of de Maistre, Bonald and Le Play had brought him rational arguments for a traditional class system; this supported (or was supported by) a traditional religion. The new ideas of modernism were naturally anathema to him, as were the social and political ideas of social Catholicism and Catholic liberalism.

In his worship of reason, however, Bourget is conscious of the excesses of his predecessors; he is prepared to accept the limits of reason, and the importance of grace. Jean Monneron, for example, in *L'Étape*, admits to M. Ferrand, the Bonaldist professor of history, that he has arrived rationally at the conclusion that science is incapable of going beyond a certain point, beyond which lies the unknown. He has gradually, by a series of rational steps, come to the idea of the existence of God and of the necessity of Catholicism. But grace is still needed for him truly to be converted, we are informed: 'On ne prouve pas la religion. ... On donne des raisons de croire, ce qui n'est pas la même chose. Une conversion n'est pas une oeuvre purement intellectuelle.'[20]

Similarly a great deal of Bourget's work is devoted to exposing the danger of the positivist claim to the domain of morality. M. Monneron *père*, for example, in *L'Étape*, has brought up his children in a non-religious atmosphere; he believes, as did many *universitaires* of his day, that humanity is capable of perfection, and that morality is a matter for the reason. What is his horror when he finds that his children have received no such lesson, and no such aid! His daughter Julie, for example, is swept off her feet by an aristocratic seducer: 'Pour elle non plus, les doctrines abstraites, par lesquelles son déraisonnable père prétendait remplacer l'efficace et vivante force de la foi religieuse, n'avaient pu être un élément suffisant de résistance morale.'[21]

Her father's ideas of a 'morality of reason' are of no use to her when she is fighting with the idea of having an abortion. 'Que valent ces quintessences et ces fumées, quand il faut agir et se décider; quand le coeur en détresse a besoin d'un secours qui vienne d'en haut, d'une certitude à laquelle s'attacher pour n'en plus bouger?'[22]

The horror of Joseph Monneron when he realises the effect of what he has taught is similar to that of Adrien Sixte, in *Le Disciple*, when he sees in Robert Greslou's crime (the cold-blooded seduction of a girl he does not love, for reasons of scientific psychological study; and the girl's subsequent suicide) the logical result of his own teachings. Bourget's message is that of the frightening responsibility of the teacher, the philosopher and the author for those who hear or read their words.

In Bourget's work, then, we find praise for reason, but a demarcation of the limits beyond which reason may not go. It may be instrumental in a conversion, but grace is essential; and it may be used to support arguments of Christian morality, as in *Un Divorce*, but has no claim to creating a morality of its own.

Philosophers Accepted not for their Methods, but for their Results

Bonald (and with him de Maistre, Blanc de Saint-Bonnet and Donoso Cortès) of course exerted a great deal of influence on various other French Catholic writers of this period, particularly on Barbey d'Aurevilly and the young Léon Bloy. But these authors accepted them primarily for the message they preached, and not for their methods of reaching their conclusions. Barbey d'Aurevilly's articles on Bonald, Blanc de Saint-Bonnet, Donoso Cortès, etc., show great admiration for their reactionary principles; but Barbey himself is not noted for his subtlety of thought. It was Barbey who introduced Bloy to the work of these authors, and again the influence seems to have been political rather than rational. Later in his career Bloy, in an attack on Bourget, whose whole Catholicism, he said, 'tient dans une demi-douzaine de phrases de Bonald,'[23] turns on Bonald himself and criticises his use of reason: 'Elle est le développement du sens critique et rien que cela, dit Bourget, son très-bon élève. La vision particulière de Bonald exclut le surnaturel, et ses disciples, quelque chrétiens qu'on les imagine, sont aussi mal placés que possible pour apercevoir Notre Seigneur Jésus-Christ.'[24]

The tendency for writers to make use of other authors in so far as they agree with their own ideas, and to judge them accordingly, is nowhere more obvious than in the case of Renan. This composite and elusive character was violently over-simplified by the average Catholic writer, who saw him, with Taine and Comte, as the arch-enemy of the Christian religion. Hello, Huysmans, Bloy, Claudel, all see him as a kind of bogey; Péguy, attempting to attack him in the same breath as Taine, finds the task a good deal more complicated, and though he devotes innumerable pages to him, never fully succeeds in tackling the problem. His eventual conclusion is that Renan, though in no way corresponding to the myth that both his detractors and his supporters have made of him, is in reality responsible for this myth, even though he may not have intended it, and must be judged accordingly:

En ce sens et dans cette mesure quand les modernes, héritiers innombrables de Renan, eux-mêmes introduisent dans le débat une certaine idée de Renan . . . *nous pouvons, nous devons. les en croire*, et l'auteur lui-même Renan est responsable de cette idée, fût-elle grossière, qu'ils ont de lui ou que du moins

ils manifestent. Les grossièretés que les modernes ont prêtées à
Renan, qu'ils ont vues ou qu'ils ont mises dans Renan, quand
même elles n'y seraient pas ... *elles y sont tout de même* ... car
il faut pour qu'aujourd'hui elles sortent et se manifestent,
qu'il ait commis cette grossièreté beaucoup plus profonde, cette
grossièreté essentielle, *cette grossièreté mère d'avoir donné la
naissance à ce peuple de grossiers qui lui attribueraient un jour ces
grossièretés. ...*[25]

At the other extreme of the Catholic camp we have Bourget,
Barrès and Maurras, all of whom express admiration for Renan's
works. Bourget's reasons are obvious to us; but what of Barrès and
Maurras?

As with the attitude of Barbey and Bloy to their sources, this
again has little to do with the scientific method that Renan used,
though they do pay lip service to it. Barrès and Maurras found in
Renan what they needed for their own purposes.

In the case of Maurras these purposes were political. As we shall
see later, it is doubtful whether his defence of Catholicism was
motivated by anything other than purely practical ends; around
him in *Action Française* he managed to gather people of all kinds of
belief, all of which could be used in support of royalism. This is
in no way to impugn his honesty; he was at all times open in his
opinions, and his eventual conversion was no doubt one of conviction, but of the conviction that the Church was necessary to the
future of France and the restoration of the monarchy.

Thus, for Maurras, 'pour l'essentiel, la politique de Renan tient
à son exposé, très diffus, mais très constant, d'un ordre aristo-
cratique opposé point par point à toute démocratie.'[26] Maurras
regrets Renan's religious history because 'sur le terrain religieux,
quand il traitait des origines de la foi, d'une question sacrée,
Renan semble raisonner à peu près constamment d'après les
principes de la nouvelle philosophie qu'il avait empruntée à
l'Allemagne. Il y était tout à fait imprégné des principes allemands.'[27] But he admires above all Renan's political ideas:
'C'est un grand malheur que Renan ait consacré une moitié de sa
vie à écrire l'histoire ecclésiastique, l'autre moitié à l'histoire du
peuple hébreu. Quelle admirable *Histoire de France* il nous eût
faite! Renan eût écrit des plus hauts points de vue de l'aristocratie,
de la religion et de la royauté, comprises toutes trois dans leur
fonction de guide naturel du genre humain.'[28]

Similarly Taine had seemed doubly valuable to Maurras; while teaching, like Le Play, that we must judge a régime by its prosperity or its decadence, he was not suspect of being right-wing, as were Bonald, Le Play and de Maistre: 'Le Play, Bonald, Maistre, hommes de centre droit ou de droite extrême, étaient frappés d'une suspicion naturelle: comment ces défenseurs-né de la vieille France auraient-ils eu quelque crédit auprès de la France moderne? Or, Taine, lui, était de gauche. Et de quelle gauche!'[29]

Taine's method, whether historical or literary, is not regarded very highly by Maurras,[30] but Taine himself is seen as politically useful. And, while Maurras smiles at Auguste Comte's attempt at a religion of positivism, he cannot avoid admiring the effort and the sincerity of the attempt, nor can he resist quoting Comte's political remarks, such as: 'Depuis trente ans que je tiens la plume philosophique, j'ai toujours représenté la souveraineté du peuple comme une mystification oppressive et l'égalité comme un ignoble mensonge.[31]

Barrès saw clearly the extent to which Maurras's apparently intellectual approach was, in fact, merely a cover for conclusions which had already been reached:

Les procédés d'argumentation régulière donnent l'illusion de la méthode scientifique. C'est un magnifique symptôme d'activité intellectuelle, mais il ne mène nulle part . . . Maurras a résolu d'avance par une adhésion inébranlable à la monarchie le problème politique; avec sa ferme et douce insistance, il a l'air de raisonner librement; mais il n'a pas le droit de se laisser convaincre.[32]

Renan, then, was admired by Maurras, as were Taine and Comte, almost entirely for his political opinions. What of Renan's influence on Barrès? Here is a paradox to beat all others; Renan, who was hated by most Catholics as the destroyer of religion, is praised by Barrès because 'Renan nous a appris à traiter le problème religieux avec gravité et avec amour.'[33] In this there is obviously some truth; the orthodox Catholics had painted Renan too black, and he certainly did not have the dastardly intentions with which they credited him; he *does* treat the religious question with respect. On the other hand, Barrès certainly seems to be going too far in the other direction. It is his own conception of religion, which is hardly orthodox, which probably leads him to this position.

Barrès, like Maurras, spent most of his life outside the Church he defended. He has been described by some people as seeing in it merely the Maurrassian idea of order and tradition; and certainly something of this attitude does enter into his religious ideas. But on the other hand it is evident that he did experience a strong religious feeling, even though it was of a very vague kind, not necessarily connected with Catholicism at every stage. This explains the mixed feelings of Catholics towards him, and the storm that greeted his *Jardin sur l'Oronte* (1922). While Barrès saw in Catholicism the guardian of order, and the spirit of France, his own religious feeling was a type of emotional religiosity related to no precise doctrine. At times one feels that he would be as much at home worshipping Rosmertha, the pagan goddess of Lorraine to whom he refers in *La Colline Inspirée*.

M. Henri Massis says of Barrès: 'Dans la religion, c'est le langage de la sensibilité qu'il retrouve, et pour nous convaincre de la haute vertu de l'Église, ce n'est pas à notre volonté intellectuelle qu'il s'adresse, mais au sentiment pur, au rêve, à ces forces profondes de l'âme qui éclosent dans le domaine obscur de l'intuition.'[34]

This approach explains Barrès's attitude to Renan. For in Renan's complex personality scientific views were constantly intermingled with a kind of poetry-laden Celtic mysticism. Renan's views were often as vague, emotional and idealistic as those of Barrès. Barrès describes the enthusiasm of the young readers of Renan thus:

> La question religieuse ne se posait pas, pour nous, comme un problème de critique historique. . . . Il y avait, tout autour de cette Sorbonne, des jeunes gens très indifférents aux données érudites du conflit, fort éloignés de tous les débats d'exégèse et de philologie, et pour qui la lecture des grandes pages de Renan était souverainement bienfaisante.[35]

A Non-Intellectual: Paul Claudel

Claudel was an extremely complex personality, full of contradictions; so much so that it is extremely difficult to make any generalisation about his attitude on any subject. On the question of religion and the intellect, for example, we find him at times playing the simple peasant, scornful of intellectualism, and at others expressing an admiration and a need for the things of the intellect.

Let us, for the moment, take the latter position, and see to what extent Claudel's philosophical preoccupations make him an exception to the anti-intellectual movement we have been describing.

Claudel was essentially a non-intellectual, even when he was playing with intellectual ideas. His reading was vast and his intelligence was, in certain facets, extremely alive. But he was incapable of the finer shades of reasoning, and of the realisation that life and thought rarely consist of absolutes. In his letters to Rivière he condemns out of hand the other's questionings about the limits of human reason; yet by the very clear-cut simplicity of this condemnation he shows himself to be completely uncomprehending of the problems that were besetting his young correspondent. The letters in question (May 1908–January 1909) read like a passage from a Chekhov play, with one correspondent ignoring almost entirely the reasonings of the other.

Poor Rivière is bewildered; he does not understand the intransigence of the generation of Claudel, nor does he realise that it may be Claudel who is at fault. His very worries show him to be of that younger generation for whom such problems were not to be answered simply; he struggles to detach himself from the comparisons Claudel draws between him and Renan and Gourmont.[36] The situation is apparently paradoxical: Rivière, the intellectual, sees the possibility that reason may be of no value; Claudel, the non-intellectual, is doggedly convinced of its importance. But this is no paradox when one looks at it more closely.

Even more surprising is the fact that it was the influence of Claudel's works and personal letters that was decisive in Rivière's approach to Christianity. Yet we have a similar situation in Bloy's conversion of Maritain. In each case a brilliant intelligence was converted by someone of essentially simple, violent opinions. The answer probably is that in each case the younger man was overwhelmed by the elder's sincere and blinding belief, it being an age where there was so little belief, in general, and so many other interests, political and temporal, within the Church. Both Maritain and Rivière might follow paths different from those of their spiritual godfathers, yet they were never to deny the overwhelming influence which they had had upon them.

Rivière's first letters had been written to Claudel in a violent, emotional desire for spiritual certitude: 'La réponse, mon jeune aîné, ô vous en qui je me suis confié, la certitude, le réponse, je la

33

veux. Je veux que vous me brutalisiez, que vous me jetiez à terre. que vous m'injuriiez; le réponse.'[37] This was in early 1907. In his desire for absolute values it was natural that he should turn to a man like Claudel. But by the middle of 1908 he is still assailed by various religious doubts, of an intellectual nature, which Claudel is incapable of understanding, let alone helping. Rivière pleads that he can only believe in what he can perceive with his senses, and that his faith in ideas and concepts has been completely destroyed by his own methods of philosophical creation, by the fact that, when writing, he is perpetually *creating* ideas which appear perfectly valid and unassailable, as a system, when seen on the page, but which are, in fact, completely factitious. Claudel replies by castigating 'le ton dégagé avec lequel vous parlez des plus hautes facultés de notre esprit'[38] and by comparing Rivière to 'l'ignoble Renan.' His next letter refers to Renan and Gourmont, and says, 'je méprise les virtuoses et je ne comprends pas les plaisants. Le ricanement, depuis Voltaire jusqu'à Anatole France, m'a toujours paru le signe des réprouvés.'[39] Claudel, in his bluster, blurs any line of argument by attributing ignoble intentions to his correspondent. The man of the absolute has lost his temper, faced with what appear to him anti-Christian and dangerous ideas. Finally Rivière, in his humility, and in his great admiration for Claudel, but not without a certain wistfulness, submits: 'Votre . . . lettre m'avait été très cruelle. Naturellement je ne doutais pas que vous n'eussiez raison. Mais j'aurais voulu que vous eussiez un peu tort.'[40] He denies, nevertheless, Claudel's accusation that he was becoming a dilettante, and playing at being a sceptic. His scepticism, he declares, is passionate and blind; there is nothing he would like more than to believe; he is continually striving to do so; but difficulties always occur, and he is tortured by doubt. Still, he declares (with perhaps a touch of acidity in his tone), 'Je vous promets formellement de ne plus vous ennuyer avec des discussions philosophiques.'

In Claudel's writings a certain amount of intellectual paraphernalia adorns what are essentially simple, violent beliefs and passions. Claudel tends to use the authors he has read only in so far as they fit in with his own preconceptions, and to distort philosophical thought in the process of simplification. This is in no way to denigrate his great poetic and dramatic works, the strength of which lies in the absolute approach, the simple directness of the

Christian beliefs, the evocative nature of the poetic language, the symbolism and the verse-rhythms, and the striking development of certain primordial situations in what one might call the 'Christian human condition'.

The Influence of Bergson

What Raïssa Maritain describes as 'le positivisme pseudo-scientifique, le scepticisme, le relativisme' of the Sorbonne teachings was challenged, at the turn of the century, by a new philosopher whose popularity and success was due in large part to the fact that he explained and supported the revulsion which the younger generation was already feeling against the scientific doctrines of the nineteenth century. Though Bergson's ideas had been in print from 1889 onwards,[41] it was his lectures, first at the École Normale from 1897 to 1900 and later at the Collège de France, which brought them to prominence. Péguy had been one of Bergson's pupils at the École Normale, and it was he who introduced his younger friends, Jacques and Raïssa Maritain, Ernest Psichari and Henri Massis, to the open lectures at the Collège de France. All these people were soon to be converted to the Catholic faith, and were all to count, among the causes of their conversion, the philosophy of Bergson. How is it that this philosopher, who was not himself a Christian, whose works were later put on the Index, and whose closest Catholic followers were to be excommunicated, should have exerted such an influence?

As Henri Massis puts it in *Les Jeunes Gens d'Aujourd'hui*,[42] it was essentially the negative side of Bergson's philosophy which influenced them. The new philosophy, in its destruction of materialism, came as a revelation of the freedom of the human spirit. As Péguy was to say, Bergson had broken their chains.[43]

The attraction of this negative side of Bergson's philosophy can be seen in the words of Jacques Maritain, who was to be such a powerful opponent of the positive part: 'M. Bergson a vu d'une manière admirable la vanité du rationalisme matérialiste et positiviste, et l'offence qu'une si aride et si orgueilleuse doctrine fait à la beauté et à la richesse de la vie.'[44] And the way in which this freedom could lead to religious belief is pointed by the statement made by Maritain's wife, Raïssa: 'Nous n'étions pas les seuls sans doute à qui Bergson rendait la joie de l'esprit en rétablissant la métaphysique dans ses droits.'[45]

In the first flood of their delight at their deliverance, it little mattered to these people the direction in which the positive part of Bergson's philosophy was likely to take them; as Raïssa Maritain says: 'Peu nous importait alors que ce fût par l'intuition qui transcende les concepts, ou par l'intelligence qui les forme; l'important, l'essentiel, c'était le résultat possible: atteindre l'absolu.'[45]

There is no point in examining here in detail the heretical implications of the positive part of the Bergsonian doctrine. It is enough to say that one of its greatest dangers lay in its individualism, more particularly in its reliance upon the individual intuition. It was this danger which became manifest in the works of the philosophical modernists.[46] For while Blondel's 'philosophy of action' was essentially anti-intellectual, it did not turn man towards revelation so much as towards self-reliance; in using our whole being in the search for truth, we are logically led to the immanentist doctrine that we must search solely within ourselves for that truth.

In the younger generation of French Catholics, a rebellion against the positive part of the Bergsonian doctrine had already formed among those very people whom Bergson had brought to Catholicism, and who, by their moderation, escaped any danger of condemnation.

This new generation of Christians—Maritain, Massis, Valléry-Radot—had a respect for the intellect (as did the young Jacques Rivière) which injected a new element into the Revival. The fact that they had been saved from Positivism by Bergson did not mean that they could follow him the whole way in his attack on reason. As Robert Valléry-Radot put it: 'C'est cette partie négative qui nous fut salutaire; la positive qui, par réaction, exagère l'infirmité de la raison et prétend démontrer l'inanité de la logique, est très dangereuse; c'est contre elle que l'Église protesta au nom de la raison.'[47]

Jacques Maritain, the spearhead of the new intellectual movement, had given much the same opinion as Valléry-Radot two years earlier, in his fine study *L'Évolutionnisme de M. Bergson*: 'On se demande parfois si la philosophie de M. Bergson peut être acceptée ou assimilée par la foi catholique. Assurément non. Une philosophie qui blasphème l'intelligence ne sera jamais catholique. Et le système tout entier, l'exposition que nous en avons faite l'a assez montré, est absolument incompatible avec la doctrine de l'Église.'[48]

For many of this generation the lectures given, in these years just before the war, by Jacques Maritain at the Institut Catholique were a revelation and a rallying-point.[49] These lectures attacked Bergson, while respecting the philosopher, and the good influence he had upon many of this generation; at the same time, they aroused a new interest in Thomism and scholastic philosophy.

The full influence of these ideas was to be felt only after the war. These young people were the advance guard, and as such had little effect on the creative literature of the period we are studying. Even among their contemporaries, the usual reaction was that expressed by Psichari in his letters to Maritain: interest, admiration, but a doubting of the positive value of intellectual Christianity.

For this generation the reaction against science no longer meant a reaction against the intellect; they were far enough from the original conflict to take a more balanced view. The symbol of this, the Church's answer both to the excesses of science and the excesses of anti-science, is Thomism, the doctrine of reason backed by faith.

Thomism

The revival of Thomist studies had been heralded by Leo XIII's famous Encyclical *Aeterni Patris*, 1879, which had proclaimed the value of Christian philosophy, and above all of the scholastic theologians. In 1880 Leo XIII published a *Motu Proprio* to promote a new edition of St. Thomas, and in the same year he proclaimed St. Thomas the patron saint of Catholic schools throughout the world. The reaction was immediate. Editions of the scholastics began to appear[50] and scholarly commentaries flourished. A new revival of religious learning appeared to be under way.

Yet what effect did this have upon the literature of the period? None that was of any value, until the arrival of Maritain; and even then the reaction was not immediate, but is to be found more in the literature of the 1920's. Until Maritain the influence of St. Thomas had been confined to scholars and theologians and had not reached the general cultural world.

Claudel, of course, had read St. Thomas, and in his later days was prepared to stress that Thomist influence in his work which his critics were only too eager to find. There is no doubt that reading the *Summa Theologica*, which he did in the years 1895–1900 on the advice of the abbé Villaume, impressed Claudel greatly. But the remarks he makes about it, and the use he makes of it, show this interest to be a strangely simple and superficial one.

Claudel said himself that he picked up the language of scholasticism as he went along; he found the text itself amazingly simple, and found the texts of the commentators far too complicated. One is left with the conclusion that he read St. Thomas much as he read other authors, dwelling only on those parts which corroborated his own ideas or furthered his own preoccupations. *L'Art Poétique*, which admittedly is claimed to be a poet's view rather than a philosopher's, is nevertheless a formless hotch-potch, in which little of the essential doctrine of St. Thomas (in which the import is so closely mingled with the form of reasoning) can be discerned.

The work in which the influence of St. Thomas is most apparent, the play *Le Repos du Septième Jour*, was written in about 1896, when Claudel was actually reading the *Summa*. The Thomist ideas come across here undiluted, in great lumps, as though Claudel, wanting the Devil and the Angel (whom the Emperor meets on a visit to hell) to talk of evil, hell, etc., has taken passages straight out of St. Thomas and presented them to us as they are. It is this that makes Act II of his play so indigestible; and not only this, but also the fact that Claudel does not seem at times to have understood the Thomist message and produces phrases which completely contradict it. Thus St. Thomas's idea of evil being merely the absence of good and not a thing positive in its own right,[51] while it is stressed throughout most of this act,[52] seems to stand in direct contradiction to the definition we are given of hell as 'le lieu où tout mal est aimé.'[53]

The serious Thomist studies, and scholastic studies in general, undertaken by Jacques Maritain and followed in greater or lesser measure by several others of the younger generation, are a very different matter. In these there is not only an understanding of St. Thomas; there is also a rigidly logical use of his philosophy.

The full influence of this movement, however, comes after the war. Much of the pre-war reaction, even among the young contemporaries of Maritain, can be seen in the attitude of Ernest Psichari, who is prepared, on the one hand, to admire the use of the human reason in religious matters, and even to react violently, in a letter to Henri Massis and Alfred de Tarde about their book *Les Jeunes Gens d'Aujourd'hui*,[54] against the idea that the Revival had an essentially 'simple' outlook, yet who is not at all convinced of the value of these things either in relation to his own personal problems, or to the problems facing Christianity at the time. Certain passages from a letter he wrote to Maritain in 1912 show this attitude well:

> Si je cherchais dans la raison des raisons de croire—et, en effet, *Fidei assensus nequaquam est motus animi coecus*—je sens que mon point de départ serait la discussion des thèses bergsoniennes du néant, de l'ordre et de la finalité. Mais ayant en ce moment plus besoin d'amour que de lumière. . . .
>
> Nous sommes en un temps où le danger de la barbarie et de l'impiété est si grand que l'on n'a plus le loisir de s'arrêter aux arguments théologiques. D'ailleurs, la *Somme Théologique* n'est pas à la portée de tout le monde. Ce qui importe avant tout, c'est de démolir toute cette racaille intellectuelle, ces tristes savants. . . .[55]

This simple approach to Christianity coupled with the sense of acceptance of divine love and guidance show as clearly as anything could do the difficult ground on which the Thomists were attempting to sow. It was for this kind of reason that the Thomist revival had little or no influence on the creative literature of the pre-war years.

The positive anti-intellectualism of the second of the two extracts from Psichari's letter expresses something which we find even more clearly in Péguy's mistrust of Thomism. For Péguy was older than Psichari, and more heavily impregnated with the mistrust of intellectualism handed on from the previous generation. He saw the Thomists as many Catholics saw the liberal Catholics; he regarded them as people who were treating with the enemy: 'Je n'aime pas les catholiques qui pactisent avec la Sorbonne; ou qui traitent avec la Sorbonne; ou qui causent avec la Sorbonne; ou qui flirtent avec la Sorbonne; et même ceux qui se marient avec la Sorbonne.'[56]

Péguy found it hard to forgive Maritain's rejection of Bergson; and he warns Thomists that they are only being used by the Sorbonne against Bergson:

> Puis-je avertir les thomistes qui ont trouvé bon accueil en

Sorbonne qu'on les aime contre quelqu'un, et que ce n'est point si je puis dire pour les beaux yeux de Saint Thomas que la Sorbonne s'est subitement senti des tendresses pour la philosophie thomiste; et que rien n'est suspect comme une tendresse de Sorbonne; et que rien n'est suspect comme une alliance, fut-elle officieuse, et fut-elle occulte, des catholiques et de la Sorbonne. . . .

Péguy was not prepared to see the dangers of Bergsonism; in his simple, loyal way he felt that opposition to this philosophy was a kind of plot, that 'ce que l'on ne pardonne pas à Bergson, c'est d'avoir brisé nos fers.'[57] He did not see the dangers; but, by his very simplicity, he avoided them; and nothing could be further from the philosophical modernists than the thought of Péguy.

In his way Péguy is the epitome of the non-intellectualism of the period. Some writers are consciously anti-intellectual, as he is; others are unconsciously non-intellectual. There are occasional exceptions, but on the whole this literary and religious movement is one of simplicity, tradition and trust in divine revelation.

NOTES

[1] Raïssa Maritain, *Les Grandes Amitiés*, New York, 1941.

[2] The term 'science' is used, throughout this book, in the sense in which it was understood in nineteenth-century France, rather than in the more specific modern sense of 'the natural sciences'.

[3] Renan, *L'Avenir de la Science: Pensées de 1848*, Paris, 1890, p. 163. Even by the time this was published, forty-two years after it was written, many of the claims in it had already proved to be false.

[4] Adolphe Retté, *Du Diable à Dieu, Histoire d'une Conversion*, Paris, 1907.

[5] Ferdinand Brunetière, *La Science et la Religion*, Paris, 1895, p. 20.

[6] Emile Littré, *Conservation, Révolution et Positivisme*, Paris, 1852.

[7] Charles Maurras, *L'Avenir de l'Intelligence*, Paris, 1905.

[8] Villiers de l'Isle Adam, *Contes Cruels*, Paris, 1883.

[9] Verlaine, *Sagesse*, 1880, I, xi.

[10] Brunetière, *La Science et la Religion*, Paris, 1895, p. 38.

[11] Ibid., pp. 31–2.

[12] Léon Bloy, *Quatre Ans de Captivité à Cochons-sur-Marne, 1900–4*, 26 December 1902.

[13] Ibid., 21 November 1903.

[14] Letter, Claudel to Rivière, 24 October 1907.

[15] Charles Péguy, *Louis de Gonzague* (26 December 1905); Pléiade, Prose I, p. 941.

[16] George Fonsegrive is almost the only exception to this, and despite his interest in modernist theories his novels are almost entirely concerned with the social and political aspects of the *Ralliement*.

[17] Bonald, *Du Divorce, considéré au XIXe siècle relativement à l'état domestique et à l'état publique de la société*, Paris, 1801.

[18] Paul Bourget, *Un Divorce*, Paris, 1904, pp. 26–9.

[19] Bonald, *Du Divorce*, Paris, 1801, pp. 9–10.

[20] Bourget, *L'Étape*, Paris, 1902, p. 22.

[21] Ibid., pp. 223–4.

[22] Ibid., pp. 343–4.

[23] Bloy, *Les Dernières Colonnes de l'Eglise*, Paris, 1903, p. 141.

[24] Ibid., p. 143.

[25] Péguy, *De la Situation Faite au Parti Intellectuel dans le Monde Moderne* (2 December 1906); Pléiade, Prose I, pp. 1053–4. My italics.

[26] Maurras, 'A Propos du centenaire de Renan,' in *Action Française*, 28 February 1923.

[27] Maurras, 'Conférence sur Anatole France'; talk given at the Théâtre de l'Avenue, 16 April 1932.

[28] Maurras, in *Gazette de France*, 11 September 1902.

[29] Maurras, in *Action Française*, 25 March 1908.

[30] See *Le Soleil*, 1 August 1897.

[31] Letter, Auguste Comte to General Bonnet, 1 December 1855; quoted in Maurras, *L'Avenir de l'Intelligence*, Paris, 1905.

[32] Maurice Barrès, *Mes Cahiers*, 1900. In an article entitled 'The *Action Française* Movement, (*Cambridge Historical Journal*, 1930), Ronald Balfour further qualifies this description of Maurras's simple attitude to intellectual problems: 'In his political works he is a journalist rather than a thinker . . . Maurras's desire is not to discover the truth but to convert others to it. . . . Yet it would be equally true to say that Maurras is a doctrinaire interested in theory rather than in practical application. And this is so despite the fact that he always maintains that he is a realist and not an abstract theorist and that he daily fills two columns with comments on current events. The explanation of this paradox is that his thought has not materially modified in thirty years. He is always occupied with current events—like a journalist; his views are never modified by experience—like a doctrinaire. All he does is to apply the same principles from day to day to his judgement of passing events; he does not desire to learn from passing events in order to perfect his principles.'

[33] Barrès, *Le Centenaire d'Ernest Renan: Discours prononcé à la Sorbonne*, 28 February 1923.

[34] Henri Massis, *Jugements*, Paris, 1923–4, vol. I, p. 258.

[35] Barrès, *Le Centenaire d'Ernest Renan*, 28 February 1923.

[36] Claudel always connected ideas with people, and used certain names as scapegoats.

[37] Letter, Rivière to Claudel, February 1907.

[38] Claudel to Rivière, 11 May 1908.

[39] Claudel to Rivière, 19 December 1908.

[40] Rivière to Claudel, 17 January 1909.

[41] *Essai sur les données immédiates de la conscience*, 1889; *Matière et mémoire*, 1896.

[42] 'Agathon,' *Les Jeunes Gens d'Aujourd'hui*, Paris, 1913.

[43] Péguy, *L'Argent Suite*, 22 April 1913; Pléiade, Prose II, p. 1219.

[44] Jacques Maritain, *L'Évolutionnisme de M. Bergson*, Montligeon, 1911, p. 75.

[45] Raïssa Maritain, *Les Grandes Amitiés*, New York, 1941.

[46] 'Philosophical modernists' is a convenient term by which to refer to a fairly heterogeneous group of philosophers who were, themselves, in no real connexion with modernists of any other kind, apart from the general characteris-

tics of unorthodoxy and compromise with modern thought, and apart from having been lumped together with others in the Papal disapproval. Where Loisy had attempted to bring biblical exegesis into line with modern scientific discoveries, the philosophical modernists attempted to bring dogma into line with modern philosophical systems and the modern mind. The main figures were Maurice Blondel, whose book *L'Action* (1893) reflected the influence of Ollé-Laprune's *La Certitude Morale* (1880) and Bergson's *Essai sur les données immédiates de la conscience* (1889), and also Edouard Le Roy, who succeeded his master Bergson in his chair at the Collège de France, and Father Laberthonnière, an Oratorian.

Bourget expresses the contemporary Catholic disapproval of this form of modernism when, in *Le Démon de Midi*, he describes Father de Malaret, who was a philosophical modernist: 'Une conception purement agnostique de l'univers a conduit ce théologien, d'abord à situer dans l'âme même le fait religieux, puis à considérer la Révélation comme uniquement intérieure, enfin à conclure que le dogme, que tout l'appareil de l'Église doivent être en constante évolution, comme cette âme' (II, 142).

Le Roy and Laberthonnière were to be condemned by the Church: Blondel was not. Though there are great differences in the details of their doctrines, it is difficult to discern the reason for the discrimination. Dr. Alec Vidler suggests that it might be the realistic one that Blondel had, like the others, used this philosophy 'as a means of commending Catholicism to those who shared the common presuppositions of much contemporary non-Catholic thought', but that 'when the philosophy of action was put forward as a substitute for scholasticism, and still more when it was applied in such a way as to call in question the traditional views of dogma in general or of this dogma or of that in particular (as it had been by Le Roy and Laberthonnière), it was unlikely to meet even with toleration from ecclesiastical authority' (A. R. Vidler, *The Modernist Movement in the Roman Church*, Cambridge, 1934, p. 187). Be that as it may, the Church's condemnation would seem to rest on the individualism of the Bergsonian doctrine, and on the apparent denial of the transcendental in the perception of God.

[47] Robert Valléry-Radot, letter, printed in 'Agathon', *Les Jeunes Gens d'Aujourd'hui*, Paris, 1913, p. 205.

[48] Jacques Maritain, *L'Évolutionnisme de M. Bergson*, Montligeon, 1911, p. 75.

[49] M. Henri Massis, for example, names them as one of the most important influences upon his own development.

[50] The complete works of St. Bonaventure were published in 1889, those of Albert the Great in 1890.

[51] See questions 48 and 49 of Section I of the *Summa Theologica*.

[52] E.g. 'Le mal est ce qui n'est pas' (Pléiade, Théâtre I, p. 824).

[53] Ibid., p. 825.

[54] Op. cit., pp. 192–3.

[55] Ernest Psichari to Jacques Maritain, 15 June 1912; quoted in *Lettres du Centurion*.

[56] Péguy, *L'Argent Suite*, 22 April 1913; Pléiade, Prose II, p. 1218.

[57] Ibid., p. 1219.

CHAPTER THREE

Non-intellectualism in History

HERE, again, there is an attack on the reign of science in the nineteenth century; and again the attack is violent. In the subjective approach to history which is so typical of the Catholic writers, Michelet is at times quoted as the model; and certainly his intuitive approach to, and interpretation of, the facts is very similar to that of many writers in this period. Added to this, however, is a sense of the symbolic nature of history, of its value not in itself, but as a series of signs given by divine revelation.

The Method v. Michelet

'A la suite de M. Taine, ils gommaient des notes, les collaient les unes à la suite des autres, ne gardaient, bien entendu, que celles qui pouvaient soutenir la fantaisie de leurs contes,'[1] writes Huysmans in 1891, referring to those who used the 'scientific method' in historical research. In this short attack, of about two pages, he sums up much of what Péguy was later to write on the same subject, stressing the appallingly unimaginative nature of the work and the eventual uncertainty of the result.

For 'Agathon' (just as it is for Huysmans), the 'method' is really a kind of mass-production, making available to all, even to those of the meanest intelligence, the possibility of doing some kind of historical research; but it is useless. 'La méthode ne vaut que ce que vaut l'ouvrier. Elle ne remplace ni l'intelligence, ni le don. Elle apporte, il est vrai, de l'assurance aux travailleurs ordinaires. Et c'est là la raison de son succès.'[2] Learning has become an industry.

The card index, or *fichier*, is for both Péguy and 'Agathon' the great symbol of the soullessness of the new culture. Even today the *fiche* often appears to be an obsession with academics. For bibliography, and for certain precise kinds of research, a card index can be invaluable; but only too often it hinders any kind of imaginative work, and a work of literary criticism or history may often be compiled by stringing together the contents of a pile of *fiches*, many of which may have been written years before. The context is often forgotten; the source itself may never be re-consulted, and quotations may even be used to prove the opposite of what they meant in their context.

As 'Agathon' puts it, 'C'est au nombre de vos fiches que l'on vous apprécie en Sorbonne.'³ The scholar most worthy of consideration is the one who has managed to collect thousands of these little cards, 'poussière de connaissance infinitésimale.' Massis and Tarde continue by quoting Anatole France's character Fulgence Tapir, who declared, 'Je possède tout l'art, vous m'entendez, sur fiches classées alphabétiquement et par ordre de matière.'⁴

The *fiche* is, moreover, for these authors, merely one example of the painstaking amassing of facts which was required of the historian. Every line of research must be exhausted, every fact must be known, before the historian dares to put down a word on paper. But, as Péguy's Clio, the Muse of History, despairingly exclaims, 'Alors moi, avec mes fiches, je suis une qui court a pied après une automobile.'⁵

For it is impossible ever to do the amount of work required. As Péguy points out, it is the lack of documents which makes it possible to write ancient history; on the other hand it is impossible to write modern history for the simple reason that there *are* documents. Clio's struggle with this mass of documentation, her concern with every detail of what she is studying, means that she is perpetually overtaken by time, and never succeeds in writing anything: 'Il me faut une journée pour faire l'histoire d'une seconde. Il me faut une année pour faire l'histoire d'une minute. Il me faut une vie pour faire l'histoire d'une heure. Il me faut une éternité pour faire l'histoire d'un jour.'⁶

In this same essay, Péguy states the basic choice which faces such a historian. Either he must forbid himself any shortening of the methods, any choice of facts, and must therefore condemn himself to sterility; or he must choose facts, and in the process risk being unfaithful to the truth.

So a choice of facts is essential, if history is to be written. Taine himself had to ignore his own methods. The question is, who is likely to make the best choice? A man who has spent his time laboriously collecting *minutiae*, or a man who has had the leisure to survey the whole subject in its broad lines? The opposition, as stated by Péguy, can be seen to be clear and simple, and at the same time false. A good historian should surely combine both qualities. He should be able to see the broad lines of the subject, and at the same time be able to do the detailed work required.

But for Péguy, and for Huysmans, all had to be in black and white. To the modern historical method they must oppose a historian of intuition, and Michelet was the example they chose. In a short article written in 1900,[7] Péguy praises Michelet, explaining his excellence by a typically simple instance from life. During Péguy's military service, he had been forced to explain to his corporal that he had perfectly good long sight, but that he had to wear spectacles to read. 'Mon caporal m'écouta longuement. Puis il me répondit, sérieusement, doucement: Je vous entends bien. Vous êtes bon visionnaire au loin. Mais de près vous vous fatiguez. Ce caporal avait raison. En définitive, ceux que nous nommons les visionnaires sont ceux qui voient. Michelet fut un bon visionnaire au loin. Parce qu'il fut un bon historien. Le temps est passé où des critiques superficiellement exactes nous empêchaient d'aimer Michelet autant que nous en avions le désir intérieur. . . .'

Huysmans stresses the uncertainty of the non-visionary nineteenth-century historians. Their system, he felt, was simple; they discovered that a certain event took place in France in a few communes, and they immediately concluded that the whole country thought and lived in a certain way, at a certain time.[8] Their generalisations were just as likely to be false as were Michelet's, and they lacked his vision.

Where Péguy and Huysmans part company is in their judgement of Michelet's truthfulness. For Péguy he was 'sans doute le plus profond, *en un sens* le plus exact et le plus vraiment historien de nos historiens.'[9] For Huysmans the most important thing was that Michelet's characters lived: 'Peu importait dès lors que Michelet eût été le moins véridique des historiens, puisqu'il en était le plus personnel et le plus artiste.'[10]

For Péguy, at this pre-conversion stage of his career, absolute truth is unattainable, but Michelet, being an approach towards it, is the best of historians. For Huysmans, at a similar stage of his development, factual truth is not so important as the effect, the evocation of the living nature of history.

Both of them agree, however, on the pre-eminence of intuition in Michelet. Péguy makes the point that the difference between Michelet and other historians is that between genius and talent; they are not to be judged on the same scale. Michelet is an 'essential' historian in the same sense that Rembrandt is a painter or Pascal a thinker. The criticisms that people make of Michelet are those that a non-musician might make of Beethoven, or a non-painter of Rembrandt. In the works of other people one can see quite well how an intelligent man, by the power of his intelligence, could do the same thing. But in 'essential' works such as Michelet's, one cannot see at all how they were written; they are 'donné', like life itself.

> L'intelligence y nuirait plutôt [he continues]. Et même on a l'impression qu'il y a entre elles et l'intelligence une antipathie, profonde, une invincible contrariété intérieure. Tous les gens intelligents que nous connaissons, et cette engeance pullule à Paris en France, haïssent mortellement le génie et les oeuvres du génie. C'est même le seul sentiment sincère qu'on leur connaisse.[11]

So intelligence is decried, and is even denied a place in genius. And the intuition or 'génie' which is opposed to it—is that a personal attribute? Only in the sense that some have it, and others do not. It is 'donné'; it is something conferred from outside. Here are the germs of that attitude epitomised by Léon Bloy, that of the historian as prophet, capable of reading the signs and symbols of which history consists, concerned not with fact but with meaning, and owing his prophetic powers to divine revelation.

Unscientific History

Despite his criticism of scientific historical writing, Huysmans was to retain, throughout his career, the system of painstakingly amassing detailed documentation upon every subject on which he wrote. This method had been learned from Zola, in Huysmans's naturalist period, and was never to be forgotten. Bloy refers, contemptuously, to Huysmans's work as 'ignorance documentée',[12] and certainly Huysmans appears on the surface to fall into just those traps which he had ascribed to the scientific historians.

The mistakes stem, however, more from the author's subjective approach to his subject than from any misuse of the objective approach. Huysmans read extremely widely, it is true, but this reading was indiscriminate, and only too often he placed his trust

46

in the faultiest of sources. What appealed to him in his reading was the extraordinary, the picturesque, the extreme; he took anecdotes as truths, and could base a whole theory upon one concrete case. Indeed, he often started with the theory, and then sought the facts to fit it.

An example of this is the idea, which he wished to express in *Sainte Lydwine de Schiedam* (1901) of the 'apotropean' succession of expiatory victims, of whom St. Lydwine was one. For this theory to stand up it was necessary to prove that St. Lydwine and St. Colette were born in the very year that St. Catherine of Sienna died, the year 1380. When he was led to believe, by a mistake in his reading of the *Acta Sanctorum* of the Bollandists, that St. Lydwine was in fact born in 1395, his horror was such that he told Dom Besse that he would have to give up the idea of writing the book. This shows that the ideas on which the book was to be based were already formed before the examination of the documents had begun.

Huysmans, despite his apparently scholarly methods, is as subjective in his attitude to history as the other Catholic writers of his time. It is this attitude which leads to the extraordinary ideas about the Middle Ages which characterise the works of Huysmans, Bloy and many others. The first part of *Sainte Lydwine de Schiedam*, for example, a study of the state of Europe at the time of St. Lydwine's birth is both superficial and personal. Both Bloy and Huysmans are misled by their over-simplified preconceptions about the period.

In many other ways writers in this period seem, consciously or unconsciously, to be following the method of Michelet, even though they may thoroughly disapprove of the ideas he expressed in his works. Claudel lists Michelet among the damned in his *Magnificat*;[13] yet his own view of history is far from objective. Most of the right-wing Catholic writers would object to Michelet's ideas as those of a 'théologien des droits de la multitude et de cet instinct populaire qui lui semble infaillible, justificateur habituel de toutes les révoltes contre les sacerdoces et les empires.'[14] yet in the simple, general nature, for example, of Barrès's ideas on the characteristics of the different races and regions of France, we can find much of Michelet's tendency to generalisation, as seen in his *Tableau de France*. Even Bourget, when he believes himself, in his novels, to be following the ideas of Taine upon heredity and milieu, is, by his over-simplification and over-generalisation of the characteristics of the inhabitants of the various provinces, and their hereditary influence on his heroes, far closer to Michelet. This similarity is in most cases unconscious; but it does point to the essentially Romantic outlook of the Catholic historians of the period. Even of Bremond this is true; as Gonzague Truc has said of Bremond's historical writings, 'Il est trop certain que ce qui s'y trouve de principal, c'est lui-même.'[15]

The Significance of History

It is only natural that Catholic authors should have had this anti-scientific approach to history, for they believed that to the Christian all events had significance in the design of God. The historian, therefore, should attempt to discover this design and transmit it to his readers. Belief in the efficacy of prayer, in the powers of vicarious suffering, in the concept of the sacrificial offering, and in that of the hidden 'sign', all leads to the conception that the design of God may be extremely hard to perceive, and that it is only the most spiritually enlightened who can find it.

It can also lead to the belief in the overpowering personal mission of certain historical characters, and of their wide mystical effect, so much greater than any material effect could be. Nations become powerful or weak, battles are won or lost, catastrophes may happen or be averted, all because of the prayers or the example of certain key figures. For Huysmans, and many others, there is the immense power of the 'compatiente', the vicarious sufferer, to expiate the sins of a whole people, or of the whole of humanity, and thus to divert from them divine trial or punishment. Certain historical figures are seen to have an importance completely different from that which is usually ascribed to them; see, for example, the views of Bloy or Massignon on Marie Antoinette,[16] or the views of Bloy, Claudel, and many others, on Christopher Columbus.[17] The great success which the cause of Naundorff (the pretended Louis XVII) was to have among the writers of the period was due to the fact that they saw in him a 'sign' and an example of a man rejected, 'déchu' from his high seat, unrecognised by man, and partaking, in kind, of the suffering of Christ. In this they were reinforced by the acceptance of the pretender by two false prophets, Martin de Gaillardon and Vintras.

Professor Louis Massignon, in his article on Marie Antoinette, states his theory of history: 'L'histoire est citation récapitulative, à comparution judiciaire, de séries successives de témoins volontaires pour une revendication de justice et de vérité; séries explicatrices, compatientes, expiatrices des crises de douleur des masses.'[18] This is a logical extension of the attitude of those writers among whom he grew up, and who were to have such a great influence on him—Huysmans above all. For Massignon, every event and every person had a supernatural significance.

Intimately connected with these ideas of the mystical significance of all human actions is the concept of a mystical symbolism, in which even such small things as the names of places or of people may have an equally great significance. A good example of this is the meaning ascribed by both Bloy and Claudel to the name of Christopher Columbus. For both of them, Columbus was significant not only as the discoverer of America, nor even merely as the man who brought the gospel to those living in darkness. For his name is a 'sign' of the true meaning of his existence: 'Christophe Colomb—la mystérieuse Colombe portant le Christ!'[19] Claudel's Columbus exclaims, in similar fashion, 'Mon nom est l'Ambassadeur de Dieu, le Porteur du Christ! Mon premier nom est le porteur du Christ! et mon second nom est tout ce qui est lumière, tout de qui est esprit et tout ce qui a des ailes!'[20] But Claudel does not, with Bloy, deduce from this that Christopher Columbus is a figuration of the Holy Spirit, in accordance with the statement 'Spiritus sanctus corporali specie sicut Columba.'[21] He confines himself to all the symbolic possibilities of the name (the dove sent by Noah to find land, etc.) and thus shows that Columbus, by his name, has a mystical place in God's pattern for the world; but he does not tread the more dangerous paths of Bloy.

These dangerous paths are peculiar to Bloy and are due, to a certain extent, to his interpretation of the exegetical system of the abbé Tardif de Moidrey. As these views were to have an immense effect on Bloy's thought in all spheres, it would be as well to examine them in some detail here.

Tardif de Moidrey and Léon Bloy

Savoir les grands événements, leurs dates, quelques-unes des circonstances principales qui les ont accompagnés, ce n'est pas savoir grand'chose [writes Bloy]. Plus je lis l'histoire et plus je m'aperçois que je l'ignore. . . . Je cherche Dieu dans l'histoire, c'est-à-dire la Main de Dieu dans tous les événements de l'histoire.'[22]

A great deal of Bloy's attitude towards history seems to stem from the ideas on biblical exegesis which were transmitted to him by the abbé Tardif de Moidrey, a priest of profound yet at times unbalanced piety, a depositary of many of the more extraordinary ideas of the period. Bloy met the abbé in 1877, and it was in his company and at his suggestion that Bloy made his first trip to La Salette in 1879. Tardif died on the trip, but this short acquaintance had had the most enormous effect upon Bloy in all sorts of ways. Bloy himself was to stress this influence, which was not purely confined to biblical exegesis, but also had a great deal to do with Bloy's subsequent devotion to La Salette, among other things. In his autobiographical novel *Le Désespéré*, Bloy describes the effect the 'abbé T . . .' had upon Marchenoir, his hero: 'Il est certain que Marchenoir tenait de lui le meilleur de ce qu'il possédait intellectuellement. Le défunt lui avait transmis d'abstruses méthodes d'interprétation sacrée qui devinrent aussitôt une algèbre universelle dans le miroir ardent de cet esprit concentrateur.'[23] This is a true description of what happened; Tardif's ideas on biblical exegesis were transformed by Bloy into something far more wild and strange.

Tardif de Moidrey's theory, to put it simply, was that every word in the Bible is to be taken as referring to the Holy Trinity. Everything is part of God's own autobiography, as it were.[24] Bloy extended this from the Bible to the whole of history; just as God, 'ne pouvant parler que de Lui-même,'[25] must necessarily be represented by both Cain and Abel, so must all historical characters and events be part of the same representation. For Bloy, the whole of history and the whole of our life have a bearing on the Holy Trinity; and the sufferings of the world are a re-enactment of the Passion of Christ. Not only this (and here is where the danger comes), every event in history becomes, for Bloy, a part of the Passion; but though at times this appears to be a symbolic parallel, and though at times one feels that he considers our sufferings here on earth to be a vicarious participation in the sufferings of Christ, only too often one finds a sense that it *is* the suffering of Christ himself that we are experiencing, and that this is an enactment rather than a re-enactment. Time does not really exist, for we are participating in a timeless drama: 'Le temps est une imposture de l'Ennemi du genre humain que désespère la pérennité des âmes. Nous sommes toujours au XVe siecle, comme au Xe., comme à l'heure centrale de l'Immolation du Calvaire, comme avant la venue du Christ.'[26]

It is the series of extraordinary correspondences which this belief produces (e.g. The Poor equals Christ, Money equals the Blood of the Poor equals the Blood of Christ, etc.) that are the cause of many of the excessive, and at times unconsciously heretical, views of Bloy, particularly with regard to suffering, with which we will be dealing later in this volume.[27]

What is needed is the power to perceive truth as a prophet, as a visionary. Bloy considers that very few historians, other than himself, have ever had this power; the methods that are valid in his case are therefore useless, he thinks, in that of others. And it must be admitted that, however factually incorrect Bloy's history may be, however personal the interpretations he gives, the emotional effect is often overpowering. Certain passages in *L'Âme de Napoléon* and *Jeanne d'Arc et l'Allemagne* are fine examples of his power of historical evocation.

As for the theories of Tardif de Moidrey, they were by no means necessarily to blame for the strange paths which Bloy's thought later took. A writer like Paul Claudel could express his admiration for Tardif de Moidrey,[28] and base his own biblical exegesis upon him, without following the same paths as Bloy. In fact, his study of Tardif de Moidrey has the title *Du sens Figuré de l'Écriture*, which shows only too clearly that he had fallen into none of the dangers we have seen. No, Bloy was right when he referred to his own effect on Tardif's theories as 'le miroir ardent de cet esprit concentrateur'. It was Bloy's own character, together with his implicit belief in the 'revelations' of his mistress, Anne-Marie Roulé, which was responsible for the excess of his theories; on the basis of a rapid and incomplete understanding of Tardif de Moidrey's ideas he constructed a universal system which in its wildness and excesses was far from its original source.

Not only was the reaction to scientific history to be expected at the time; it was also natural to find it manifesting itself in Catholic authors. Rather than amass meaningless facts they sought the hand of God in the events of history; for them everything had some possible significance. This mystical approach to history, and the over-simplification that the reaction against the scientific method entailed, had an immense effect upon the thought of the period in every field. In their rejection of the scientific method and their concentration on the symbolic aspects both of the Bible and of history, writers such as Claudel and Péguy felt themselves to be returning to the analogical, anagogical and allegorical traditions of the biblical exegesis of the Middle Ages.

NOTES

[1] J.-K. Huysmans, *Là-bas*, Paris, 1891, Ch. 2.

[2] 'Agathon', *L'esprit de la nouvelle Sorbonne*, Paris, 1911, p. 35.

[3] Ibid., p. 38.

[4] Anatole France, *L'Ile des Pingouins*, Paris, 1908; quoted in *L'Esprit de la Nouvelle Sorbonne*, p. 38.

[5] Péguy, *Clio*; Pléiade, Prose II, p. 237.

[6] Ibid. p. 240.

[7] Péguy, *Réponse brève à Jaurès*, 4 July 1900; Pléiade, Prose I, p. 278.

[8] Huysmans, *Là-bas*, ch. 2.

[9] Péguy, Réponse brève à Jaurès; Pléiade, Prose I, p. 278. My italics.

[10] Huysmans, *Là-bas*, ch. 2.

[11] Péguy, *De la Situation Faite à l'Histoire et à la Sociologie dans les Temps Modernes*, 4 November 1906; Pléiade, Prose I, p. 1009.

[12] Bloy, *Le Mendiant Ingrat*, 1892–5.

[13] Claudel, *Troisième Ode, Magnificat*, 1907; Pléiade, Poetry, p. 261.

[14] Maurras, *Trois idées politiques: Chateaubriand, Michelet, Sainte-Beuve*, Paris, 1898.

[15] G. Truc, *Histoire de la Littérature Catholique Contemporaine*, Paris, 1961, p. 142.

[16] Bloy, *La Chevalière de la mort*, Gand, 1891. Louis Massignon, 'Un Voeu et un Destin: Marie-Antoinette, Reine de France'; in *Lettres nouvelles*, September–October, 1955.

[17] Bloy, *Le Révélateur du Globe: Christophe Colomb et sa béatification future*, Paris, 1884; *Christophe Colomb devant les Taureaux*, Paris, 1890. Claudel, *Le Livre de Christophe Colomb*, 1927; Pléiade, Théâtre II.

[18] Op. cit., p. 1.

[19] Bloy, *Le Révélateur du Globe*, Paris, 1884, p. 8.

[20] Claudel, *Le Livre de Christophe Colomb*, 1927; Pléiade, Théâtre II, p. 1146.

[21] Bloy, *Le Révélateur du Globe*, p. 3.

[22] Bloy, *Histoire de France racontée à Véronique et Madeleine* (*Introduction inachevée*), printed at the end of *La Porte des Humbles*, the last section of the Journal, 1915–17.

[23] Bloy, *Le Désespéré*, Paris, 1886, p. 37.

[24] 'Cette science, telle que je l'ai conçue ou inventée, partant de ce point que *l'Ecriture*—c'est-à-dire la Vulgate—n'est que *l'Autobiographie divine*, peut

et doit se définir: L'ILLUMINATION, lieu d'embarquement de tout enseignement théologique et mystique.' Bloy, *Cochons-sur-Marne*, 4 April 1903.

[25] Bloy, *Le Salut par les Juifs*, Paris, 1892, p. 140.

[26] Bloy, *Jeanne d'Arc et l'Allemagne*, Paris, 1915.

[27] See Ch. Eight.

[28] Claudel, *Du sens Figuré de l'Écriture: introduction au Livre de Ruth commencé
par l'abbé Tardif de Moidrey*, Paris, 1937.

CHAPTER FOUR

Simplicity and Reality of Belief

The Night of Trust

> Me voici. Je ne suis qu'un homme.
> C'est Vous qui éclairez la nuit.[1]

This statement by Francis Jammes of an infinite trust and reliance in God is an expression, both by its form and its content, of that simple approach to religious matters which characterises many of the writers of this period, and which numbers among its causes those anti-intellectual trends we have been examining. Time and again writers deny the value of intellectual commentaries and explanations; God is to be trusted, and we gain knowledge of ultimate truth through simple acts such as prayer and through the imitation of Christ's example.

The image of Night is one common to all the main Catholic authors of the period. In their thought Night equals Ignorance (the ignorance of human reasonings) which equals True Knowledge. Claudel, for example, writing to Gide in 1903, rejoices in the defeat of nineteenth-century science, and cries: 'Nous allons enfin respirer à pleins poumons la sainte nuit, la bienheureuse ignorance.'[2]

Péguy's is in many ways the best expression of these trends. He devotes almost the whole of his two great mysteries, *Le Porche du Mystère de la Deuxième Vertu* (1911) and the *Mystère des Saints Innocents* (1912), to a thorough examination of the problem; though if we take him as an example we must always remember that most of these opinions are shared by many of his Catholic contemporaries and predecessors. He does not expand or develop the ideas very far, but he does express them clearly and memorably and with a wealth of metaphorical illustration.

In the *Mystère des Saints Innocents* his main illustration for man's need to place himself in the hands of God is Night, as being the time when man's conscious defences are at their lowest. God, says Péguy, will not only reveal to man all that is necessary (and as for the rest, what is the point of trying to find it out?); he will also take care of him far better than he could take care of himself. Péguy depicts God, in this poem, as glorifying Night because it somehow manages to obtain that most difficult of things, man's abdication of his personal judgement:

Le désistement de l'homme.

L'abandonnement de l'homme entre mes mains.[3]

Still speaking in the person of God, however, Péguy stresses man's liberty, and describes it as 'le mystère des mystères.' This might at first seem a contradiction; but it must be considered in relation to the concept of liberty which Péguy shared with many other writers, including Claudel. They hold the perfectly orthodox doctrine that, while it is man's liberty that has produced sin in this world, it is this same liberty which has provided the means of redemption and the possibility of sanctity. They are thus in no way opposed to the idea of liberty; it is their *definition* of liberty which places this idea in line with the rest of their religious philosophy. For them, entire reliance on God in no way involves any abdication of personal liberty, because the decision to place one's trust in God is in itself a free decision. Once it has been taken, however, man should abandon himself entirely to the mercy of God and let Him decide.

This concept of 'freedom to obey' can lead to extraordinary consequences, particularly in the political field. It is, however, the perfectly logical contrary to what one might call the 'necessity to disobey' which characterises the work of so many of the secular writers of the time.

All Péguy's God demands is that man should let himself go and forget his ridiculous thoughts, which anyway are never of any use:

Que sa tête surtout ne marche plus. Elle ne marche que trop, sa tête. Et il croit que c'est du travail, que sa tête marche comme ça.

Et ses pensées, non, pour ce qu'il appelle ses pensées . . .

Quand on voit ce que c'est, ce qu'il appelle ses idées.

Pauvre être.[4]

Man is continually wishing to do God's job, which is to look after the morrow:

Ils veulent toujours faire mon métier, qui est de peser le lendemain.

Ils ne veulent jamais faire le leur, qui est de le subir.[5]

All man needs to do is trust and pray:

> Il ferait mieux de faire sa prière.[6]

In all this Péguy is still following the religious ideas of his time.[7] But whereas most of his contemporaries would follow Péguy in his conception of the Night of trust, the Night both of ignorance and and of true knowledge, few of them would agree with him in his claim that every word of God as expressed in the Bible is essentially simple and to be taken at its face value. Bloy, for example, with his whole system of symbolical exegesis, would be appalled at the suggestion.

For Péguy, Christ's words are simple and clear. There is no point in searching for hidden meanings in them. Christ did not have much time in this world, so surely he would not waste his time trying to mislead us?

> Il n'avait pas de temps à perdre, il n'a pas perdu son temps à
>   nous conter des fariboles et à nous donner des charades à
>   deviner.
> Des charades très spirituelles.
> Très ingénieuses
> Des devinettes de sorcier.
> Avec des mots à double entente et des malices et de misérables
>   finesses de finasseries.
> Non, il n'a pas perdu son temps et sa peine,
> Il n'avait pas le temps.[8]

It is only idiots, 'qui cherchent midi à quatorze heures,' who go looking for hidden meanings. For nothing is so simple as the word of God. He tells us ordinary things, in an ordinary way:

> Il est venu nous dire ce qu'il avait à nous dire.
> N'est-ce pas.
> Tout tranquillement.
> Tout simplement, tout honnêtement.
> Tout directement. Tout premièrement.
> Tout ordinairement.
> Comme un honnête homme parle à un honnête homme.
> D'homme à hommes.[9]

This is a natural extension, in Péguy's mind, of the concept of man's simple approach to God; it is also a reflection of his view of the importance of the human element in the Incarnation, with Christ the simple peasant whom we see in Madame Gervaise's description of the Passion, in the *Mystère de la Charité de Jeanne d'Arc*. But not many of his contemporaries and predecessors would have accepted this extension. For them, an element of mystery was essential in Christian belief, and the transcendental element of Christ was far more important than the human. The simple approach to Christianity meant, to them, blind trust, whether they understood everything or not; they would not necessarily expect all to be laid simply before them, except by exceptional divine relevation.

The Innocence of the Child

> Petit Jésus qu'il nous faut être,
> Si nous voulons voir Dieu le Père,
> Accordez-nous d'alors renaître
>
> En purs bébés, nus, sans repaire
> Qu'une étable, et sans compagnie
> Qu'un âne et qu'un boeuf, humble paire;
>
> D'avoir l'ignorance infinie
> Et l'immense toute-faiblesse
> Par quoi l'humble enfance est bénie.[10]

In these lines by Paul Verlaine we find once again the plea for ignorance, for the lack of human knowledge; yet implicit in this statement is the feeling that this 'ignorance' we are seeking is in fact true knowledge. Children, in their simplicity and purity, enjoy that understanding of the true nature of things which is gradually broken down, as they grow up, by the increase of purely human knowledge. Their simple trust and innocence are a form of spiritual greatness which man will try in vain fully to achieve, or indeed regain.

This view of the primal innocence of children is not, of course, peculiarly Christian. Truth and innocence have often been associated by non-Christian writers, and so it is no surprise at all to find Francis Jammes, even before his conversion, writing: 'Pour être vrai, mon coeur a parlé comme un enfant.'[11] Both before and after his conversion Jammes is remarkable not only for his extreme simplicity of style but also for an equal simplicity of subject-matter. In those poems which contain a Christian message, this message is conveyed by the most simple exterior descriptions, and by the evocation of the faith of children and peasants.

As Péguy says, 'C'est l'innocence qui sait et c'est l'expérience qui ne sait pas.'[12] The whole of his work *Le Mystère des Saints Innocents* is based on this apparently paradoxical contrast. The title of this work has a significance far beyond the historical event with which so small a part of it is specifically concerned, for the whole work is a study of the mystery of the relation between holiness and innocence.

The contrast between children and their parents is gradually built up in this work. Péguy's God is mystified by the fact that children are sent to school:

> On envoie les enfants à l'école, dit Dieu.
> Je pense que c'est pour oublier le peu qu'ils savent.
> On ferait mieux d'envoyer les parents à l'école.
> C'est eux qui en ont besoin.
> Mais naturellement il faudrait une école de moi
> Et non pas une école d'hommes.[13]

As human knowledge grows, divine knowledge disappears. The parents know nothing, the children know everything:

> Car ils savent l'innocence première
> Qui est tout.[13]

Life, too, is a school, so they say; in it one gathers experience. Yet of what use is that? It is an equally empty form of knowledge:

> Singulier trésor, dit Dieu.
> Trésor de vide et de disette,
> Trésor de la disette des sept années, trésor de vide et de flétrissure et de vieillissement.
> Trésor de rides et d'inquiétudes.
> Trésor des années maigres. Accroissez-le, ce trésor, dit Dieu.
> Dans ces greniers vides
> Vous entasserez des sacs vides
> D'une Égypte vide.[14]

The great example of the power and truth of innocence, says Péguy, is the immediate admiration which is aroused among men when they hear a 'mot d'enfant,' a child's simple and innocent phrase. This sincere, profound admiration, he says, is almost enough to redeem them; they laugh, and say, 'Il est bon, celui-là, je le retiens.' They intend to repeat it to their friends, but when they try to do so they find that it has disappeared from their memory:

> C'est une eau trop pure qui a fui de votre sale mémoire, de votre mémoire souillée.[15]

The sense of a lost paradise of truth, which must be sought again if man is to be saved, is thus intimately connected with the innocence of childhood. Man must 'apprendre à désapprendre.'[16] Péguy's is the most complete treatment of this theme; but it is the summing-up of the attitude of a great many writers, who see in the child an example of divine knowledge, innocence and trust. Unfortunately some writers, particularly some of the minor Catholic poets (for example, Amélie Murat and Louis Lefebvre), turn this image into one of a rather maudlin sentimentality, far from the effective treatment given to it by Jammes and Péguy.

The Common Sense of the Peasant

For many of the writers of the period (Bazin, Péguy and Claudel, for example) the peasant stands for the great principles—Tradition, Loyalty, the Family, the Land. A nation, for them, rests on the broad shoulders of its peasants.[17] But what concerns us here are those characteristics which make the peasant in one sense a parallel to the child—his common sense, his trust and his simplicity.

The peasant is regarded as the man whose intuition shows him the right course when more intelligent men are taking the wrong one. In Jean Nesmy's novel *Les Égarés*, for example, the peasants are not taken in at all by the intellectual arguments in favour of pacifism, put forward by a young schoolmaster. The meeting breaks up in disorder amidst shouts of 'Vive l'armée! Vive la France!' Their natural instinct, we are told, was the right one: 'C'était la réponse des simples aux insultes d'intellectuels, qu'ils avaient entendues.'[18]

For the peasant was above all the Catholic of tradition, who had remained untouched by the intellectual movements of the capital and had thus escaped the dangers of that unbelief from which most of the Catholic authors of the time had emerged as converts. As such, the peasant represented the continuity of Christianity, the unshakeable faith which these converts were seeking. He does not get bound up in complicated arguments; he works, and God is with him. Claudel's Anne Vercors, in *L'Annonce faite à Marie*, stresses the mysterious spirituality of the peasant's simple life:

O bon ouvrage de l'agriculteur, où le soleil est comme notre boeuf luisant, et la pluie notre banquier, et Dieu tous les jours au travail notre compagnon, faisant de tous les mieux!

La terre tient au ciel, le corps tient à l'esprit, toutes les choses qu'il a créées ensemble communiquent, toutes à la fois sont nécessaires l'une à l'autre.[19]

Joan of Arc, of course, was popular with Catholic writers for a great many reasons—patriotism, the assurance of France's Christian mission, anti-pacifism, etc.—but though Claudel and Péguy value her for these reasons too, it is primarily as a peasant that they see her, simple and trusting. Much of Péguy's work is concerned with this saint.

Péguy's peasants are far from the idealised picture given by other writers, many of whom would have been horrified to meet a real peasant. In Bazin's novels, for example, as Henry Bordeaux (himself not entirely guiltless in this respect) says, 'Ça ne sent pas assez le fumier; mais ça embaume les fleurs des champs.'[20] In Barbey d'Aurevilly's works the peasants merely provide delightful local colour, and in many of the Catholic poets they are only pale literary shadows, two-dimensional symbols of an innocence which the poets themselves did not fully understand.

It is in Péguy and Jammes that we find the most worthy treatment of the peasant. Whatever symbolic use they may put him to, he is *real*. Jammes, who spent almost the whole of his life in or near Orthez, in the Pyrenees, remained a poet of the countryside not from literary fashion or from religious symbolism but because he *was* a countryman. His simple descriptions are at all times three-dimensional and never give an impression of factitious invention. Péguy on the other hand spent most of his career in Paris, but his roots remained with his peasant mother in Orleans, whom he often visited. In *Solvuntur Objecta* he explains that he himself is a true peasant, however much he may have tried, when younger, to cover this up under a veneer of 'École Normale' sophistication. Such an attempt is now not only impossible, he says, but not in the slightest bit desirable. For he is proud of his peasant nature, of 'ma grand mère qui gardait les vaches, qui ne savait pas lire et écrire . . . à qui je dois tout, à qui je dois, de qui je tiens tout ce que je suis.'[21] Above all he is not a 'literary' peasant like La Fontaine's peasant of the Danube, or Ronsard's woodcutters of the forest of Gastine, or like so many peasants in contemporary Catholic literature: 'Tout concourt à faire de moi un paysan non point du Danube, ce qui serait de la littérature encore, mais simplement de la vallée de la Loire, un bûcheron d'une forêt qui n'est pas même l'immortelle forêt de Gastine, puisque c'était la périssable forêt d'Orléans.'[22]

In Péguy's works the peasants are real people with real worries. They have faults, like other men; and even their virtues may at first sight seem faults. The cunning of the peasant, for example, is seen by Péguy as a virtue. He describes the sheaves of corn in the fields as being, like gothic arches, an example of this peasant cunning, with shapes that are deceptively innocent in appearance but remarkably effective as a protection against wind and rain: 'Innocentes courbes et formes, dites-vous; innocentes, apparemment; astucieuses en réalité, astucieuses et très habiles, d'une patiente et invincible habileté paysanne, invinciblement astucieuse contre la pluie oblique et le vent démolisseur.'[23]

This cunning is the peasant's practical protection against a hostile world; it is through this protection that he can continue to do that temporal work which is the highest form of spirituality. As Péguy says, comparing the workers of previous generations with the strikers of the twentieth century: 'Ils disaient en riant, et pour embêter les curés, que travailler c'est prier, et ils ne croyaient pas si bien dire.

'Tant leur travail était une prière. Et l'atelier un oratoire.'[24]

The peasant's situation is similar to that of these workers. To work is to pray. To work successfully is to pray successfully. And peasant cunning is not only the way to successful work; it is also the symbol of the practical bent of the peasant. When Péguy discerns this characteristic within the works of Renan, the man he is attempting to refute, he is incapable of concealing a kind of grudging admiration:

Il est incroyable déjà qu'un intellectuel ait pu, aussi constamment, déployer, comme on dit, tant d'astuce. On dirait d'un paysan. Il faut que toute la vieille rouerie des ancêtres marins et pêcheurs et des ancêtres paysans se soit maintenue en dessous, ait nourri son homme. . . . Une telle ruse, une telle astuce, d'une telle constance, d'une telle perfection, est beaucoup trop accomplie pour être une simple astuce intellectuelle. Il faut que ce soit une astuce de paysan, une astuce héréditaire demeurée toujours vigilante, et infatigable.[25]

This virtue of cunning is matched, in Péguy's thought, by that other peasant virtue: obstinacy.[26] It is a characteristic possessed, above all, by Péguy's Joan of Arc. In a long argument she has with the nun, Madame Gervaise, at the end of the *Mystère de la Charité de Jeanne d'Arc* (1910), this quality is stressed by her simple, repetitive answers to all the reasonings which are put before her. Her mind has one track only, and often we feel that she is not even listening to Madame Gervaise.

As Péguy himself says, 'Nulle Jeanne d'Arc n'est historique, nulle Jeanne d'Arc n'est dans le tissu de la réalité de l'histoire qu'une Jeanne d'Arc profondément et éternellement peuple';[27] so it was only natural that it should be this Saint who took up such a great amount of his poetic writings. Of all the French writers of the period who used this theme, he was the only one to make her truly a peasant.[28]

Péguy was not the only Catholic author of the time to come from peasant stock. The poet Loys Labèque, for example, was the son of a shepherd. But Péguy's peasants, and those of Jammes, are the only ones that truly convince the reader.

Péguy and the Incarnation

Péguy's admiration for peasant virtues, his association of the peasant with all that is best and most real in Christian belief, can be seen in what is the most impressive and the most moving piece of verse he ever wrote: the long description of the Passion[29] told by Madame Gervaise in *Le Mystère de la Charité de Jeanne d'Arc*. Here the Virgin Mary, through whose eyes much of the Passion is seen, is a peasant woman, bewildered, anguished, uncomprehending:

> Elle suivait, elle pleurait, elle ne comprenait pas très bien.
> Mais elle comprenait très bien que le gouvernement était
>   contre son garcon.
> Ce qui est une mauvaise affaire.

Her reactions are those of an ordinary mother:

> On a souvent beaucoup de mal avec les enfants . . .
> Quand ils grandissent.
> Elle l'avait bien dit à Joseph.
> Ça finirait mal.

She shows the peasant respect for a man of importance like Joseph of Arimathea. Jesus's friendship with this man (no one would give up their sepulchre to anyone 'avec qui on n'était pas bien') showed, she thought, that Jesus could not be the good-for-nothing vagabond which the chief priests were trying to make him out to be. (Even though he had been going around a lot lately with 'des gens qui n'étaient pas des ouvriers qui travaillaient.')

Jesus, too, is credited with some of the reactions of a solid peasant. He cast the merchants out of the temple for very good reasons: they were desecrating the house of God, and by driving them out he was fulfilling the Scriptures. But all the same, he also has the peasant's mistrust of merchants:

D'ailleurs il n'aimait pas les commerçants.

Ouvrier.

Fils d'ouvriers.

Fils nourricier.

Fils nourri

De famille ouvrière.

D'instinct il n'aimait pas les commerçants.

Il n'entendait rien au commerce.

Au négoce.

Il ne savait que travailler.

Il était porté à croire que tous les commerçants étaient des voleurs.

All this is done not to lower Christ and his mother, but rather to stress more vividly the meaning of Christ's Incarnation. For Christ was made man as a member of a working family, in a certain place, at a certain time. For Péguy, the peasant was the most noble form under which Christ could be made man. Péguy's *Passion* is, in fact, a form of shock tactics to stress the temporal aspect of the Incarnation, which he felt was neglected by other Christians: 'Ils ne la considèrent guère que venant de l'éternel, du côté de l'éternel, procédant de l'éternel, *ab aeterno, ab aeternitate.*'[30]

Throughout his works the message is hammered home, time and again, that in the Incarnation the temporal and the eternal are inextricably intermingled. In fact the Incarnation is the extreme case of a general law applying to all creation: 'L'incarnation n'est qu'un cas culminant . . . de cette (toute) mystérieuse insertion de l'éternel dans le temporel, du spirituel dans le charnel, qui est le gond, qui est cardinale, qui est, qui fait l'articulation même, le coude et le genou de toute création du monde et de l'homme. . . .'[30]

And nothing can detach man from his earthly connections, not even sanctity. If sanctity is detached from the earth, it is valueless: 'Il ne faut pas qu'elle en soit préalablement, arbitrairement, intellectuellement déracinée, déplantée. Alors on n'a plus que des miracles de pacotille.'[31] It is for this reason, among others, that Péguy's favourite Saints are Joan of Arc and St. Louis.

Péguy's stressing, in this *Passion*, of the factual, the real, does not mean that he neglects the spiritual and eternal nature of Christ and his mother. These are brought home to us with great effect at certain moments, and are set off in sharp relief against the perfectly realistic description. For example, the mother is asking herself again and again what her son could possibly have done to bring all this upon himself, when suddenly, starkly, we are told:

'Je vais vous le dire:
Il avait sauvé le monde.'

Similarly, in the middle of a most realistic description of the way in which Mary's grief had aged her, we are brought up short by the words:

'Elle était devenue Reine,
Elle était devenue Reine des Sept Douleurs.'

It is completely impossible to give any idea of the emotive effect of this *Passion* without quoting the whole immensely long text. This is one of the masterpieces of expression in the French language. It is also a profoundly religious work, with no hint of disrespect to Christ or to the Virgin Mary. Yet Claudel felt strongly about Péguy's vision of the Holy Family, and no doubt spoke for many when he said: 'Je n'aime pas, comme chrétien, je n'aime pas du tout, par exemple, l'idée qu'il se fait de la Sainte Vierge qu'il dépeint comme une bonne femme somme toute un peu comme sa mère, qui était une rempailleuse de chaises. Moi je vois la Sainte Vierge d'une toute autre manière.'[32]

One is tempted to quote here Péguy's judgement on another opponent: 'Il ne peut point pardonner à M. Péguy ce christianisme peuple, directement sorti du peuple. Il aimerait mieux un christianisme plus élégant. Distingué.'[33] But this is to some extent unfair. Claudel's main objection to Péguy, as expressed to Gide, was that he saw in his approach to God hints of Protestantism. As Claudel tended to see Protestants under every stone this accusation need not be taken too seriously, but it does show Claudel's objections to Péguy's *Mystère de la Charité de Jeanne d'Arc* to have been based on more serious grounds than simple *snobisme*.

Reality

In all this concentration on the 'real' Péguy was not as far from his Catholic contemporaries as he liked to think. While they might not have followed him in his extreme view of the peasant Christ and Virgin, a great many of them were in fact brought, by their simple approach to religion, to a concentration on the most immediately comprehensible outward attributes of Christian belief. Just as Péguy's Hauviette, referring to Joan of Arc in *Le Mystère de la Charité de Jeanne d'Arc*, had stressed the importance of the senses in Joan's intuitive approach to religion—'Tu vois, tu vois. Ce que nous savons, nous autres, tu le vois. Ce qu'on nous apprend, nous autres, tu le vois'—so we find that many other authors of the period were concerned with the external reality of things.

Even those most avid in their researches into mysticism—Huysmans and Bloy, for example—ignored almost completely the more spiritual complications and concentrated on the external, the extraordinary, the miraculous, all that is most appealing to those of simple faith. As Jean Lhermitte says in his study *Huysmans et la Mystique*, Huysmans was 'préoccupé sans relâche par l'extraordinaire, le merveilleux, que les âmes simples et les esprits insuffisamment informés considèrent comme la marque spécifique de l'expérience mystique.'[34] Similarly Bloy, so M.-J. Lory informs us, had an unconscious tendency to 'confondre le surnaturel avec le merveilleux.'[35] He was far more impressed by the lives of the desert fathers than by their teachings; the real, concrete descriptions of the visions of Anna Katharina Emmerick, who saw in detail scenes from the life of the Virgin and the Passion of Christ, had much more effect on him than the mystical visions of St. Theresa of Avila.

For Huysmans 'la Mystique est une science résolument exacte,' of which he had been able to verify one or two of the results. He did not need miracles and signs in order to believe, like so many of his contemporaries, because he felt that he knew already, from his religious reading, that such miracles could happen: 'Je ne tiens pas à voir des miracles; je sais très bien que la Vierge peut en faire à Lourdes ou autre part.'[36] In his works Huysmans unquestioningly accepts all the miracles ascribed to Saints, even those of the most dubious nature. He accepts sources which no self-respecting Catholic historian would nowadays trust. As Huysmans's friend, Lucien Descaves, is said to have remarked, for Huysmans 'credo' meant 'Je suis crédule.'

Such a physical approach to mysticism accounts for many of the more doubtful characteristics of this period of Catholic thought: the concentration on the miraculous; the seeking for a Sign; the almost mechanical, physical application of such doctrines as vicarious suffering; the immediate acceptance, by some people, of the most suspicious doctrines, because of apparently conclusive external signs;[37] the violent devotion to La Salette, despite the Church's official doubts on the matter, and the acceptance of its message; and, stemming from this, the belief in the imminent end of the world, and in the coming, *physical* Third Reign, that of the Holy Spirit, on this earth.

All this we shall see later;[38] what concerns us here is the mood engendered by the physical approach to belief, a mood which can descend at its most extreme to a positive need for physical *proof*, for a sign of God's intentions. This extreme we find in Ernest Hello, that strange, brilliant but erratic writer whose life of physical and spiritual suffering was so unbearable to him that he awaited with impatience the coming of God's justice at the end of the world, an event which, he believed, must be at hand. Above all, if he was not to despair completely he demanded physical signs from God. Writing to Léon Bloy, he said, 'Les idées ne me suffisent pas; il me faut des faits, des faits evidents, palpables, sensibles, grossiers et actuels.'[39] In the same letter Hello continued:

Concentrez toute votre prière et toute celle de vos amis sur cette nécessité de faits actuels. Il nous faut absolument des témoignages terrestres. Car ce sont l'eau, le sang et le feu qui rendent témoignage sur la terre. Des faits! Des faits! Des faits! Des signes! J'aime mieux un *tiens* que cent mille *tu l'auras*. Précipitez toutes les prières possibles sur ce même point, et, puisque je n'en peux plus, obtenez que je VOIE *aujourd'hui*.[40]

These are the extremes to which one aspect of the pursuit of reality could lead, when taken to excess. Writers like Hello often failed to see that, in the miraculous, the external is the outward expression of an inner truth which exists in its own right, and that it is the means of expression rather than an end in itself. As Péguy had said, the eternal and the temporal are intertwined; excess in one direction or in the other leads to imbalance.

But far more than in this physical approach to Christianity, Péguy is representative of contemporary Catholic thought in his concentration on the temporal aspect of the Incarnation of Christ.

Just as Péguy's Joan of Arc had envied those who had lived at the time of Jesus and had actually seen him in his physical reality, so Claudel's Anne Vercors, in *L'Annonce Faite à Marie* (1910), wishes to behold the great hole which the Cross had made in the ground. His wife tries to restrain him, declaring that God is always with us, in the tabernacle; but Anne requires this physical contact with the reality of Christ Incarnate.[41] In this he is the figure of all pilgrims, all those who, by visiting the Holy Land, wish to 'see that blessed land' and to 'honour personally, *in the Holy Places where Christ was born, lived, died and ascended to Heaven after his resurrection,* the first mysteries of our faith,' as Pope Paul VI has so recently said. It was the reality of Christ made man, and his example, which caused Charles de Foucauld to follow in his steps as a humble worker in Nazareth.

NOTES

[1] Francis Jammes, *L'Église Habillée de Feuilles*, Paris, 1906.

[2] Claudel-Gide correspondence.

[3] Péguy, *Mystère des Saints Innocents*, 24 March 1912; Pléiade, Poetry, p. 682.

[4] Ibid., p. 683.

[5] Ibid., p. 708.

[6] Ibid., p. 683.

[7] These ideas are extremely clearly stated in a letter from Charles de Foucauld to his friend Henri de Castries, in which he stresses the need for guidance rather than individual mental effort. Praising Castries's brilliant understanding of scholastic philosophy, Foucauld nevertheless denies it any value in Christian experience: 'Vous en avez fait l'expérience, ce n'est pas là que nous trouvons la lumière: nous la trouvons dans la prière, "demandez et vous recevrez"; nous la trouvons dans la persévérance à suivre les conseils d'un bon confesseur, "qui vous écoute m'écoute"; nous la trouvons dans l'imitation de Jésus, "si quelqu'un me veut servir, qu'il me suive. . . ." Et en faisant ces trois choses, nous entrons infailliblement dans ce plein jour qui nous fait dire avec David: *nox illuminatio mea in deliciis meis*.' 14 August 1901.

[8] Péguy, *Le Porche du Mystère de la Deuxième Vertu*, 24 September 1911; Pléiade, Poetry, p. 596.

[9] Ibid., p. 597.

[10] Verlaine, *Noël*; Liturgies Intimes, III.

[11] Jammes, Introduction to *Vers*, Orthez, 1893.

[12] Péguy, *Mystère des Saints Innocents*, 24 March 1912; Pléiade, Poetry, p. 786.

[13] Ibid., p. 783.

[14] Ibid., p. 785.

[15] Ibid., p. 790.

[16] Ibid., p. 786.

[17] See Chapters Ten and Eleven.

[18] Jean Nesmy, *Les Égarés*, Paris, 1906, p. 201.

[19] Claudel, *L'Annonce faite à Marie*, 1910; Pléiade, Théâtre II, p. 39. Claudel

often uses folk-songs in his works, with remarkable dramatic effect; in their simplicity they indicate symbolically yet clearly the truths that the characters are seeking.

[20] Henri Bordeaux, *Les Écrivains et les Moeurs*, Paris, 1900, p. 213.

[21] Péguy, *Solvuntur Objecta*, 23 October 1910; Pléiade, Prose II, p. 666.

[22] Ibid., p. 668.

[23] Péguy, *De la Situation Faite au Parti Intellectuel dans le Monde Moderne devant les Accidents de la Gloire Temporelle*, 6 October 1907; Pléiade. Prose I, p. 1183.

[24] Péguy, *L'Argent*, 16 February 1913; Pléiade, Prose II, p. 1052.

[25] Péguy, *De la Situation Faite à l'Histoire et à la Sociologie dans les Temps Modernes*, 4 November 1906; Pléiade, Prose I, p. 1015.

[26] Hard-headed peasant obstinacy is better described by the French adjective *têtu* than by any English equivalent.

[27] Péguy, *Un nouveau theologien: M. Fernand Laudet*, 24 September 1911; Pléiade, Prose II, p. 845.

[28] In this, for different reasons, he comes near to the conception of Joan held by Bernard Shaw.

[29] Pléiade, Poetry, pp. 438–483. This whole description was added to the play at proof stage.

[30] Péguy, *Solvuntur Objecta*; Pléiade, Prose II, p. 729.

[31] Ibid., p. 721.

[32] Claudel, *Mémoires Improvisés*, Paris, 1954, p. 298.

[33] Péguy, *Un nouveau théologien: M. Fernand Laudet*, 24 September 1911; Pléiade, Prose II, p. 848.

[34] Jean Lhermitte, Huysmans et la Mystique, *Tour St. Jacques*, May–June 1957, p. 126.

[35] Marie-Joseph Lory, *La Pensée Religieuse de Léon Bloy*, Paris, 1951, p. 41.

[36] Huysmans, *Les Foules de Lourdes*, p. 25.

[37] E.g., the acceptance of the Vintrasian doctrine because of the 'miraculous' bleeding hosts.

[38] See Chapter Seven.

[39] Bloy, when he reprinted this letter in his pamphlet *Ici on assassine les grands hommes*, noted at this point: 'Je voudrais un miracle *naturaliste*, me disait un jour Huysmans.'

[40] Ernest Hello to Léon Bloy. No date, but certainly somewhere between 1876 and 1881. Reprinted by Bloy in his pamphlet *Ici on assassine les grands hommes*, Paris, 1895.

[41] Claudel, *L'Annonce faite à Marie*; Pléiade, Théâtre II, p. 32.

CHAPTER FIVE

Violence and Exaggeration

IN the average second-feature Western the good men tend to wear white hats and the bad men black ones. The nations of Western Europe, and particularly England, looking at recent events in the United States, ascribe the over-simplification of political and social ideas which are at the basis of all such acts of terrorism and intolerance to the same type of mentality, that of the horse opera. They are a young nation, muse the reporters wisely, and they have yet to grow up into a form of civilisation such as ours.

Yet in any country, at moments of great stress, such over-simplification of issues occurs. It is not a question of civilisation or otherwise; if people feel strongly about something, and see it threatened, that is all they need to start seeing everyone who is not of their opinion as an opponent, and to start branding all these opponents as the most dastardly villains. Not only that, but they will tend to see danger under every stone, complicated plots where none exist, alliances between the coolest of friends.

In France, that most civilised of European nations, exactly such an atmosphere existed in the period preceding the 1914–18 war; and the greatest violence of all was displayed among what should be the most civilised part of the community—the writers. Both sides felt themselves threatened, and acted accordingly.

It would be easy to try to link the violence of the opinions of the Catholic writers to that simplicity of outlook which we have seen to have characterised their religion; but it would also, to some extent, be misleading. This simplicity of outlook contributed, no doubt, to laying the foundations on which simple and violent passions could flourish, but it in no way explains the fact that the opponents of the Catholic writers were equally virulent. The whole country was in a state of ferment, split from top to bottom by such issues as lay education and the laws against the Congregations. Excess led to excess on both sides until the 1914–18 war in part healed the wounds, leaving the extremists still facing each other, but providing a healthy buffer of moderate opinion between them. Many of the prejudices produced by the pre-1914 world still exist today, however; the older generation cannot forget, however hard they try, the lessons of their youth. Violent anti-clericalism, for example, still flourishes, though it no longer has the power it had before the 1914–18 war; and the political and national ideals of that epoch still live on in the words (and, one must concede, in the mind) of President de Gaulle. Much of France, and that not the least important part, is still turned back towards that period of stress, and we must not forget this when striving to interpret the events of our own day.

In such a study as this we shall naturally have to concentrate on the examples of violence to be found in the Catholic writers, and this will unavoidably give something of a one-sided effect; let us not forget, therefore, that attacks from the other side were equally naïve, and equally virulent. The vicious attacks made upon Catholicism by the Combes administration (1902–5), for example, were in part the result of the heightening of the tension and the added simplification of the 'images' produced by the Dreyfus Affair, and in part an expression of Combes's own fear of religious education, and of Catholic political intrigues (he himself was originally educated in a Catholic seminary). Fear, on both sides, made demands and actions more violent, and made originally unjustified fears only too justified. It was a vicious circle. Waldeck-Rousseau's law on the Congregations, originally moderate in intention, fell, amid the general extremism engendered by the Dreyfus Affair, into the hands of Combes, and was applied with great rigour.

Some of the best examples of this anti-clerical violence are the newspaper attacks, such as those which Péguy describes in *Casse-Cou*.[1] He quotes an article from *La Petite République* (26 October 1900), describing the reception given at a meeting of the *Coopération des idées* to a priest who had come to speak on 'Le rôle social du christianisme' (the scene is very similar to one in Bourget's *L'Étape*, (1902)):

> Nos camarades du faubourg Antoine se sont chargés de la résoudre [the question of free schools] avec autant de simplicité que de promptitude: ils ont mis le 'curé' à la porte. . . . Et je me suis réjoui de les entendre crier 'A bas la calotte.' Quand il s'agit de réfuter la doctrine du bayado, je goûte fort les objections présentées sous cette forme vigoureuse et synthétique.[2]

Not all attacks were as frontal as this. Just as dangerous, if not more so, was that pretence of tolerance so common to liberals, which turns out so often merely to be tolerance towards those ideas with which they agree. Only too often, indeed, this form of intolerance was hidden even to themselves. M. Monneron, for example, in Bourget's *L'Étape*, believes himself to be broadminded; yet he is violently anti-Catholic. He opposes the project that a Catholic priest should speak on social work to the 'Union Tolstoï', producing in his support the excuse that one cannot be tolerant to the intolerant. In other parts of this book M. Monneron, after saying that his children are perfectly free to choose whatever belief they wish, declares how shocked he would be if they should become Catholics, because the beliefs are so wrong. As M. Ferrand, the Bonaldist Catholic professor, says, 'Monneron se croit tolérant. C'est un fanatique à rebours.'³ It must be admitted, however, that Bourget himself is equally intolerant in his tacit condemnation of the liberal Catholic priest's attempts at understanding and agreement with the other side.

Monneron's fanaticism is unconscious; he believes himself to be completely unbiased in all things. Despite Bourget's own extremism, there is much that rings true in Monneron; his attitude to Catholicism is, to this day, that of any number of well-meaning liberals in all countries who do not realise that anti-Catholicism can become the anti-Semitism of the liberal intellectual.

The Catholics in this period felt themselves to be a minority, threatened by multiple dangers. There was the political danger; the Church, having for so long been associated with right-wing, monarchical movements, was perpetually threatened by the Republican régimes. There was the danger of individualism, as seen in Protestantism and in the philosophy of Kant. There was, very strongly, the danger of that individualism and freedom from restraint which was preached by Gide and followed by so many of the younger generation. There was the danger of the reign of science, though by the turn of the century this was receding. And there were many other dangers, great and small. But, above all, there was the danger from within the Church. Heresy appeared to be rearing its head, in different forms, and must be stamped out. Small wonder that so many of the Catholic authors, in this apparently desperate position, should have stood firm on orthodoxy and tradition, order and discipline, denied anything that savoured of dealing with the enemy, and violently counter-attacked whenever possible. Small wonder that they should have mistrusted the liberal Catholics' dealings with the Republic, the exegetical modernists' use of scientific methods, the philosophical modernists' tendency to individualism. Their opinions became massive and monolithic; they were blind to the opinions and beliefs of others, and even mistrusted those who appeared luke-warm on their own side. 'Vae tepidis',[4] as Péguy was to say. He who was not with them was against them, and to be with them a man had to be thoroughly committed. As Léon Bloy put it: '(Règle sans exception.) Il ne faut jamais rien accorder à l'ennemi, rien, rien, RIEN.'[5]

'*Vae tepidis*'

The violence of Catholic views in this period stems in part from conscious, in part from unconscious causes. There were those who saw the irrationality of the course they were taking but justified it by appealing to expediency; and there were those who followed naturally the simple and violent demands of their temperament. Claudel was, to some degree, in the first of these groups, and in the important conversations he had on the radio in 1951 and 1952 with Jean Amrouche he explained the attitude of mind to which he had held throughout his career. Having said that all error has some truth in it, and that one has to decide which side to see, he continued: 'Or, moi, j'ai eu à lutter toute ma vie contre l'erreur. Je me suis trouvé seul, j'ai eu à lutter très durement at très énergique-ment contre un tas de mensonges qui tâchaient de s'imposer a moi, et j'ai dû réagir avec la plus grande violence, avec la plus grande brutalité, à ce sujet là.'[6]

Many of Claudel's enemies were to call him a Pharisee, and the frequency with which the word appears to have occurred in his letters and his conversation shows that he himself was perhaps worried by the applicability of this term to him. Writing in a letter to René Schwob about his attitude to Gide, he contrasts his own attitude with the ineffectual moderation of many other Catholics (he is writing in 1933): 'Il n'y a pas de pharisaïsme à l'attaquer, c'est au contraire un devoir. Un tout autre ton, en tout cas, est de mise que celui d'une indulgence attendrie. Mais c'est le ton veule et bénisseur qui est aujourd'hui à la mode chez beaucoup de catholiques.'[7]

It was Claudel's misfortune, in a way, to outlive so many of his Catholic contemporaries who died in or before the First World War, and to remain as an outpost of a previous age in a time when Catholic attitudes were changing. Far too many people ascribe to Claudel personal characteristics which are not his, and make of him an ogre. Claudel's were the ideas and attitudes of his age; he changed them little, and perhaps became more entrenched in them as time went by, but it is against the atmosphere that surrounded his youth that we must see him, if we wish to judge his person. A threat to Christianity gives rise to violent reflexes in a Christian author, and it is sometimes difficult for him to realise when the danger is past.

In the Catholic world before 1914 many people felt that there was no room for softness towards the enemy. To a certain extent this attitude was justified by the suspicion with which the enemy received any such approaches. Bourget attacks the liberal Catholics, and accuses them of, in effect, sympathising with the other side in the political battle; when Savignan's son, in *Le Démon de Midi*, claims that they stand for broadmindedness both to left and right, Savignan denies this, saying that they are broad to the left, narrow to the right:

> Un catholique libéral est un catholique qui aime beaucoup les libéraux et très peu les catholiques. Ah! l'étrange déviation de la conscience! Elle consiste à servir, sous son drapeau, loyalement d'ailleurs, en détestant, en critiquant les gens qui servent sous le même drapeau, et à réserver toute son admiration, toute sa sympathie pour l'ennemi.[8]

One finds similar attacks in the works of many others.

Liberal Catholicism had some success among the intellectuals, but there its influence could be said to end. The mass of believers were either already entrenched in their traditional beliefs or were reinforced in them by the writers of the Catholic Revival. In journalism liberal Catholic power was slightly greater, though it was faced by the might of Drumont in *La Libre Parole*, Cassagnac in *L'Autorité*, Father Bailly and the Assumptionists in *La Croix*, and later Maurras and Daudet in *L'Action Française*. In the novel, the theatre and poetry it was almost non-existent.[9]

In other fields, too, moderates were viewed with great suspicion; any sign of moderation was regarded as treating with the enemy. Thus Péguy accuses the Thomists, in their attempt to reconcile

Catholicism and intellectualism, of voluntarily or involuntarily helping the intellectual party at the Sorbonne,[10] and Claudel contemptuously dismisses Blondel, the philosophical modernist, as a 'Protestant'.[11] Fear is another emotion ascribed to the moderate, even if it is, as in Péguy's attacks on lukewarm Christians, merely the fear of ridicule: 'Il s'agit ici de l'homme qui ne s'occupe point de savoir s'il croit ou s'il ne croit pas. Il s'agit de l'homme qui n'a qu'un souci, qui n'a qu'une pensée: *ne pas faire sourire M. Anatole France*. Il s'agit de l'homme qui vendrait son Dieu pour ne pas être ridicule.'[12]

All these writers see the greatest danger as coming from within the Church; if only the Church were strong and united, violent and powerful, no enemy could deal with it. Some of the most violent attacks made by Catholic writers are against the clergy of the day and the Catholic laity, who, they believed, even when they were not heretical, were cowardly and somnolent. Catholics must be not only true believers but also fighters in a violent cause. Those who were prepared to co-exist with the Republic were condemned by many, despite the Pope's call to *Ralliement*; and apathy in the face of anti-clerical measures was regarded by these writers as a prime reason for the downfall of the Church.

In political and religious matters there were, for the Catholic writers of our period, no possible shades of opinion. Nothing could be grey; everything had to be black or white. One of the most fantastic examples of this is Adolphe Retté, who in a sudden conversion changed from a rabid left-wing anti-clerical into a violent right-wing royalist Catholic. This is an extreme example, but it does point to the trends of the time. Most Catholic writers despised moderates and their attempts at reconciliation.

The Enemies

In the perpetual simplification of issues which was typical of the thinking of the period, there were certain stock enemies who returned time and time again in the writings of Catholic authors, to be blamed for the unfortunate position in which the Church and the country found themselves. The attacks against them were violent and excessive. Though one is perpetually amazed to find that there is usually an element of truth in the original dangers envisaged, the attacks often tend to deteriorate into the unreasonable.

The main enemies were by no means the same for all the authors of this period. Each appeared to have his own *bête noire*, which dominated the other prejudices he might hold. Thus, to take some examples, one might say that for Péguy the greatest enemy was the Sorbonne, and intellectuals in general; for Claudel, Protestantism and individualism; for Drumont, the Jews; for Maurras and Barrès, all foreigners within France; for Huysmans, the unworthiness of the Catholics themselves; for many writers, the Freemasons; and for almost all, 'La République Française athée, rénégate, apostate, sacrilège, parricide, infanticide et concordataire.'[13] Many of these opinions were shared in various degrees by most of the contemporary Catholic writers, though there were always exceptions, particularly on the vexed question of anti-Semitism.

Much of this, even stated in this form, would appear excessive to our modern eyes; but we must remember, firstly, that the dangers on the spiritual side (i.e. the reign of science and the cult of individualism) *had* proved to be real, and that, on the temporal side, appearances often tended to point to the power and potential danger of the groups whom the Catholics feared. The Freemasons, the Jews, and the Protestants were all closed groups, existing on mutual help inside the group, and they all held immense power in different forms. The Freemasons infested the government, the Jews controlled an immense amount of the banking and big business of the country, and the Protestants controlled much of the administration.[14] These three groups also tended to have interests opposed to Catholicism and right-wing politics (in the case of the Freemasons, this was an extreme of rabid anti-clericalism), and to be among the staunchest supporters of the loathed Republic. Nor must we underestimate the more particular dangers to Catholicism presented by these groups, especially by the Freemasons. The 'affaire des fiches', a scandal which came to light in 1905, shows us to what lengths anti-Catholicism could lead. A card-index was being kept, it was discovered, of every officer in the French Army, with details of whether he was a practising Catholic or not. Those who were, were passed over for promotion. The main organisation of the gathering of this information was performed by the local lodges.

There is no denying, nevertheless, that many of the attacks made were over-violent and exaggerated; nor can we gloss over the fact that once these writers had seen an enemy, they tended to attack him by any means at their disposal, true or untrue, fair or unfair. Fear produced the original hatreds, but violence soon overshot the original causes of the fear and produced other weapons of attack. It is thus that Drumont, for example, claiming that his anti-Semitic attacks were based purely upon the economic draining of France by these 'foreign' interests, did, in fact, use the full barrage of anti-Semitic technique (though he did not, as he rightly claimed, touch on the Jewish religion); and his example was followed by many others who indulged in conscious or unconscious anti-Semitism at the time. Similarly Léon Daudet, when he attacked Republican dignitaries, sometimes forfeited the effect of even his justifiable attacks by a flood of personal abuse.

In a time of complicated political plots and counter-plots, it is hardly surprising that many should have felt that innumerable shady undercurrents surrounded every big event. Huysmans was convinced that the Dreyfus Affair had been mounted in order to destroy the Church; his autobiographical character, Durtal, seems to speak his opinion in *L'Oblat*: 'L'affaire Dreyfus a avancé les affaires de la maçonnerie et du socialisme de plus de vingt ans; elle n'a été, en somme, qu'un prétexte pour sauter à la gorge de l'Église; c'est la sortie en armes des juifs et des protestants.'[15]

If one looks at this view from our distance, it naturally seems ridiculous. But, on the other hand, there is no doubt that the forces opposed to the Church *did* make the fullest use of the Dreyfus Affair, in the way that political forces always do make use of moral issues. In this Affair there often seems little to choose between the sides; in fact, apart from a small group of sincere idealists, the pro-Dreyfus side often seems the more unpleasant. Most of those against Dreyfus were fighting not so much for injustice on an individual issue but for their own survival on the more general issue, faced by the political forces which had been raised by the other side. And in the results of the Affair we see those dangers which the *anti-dreyfusards* had feared, and which were to disgust Péguy with the side he had supported.

The *dreyfusards* had found a situation, and had used it. But they had, one might say, played it by ear. The idea of a complicated plot such as Huysmans suggests, with the Affair 'un tremplin installé par les juifs et les protestants, pour mieux bondir à la gorge de l'Église et l'étrangler,'[16] is ludicrous. Yet would it necessarily have seemed so to a man ignorant of political reality at the time? There is no doubt that the Third Republic did cover a great many shady plots and combinations, many of them extremely intricate, and that often the most incredible accusations have turned out to be the most true. The Third Republic had many shameful secrets, and some of the plots and counter-plots appear to be the imaginings of a successful popular novelist. It is hardly surprising that people should imagine still stranger combines. The fear of the methods of the politicians of the Republic still continues; and some of the imagined plots of our own time seem ridiculous, until they are placed in relation to the real ones of which we have evidence.

The Scapegoats

In the tendency to simplification, many writers took individuals as examples of all they hated in one particular direction. This personification of issues could naturally tend to be unjust. We have already seen, in the case of Renan, how authors tended to over-simplify his complex personality in order to make of him their natural enemy. In many cases this simplification is unconscious; but Claudel makes his position clear when he says that in Goethe, Renan, Rousseau, etc., there is no doubt a certain amount of good, but that all depends on the way you look at them. Some, like Bremond, says Claudel, try to see the best in people: 'Moi, je suis différent. Le mensonge et l'erreur, ce que je considère comme le mensonge et l'erreur—m'inspirent une violente aversion, n'est-ce pas, que je traduirais volontiers aux dépens de ceux qui les professent. ... Je le reconnais.'[17] In Claudel's opinion, people like Goethe and Renan were to be either ignored or violently attacked. They serve him as the great targets:

> Ne me perdez pas avec les Voltaire, et les Renan, et les Michelet, et les Hugo, et tous les autres infâmes!
>
> Leur âme est avec les chiens morts, leurs livres sont joints au fumier.
>
> Ils sont morts, et leur nom après leur mort est un poison et une pourriture.[18]

For Claudel, the 'homme d'absolu', there was no hesitation in relegating such people immediately to hell. Gide, too, would end up there, he foretold.

After his big break with Gide, Claudel saw in him all the horrors and dangers of that individualism he abhorred. Tending, as he did, towards absolute judgements, Claudel amassed in the person of Gide all those trends he disapproved of. Gide's individualism is seen as a form of Protestantism, which Claudel describes as resting on 'une perversion monstrueuse, c'est-à-dire sur le principe que Dieu est fait pour l'homme et non pas l'homme pour Dieu, que Ses paroles ne sont recevables pour nous qu'autant qu'elles ont passé le contrôle de notre raison, de notre jugement et de notre sentiment particulier. C'est en nous-mêmes que nous trouvons les règles suprêmes.' This, says Claudel, is a principle to which Kant gave a formula when he said that one should always act in such a way that the principle of your act can be erected as a universal principle. And, in the same letter to René Schwob from which these opinions are taken, Claudel continues by drawing a grand design in which Gide, the Protestants and Kant are all seen to be intimately connected with Satan, and in which Gide's sodomy is seen as a parallel, on the human plane, to the spiritual 'inversion' which Protestantism signified:

> Quoi de plus logique que cette monstrueuse aberration morale et intellectuelle se traduise par une égale déformation physique, et que la perversion de l'intelligence aboutisse à une inversion de l'instinct? Que l'homme conseillé par le diable enfouisse dans les excréments le pouvoir de création et d'éternité dont Dieu l'a fait dépositaire? . . . Gide . . . est tout à fait dans la ligne de Luther et de Calvin, et des autres fils *du Suprême Hérésiarque*. Tout ce qui nous détourne de Dieu, que ce soit le paganisme ou l'hérésie, aboutit toujours a *l'inversion*, a cette communion hideuse avec Satan qui est une parodie du Grand Sacrement.[19]

All this is very typical of the pre-1914 mentality, where single personalities came to bear the brunt of attacks bearing on policies or philosophies. Even Péguy, when carried away, turned his attack against persons in whom he could incarnate ideas. Thus Lavisse, Lanson and Langlois are pilloried as examples of various aspects of the Sorbonne; poor inoffensive Laudet, who did not even write the article on Péguy to which Péguy is ostensibly replying in *Un nouveau théologien*, becomes the example of the lukewarm Catholic; and Jaurès becomes the point of attack for Péguy's ideas on international pacifism. In this last case, Péguy is more than violent; he is deliberately unjust in his exaggerated picture of Jaurès as a kind of German spy: 'Ce représentant en France de la politique impérialiste allemande, capitaliste allemande, et particulièrement coloniale allemande est tombé dans un mépris universel. Ce traître par essence . . . a essayé de trahir la France même au profit de la politique allemande.'[20]

Of all the writers of this period Barrès is perhaps the man who has been most often accused of hatred and injustice towards others; but he is, in fact, something of an exception to the attitudes we are describing. If he was convinced of a man's personal unworthiness, nothing would restrain his attacks, but he did not make the mistake of confounding personalities with policies. His admiration and friendship for Jaurès, for whose policies he had just as much hatred as had Péguy, show us a moderation and humanity which are typical of this unjustly forgotten magnanimous side of his character. In his *Cahiers* we find frequent expression of this closeness to a man who should have been his enemy, a closeness which led him to go to Jaurès's funeral despite the remonstrances of many of his supporters:

Il ne faut pas me demander de haïr Jaurès. Je ne le peux pas, et après examen, je ne le dois pas. S'il y a chez lui de mauvais services rendus à mon pays et qui m'opposent à lui, qui font de moi un soldat contre lui, ce qu'il y a de plus intime et de plus élevé dans sa nature ne m'est pas étranger, et parmi ceux avec qui je dois combattre, il en est qui sont démunis de ce saint des saints, de cette valeur vraie, de cette sensibilité généreuse que je voyais vibrer au centre de son être.[21]

Léon Bloy could never see anything except at the personal level; he described himself as being 'anticochon', and all his most successful attacks were personal. He saw certain people as the prime examples of those human qualities he most hated, and immediately attacked without thought of consequences, or with enjoyment if he did think of them. The literary party described in his novel *Le Désespéré*, in which he violently attacked, under the most flimsy disguises, such influential people as Catulle Mendès, Francisque Sarcey, Aurélien Scholl, Jean Richepin, Alphonse Daudet, and others, is matched by the articles in which he tackled such people even more openly by their names. The titles of some of them give one an idea of the violence of the attack; L'Eunuque (Paul Bourget), Eloi ou le Fils des Anges (Péladan), Les premières plumes d'un vieux dindon (Edmond de Goncourt), and the article on Albert Wolff which he printed in *Le Désespéré*: L'Hermaphrodite Prussien, Albert Wolff.

The whole of Bloy's polemical writing is a flow of unchecked fury at the modern world, modern Catholics and modern literary corruption. Obsessed as he was by the world's acceptance of false Christian virtues, Bloy let himself go completely and often passed all bounds of ordinary feeling. Death, for him, was no reason to restrain his violence; and it was after their deaths that many of his targets received their worst attacks. False ideas of Christian charity are attacked in his article on the Duchess of Galliera, Les Fanfares de la Charité (1888); appearing as it did, just after her death, amid the 'jérémiade clichée sur la beauté d'âme des défunts pourvus de millions,'[22] this article spared neither the dead woman, nor all those others like her who were still living. Once again, Bloy had taken a single example as his point of attack.

While the whole of Paris was mourning the victims who were burned to death in the fire which in May 1897 destroyed the Bazar de la Charité, an annual event at which ladies of fashion served behind stalls for the purposes of raising money for charity, Bloy delivered a blistering attack on this whole concept of charity, and saw the fire as the judgement of God on hypocrisy. And his description of the fire at the Opéra-Comique, in *La Femme Pauvre* (1897; the fire actually took place in 1887), is similarly uncompromising: 'Les premières étincelles avaient voltigé, a neuf heures cinq, sur l'abjecte musique de M. Ambroise Thomas, et l'asphyxie ou la crémation des bourgeois immondes venus pour l'entendre commençait, sous l'odorante pluie tiède'.[23] Death never caused Bloy to lower his tone. His book *Sur la tombe d'Huysmans* is full of violent polemic, and one of his most unforgettable scenes is the description, in *Les Dernières Colonnes de l'Église*, of Pope Leo XIII (who was on his deathbed when this attack was being written) arriving in heaven and attempting to excuse himself for his misdeeds. It is an incredible piece of polemic, stemming from an attack on Brunetière, that new 'colonne de l'Église' of whose moderation, and attempts to reconcile science and religion, Bloy so heartily disapproved. What has happened? says Bloy. He has been converted through being received by the Pope! All Bloy's disgust with Leo XIII then comes flowing forth:

A l'heure ou j'écris, le successeur de Pie IX est sur le point de mourir. Peut-être est-il déjà mort et devant Dieu, face à face.

Que va-t-il dire au Pasteur qui lui redemandera son troupeau? Quel compte rendra cet intendant qui a enfoui le talent de son Seigneur, ce berger qui a sacrifié les brebis pour réconcilier les chiens avec les loups? Que répondra-t-il à son Maître, ce premier de tous les Vicaires du Fils de Dieu qui ait encouragé la Canaille et restitué la parole à la servante de Caïphe, silencieuse depuis tant de siècles? Alléguera-t-il 'le côté d'où vient le vent', 'la queue de la poële', ou 'l'assiette au beurre', au milieu du ruissellement des Anges et parmi les cataractes de la Lumière?

Enfin ce dissipateur du *Syllabus* fera-t-il à son Juge cette déclaration prodigieuse: —Autant que je le pouvais, j'ai détruit la foi en frappant au coeur l'obéissance des peuples et la discipline du clergé. Je me suis tu chaque fois que les forts massacraient les faibles et j'ai donné ma bénédiction à ceux qui Vous outrageaient. Les victimes de la violence ou du mensonge qui me nomment leur Père ont en vain crié vers moi.

A cause de moi, la France est au désespoir.

Enfin, le danger de mes doctrines républicaines et la parfaite abomination de mon inertie pontificale ont été un scandale comme on n'en avait jamais vu.

Seulement, voici Brunetière qu'aucun autre pape n'aurait pu séduire. Ce précieux bavard n'est-il pas de vos plus fermes Colonnes? L'ai-je payée d'un trop grand prix, ô Seigneur?[24]

Bloy's violence held no fear. He was prepared to express himself anywhere, at any time, on any subject or on any person. Some other authors of the time, though many of their feelings were equally violent, preferred to attack on the more general issues, and leave personalities out of it as far as possible. Huysmans, for example, originally wished his novel *L'Oblat* to be in part a violent attack on the contemporary Church, the monasteries, and the Pope. In fact he wrote joyfully to his friends about what a scandal its publication would cause. But by the time he wrote it he had decided to tone it down a good deal, and later described it as being 'malgré quelques coups de patte, bénévole.'[25]

The Main Polemical Writers and their Styles

If a list were to be made of the masters of polemic in France since 1870 well over half of the names mentioned would be

Catholic writers; Veuillot, Barbey d'Aurevilly, Bloy, Drumont, Léon Daudet, Péguy and Bernanos are among the most prominent who come to mind. In their hands the French language became a violent weapon of attack. We have already seen some of the causes for this violence; let us now examine some of the ways in which this weapon was used.

Some of the most brilliant writing in the Catholic literature of the time was polemical; it is a pity that this form becomes so quickly dated, not because of faults in the style, but because of the distance, for the modern reader, of the enemies who were being attacked. This cannot, however, prevent admiration for the skill of the writers, nor wonder at the expressive nature of the language they used.

Those polemical writers who interest us most, naturally enough, are those who use works of imagination for their purpose; but we must also deal with the outstanding polemical journalists who had such influence on those around them.

Louis Veuillot, whose active journalistic career ended in 1879 when he handed over his newspaper *L'Univers* to his brother Eugène, was one of the greatest French polemical writers of all time. Though the greater part of his career lies in the Second Empire, his ideas and his polemical violence were to be of great influence on later writers. Above all his capacity for a clear, memorable statement of issues in a short, crisp form meant that he was continually quoted in the works of those who were in sympathy with his ideas.

His views were those of an extreme Ultramontanism, demanding for the Pope all power, both temporal and spiritual. His bases were Bonald and de Maistre, but he added to their cold logic a fiery enthusiasm and a rigid intransigence. All those who did not follow the same opinions as himself were attacked mercilessly, and sometimes unjustly. The opponents against whom a great deal of his fire was directed were the moderate Catholics, including Cochin, Montalembert, Falloux and Dupanloup. The intransigents were gathered round his paper, *L'Univers*, the moderates around *Le Correspondant*. *L'Univers* had many difficulties, including suspension by the Archbishop of Paris in 1853, governmental intervention in 1861 and a further suspension in 1874.

His influence on later writers was immense not only because of the causes which he so ably defended but also because of his tone.

He could be violent, unjust and unreasonable; he aimed at the persons themselves; he chose the most wounding epithets; he admitted himself that he sometimes refused to deprive himself of a 'bon mot' merely because it might be untrue; and his language was, for the age in which he started writing, wildly original. As Huysmans describes it in *À Rebours* (1884), it was 'une langue particulière, ou il y entrait du La Bruyère et du faubourien du Gros-Caillou. Ce style mi-solennel, mi-canaille, brandi par cette personnalité brutale, prenait un poids redoutable de casse-tête.'[26]

Despite this violence, however, Veuillot's style remained clear, precise and uncomplicated; in it there is never any part of a sentence which does not fulfil the purpose the author intends. Take, for example, his judgement on liberal Catholics: 'Le libéralisme est une maladie qui se manifeste par une absence d'horreur pour l'hérésie, par une perpétuelle complaisance envers l'erreur, par un certain goût des pièges qu'elle tend et, souvent, par un certain empressement à s'y laisser prendre.'[27]

'That cad Veuillot', as Charles Scott Stokes described him in a letter to J. H. Newman,[28] was, as well as being the main mouthpiece, before the Catholic Revival, of the extreme views which were to find so much favour with that movement, a purveyor of polemical insult on a grand scale. His methods as well as his ideas were to be taken over by later Catholic writers, though rarely could they achieve his searing effect.

In its measured clarity, Veuillot's work lies in the direct line of French style. Later polemicists were to have a far more complicated, colourful approach; their epithets were more highly coloured than Veuillot's (though many of his personal epithets appeared violent in the age in which he lived), their sentences more dislocated. Though this is on occasions most effective, they nevertheless sometimes tend to lose sight of the main aim of polemic, which is to hit, and to be seen to hit.

Barbey d'Aurevilly, strangely enough, despite the immense complexity of his sentence-form as a novelist, seems to realise that in polemic a clearer form of phrase must be used. Nevertheless his flamboyance comes forth in other ways, particularly in an overwhelming desire to make 'clever' remarks, which occasionally make his works of criticism rather difficult reading. Wit is immensely effective when it is sparingly used; but when it is liberally scattered throughout a man's writing it is wearisome and misleading. The perpetual desire to be witty can lead a man to say things he does not mean; the search for an unusual and telling metaphor can do the same thing. Barbey is as intransigent and violent as Veuillot in his opinions, yet the highly-coloured nature of his style weakens rather than strengthens his effect.

Bloy's polemical style is magnificent, though it breaks all the rules. His contorted sentences might be expected to mislead and bewilder the reader, his blatant exaggerations might be guaranteed to repel him, and his predilection for what one might call 'lavatory-epithets' to revolt him. Yet the reader is swept along by a feeling of tortured urgency, a sense of frustrated hatred for all around the author. Bloy's violence is real. The man's personality appears in every word he wrote, and we are bludgeoned into following his hammering succession of insults, his rushing flow of fury. Some of the best moments are those of scorn, such as the following passage from his article L'Eunuque, where he is describing the works of Paul Bourget:

> Ses *analyses* boréales amalgamées de Renan, de Stendhal et de quelques pions germaniques, où l'absence infinie de style et de caractère est symétrique au double néant du sentiment et de la pensée, furent sucées avec dévotion par tout un public de mondaines, ravies qu'un auteur qui leur ressemblait condescendît, en leur présence, de ses pâles doigts en glucose, à traire les vaches arides qu'elles gardent avec tant de soin dans les ravissantes prairies de leurs coeurs.[29]

The immense complexity of the sentence here seems to add to rather than detract from the effect, ending as it does on such an outrageous metaphor. This is one of the most characteristic tricks in Bloy's polemical style; the complication, instead of bewildering the reader, gives the impression of insult after insult breathlessly being piled up by an infuriated writer. Take, for example, Bloy's description of Marchenoir's disgust at modern Christians, in the novel Le Désespéré:

> Investi des plus transcendantales conceptions, il considérait avec d'horrifiques épouvantements ce collège oecuménique de l'Apostolat, cette cléricature fameuse qui avait été réellement 'la lumière du monde', —si formidable encore que la dérision ne peut l'atteindre sans rejaillir sur Dieu une tempête de fange, —devenue pourtant le décrottoir des peuples et le tapis de pied des hippopotames![30]

Bloy's epithets are always vivid and violent. In their violence they often turn to the anatomical and the sexual. No epithet is bad enough to fling at an enemy, and the title of Caïn Marchenoir's article, 'La Sédition de l'Excrément', which is mentioned in *Le Désespéré*, shows us clearly the nature of much of Bloy's own polemic. As Bloy says of his own autobiographical character, 'Marchenoir avait la réprobation scatologique.'[31]

Despite the physical side of Bloy's imagery, and despite the amount of space that actual physical description of his opponents takes up in his polemic, one is still carried along by the fury and abandon of his attacks. Nothing could be further from Veuillot than the apparent disorder and complexity of Bloy's style; yet some people called Bloy a 'sous-Veuillot'. Their attitudes, their hatreds, their violence are similar; but nothing could be more different than their styles.

Bloy uses his novels as bases for violent attacks on his enemies. Many appear there under transparent pseudonyms;[32] some under their own names.[33] He also uses these novels to put forward all his ideas on the main issues of life and religion, which naturally leads to attacks on all those of other opinions. Many other authors of the time, in the course of putting their own opinions into their novels, indulge in a form of polemic; Bourget, for example. Yet never does it overshadow the work so powerfully as in Bloy's novels, and rarely is it so direct.

In Huysmans's novels the autobiographical element naturally leads to frequent discussion of the author's own ideas, and to condemnation of those tendencies in contemporary Christianity which disturb him. Yet names are mentioned rarely, compared with Bloy, and the attacks are more general. Also the tone is reflective rather than impassioned, and every statement is muffled in that 'écriture artiste' of which Huysmans was such an exponent. There is no denying his disgust at the contemporary situation, however. Speaking of the mediocrity of the clergy, he writes that it is the laity's fault: 'Si ces gargotiers d'âmes avaient du talent, s'ils servaient à leurs pensionnaires des nourritures fines, des essences de théologie, des coulis de prières, des sucs concrets d'idées, il végéteraient, incompris des ouailles!'[34]

Huysmans does tend, like Bloy, to exaggerate beyond belief, to apply the most outrageous epithets to people. His language is often as violent as Bloy's, even to the point of scatology. The last lines of the novel *Là-bas*, consisting of an exchange between the two characters Des Hermies and Durtal, show this:

> Ce siècle se fiche absolument du Christ en gloire. Il contamine le surnaturel et vomit l'au-delà. Alors, comment espérer en l'avenir, comment s'imaginer qu'ils seront propres, les gosses issus des fétides bourgeois de ce sale temps? Élevés de la sorte, je me demande ce qu'ils feront dans la vie, ceux-là?

> Ils feront, comme leurs pères, comme leurs mères, répondit Durtal; ils s'empliront les tripes et ils se vidangeront l'âme par le bas-ventre!

Yet such moments of fury are rare; Huysmans's attacks on the modern world are more often marked by a grim kind of humour, an attribute which is completely lacking in Bloy. Huysmans's polemic is often entertaining. It lacks the note of hysteria we find in Bloy, and is consequently less subjectively gripping. The over-conscious use of artistic language and complicated sentence constructions often distract us from the object of attack. But much can be forgiven for a moment such as this:

> Le scepticisme et la corruption raffinée du temps moderne ont construit la Trinité, cette Église fumoir, ce prie-Dieu sopha où l'ylang et le moas-rosa se mêlent aux fumées de l'encens, où le bénitier sent le saxe parfumé qui s'y trempe, cette église d'une religion de bon goût où l'on a sa loge à certains jours, ce boudoir coquet ou les dames de M. Droz flirtent à genoux et aspirent à des lunchs mystiques, cette Notre-Dame de Champaka, devant laquelle on descend de sa voiture comme devant la porte d'un théâtre.[35]

Huysmans's attacks betray exasperation rather than the prophetic fury of Bloy; and his novels, autobiographical as they are, do not become mere vehicles for polemic, as Bloy's only too often do. They are the history of a human soul in its search for truth. The characters are real, especially the hero, and never become the two-dimensional caricatures which Bloy's novels place before us.

Most of the Catholic novels of this period are, to some extent, *romans à thèse*; but rarely does polemic become the overriding feature. A remarkable novel in which it does is Barrès's magnificent diatribe against the deputies involved in the Panama scandal, *Leurs Figures*; this novel is not, however, a Catholic novel in any sense of the term, even though we shall find its author having a great effect on Catholic literature in other connections.

In political journalism, Charles Maurras and Léon Daudet, who from 1908 onwards were in charge of the newspaper *Action Française*, were among the most brilliant writers. Maurras, who was not at that time a Catholic, nevertheless supported Catholicism strongly, as a binding force which was a great strength on the side of the monarchism and patriotism which were his main beliefs. By his stirring, powerful and rolling phrases and his perpetual calls to honour, patriotism and order, he built up an enthusiastic following among young people, many of whom became 'Camelots du Roi', officially sellers of the newspaper, but unofficially powerful groups of action troops for use in riots.

Maurras made sparing use of personal insult in his writings, compared with his colleague Léon Daudet. Daudet's polemic, used almost entirely for political purposes though he was himself a staunch Catholic, amasses vile personal insults, descriptions, etc., and attributes to his opponents the most sordid sexual habits. His perpetual violence is matched by his incredible world of make-believe, which is illustrated by his belief that the condemnation of *Action Française* in 1926 by Pope Pius XI was the result of a blackmail of the Pope by Republican politicians; or by his belief that both Briand and Berthelot were in the pay of Germany. His style is brilliantly effective in its ice-like fury, its careful amassing of insults, its searing malice and its satirical pungency. But we are left with little sympathy for the writer himself, except in those passages of profound grief and reclamation of justice which he wrote after his son's death.

One of the greatest of polemical journalists, if one counts the effect on the reader as the sign of a good polemicist, was Edouard Drumont. As Editor of *La Libre Parole* from its foundation in 1892 and as the author of such books as *La France Juive* (1886) and *Le Testament d'un Antisémite* (1891), he devoted most of his writings to a violent attack on the Jews in France. But here we are not so much concerned with the contents of his writing as with his polemical style. This, at first sight, is dogged and almost monotonous. He gathers his evidence and lays it before the reader calmly, with an almost detached manner, yet with an underlying bitterness which is always present. The whole of his strength lies in this restraint, in this impression of suppressed fury, so different from the wild, unrestrained shouts of his contemporaries. As Bernanos, his great admirer, says, comparing him with these other polemicists:

Les portraits de Veuillot trop scolaires, les cris déchirants de
Léon Bloy, les fureurs lyriques de Léon Daudet, l'éloquence
antique, la colère sacrée de Maurras, ne sauraient donner l'idée
de cette férocité bonhomme et familière, dans son déroulement
un peu monotone, où passe tout à coup un frémissement
tragique, tout le souffle de la puissante poitrine, pareil à un râle
de lion.[36]

The movement is slow in a chapter by Drumont, and it is
impossible to give the effect by quotation. The section of *Testament
d'un Antisémite* entitled 'Le Clergé Fin de Siècle', for example, in
which Drumont attempts to find reasons for the success of anti-
Catholicism in the Government's actions, and finds them in the
mediocrity of the clergy and Catholic laity, and their unwillingness
to stand up to the government, is a masterpiece of painstaking
amassing of evidence, which gradually adds up to an overwhelming
indictment. In the same book, the chapter 'Léo Taxil et le Nonce
du Pape' is a magnificently organised onslaught on the contemporary Church and its acceptance of the two-faced scoundrel Léo
Taxil.[37] Drumont's violent anti-Semitism brings him little
sympathy in this present age. But he must nevertheless be regarded
as a great polemist; not a stylist, in the literary sense of the term,
but a most effective mover of men.

Péguy and Claudel both use polemic occasionally in their works.
The vast litany of hatred in Péguy's *Ève*, for example, is extremely
effective. For more than two thousand lines, in the middle of this
poem, Péguy gives himself up to a monotonous, repetitive list of
all those aspects of the modern world which he dislikes. None of
these things, he says, will be of value on the Judgement Day:

Et ce n'est pas des tas de sociologies
Que nous emporterons le jour du jugement
Et ce n'est pas des rats de bibliographies
Que nous emporterons le jour du règlement.

Et ce n'est pas des sots et des sociologues
Qui rameront pour nous sur nos pauvres trois-mâts
Et ce n'est pas des mots et des archéologues
Qui penseront pour nous dans ces derniers frimas. . . .

The list goes on and on, monotonously, yet with mounting effect.
And every so often it is broken by a more positive statement, which
gains its effect from the vast expanse of negation which lies around

it and whose monotonous rhythm it has broken. Within these interruptions there is often a new interior repetition of their own; but this repetition stresses, not the multitude of mediocrity, but the uniqueness of the one True Being: . . . 'Un autre, un Dieu . . . Un autre, un Dieu . . .' and 'Parce que c'est Jésus . . . parce que c'est Jésus . . .'

This is effective, but by no means so much so as Péguy's polemics in prose. In *Un nouveau théologien: M. Fernand Laudet* and *L'Argent Suite*, the best examples of Péguy's polemical writing are to be found, though there are innumerable examples throughout the rest of his work. Péguy's best characteristic in this type of writing is an irrepressible sense of humour. One can see, in his treatment of Taine's edition of La Fontaine,[38] and of Lanson's lectures on the French Theatre,[39] to what extent his technique is one of ironical deflation of pomposity and intellectual self-sufficiency. Often his most barbed comments are those which are almost asides. For example, in his surprise at the way Rudler, a pupil of Lanson's, had praised his master in an article, Péguy says: 'Je ne sais pas si vous êtes comme moi. Il me paraît un peu raide qu'un disciple écrive de son maître publiquement en de tels termes. Car enfin, si on parle en ces termes de M. Lanson, en quels termes parlera-t-on d'un écrivain?'[40] Here the last word has a completely unexpected effect, in a 'throw-away' line of great acerbity. Péguy sees through his enemies, and makes them ridiculous:

On ne saura jamais ce qu'un froncement de sourcils de Herr aura fait, ce qu'il aura eu d'influence sur les destinées de la troisième République. Car Herr fronce aisément ses gros sourcils; et il gonfle volontiers sa grosse voix; et il jure et il sacre; et les *Nom de Dieu* font sa ponctuation la plus modeste; et M. Lavisse, qui ne s'y connaît pas beaucoup, croit que c'est cela de la force, et que c'est cela de courage, et que c'est cela de l'énergie.[41]

There are, however, many other facets to Péguy's attack; the immense, almost Rabelaisian enumeration of facts or faults in the opponent's argument, for example. This is to be found in the long list of paragraph-headings from Taine's edition of La Fontaine (in *Zangwill*), or in the passage where, taking Laudet's[42] statement that only Joan of Arc's public life is of any use to us, he lists all the attributes of obscure, little-known saints which would be lost to us if this were so:

Quand on prend de l'hérésie, on n'en saurait trop prendre. M. Laudet exclut, retranche de la communion des saints et de la réversibilité des souffrances, des épreuves, des exercices, des travaux, des Vertus, des grâces, des mérites, des prières ces innombrables souffrances, ces innombrables épreuves, ces innombrables exercices, ces innombrables travaux, ces innombrables Vertus, ces innombrables grâces, ces innombrables mérites, ces innombrables prières. Il dépeuple littéralement la communion des saints et la réversibilité des grâces.[43]

And some of the greatest moments of Péguy's polemic are those where, filled with a spirit of anger or anxiety, he sweeps along in vast sentences filled with repetitive phrases, in which the words seem almost to be tumbling over each other, but in which a subtle rhythmic pattern sets some into relief and insistently points up others, maintaining all the while a magnificently rhetorical phrasing, lost if read to oneself but resounding with the fire of passion when declaimed out loud. Nobody should ever read Péguy to himself; the printed text cries out to be heard. In the persistently shifting rhythms of Péguy's prose there is much of the character of his free verse; and it can be, almost always is, equally effective.

Péguy has created a new rhetoric; a rhetoric, however, in which many of the lessons of the old have paradoxically been pressed into service. The sentence forms may lack the balance and measure taught in the classical text-books, but the insistent repetitions, the parentheses, the antitheses, all have the effect assigned to them by the old rhetoricians. And the apparent incoherence of certain passages is one form of rhetorical effect; the simple, man-to-man style of most of Péguy's best prose is here transformed into an insistent determination to say all that is to be said, unequivocally and simply. The peasant simplicity of Péguy turns the search for the *mot juste*, which had forced poets such as Mallarmé to a sterile economy, into a torrent of almost similar phrases, each qualifying the other. Through all this we glimpse the peasant, Péguy, speaking simply to those around him; for by this constant repetition we are not bewildered but reinforced in a few simple, forthright opinions.

Paul Claudel's plays serve rather unsuccessfully for polemic, on the occasions when he uses them for it. The reason is that the side which he is opposing is portrayed always in such black colours that it is difficult for the spectator not to feel a sense of unreality. Such

black-and-white representations can be effective as adjuncts to the
main plot of a novel, though even there, if they become the main
plot itself, they will tend to be unsuccessful. In the theatre, where
we see the persons actually before us, the effect is doubly unfortunate.

Thus in *Jeanne d'Arc au Bûcher* the attack on those who condemned Jeanne d'Arc is one of hatred and mockery; these men are
seen as being utterly evil, with no redeeming features, and they
become in this play ignorant and vicious animals. Bishop Cauchon
is represented as a 'cochon', the assessors as sheep, etc. The whole
scene of the trial is a ridiculous farce. Evil many of these people
may have been; but this is so far from good polemic that it leaves
the spectator with the sense that all the scales are weighted on one
side. It would have been far better to show these enemies as being
mixtures of good and evil, like all men. Then their evil side would
have been convincing. Claudel's procedure here lacks charity and
justice; it was an atheist, George Bernard Shaw, who was to
produce in his play *Saint Joan* the most 'Christian' portrayal of
St. Joan's judges.

Claudel makes a similar mistake in his play *La Nuit de Noël
1914*. This is, of course, a piece of war propaganda against the
Germans, and Claudel should not be judged for the exaggerations
which are so necessarily a part of such literature. But even here the
effect must surely have been lost, even in wartime, by the piling
up of horrors. The ghost of child after child appears, telling how
they have been killed by the wicked Germans—'C'est un gros
homme gris qui m'a tuée à coups de sabre, j'avais beau me
cacher . . .' etc.—and the priest's prayer is full of heavy irony of an
unsuccessful sort: 'Prions donc pour nos bourreaux. Mais Seigneur, vous savez qu'il n'est pas facile de prier pour un Allemand.
Ce sont des gens si parfaitement honnêtes, et vertueux, et sûrs de
bien faire, même quand ils assassinent des enfants. . . .'[44]

It would seem that the polemical scenes are the least effective in
Claudel's plays. Those virtues of strong belief and violent passions
which are the making of so much of the rest of his work here fail by
their very extremeness. What is remarkable, however, is to see how
much more successful he was in conversation,[45] when he wished to
attack someone. Here, instead of making violent and categorical
condemnations, he often uses a completely different technique, of
pretending to hold himself back as though hesitant to attack. In

his letters, too, he often strikes more accurately and tellingly, though again his violence often undoes him.

One often finds, in the study of polemical literature, that the man whose polemic fails to convince is often the more honest man. To be a successful polemist one has to attack with care and premeditation; violence of feeling can often, though not always, destroy this attempt. It is those who manage to combine these two apparently contradictory qualities who are the best polemists; but they are rare.

What we have seen of the violence and simplicity of the opinions of the authors of the Revival is symptomatic, also, of much of their attitude towards the doctrines of their Church. Many of these writers were converts, and in the enthusiasm typical of the convert they often tended to take the most extreme parts of Catholic doctrine and place their whole emphasis upon those, to the detriment of other parts. In most cases this is more a question of degree and of false emphasis than of actual heresy. But the danger of heresy is always there in the background, and we shall sometimes see authors perilously near to this danger, particularly in the early years of the Revival. The first large wave of conversions in the generation of Bloy and Huysmans is the one where this danger is strongest, and where the opinions and beliefs are most extreme. By the time we reach the main works of writers like Claudel and Péguy it is clear that in most fields the attitudes have become more moderate, though there still remains much in their Catholic beliefs which can only be explained in the context of the religious generation in which they grew up.

Not all the great Catholic literary figures of this time took up such violent stances. Jammes, for example, appears in most of his work to be completely cut off from the political scene. In general, however, the violence which has been described in this chapter remained constant throughout the period. Catholic writers were perpetually on their guard against their opponents in both the temporal and spiritual fields and were unwilling to countenance any form of compromise with them. There were moments of apparent abatement of the struggle—for instance, the time of the 'new spirit', 1893–8, when the moderate elements on both the Republican and Catholic sides seemed to be working towards a reconciliation, before the Dreyfus Affair destroyed any such possibility—but these were not reflected in the writings of the principal Catholic authors. These men continued in their intransigent attitudes and condemned all moderates as conscious or unconscious traitors to their cause.

NOTES

[1] Péguy, before his conversion, was one of the few on the left wing to object to the intolerance of anti-clerical writings.

[2] Quoted in Péguy, *Casse-Cou*, 2 March 1901; Pléiade, Prose I, p. 331.

[3] Bourget, *L'Étape*, Paris, 1902, p. 23.

[4] Péguy, *Un nouveau théologien: M. Fernand Laudet*, 24 September 1911; Pléiade, Prose II, p. 895.

[5] Bloy, letter to Bernaert, 5 October 1899; quoted in Bollery, *Léon Bloy*, Vol. 3, p. 302.

[6] Claudel, *Mémoires Improvisés*, Paris, 1954, p. 223.

[7] Claudel, letter to René Schwob, Washington, 27 January 1933.

[8] Bourget, *Le Démon de Midi*, Paris, 1914, vol. I, p. 282.

[9] Among the few examples of the liberal Catholic novel are the works of Fonsegrive and a work by a minor author, Jean Nesmy, called *La Lumière de la Maison* (1910).

[10] Péguy, *L'Argent Suite*; Pléiade, Prose II, p. 1219.

[11] See letter from Rivière to Claudel, 3 October 1907.

[12] Péguy, *Un nouveau théologien: M. Fernand Laudet*; Pléiade, Prose II, p. 895.

[13] Bloy, *Quatre Ans de Captivité à Cochons-sur-Marne*, 1900–4, Paris, 1905.

[14] As Maurras was to point out later in his *L'État Monod*, a study of the many ramifications of the Monod family, who were Protestants of foreign origin.

[15] Huysmans, *L'Oblat*, 1903, p. 46.

[16] Ibid., p. 235.

[17] Claudel, *Mémoires Improvisés*, p. 223.

[18] Claudel, *Magnificat* (Troisième Ode); Pléiade, Poetry, p. 261.

[19] Claudel, letter to René Schwob, New York, 25 June 1931. The basis for this comparison would seem to rest on a statement by Charles du Bos about Gide's 'inversion spirituelle', a statement which was seized upon and made more violent by such polemicists as Claudel and Massis.

[20] Péguy, *L'Argent*, 16 February 1913; Pléiade, Prose II, p. 1057.

[21] Barrès, *Mes Cahiers*, 1915.

[22] Bloy, 'Les Fanfares de la Charité', 1888; reprinted in *Belluaires et Porchers*, 1905.

[23] Bloy, *La Femme pauvre*, 1897, Part II, Chapter 26.

[24] Bloy, *Les Dernières Colonnes de l'Église*, Paris, 1903, pp. 55–7.

[25] See Baldick, *The Life of J.-K. Huysmans*, p. 363.

[26] Huysmans, *À Rebours*, Chapter 12. Gros-Caillou was a working-class district of Paris.

[27] Louis Veuillot, *Mélanges*, third series, vol. III.

[28] Charles Scott Stokes, letter to John Henry Newman, 1870; quoted in Meriol Trevor, *Newman: Light in Winter*, p. 482.

[29] Bloy, 'L'Eunuque', in *Belluaires et Porchers*, Paris, 1905.

[30] Bloy, *Le Désespéré*, Paris, 1886, Part I.

[31] Ibid., Part IV.

[32] E.g., Huysmans (Folantin), Bourget (Alexis Dulaurier), Mendès (Properce Beauvivier), Richepin (Hamilcar Lécuyer), Maupassant (Gilles de Vaudoré), Alphonse Daudet (Gaston Chaudesaigues) and many others.

[33] E.g. Ohnet and Wolff.

[34] Huysmans, *En Route*, p. 3.

[35] Huysmans, *L'Art Moderne*.

[36] Georges Bernanos, *La Grande Peur des Bien-pensants*, Paris, 1931, p. 234.

[37] Bernanos explores brilliantly, in his book on Drumont, the construction of this chapter.

[38] Péguy, *Zangwill*, 30 October 1904; Pléiade, Prose I, p. 681.

[39] Péguy, *L'Argent Suite*, 22 April 1913; Pléiade, Prose II, p. 1121.

[40] Ibid., p. 1109.

[41] Ibid., p. 1203.

[42] In fact, Le Grix's. Péguy in this essay pretends that the article he is attacking was, in fact, written by the editor of the journal in which it appeared.

[43] Péguy, *Un nouveau théologien: M. Fernand Laudet*, 24 September 1911; Pléiade, Prose II, p. 850.

[44] Claudel, *La Nuit de Noël 1914*; Pléiade, Théâtre II, p. 576.

[45] There are several examples in the *Mémoires Improvisés*, particularly in the references to Bernanos in the 32nd conversation.

PART TWO

Some Early False Steps

CHAPTER SIX

Romantic Catholicism

AMONG the accusations levelled at the first generation of the Revival none is more common than that of 'Romantic Catholicism'. It is a vague term, rarely defined, which shelters beneath its umbrella all kinds of trends; and together with its opposed counterpart, 'Political Catholicism', it is often held to have been responsible for a completely false start (from the religious point of view) in the revival of Catholic literature. Nothing could be further from the truth. While the converts of this period were often brought to Catholicism in highly mysterious ways, and while they often retained, in their approach to religion, various characteristics of these original attitudes, rare are the cases where these were not superseded by more specifically Christian views, with which they had to conform or be forgotten. Huysmans might retain a certain amount of his aesthetic approach to religion, yet this need in no way invalidate his beliefs; in fact his later writings and his own approach to death show his religion to have been based on far stronger foundations. Similarly, a belief in the political uses of Catholicism need not necessarily denote any lack of religious feeling, nor even any false emphasis within religious belief itself.

What is interesting to us here is the way in which, in these men, the combination of a strong Christian belief and of diverse elements left over from their pre-conversion ideas produced an extremely varied and exciting literary movement. Elements of 'Romantic Catholicism' remain in the aesthetic and liturgical interest of these authors, in the erotic element in some of their works, and in their fascination with the occult; and, on the other hand, the natural exuberance of the convert leads to an exaggeration of Catholic doctrine, which, while on the whole remaining by a hair's breadth within the realm of orthodoxy, does mingle with these other elements to present the reader with all kinds of unusual and interesting effects. The Revival restored to French literature some of the

97

enthusiasm which, by the late nineteenth century, it at times seemed to be lacking. It was a turbulent, untidy, at times incoherent literary movement, for the very reason that it was primarily a religious movement; but its influence on the course of French literature has been incalculable, right down to the present day.

Among the characteristics of the Revival are several which can be traced to sources not specifically Catholic; and of these, some do indeed come under that vast blanket term, 'Romantic Catholicism'. Let us examine more closely one or two of the ways in which our authors were brought to their conversion.

Dilettantism

For many of the Romantic authors, details of Catholic belief, liturgy and decoration had been a form of local colour highly suitable for inclusion in their works. The evocative nature of these details did not in any way mean that the authors who used them had any idea of their true significance. Any religious feeling that the average Romantic author might have was likely, at the most, to be a vague form of deism, as in the case of Lamartine. These authors usually show little understanding of the Christian religion; yet they often use its themes in their works, for they see in them a power of evocation which is all the more effective for being beyond their comprehension. These Christian themes are often mingled with others from pagan sources or from other religions; they appear for their effect upon humanity, rather than for any intrinsic truth the author might see in them.

Strangely enough, it is in an author who was ostensibly converted to Catholicism that this dilettantism appears at its strongest. Barbey d'Aurevilly's conversion was no doubt part of that elaborate world of make-believe which surrounded him. Living in a past which had never existed, Barbey reacted against the modern world with a false dandyism which, by its very extravagance and eccentricity, defeated its own ends. This spiritual dandyism had more form than content, a failing which one can see reflected in his literary style. Traditionalism, monarchism, all his reactionary views were flaunted before his contemporaries with more desire for immediate effect than for anything else. The essential thing was to be different, and one can imagine Barbey's horror if he had seen a great many people converted to his opinions. His Catholicism was one more pose among many. Though Bloy, who met him when extremely young and impressionable and never lost his admiration for the man, was to describe him as 'le plus grand de nos ecrivains catholiques,'[1] we must agree rather with the opinions of contemporaries such as Veuillot, who saw in him an author using Catholicism as a means rather than accepting it as an end.

Nowhere is this more obvious than in his novel *Un Prêtre Marié* (1865), which was a consciously Catholic novel. The action and the characters of this novel, typical of any of Barbey's earlier works, are impregnated with his particular brand of Romantic decadence; Catholicism is merely an added Romantic trait. The perpetual desire to make the reader's flesh creep, which is found in all Barbey's works, is here aided by the religious horror of eternal damnation. Barbey has exhausted the possibilities of sexual excitement, and now turns to this.

Sombreval, the hero of the novel, has left the priesthood and married; in so doing he has, Barbey tells us, 'tué Dieu'. By resuming the priesthood while still an unbeliever he has damned himself still further. But Sombreval is, in fact, one more reflection of the Byronic figure. He is what Signor Mario Praz would describe as a 'metamorphosis of Satan', the fallen angel who remains great. He is one of Barbey's most successful creations; we feel more sympathy for him, in his solitude, his pride, and his obsessive love for his daughter, than for anyone else in the book.

Calixte, the daughter, is likewise a descendant of the pale, ailing beauties of Romanticism. Like Léa, the heroine of a story Barbey wrote in 1832, one feels that she would die at the first kiss she received. Her frequent attacks of coma and her sleep-walking are all caused by her emotional reaction to her father's crime. She is suffering to expiate her father's sins; but the idea of vicarious suffering is here merely a Catholic means to a literary end.

Néel, the dashing Romantic hero of violent courage and brilliant horsemanship, prefers, like so many of his kind, the fragility, pallor, and sick-bed beauty of Calixte to the buxom healthiness of the girl to whom he is engaged. All these people have the predictable characteristics of the heroes of Romantic fiction, and the plot itself is as full of sinister prophecies by an old witch, La Malgaigne, as of statements of Catholic belief. It is impossible to tell whether God, Satan or some mysterious third force is ruling the action, for despite a priest's statement that it is never too late for repentance and salvation, and despite Calixte's sacrifice for her father, it is the witch's prophecies which are fulfilled.

This novel by Barbey d'Aurevilly is one of the extreme examples of the lengths to which literary dilettantism can lead. It is regarded as one of the great Catholic works of its age for the simple reason that there is so little of value around it. Barbey's generation produced little in the way of valid Catholic fiction; where Catholicism appears, it is merely one attribute among many used purely for literary effect. It is in the subsequent generation, that of Bloy, Huysmans, Verlaine and Nouveau, the age of the conversions, that we find Catholicism becoming a literary end in itself, interdependent with the literature which has arisen around it. The first approach to religion may, in the case of some authors, have been as purely literary as that of the previous generation, but the resultant writings are a very different matter.

One of the most clear-cut examples of this is the case of Joris-Karl Huysmans. His original outlook was very much that of the professional writer. Feeling that the impact of naturalism had been exhausted, and looking around for an escape from the materialism which was at the basis of it, he turned first of all, in his novel *À Rebours*, to an escape into the realms of aesthetic experience. Then, in *Là-bas*, this reaction against materialism took the form of an excursion into the occult and an examination of Satanism. Too many people, knowing of Huysmans's subsequent conversion, see in all this the beginnings of religious belief; and there is no denying that it was through his consciousness of a world beyond reality that Huysmans *was* brought to the point of conversion. But though these undercurrents were present, at the time of the writing of *Là-bas* his main reasons for this departure would seem to have been far more prosaic. They would seem to have been partly a question of literary effectiveness and originality, and partly a detached curiosity with regard to extraordinary phenomena.

In the first chapter of *Là-bas*, Huysmans's autobiographical hero, Durtal, muses on the shortcomings of the naturalist novel and tries to think of a new *genre* which will escape the sterility that threatens it. At first he can see no escape: 'Durtal ne voyait pas, en dehors du naturalisme, un roman qui fût possible, à moins d'en revenir aux explosibles fariboles des romantiques, aux oeuvres lanugineuses des Cherbuliez et des Feuillet, ou bien encore aux lacrymales historiettes des Theuriet et des Sand!'² Eventually, however, he works out the possibility of a new type of novel in which the documentary truth and detail of naturalism would remain but in which the author would become a 'puisatier d'âme'. Mystery would have its place in this type of novel, and would not be explained away as an aberration of the senses. Beside the realistic plot there would be another one, parallel to it, yet at the same time intermingled with it, a spiritual plot dealing with matters of the soul. The intention would be to create a kind of 'naturalisme spiritualiste'.

The intention, in other words, is originally literary; and though here Huysmans obviously does believe in a world of mystery beyond reality, his approach is more one of curiosity than of involvement. Throughout *Là-bas* we see Durtal as a detached onlooker, intrigued yet repelled by the details of contemporary Satanism. He asks questions, and other people expound the theories of Satanism; the 'novel within a novel' which he is writing, a history of Gilles de Rais, makes use of the detailed knowledge he has been gathering. Yet the actual author, Huysmans, never declares at what point he believes these theories to coincide with mystical reality. Within all this apparent dilettantism, however, there were the germs of belief, and when we look at the whole of Huysmans's odyssey we can see, at this point, that belief in the power of an 'au-delà' which had already been hinted at in previous works, and particularly in *À Rebours*. The main intention in writing *Là-bas* may have been purely literary; but already Huysmans's conscious intentions may have been being stampeded by subconscious desires.

It is when we come to the point of conversion itself that we see these two sides of the matter most clearly in opposition to each other. Even while he was writing *Là-bas*, Huysmans had been publicly declaring that, when he had finished his 'black' novel, he might well turn his mind to writing a 'white' one; in fact, having written about one type of mysticism, he might as well see if there was anything in the other type. He talked about this much as though it were an interesting subject for research. Now, while we must not discount the fact that Huysmans, like so many people, had the habit of varying his tone to suit his interlocutors or his correspondents, and while there is no doubt that religious conviction *was* growing within him at this time (spurred on by the unlikely influence of the abbé Boullan), it is fairly certain that his original plan was that *En Route* should be as detached a study of unusual phenomena as *Là-bas* had been.

This is made clear by a study of the unpublished manuscript which was to have been Huysmans's 'white' novel. Though it was unfinished, a great deal of this novel had been written before Huysmans decided to scrap it completely and start afresh with *En Route*.[3] This novel, written between about March 1892 and May 1893, is centred around La Salette, to which the hero makes a pilgrimage with the abbé Gévresin and Madame Bavoil in the second part; and the reasons which have, in the past, been given for its destruction include the suggestion that the whole question of La Salette was too dubious and dangerous in the eyes of the Church, and that Huysmans had feared to publish a novel devoted to the question. Yet when we examine the text we find that most of the conversations devoted to La Salette follow the pattern of the conversations about Satanism in *Là-bas*; Durtal asks questions and is given all the details, in a straightforward manner. The story of La Salette is given in a manner no different from any of the pamphlets of the time (except that stylistically, of course, it is much better), and it is interlarded with sceptical comments by the questioner, Durtal, who is never depicted as being convinced either of the truth or of the falsehood of the story. He is as detached in relation to these miracles as he had been to the question of Satanism. The author's unbelief or belief are equally hard to establish from the reader's point of view.

There is nothing dangerous here; Huysmans has not committed himself. La Salette could not have been the cause of the abandonment of the manuscript, in this sense. But in another it well might. Huysmans, in his search for an extreme example of nineteenth-century Catholic mysticism with which to balance the extremity of Satanism in his previous book, naturally chose La Salette. And his treatment of this subject justifies, to a certain extent, the epithet of 'pur dilettantisme' which was applied to his work and to his religious leanings at the time. But meanwhile his own religious progress had taken him far from the dilettante approach, and those undercurrents of serious belief which had underlain his most detached questionings had begun to take the upper hand. We see the contrast in various letters written about Huysmans's own visit to La Salette. Some, to unbelieving friends, are fairly flippant, keeping up the game of detachment. Others betray a far more serious impression. There is not necessarily deception here; rather these letters seem to reflect a basic split in Huysmans's own mind at the time.

So it may be that, by the time he had written a good deal of this new novel, Huysmans suddenly realised that it no longer conformed with his attitude towards the Christian religion; and La Salette, now that he had visited La Trappe d'Igny, was no longer so suitable, in his opinion, for the centre of the novel.[4] What was needed was not a detached study of extraordinary mystical phenomena (such as he was to return to in his later novels) but the intimate study of a conversion. He will have the opportunity later, in *La Cathédrale*, to describe La Salette; in *En Route* he takes us to the solitude of La Trappe d'Igny, in which the conversion of a soul can be more clearly described. There is no doubting Huysmans's sincerity, either in *En Route* or in his later works. We see all his doubts, his disbeliefs, and even his shallow reasons for digging his heels in against conversion: 'Et si je me décide . . . ah! non, par exemple . . . car alors il faudra s'astreindre à un tas d'observances, se plier à des séries d'exercices, suivre la messe le dimanche, faire maigre le vendredi; il faudra vivre en cagot, ressembler à un imbécile!'[5] This, and other such statements, do not necessarily point to shallowness in the author. He is depicting his whole personality in the face of an internal religious upheaval, and he must depict as part of that personality the dilettantism which had been so strong in him. In the same way much of his old sceptical irony comes out in his own attempts at self-depreciation: 'Il faut que, décidément, la société soit bien immonde, pour que Dieu n'ait plus le droit de se montrer difficile, pour qu'il en soit réduit à ramasser ce qu'il rencontre, à se contenter pour les ramener à lui, de gens comme moi!'[6]

These lighter moments are all part of a spiritual 'bouleversement' which, in other parts of the novel, is expressed with greater solemnity. One feels in the character of Durtal the workings of grace, against which no struggles have any effect. The Durtal who is moved by Catholic prayers and impressed by religious art and music but who has no desire to take any decisive step becomes an ardent convert under the influence of divine grace, and by the end of the novel is unrecognisable as the same man. A confessor himself, Father H. R. T. Brandreth says of the first part of *En*

Route: 'It is not possible for anyone whose conversion was a mere literary device to portray so accurately just those hesitations and procrastinations which beset Durtal and which any confessor can at once recognise as genuine.'[7]

Of all the Catholic writers of this period it was to Huysmans that the epithet 'dilettante' was most often applied; and yet when one examines his work one finds a gradual change of approach resulting from his conversion which makes his religious belief interdependent with his literary creation. Despite the fact that he retains many characteristics of his pre-conversion way of thinking and writing, these have become metamorphosed by the change of emphasis which is given to him by his firm religious belief. What is true of Huysmans is true of other Catholic writers of his generation—Verlaine and Nouveau, for example. They could not be accused, like the writers of the earlier part of the century, of using Christian motifs for purely emotional or decorative effect. These motifs are part and parcel of their work, no matter to what extent they had used them for other reasons in their pre-conversion writings.

The Aesthetic Approach

A trend which can trace its origin back to Chateaubriand, the creator of a great many current illusions about the nature of Catholicism, and which must therefore be classed as yet another facet of the elusive movement 'Romantic Catholicism', is what one might call the 'aesthetic' approach to Christianity. In various forms, accusations of such an attitude have been levelled at several authors of the Revival; and, indeed, it was often this side of Catholicism which attracted the writers of the *fin de siècle* to an interest in Christianity. Of those who actually became converted, however, the greatest managed to subordinate this trend to the rest of their Christian belief, and it is only in minor poets of the time that we find aestheticism running riot. As an adjunct to Christian belief, such an approach was an advantage to literary creation; but as the central reason for belief, it tended to produce a vapid, hothouse literature of no great strength.

Chateaubriand, attempting to defend the Christian faith in the wake of the eighteenth century Age of Reason, was in a situation where those who opposed him felt it to be impossible that any man of intelligence could be a Christian. To a certain extent this situation is mirrored in that of the authors of the Revival, faced by the incomprehension of the positivists. But in place of that form of anti-rationalism which we have seen these later authors using, that reliance on God's revelation to man (an argument which is only convincing to the man to whom truth has already been revealed), Chateaubriand took the more dangerous path of proselytism, attempting to persuade unbelievers not through their minds but through their senses. His main aim was not necessarily to prove that Christianity was true, but to show that it was beautiful. Where the Revival of the end of the nineteenth century was to be defensive, stressing the most difficult and unacceptable parts of Christian doctrine in an attempt to repel those of little faith and strengthen believers with a sense of being apart, Chateaubriand's attitude was one of attack, desiring to convince those outside it that 'la religion chrétienne est la plus poétique, la plus humaine et la plus favorable à la liberté, aux arts et aux lettres.'[8] These are two opposed reactions of a minority: one a stubborn turning inwards, the other an attempt at persuasion of one's opponents which, in effect, distorts one's own beliefs. Each is wrong, in its excess.

This great difference of outlook might seem to invalidate the connection which has so often been made between the methods of Chateaubriand and those of the Revival; and certainly in the main authors of the Revival there was an intransigence which has little to do with the 'God is beauty' approach. Nevertheless this danger was perpetually present in those who played with belief and never became converted, and in the original attraction of Christianity for many who were later to develop more orthodox ideas, and in the works of minor poets who, though Catholics and contemporaries of the Revival, cannot be considered to have been in any way a part of that vital and original movement, but were rather a prolongation of a less virile tradition of Catholic poetry.

In Chateaubriand's apologetic we must distinguish between two trends, both of which were to have great influence: firstly, the argument for belief in God, drawn from a consideration of the magnificence and the beauty of nature; secondly, the argument for the attractiveness of the Catholic religion drawn from the beauty of Catholic art, music, architecture and liturgy.

In the early years of the century one of the adherents of this form of 'Romantic Catholicism' had been Maurice de Guérin (1810–39). Barrès, in his remarks on this young poet's attitude to

Christian belief, was to point out the basic weakness of this form of Christianity:

> Voilà un problème: la religion (qui tient en mépris les biens de ce monde et qui redoute les séductions terrestres) peut-elle s'accorder avec cet amour de la nature? Maurice de Guérin voulait croire que l'homme était l'élu qui devait adorer le Seigneur, en le félicitant de son oeuvre. C'est un rôle, une fonction. Mais d'une falaise, s'il domine la mer, il n'aperçoit pas a l'horizon le Dieu crucifié. Les dieux ne sont pas loin.[9]

This form of Christianity is never far from a certain type of paganism, and by far the best part of Guerin's work is that of a purely classical, pagan nature, such as his masterpiece *Le Centaure*. Beside this and his other prose poem *La Bacchante* much of the rest of his work appears insipid. The classical influence on Romantic poetry was great precisely because of this pantheistic love of nature. It is hardly surprising, therefore, that Romantic views of religion should so often have been nearer to classical paganism than to Christianity.

The case of Germain Nouveau is a perfect example of the change which could overtake both the life and the poetry of a man as a result of a violent conversion. For Nouveau this moment of truth was 14 May 1891; the physical manifestations of the sudden access of belief were such that for a time he was shut up in the mental hospital at Bicêtre. Manic depression may have taken a great part in these manifestations.[10] Imbalance at this moment of conversion certainly did, and there was much in Nouveau's life before this date that would denote similar imbalance. Yet it is in an extreme case such as this that we see most clearly those changes of emphasis which are more gradual in other authors.

Germain Nouveau had written a large collection of Catholic poetry, called *La Doctrine de l'Amour*, before this date, in the years 1879–81. This collection is a perfect example of the dilettante approach to Christianity of many of the *fin de siècle* writers. He was merely playing with belief, and in the years after it he was still to write perfectly pagan poetry of erotic love in the collection *Valentines* (1885–7, published in 1922), which has been described as an 'oeuvre érotique absolument unique dans les lettres françaises.'[11] Certain critics have been so misled by the nature of these two collections that they have neglected to look at the chronology, and have claimed that the *Poésies d'Humilis* (the title under which the

Doctrine de l'Amour was first published in 1910) were written *after*
the *Valentines*. This is, of course, untrue; and if one looks at the
Doctrine de l'Amour one can see in it a completely different form
of Christianity from that of Nouveau's later Christian poems.

The *Doctrine de l'Amour* is a work of aesthetic Christianity. As
Marcel Arland says, 'le goût de la beauté et de ses pompes, voilà ce
qui entraîna surtout Nouveau vers la religion; on le sent nettement
dans les *Poésies d'Humilis*, qui sont une enluminure ajoutée aux
innombrables splendeurs de la cathédrale antique.'[11] For Nouveau,
at this stage of his career,

Dieu, c'est la beauté, Dieu, beauté même, a parlé
Dans le buisson de flamme à son peuple assemblé.[12]

God speaks to him out of the whole of Nature, as he had to the
Chateaubriand of the *Génie du Christianisme*:

Voyez le ciel, la terre et toute la nature;
C'est le livre de Dieu, c'est sa grande écriture;
L'homme le lit sans cesse et ne l'achève point.
Splendeur de la virgule, immensité du point![13]

And we are left with the vast and splendid generalisation:

Partout où l'homme écrit 'Nature', lisez 'Dieu'.[14]

It is not only this one aspect of Christianity *à la* Chateaubriand
which is stressed. There is also the attraction of Catholic art, the
magnificence of the cathedral with 'le vitrail tout en flamme au
cadre des ogives,'[15] and the beauty of the mysteries of the liturgy.
All this shows one form of attraction to Christianity; but what of
the Nouveau of after his conversion, the man of great humility,
who took upon himself a life of abject poverty and vagabondage in
order to lower himself as far as possible in his unworthiness; the
man who took as his patron St. Benedict Labre, the saint of poverty,
and who was to describe his poverty as 'Cette vertu du chrétien,
cet état de Notre-Seigneur, cette vocation de saint Labre'?[16] There
is a feeble trace of this in the poem *Humilité*, but this is a humility
to order, a humility of beauty, 'parfum du fort, fleur de petit,'[17]
far from the harsh rigour of Nouveau's later conception of this
virtue:

Si quelque affreux crachat qui passe
Vient à tomber près de mes pieds,
Ma langue en boit jusqu'à la trace:
Ceux qui sont empreints sur Sa Face
Seront-ils jamais expiés![18]

The poetry of *La Doctrine de l'Amour* is that of a man impressed by Christianity yet living a life basically unaffected by any beliefs this feeling may have brought to him. It is a collection of verse magnificent in its colour, its vitality, its sensuous rhythms, its concentration on sound and on evocative effects. The poetry of Nouveau's second period, however, is that of a man of absolute faith, who lives according to the strongest demands of a fanatical humility. It is perhaps less impressive, as poetry, at first sight; yet its strength and simplicity have a lastingly effective quality which make of this later work the crowning achievement of Nouveau's literary career.

In Nouveau the change brought by conversion is sharp, and fits the extreme nature of his own character. In his desire for the absolute he seems to wish to throw off all that had been part of his outlook before the change. Few traces remain of that aesthetic approach which had originally brought him to Christianity. In other authors the change is less accentuated, and often a great deal of this aestheticism remains in their later work, modified in accordance with their new outlook and subordinated to their new beliefs.

Thus we find in Huysmans an overriding interest in Catholic art and liturgy which, originally, in his dilettante period, was one of the attractions which brought him to Christianity. In his later writings this aesthetic approach is still very much to the fore; the descriptions of plain-song in *En Route* and *L'Oblat*, the minute examination of architecture in *La Cathédrale*, the detailed examination of the liturgy in *L'Oblat*, would all seem to be reflections of the detailed aesthetic descriptions of colours, book-bindings, etc., which the reader has already seen in the novel *À Rebours*. And there is no doubt that Huysmans has retained a good deal of his interest in aesthetic questions. But his descriptions of these things have now gained an added dimension, that of *meaning*, and it is the symbolism of the liturgy and of religious art which now pervades the works of Huysmans. With all the powers of documentation which he retained from his naturalist training he provides us, above all in *La Cathédrale* and *L'Oblat*, with an immense lesson in Christian history and symbolism as seen in architecture and liturgy. And though his love of all that is beautiful in Christian art remains and enriches his work, the effect which he describes is no longer purely aesthetic; plain-song at one moment lifts him into the joy of exultation, and at others, at the moment of the *Tenebrae* services, instils in him a salutary remainder of the need for suffering. Huysmans's is a hard religion, a religion of suffering, far from the aesthetic delights of a *fin de siècle* dilettante. In Christian art, too, he comes to look for a depiction of that suffering, in a conception of beauty far from that of the conventional Church art of his day. The twisted forms of a Grünewald crucifixion contain more impact and meaning for him that any religious art created since. Huysmans's religion was no aesthetic game; he still loved beauty in Church art when it was compatible with his beliefs, but for him the main thing was the meaning of this art in religious terms.

It was nevertheless Huysmans who became the target for all those who wished to criticise aesthetic Catholicism. Seeing religious art as the attraction which originally drew him to Catholicism, and perceiving so much of his work to be still devoted to this question, his critics classed him as a shallow believer of aesthetic leanings. Léon Bloy, in a furious attack on this attitude in his novel *La Femme Pauvre* (1897), contrasts his own character Léopold (in whom there is much of Bloy himself) with a thinly disguised Huysmans, who is given the name of Folantin (a character in one of Huysmans's early novels):

> Léopold n'était pas de l'école des *Rares* qui découvrent tout à coup le catholicisme dans un vitrail ou dans un neume du plain-chant, et qui vont, comme Folantin, se 'documenter' à la Trappe sur l'esthétique de la prière et le galbe du renoncement. . . . Il ne pensait pas non plus qu'une architecture spéciale fût indispensable aux élans de la dévotion et ne songeait pas, une minute, à se demander s'il était sous un plein cintre ou sous un tiers-point, quand il s'agenouillait devant un autel.[19]

Bloy's attack is violent and unimaginative. He does not credit Huysmans with any of that solid belief which characterises his work. The false emphases in Huysmans's beliefs may at times have been extreme; but it is difficult, in the face of his later writings and of his attitude to his own sufferings, to class them as 'purely aesthetic' Christianity.

If it is in Huysmans that the greatest trace of the influence of aesthetic Catholicism is to be found, there are nevertheless, in the conversion of many another Catholic author of this and the ensuing generation, hints of this influence. Often it is combined with other, more urgent causes of conversion; but it is still there, in however small a quantity. Among the influences working on young Ernest

Psichari, for example, out in the desert of North Africa, there is not only the whole question of order, military and religious, nor merely the tremendous impression of faith given by the example of Islam; mingled with these there is the influence of the desert itself, not merely as a place of solitude which allows man to think more clearly, but as a place containing that beauty which brings man closer to God:

> Minute impérissable! C'était au milieu d'une lande qu'ils reposaient, et des touffes de plantes y poussaient à l'envi, dont le vert pâle était celui des bruyères du pays de Galles. Une rosée abondante couvrait le sol, car déjà l'influence de la mer amollissante se faisait sentir. Vers l'est, les sombres dentelures de l'Adrar Souttouf apparaissaient, couronnées de brumes légères. L'air était allégé, décanté dans les laboratoires du matin, et il apportait, en brises tièdes, des parfums de terres mouillées. Quelques gouttes de pluie tombèrent dans le silence. Maxence, debout vers l'Orient, saluait la naissance du monde. Alors Sidia, un Maure de l'escorte, s'approcha de lui, et, faisant un grand geste du bras droit vers l'horizon:
>
> —Dieu est grand! dit-il.
>
> Sa voix tremblait un peu. . . . Il n'y eut pas d'autres paroles de dites ce matin-là.[20]

Many authors, too, shared that feeling of awe at the ceremonies and liturgy of the Catholic Church which Claudel describes in his article 'Ma Conversion'. Among his first reasons for thinking of religion was the feeling that it might be interesting to write about it: 'Il me semblait que dans les cérémonies catholiques, considérées avec un dilettantisme supérieur, je trouverais un excitant approprié et la matière de quelques exercices décadents.'[21] But later, when he attended a religious ceremony, he was completely overwhelmed by the power of the liturgy:

> Ah, ce n'était plus le pauvre langage des livres de dévotion! C'était la plus profonde et la plus grandiose poésie, les gestes les plus augustes qui aient jamais été confiés à des êtres humains. Je ne pouvais me rassasier du spectacle de la messe et chaque mouvement du prêtre s'inscrivait profondément dans mon esprit et dans mon coeur. . . . Tout cela m'écrasait de respect et de joie, de reconnaissance, de repentir et d'adoration! Peu à peu, lentement et péniblement, se faisait jour dans mon coeur cette idée que l'art et la poésie aussi sont des choses divines, et

que les plaisirs de la chair, loin de leur être indispensables, leur sont au contraire un détriment.[22]

This statement must, of course, be placed beside those other, more important reasons for Claudel's conversion: the reaction against materialism, the influence of Rimbaud in showing him that something *did* exist beyond the real, and above all that rooted fear of death and nothingness that is to be found in all his early works. In Claudel's works themselves aesthetic interests take a low place in the list of priorities. Nevertheless, even with Claudel the aesthetic approach of 'Romantic Catholicism' had some bearing upon his conversion.

In the works of almost all the writers of this period the liturgy has an immense effect, on both form and content. This is perhaps because in the liturgy itself form and content are impossible to disentangle. Authors, therefore, by using liturgical effects, are adding one more dimension of meaning to their text, and this 'fourth dimension' can have as great an effect on the emotions as on the intellect. Catholic art, at all times, has this power of stylised evocation; and the use of the liturgy in literary works need not necessarily mean any concentration on purely aesthetic effect on the part of the author. The aesthetic effect of the liturgy is merely one among many. At the end of the nineteenth century it was often this aspect which interested writers initially; but rarely did they fail, later, to see its other attributes. A study of the influence of the liturgy upon the style and content of Catholic literature would be an interesting undertaking; it does not, unfortunately, fall within the scope of the present work.

We have seen that in the greater Catholic writers of this period any aesthetic leanings which their religious belief may have had at the time of their conversion became either supplanted or overwhelmed by other religious attitudes, with which they might mingle, but which they might never rule. In lesser writers, however, this essentially false attitude to Christian belief was at times allowed to run riot, and the interesting thing is that what, from one angle, is a religious weakness, only too often turns out to be a literary weakness as well. The excessive concentration on the beauty of Christianity can become a cloying, sticky thing which is aesthetically repulsive. The worst examples of this type of Catholic literature are timeless; they are always with us, and their appearance in the same years as the starker, more exciting works of the

Revival does not in any way mean that they had any connection with that literary movement.

Occasionally one of these writers rises above his fellows and gives us a glimpse of a pagan delight in beauty, a delight almost untouched by Christianity. Such, strangely enough, was Louis Le Cardonnel, a priest as well as a poet, in whose poems we find the harmonious beauty of classical Italy. He succeeds where the others fail, because his is poetry, rather than Christian poetry, and because the delight in beauty leads him neither to a lowering of what is infinitely great, nor to a wallowing in pious sentiment. In this poetry we find none of that concentration on the words 'beau', 'doux', 'lys', 'fleur', 'lumière', 'baume', etc., which mars the verse of lesser writers. Instead we find a calm, almost reverent love of natural beauty and of the Italian countryside. In his *Carmina Sacra* (1912) we find the best of this poetry; it is reflective, flowing, calm, like the pilgrim of whom Le Cardonnel writes:

Il lui faut le repos dans la stabilité,
D'ardents amis, un bel, un lumineux été,
Un automne, avec lui, songeant, le long des vignes,
De purs coteaux, menant d'harmonieuses lignes,
Des foyers où s'asseoir, toujours sûr de l'accueil.[23]

This collection is primarily a hymn to the beauty of the Tuscan countryside; if Christianity enters it is incidental, and the thought of it is prompted by the landscape. It is Assisi itself which speaks of St. Francis:

Que les verts oliviers, le ciel, la terre, l'eau,
Tout leur parle à la fois du grand *Poverello*.[23]

As the poet says, it is here in Italy that he has left his heart:

Au val d'Arno, c'est là que mon coeur est resté.[23]

How far all this is from the hothouse effect of the poetry of Maurice Brillant (1881–1953), where the suavity of the verse is matched by the banality of the luxuriant epithets applied to the Virgin, and where we wallow in waves of lilies, roses, narcissi, sweet smells, soft sounds and rich colours. Brillant is an extreme example of a deplorable trend which extends itself, in greater or lesser degree, to many other poets of his period, including Jean Lebrau (b. 1891), Charles Grolleau (1867–1940) and Guy Chastel (b. 1883).

The purely aesthetic approach, then, can be seen to confine itself mainly to minor Catholic poetry of no great value. In only one case, that of Le Cardonnel, does it raise itself, and that because his poetry contains so much of the pagan and so little of the Christian attitude to life. In all the greater writers of this period 'aesthetic Catholicism', where it remains after their conversion, is subordinated to the greater demands of orthodox Christianity. In this way not only is a more balanced Christian belief obtained but also a more healthy and successful form of literature.

Sentimentalism

Sentimentalism is not always the literary drawback that it is represented to be. In the literature of the eighteenth century, for example, when not taken to excess, this attribute made a contribution of some worth. In the Christian religion, however, sentimentalism is a perpetual danger, with its capacity for distorting religious values. The combination of Catholicism and sentimentalism produces a form of literature which is both religiously and aesthetically regrettable; a smug, comfortable and kindly reading-matter for unthinking *bien-pensants*.

Fortunately, anyone who looks for signs of sentimentalism in the major authors of the Catholic Revival is doomed to disappointment. Their outlook was vital and exciting; their Christianity was hard and demanding; their writings were taut and explosive. In fact they all reacted strongly against the sentimentality of contemporary Catholic life and thought. Huysmans, Bloy, Drumont, Péguy, Claudel and many others inveigh against the mealy-mouthed piety of the *bien-pensants* as seen in contemporary Church life, in Catholic art and in the writings of those minor Catholic authors who remain in a literary and religious tradition alien to the new ideals.

It is in these minor writers, so maltreated by those of the Revival, that one more part of what we have called 'Romantic Catholicism' lives on. For it was in the Romantic era of the beginning of the nineteenth century that that sentimentalism which is always present in certain areas of Christian thought became magnified by contact with the literary sentimentalism of the eighteenth century, and of the early Romantics. Chateaubriand's conversion, in 1798, sets the pattern for early nineteenth-century Catholicism. 'J'ai pleuré et j'ai cru', he wrote. When we look at Chateaubriand's writings, we must consider him as firstly a Romantic and only secondly a Catholic. His conversion is the conversion of René; and it contains in it emotions worthy of Byron, Werther and the whole Romantic hierarchy. It sets the scene for the century.

Of the writers of the first half of the new century, Eugénie de Guérin (1806–48) is a prime example of this trend. She was the sister of Maurice de Guérin, whom we have already discussed. Maurice died young and his work had not had time to gain force and power. Nevertheless, one wonders whether his Christian writings would ever have risen above a charming but shallow melancholy. His sister Eugénie's journal and letters are several steps further in the direction of sentimentalism. They are the pious outpourings of a young maid's heart, and Huysmans's strictures upon these writings, in *À Rebours*, are only too true. They are filled with what one might call the 'petitesses de dévotion', and with sentimental references to nature. The journal, written for her brother, and in devout admiration of him, meanders on until the death of Maurice, after which, as Huysmans so well describes it, Eugénie wept for him 'en de nouvelles pages, écrites dans une prose aqueuse que parsemaient, ça et là, des bouts de poèmes dont l'humiliante indigence finissait par apitoyer des Esseintes.'[24] It is surprising to find, in the generation of Huysmans, authors who do not share the opinion of his hero, Des Esseintes. One of the most remarkable is Maurice Barrès, who, though he certainly did not see her as a great writer, was bowled over by her personality:

> Il ne faut pas que l'on dise qu'Eugénie de Guérin est un grand écrivain, c'est mal s'exprimer. Il faut dire qu'en écoutant les confidences de son *Journal* intime, on l'entend respirer et que c'est une respiration sublime; il faut dire que cette âme aimante faisait du sentiment avec les plus humbles détails du ménage et tous les instants de la nature; il faut dire enfin que c'est là et nulle part ailleurs, comme dans une petite église de la campagne française, que l'on goûte la poésie profonde du coeur.[25]

In the writings of the period after 1870, particularly in the poetry, there are frequent reflections of that sentimental approach to religion which is to be found expressed in so much of the Church art and architecture of the Second Empire and the Third Republic. It is unnecessary to name all the minor poets responsible; one has only to open a modern anthology of Catholic poetry to find many examples, ranging right up to the present day. It is interesting, nevertheless, to find François Coppée, whose own approach to life and poetry had already been sentimental, converted to a Christianity of even greater sentimentality; and among the novelists we must pick out Henry Bordeaux, 'chantre du pot-au-feu à l'eau bénite',[26] as Adolphe Retté was to call him, but who nevertheless occasionally managed to rise above this description.

And, just before the 1914–18 war, it is interesting to see a novel of somewhat greater stature, André Lafon's *La Maison sur la Rive*, which, despite the fact that it deals with various religious problems of some weight, is nevertheless written in an insipid style worthy of Eugénie de Guérin herself, whom the author so admired. In fact it is written in the form of a young girl's diary. In the work of André Lafon there is much that is good; his poetry is impressive by its restraint and its simplicity; yet in this novel he strikes a false note which destroys the intentions he must have had when writing it. We are not convinced of his heroine's sacrifice in marrying the wrong man, for the simple reason that we can never be certain of the depth of her sentiments; and the whole novel is bathed in the immature piety of an adolescent girl. Themes which have great vigour and religious and emotional force in other writers are here debased by insipidity of style and thought.

The Erotic Element

In that decadence of Romanticism which Mario Praz so skilfully diagnoses in his book *The Romantic Agony*, one of the strongest elements is an obsessive eroticism. In fact when Signor Praz's work first appeared it was mistaken, by some critics, for a treatise on pornography; and their criticisms at times failed to recognise the serious intent and the voluminous scholarship of the work. Amid the many manifestations which Signor Praz sees of the search for new forms of erotic excitement, there stands out that form of decadent Catholicism which will always find extreme sexual excitement in the concepts of sacrilege and damnation.

To find such excitement men need not necessarily be practising Catholics. As Adolphe Retté points out in an article (written long before his conversion) criticising this trend, people who have been brought up in a Christian manner tend to retain the concept of sin and sacrilege, and fear of God's justice, however far they may have strayed from the practice of Christianity. And, as one can see in any number of works of the *fin de siècle*, fear can add a sexual element which makes the joy of transgression more vivid: 'Les uns, imprégnés du christianisme, bien que ne pratiquant plus, bien que se complaisant à discuter leur croyance, gardent infuse la notion qu'ils sont en état de péché lorsqu'ils commettent l'acte charnel. De là, le plaisir de transgresser les commandements de l'Église leur vaut une volupté intense.'[27] This is true of authors who never took the step of placing themselves within the Church which afforded them such erotic pleasure. What, then, of those writers whom one might term decadent, and who were indeed professing Catholics?

Jules-Amédée Barbey d'Aurevilly (1808–89), Jean-Marie-Mathias-Philippe-Auguste de Villiers de l'Isle Adam (1840–89) and 'Sâr' Joséphin Péladan ('Sâr Merodack,' 1858–1918) are three Catholic authors in whom this erotic element was particularly strong. Anatole France, writing about Villiers, groups him with Barbey and Péladan in the following manner:

> Il était de cette famille de néo-catholiques littéraires dont Chateaubriand est le père commun, et qui a produit Barbey d'Aurevilly, Baudelaire, et, plus récemment, M. Joséphin Péladan. Ceux-là ont goûté par-dessus tout dans la religion les charmes du péché, la grandeur du sacrilège, et leur sensualisme a caressé les dogmes qui ajoutaient aux voluptés la suprême volupté de se perdre.[28]

The diagnosis would seem to be accurate, though the addition of Baudelaire to this unholy trio is rather odd; and Signor Praz's additions to the list, which he makes after quoting Anatole France's remark in *The Romantic Agony*, seem even odder. Huysmans, Verlaine, Barrès, Bloy and Montherlant are all lumped together as examples of 'this type of confused Christianity'. The confusion is here Signor Praz's. Occasional erotic elements may enter the works of these other writers, and in the early, pre-Catholic writings of Huysmans they are certainly to the fore, but the approach of these writers to their religion is very different from that of the Barbey–Villiers–Péladan trio, who represent a completely different strain of belief from that of the Revival proper.

We have already seen, in the case of *Un Prêtre Marié*, some of the uses to which Barbey put Catholicism; and in his collection of short stories *Les Diaboliques* one sees a series of variations on sexual excitement in which, as Signor Praz says, 'pleasure and horror are closely intertwined.'[29] They reflect much of the sadism and strange deviations which we find in earlier novels by Barbey, such as *Une Vieille Maîtresse*; but here another dimension of horror is added. Yet Barbey's 'decadence' is strangely superficial; one is left feeling that there is little true blasphemy in his own outlook, and that it is purely a literary pose.

Often, in Villiers, we find the same obsession with sexual deviation and with sadistic forms of suffering, particularly in such stories from the *Contes Cruels* as 'Sylvabel', 'L'Incomprise' or 'La Torture par l'Espérance'.[30] And we see his fascination for the macabre and the mysterious in such stories as 'Le Convive des Dernières Fêtes',[31] where a rich young sadist, obsessed with executions and himself an enthusiastic amateur executioner, dines with unsuspecting strangers on the eve of performing his grisly work; or in 'Duke of Portland',[31] a story about a rich young English lord who shuts himself away mysteriously in his castle and is never seen except in a black mask, having contracted a severe form of leprosy. It is in a story such as 'L'Enjeu'[32] that we see the full attraction of sacrilege; as a priest, gambling in a salon, wagers 'le secret de l'Église,' one of the bystanders cries: 'L'abbé! savez-vous bien que vous avez l'air du . . . Diable?'

Barbey d'Aurevilly wrote of Péladan, in his Preface to the latter's novel *Le Vice Suprême*: 'Il y a, en effet, une triple raison pour que le scandale soit la destinée des livres de M. Joséphin Péladan. L'auteur du *Vice Suprême* a en lui les trois choses les plus haïes du temps présent. Il a l'aristocratie, le catholicisme et l'originalité.'[33] This would almost seem to be Barbey's most flattering opinion of himself; and if we add that other characteristic of Barbey's, superficiality, we are well on the way to getting a true picture of Péladan: false aristocrat, false Catholic, and original only in his eccentricity. Dabbling extensively in the occultism which had become so fashionable in this period, Péladan set himself up as a 'magus' and, giving himself the resounding and kingly title of 'Sâr Merodack', growing a long and unkempt beard, and wearing flowing robes of Oriental design, became one of the most extraordinary figures of Paris. In 1888, with Stanislas de Guaïta and Oswald Wirth, he became one of the founder-members of the *Ordre Kabbalistique de la Rose ✠ Croix*; but partly because the others, who took their occultism seriously, saw in him a superficial and flamboyant mystifier with little true knowledge of the subject, and partly because they were more and more annoyed with the resounding titles he gave himself and the important 'mandements' he issued in the name of the Order, and partly, on the other hand, because he himself, who thought himself a Catholic, resented the non-Catholic tendencies of the group, he soon broke off from the *Ordre Kabbalistique* and founded a new Order of Rosicrucians, *Le Tiers-Ordre de la Rose ✠ Croix Catholique*. This new Order devoted itself to the artistic and literary expression of its ideals and held several *salons* in which the works of artists such as Félicien Rops were exhibited.

Péladan's writings are full of the erotic elements we have been describing, and he had a particular *penchant* for accounts of Lesbianism and descriptions of an androgynous nature. In his works we find all the features of what one might call 'decadent Catholicism' magnified beyond measure. To add to this, the works are extremely badly written.

A natural result of the unhealthy interests of these Catholic writers was a dabbling in Satanism. Retté, in the article already mentioned, continues: 'Beaucoup de ceux-là versent dans le satanisme, polluent les hosties, s'accouplent à des prêtres rénégats, chevauchent des incubes et se livrent à maintes saletés du même acabit.'

The influence of the decadents was merely one among many which produce the vogue for Satanism and for the more extreme forms of occultism which we find at the end of the nineteenth century and which will be discussed in more detail in the next chapter. Let it be said here, however, that this Romantic influence exerted itself in a more shallow manner than some others, and that one is often uncertain as to the extent to which authors themselves believed what they preached. The impression is often merely one of an immense façade. If we look back to the poetry of Baudelaire, for example, we find on the one hand what is obviously a sincere inward struggle of belief, and a form of Manicheism which polarises the strong forces of good and evil; but on the other hand we find, on the surface of the poetry, occasional glimpses of that Romantic *panache* and desire to shock which have moved Yves Bonnefoy to say 'Certes, le satanisme de Baudelaire n'est qu'un décor.'[34] Baudelaire's external manifestations of Satanism have little to do with whatever inner beliefs in the power of evil he may have had, which come out in far more subtle ways.

Barbey's *Diaboliques* are sadistic rather than satanic, and even here the main aim seems to be to impress the reader. Huysmans, in *À Rebours*, expresses great admiration for Barbey and is astonished at the Church's calm attitude towards 'cet étrange serviteur qui, sous prétexte d'honorer ses maîtres, cassait les vitres de la chapelle, jonglait avec les saints ciboires, exécutait des danses de caractère autour du tabernacle.' But the Church knew what it was about and saw no great danger in Barbey's bluster. Retté might well claim, speaking of the authors of the decadence, that 'ils violeraient volontiers une religieuse'; but in the case of Barbey the judgement of Zola would seem nearer the mark: 'C'est un bourgeois dévoyé et enragé. . . . Il n'a encore assassiné personne et il n'a même pas violé une duchesse. Pauvre homme, il est comique, il est touchant.'

Barbey and Villiers are the representatives of a form of Romantic Catholicism which is continued into the time of the Revival by Péladan and other, lesser figures; it is a Catholicism rooted in erotic and sadistic delight, in blasphemy or occult mystery; at the same time it is an extremely shallow and superficial form of religious belief. None of these three authors can compare with the authors of the Revival for fervour, humility or profundity of belief. Where erotic elements are to be found in such men as Huysmans and Bloy, they are not the basis of belief so much as appendages to it. In the case of Huysmans, what may have started as a superficial interest in this side of the coin swiftly became transformed by the new beliefs brought to him by his conversion.

Distinction must be made between Romantic Satanism, an essentially simple façade with no great belief involved, and the other forms of occultism and Satanism in this period, with which we shall be dealing in the next chapter.

Of the many different literary trends which could be classed under the heading 'Romantic Catholicism', few had anything which might be called a major influence upon the literature of the Revival. The dilettantism which made some Romantics toy with Christian doctrines and images was no doubt instrumental in arousing, in some authors, the first glimmerings of a far more serious belief; and the aesthetic side which appealed to the authors of the end of the century undoubtedly brought some of them to the Christian faith, but then almost certainly paled into insignificance beside more important aspects of the Christian life. As for that sentimentalism which seems so much a part of the nineteenth-century

I

approach to religion, it has no place in the sterner faith of the authors of the Revival, who condemned it bitterly at every opportunity. And in the decadent Romantic search for erotic excitement and originality, the Catholic religion no doubt played its part, but again as a form of that dilettante religion we have already seen. Its excesses are still far from that more real and frightening excursion into error that we see in such men as the abbé Boullan; and, while this Romantic Satanism may have appealed to many men in the days before their conversion, it was not the stuff of which conversions were made. A belief in the power of evil can produce a belief in the power of God; but the erotic fantasies of Romantic decadence could do no such thing.

NOTES

[1] Bloy, letter to Charles Buet, 1 February 1892.

[2] Huysmans, *Là-bas*, Chapter 1.

[3] It is only by the most extraordinary of chances that this manuscript is still in existence. At the time of the writing of Dr. Baldick's great biography it was still believed to have been destroyed by Huysmans (Baldick, p. 224). The torn manuscript is now in the possession of an American collector, Mr. Artinian, and a critical edition of it is soon to be published, with notes and comments by M. Pierre Lambert and M. Pierre Cogny. Through the kindness of M. Pierre Lambert, I was allowed to read a copy of the text.

[4] There are other possible reasons for the abandonment of the manuscript. We have seen that the progression of Huysmans's faith and the visit to La Trappe (which took place during the writing of this manuscript) were probably the main reasons; but other events which took place during the year of its writing may well have had a subsidiary effect. It was in this year that Boullan died, and though it was not till the summer of 1894 that Huysmans, examining his papers, fully realised the hidden evils of that man's doctrine, nevertheless hints of this may have made him wish to forget the journey he made to La Salette in his company. In this year, also, Huysmans's mistress Anna Meunier was finally committed to a lunatic asylum.

[5] Huysmans, *En Route*, Chapter 2.

[6] Ibid., Chapter 9.

[7] The Rev. H. R. T. Brandreth, O.G.S., *Huysmans*, 1963, p. 89.

[8] Chateaubriand, *Le Génie du Christianisme*, Chapter 1.

[9] Barrès, *Mes Cahiers*, 1910.

[10] A schoolmaster, he knelt before his pupils crying: 'Ah mes enfants, que Dieu est grand!' The doctor's certificate on him reads thus: 'Délire mélancolique, stupeur, hallucinations de l'ouïe, génuflexions extravagantes sur la voie publique. Idées mystiques: récit continu de prières, fait par terre des signes de croix avec sa langue. Ce malade est dans un état mental qui exige son placement dans un asile d'aliénés.'

[11] Quoted in the Preface to *Germain Nouveau: Oeuvres Poétiques*, Gallimard, 1953.

[12] Nouveau, 'Dieu'; in *Doctrine de l'Amour*, Gallimard, vol. I, p. 155.
[13] Nouveau, 'Immensité'; ibid., p. 152
[14] Ibid., p. 154.
[15] Nouveau, 'Les Cathédrales'; in *Doctrine de l'Amour*, p. 179.
[16] Nouveau, letter, 21 April 1892.
[17] Nouveau, 'Humilité'; in *Doctrine de l'Amour*, p. 200.
[18] Nouveau, *Memorare*.
[19] Bloy, *La Femme Pauvre*, Part II, chapter 8.
[20] Ernest Psichari, *Le Voyage du Centurion*, 1915, p. 132.
[21] Claudel, 'Ma Conversion'; in *Oeuvres Complètes*, vol. XVI, p. 191.
[22] Ibid., p. 194.
[23] Louis Le Cardonnel, *Carmina Sacra*, 1912.
[24] Huysmans, *A Rebours*, chapter 12.
[25] Barrès, *Mes Cahiers*, 1910.
[26] Retté, *La Basse-Cour d'Apollon*, 1924, p. 232.
[27] Retté, 'Rapports Sexuels', 1897; in *Oeuvres Complètes*, Prose I (1898), p. 12.
[28] France, *La Vie Littéraire*, third series, p. 121.
[29] Mario Praz, *The Romantic Agony*, p. 347.
[30] All three from *Nouveaux Contes Cruels*, 1886.
[31] *Contes Cruels*, 1883.
[32] *Nouveaux Contes Cruels*, 1886.
[33] Introduction to *Le Vice Suprême*, 1884.
[34] Yves Bonnefoy, Les Fleurs du mal; in *L'Improbable*, 1959, p. 45.

CHAPTER SEVEN

Heresy, Occultism and Satanism

A PREOCCUPATION with the *au-delà*, a 'beyond' which must be reached in order for the true poetic message to be conveyed, is something common to many poets of the nineteenth century in France. Too often, however, critics have tended to see a uniformity in this search where no true uniformity is to be found. There is little in common between the search for a pure world of essence undertaken by Mallarmé and the delvings into the human unconscious which we find in the poetry of Rimbaud; and there is even less in common between the rather puerile spiritualism of Hugo, the more coherent illuminism of Nerval, and the super-real explanation of natural phenomena undertaken by Baudelaire. It is useless to follow the example of certain Catholic critics and class the whole tendency under the vague heading of 'mysticism', for there is little of the mystical in the philosophical speculations of Mallarmé and Valéry, and indeed even in the case of Rimbaud Claudel's description of him as a 'mystique à l'état sauvage' is grievously wide of the mark. But there is one way in which Claudel's view of Rimbaud tells us an essential truth which unites all these tendencies in one common characteristic. Claudel's own conversion was to a great extent caused by his reading of Rimbaud, because he saw in Rimbaud an impatience with the world of reality and a consciousness of some more real reality beyond the physical. It is this reaction against the materialism of the age in which they lived which provides the common factor which may link these poets and their ideas, and it was the same reaction against materialism which was to spark off many of the conversions which made up the Revival. To that extent, and to that extent only, these poets can be seen as predecessors of the religious literary movement that we are studying; but any attempt to make further generalisations and links is a very risky matter indeed. A study of the question of the *au-delà* in the Romantic and Symbolist poets is a complicated task which a blanket term such as 'mysticism' could not hope to cover. What is important for our purposes, however, is to see in the general tendency away from materialism a reflection of those aspirations which we also find in the thought of the Revival.

One of the most important, and dangerous, trends which the reaction against the excessive materialism of the age had brought about in the late nineteenth century was a fashion for the occult; and in its preliminary stages the Revival often looked as though it might lean rather heavily in this direction. The fashionable occultism of the *cénacles* of the '70's, '80's and '90's was not, however, the greatest danger; while it might influence what one might call the 'Romantic Catholics', Barbey d'Aurevilly, Villiers de l'Isle Adam, etc., by its mystery, its secrecy, and the romantic aura surrounding it, their interest tended on the whole to be a superficial one, concerned above all with the impression they might make on those around them by professing these mysterious beliefs. While an occultist like Stanislas de Guaïta no doubt seriously believed the value of the doctrines he was professing, one gains the impression that those ostensibly Catholic authors who took an interest in these things had far more the attitude of a muddled exhibitionist like 'Sâr' Joséphin Péladan, whose actual knowledge of things occult was far less obvious than his delight in parading his mysterious beliefs, and whose life of make-believe was governed far more by personal impulses than by any coherent doctrine. Where Catholic authors show an interest in the occult fashions of the society of their time, it is either through this desire for a superficial impressiveness or through a morbid curiosity such as that shown by Huysmans before his conversion.

Far more danger lies in a different form of occult doctrine. In the declarations and revelations of various prophets of the nineteenth century, in such men as Vintras, we find certain forms of gnostic belief which were bound to appeal to the authors of the Revival. For gnostic forms of belief (despite the fact that many writers have seen in the various forms of early gnosticism an intellectual attempt to bring Christian belief into line with a philosophical system) are essentially anti-intellectual and anti-rational. In many forms of gnostic belief the *gnosis* or higher knowledge is not attainable by ordinary intellectual processes but only by spiritual enlightenment. Supreme knowledge is thus given to us only by supernatural means.

In their reaction against an intellectual approach to Christianity, therefore, and in their reliance upon revelation, the authors of the Revival possessed a form of Christian belief which in itself could be perfectly orthodox but which, if taken to extremes, contained qualities which could create a tendency to gnostic error. In the early years of the Revival such extremes were at times reached. The sense of being a minority, which we have already noted in these authors, may have been one of the causes for the desire which we so often find in them, a desire to be themselves the depositaries of a true knowledge unknown to others. In Hello and Bloy above all we find an obsession with secret messages, with apocalyptic predictions, with allegorical commentaries on holy writings and with mystical experiences. Much of this, and more, we find in the beliefs of the Vintrasian sect, and also of its Boullanist offshoot. Whether Bloy was directly influenced by Vintrasian doctrine or not is a moot point; later in this chapter something of the relationship will be discussed. But there is no doubt that this questionable form of mysticism was in the air at the time, and that Bloy could possibly have arrived at some of the same forms of belief as Vintras and his followers without having had any actual contact with them. On Huysmans the influence of Boullan was a direct one, and while Huysmans's religious views were never as unorthodox as those of Bloy, they nevertheless retained certain characteristics of Boullanist belief.

Around the miracle of La Salette and the Secret of Mélanie many of the more questionable aspects of religious thought of the time gathered, for this event contained many of those elements which most appealed to the stranger sects of the time. It may well have been for this reason that the Church was so wary of approving this miracle.

When we come to the question of Satanism we must make something of the same definition and division that we have done for occultism in general. At one extreme Satanism is merely used as an effective literary expedient, as a method of evoking horror, amazement or a form of erotic delight. Authors who use it in this superficial way do not need to have any extended knowledge of Satanic doctrine nor even any positive belief in it. At the other extreme we have 'le satanisme pur, avoué, voulu et militant',[1] as Stanislas de Guaïta describes it, a form which is mercifully rare but which at certain periods, such as the late nineteenth century, is unexpectedly active. The practices of this form of Satanism are naturally secret and its adepts dare not declare themselves as such. For this reason it would be extremely difficult to give any coherent view of the situation at the end of the nineteenth century, save that this perversion appears to have flourished; and its only effect on the literature of the time appears to have been the arousing of the morbid curiosity of various writers, including Huysmans, who in attempting to depict its rites did not himself intend to become involved.

In between these two extremes, however, there are various forms of conscious and unconscious Luciferism and Satanism, which may be arrived at through various distortions of Catholic belief. In some of these, Lucifer is seen as the principle of light, the incarnation of good. Bloy unconsciously, through certain aspects of his symbolic view of history and his belief in the mission of the outcast, often comes perilously near to a form of Luciferism. In a recent book[2] M. Raymond Barbeau has tried to make of Bloy a conscious Luciferian; but in attempting to construct a coherent doctrine from Bloy's often chaotic beliefs M. Barbeau appears to be doing him an injustice. Nevertheless the dangers of an excessive reliance on miraculous revelation, on signs and wonders which may often be the result of hysteria, are nowhere more clear than in the writings of Bloy.

The influence of the occult and of gnostic forms of revealed truth had a short-lived influence on the Revival. Though it lingered on in the works of Bloy, by the beginning of the twentieth century it had disappeared from the works of Catholic writers or had at least been planed down to size. While the influence lasted, however, it was a dangerous path down which the Revival as a whole might well have turned.

In this chapter we will be examining some of the more important aspects of this influence; and the best starting-point will no doubt be a study of two important figures, Vintras and the abbé Boullan.

Vintras

Eugène Vintras, later to be known as the 'prophet of Tilly', was born in 1807 at Bayeux. He was of peasant stock, the bastard child of a poor working girl. His early life gives no hint of the extraordinary; he had a series of poor employments, each one worse than the other. Suddenly, in 1839, his whole life was irrevocably changed by a vision he received at Tilly, a small village near Caen, in which the

Archangel Michael appeared to him and announced to him his mission. The end of the world (that is, the world of the Second Reign, that of Christ) was at hand, and it was Vintras's mission to prepared for the coming of the Paraclete. He was given the names Pierre-Michel, though subsequent visions made of him a rein-carnation of the prophet Elisha; indeed, after a mystical experience in 1850 he was usually referred to simply as 'Élie' or as 'Strathan-aël'. After the first vision Vintras experienced frequent trances in which further details of obscure points of doctrine were revealed to him. The prophecies of destruction which abound in his message are common to many other visions of the nineteenth century, even that of Mélanie at La Salette, but there are many other more extraordinary features of his doctrine.

From the first Vintras's impact was enormous. And while we may attribute some of this effect to his own personal 'presence', which was apparently tremendous, we must also conclude that there was much in his doctrine which appealed to the aspirations of the believers of the day. He founded the 'Carmel' or *Oeuvre de la Miséricorde*, which was to prepare for the Second Coming by rites which aimed at the regeneration and redemption of erring mankind. People flocked to join this new Church, with its new priesthood which was to replace the 'corrupt' priesthood of the contemporary Catholic Church. Under the complicated Hebrew names which the followers of the sect now possessed (the names of those angelic natures which they had been before their entry into earthly life) were disguised priests, scholars, peasants, aristocrats—in fact people from every walk of life. The brothers Baillard, whose story Barrès tells in his novel *La Colline Inspirée*, were but three of the priests who were led astray into this new doctrine, and at the time of the abbé Boullan's claim to be the successor of Vintras there were nineteen bishops of the Vintrasian Church. Among the members of the Carmel, too, was Naundorff, the pretender to the throne of France, the 'Louis XVII' whose recognition had been yet another part of Vintras's revelations.

Among the miracles accorded to Vintras none was more impres-sive than the miraculous hosts which used to appear on his altar. Often these hosts were bleeding, in different places; some bore the stigmata, others bore letters of blood. They seem to have appeared in some profusion, for Vintras often used to give them to his followers.[3]

Vintras's life was a stormy one. He was put in prison for fraud in 1842, after the Bishop of Bayeux had seized hundreds of the bleeding hosts, and shortly after his release he left France, going first to Belgium and then to London, where he was to spend several years. Eventually he returned to France, to Lyon, which was henceforth to be recognised as the true centre of the sect. Here he died in 1875.

Later in the century the general public's memories of Vintras were to be aroused in a most mysterious manner. In the year 1896 the inhabitants of Tilly and of various nearby villages saw a vision of the Virgin. Whole crowds of people, whose names were taken, witnessed the event; and the vision recurred several times throughout the year. Many people looked back to Vintras, who had foretold that such miraculous events would take place.

Probably the most important of the doctrines of the Vintrasian sect and one which fitted in extremely well with other contemporary views was the belief that the world was approaching the end of the Second Reign, the New Testament Reign of the Son, and that the Third Reign was at hand, that of the Holy Ghost. This Third Reign was seen as taking place upon this earth, and it would also be heralded by the return of Christ in glory. The signs of the closeness of its coming were to be seen in the confusion of the century, in the increasing blasphemy and sacrilege.[4]

In such times as these an *élite* of chosen people was needed who could carry on their shoulders the faults of other men. These were the 'Carmel', the followers of Vintras, who by the performance of various acts and rites might speed the coming of the glorious Third Reign. These rites were sacrificial in nature, and they enabled those who performed them to receive the merits of 'redemption', and to participate in the preparation for the coming of the Paraclete. The belief in the efficacy of a specific rite in freeing man from the fetters of matter and bringing him nearer to the spiritual redemption which would announce the Third Reign is very near to that of most gnostic sects, for whom the method of redemption consisted not so much in the profession of certain opinions or virtues as in the practice of certain rites. In the Vintrasian sect the two main rites were the *Sacrifice Provictimal de Marie*, a cleansing rite of the type just mentioned, and the *Sacrifice de Gloire de Melchissédech*, a rite of the future, looking forward to the Reign of the divine Paraclete. Where the Mass is the renewal of Christ's sacrifice and looks backward to that event, the *Sacrifice de Gloire de Melchissédech* looks forward to the glory which is to come.

In the extremely complicated doctrine which Vintras built up there are various other characteristics which will interest us. Firstly, there is the place of women in the cult. Women were permitted into the priesthood of the rite, in fact they held a very important place, for it was through Woman that salvation was to come. And in the attitude towards the Virgin Mary we find a conception of her as 'created Wisdom', the invariable reflection of 'uncreated Wisdom'. This can be seen to be very close to one form of Valentinianism, a gnostic belief in which *Sophia*, or Wisdom (a divine principle which had fallen from the realm of light into the realm of matter) was conceived as being a double figure. The higher *Sophia* remained in the sphere of light, the lower *Sophia* had sunk into darkness. Through this duality *Sophia* became the fallen divinity through whom the mingling of light and dark, of spirit and matter, in the world, had been achieved; she was also seen as the intermediary between the lower and higher worlds and an instrument of redemption. The place of the Virgin Mary in the Vintrasian rite was similarly one of intercession and redemption. Take for example, the following passage from the *Sacrifice Provictimal de Marie*:

> O Sagesse créée, qui êtes à jamais l'invariable réflexion de l'incréée Sagesse, auguste Reine, ineffable Shahaël . . . la lumière de la foi qui nous éclaire comme un phare de salut, nous apprend qu'après notre chute céleste, ce fut uniquement à la grâce de vos prières et de votre médiation maternelle, que la loi de la pénitence nous a permis d'espérer notre réascension, pour atteindre la fin suprême de notre création angélique.

Vintras announced, too, the doctrine of the Immaculate Conception, years before the promulgation of the dogma. But here he was in line with a trend which runs right through the religious thought of his time and which was to culminate in the proclamation in 1854.

Among other Vintrasian doctrines which we shall find reflected in certain authors of the Revival there is that of the non-eternity of hell, and also the Naundorffism which was to play such a large part in the thought of the time.

Naundorff is now known to have been an impostor; but in proclaiming him the true Louis XVII, who had escaped from the

Temple and was thus the true heir to the throne, Vintras was well in the line of other prophets of the age. Thomas Martin, a peasant from Gaillardon in Beauce, had already proclaimed to Louis XVIII at the beginning of his reign that he was not the true successor to the throne; and many people have felt that this may have been one reason why Louis XVIII was never anointed king in the accustomed way. Martin divulged the same news to Charles X, and shortly before the end of his life he pointed to Naundorff as the pretender to whom he had been referring. Naundorffism, supported by all these prophecies, became extremely popular, for both political and religious reasons. Royalists and traditionalists saw in it a political resource and mystics saw in Naundorff himself an example of the Lord's Anointed suffering in ignominy, the great man thrown down from his high seat. Such beliefs were not confined to Naundorff. In 1896 a young girl living in the rue du Paradis, whose visions had brought half Paris to her door, foretold the revelation of a king, now living, who was the rightful heir to the throne of France *although he was not descended from Louis XVI*. Vague references to a 'younger son who had reigned' made all the believers in this visionary think of the legend of the Man in the Iron Mask, the elder brother of Louis XIV, of whom it was said that he was kept in prison all his life. Such beliefs did not seem at all ridiculous to an age when such revelation appeared more real than actual fact.

Certain of the accusations levelled against Vintras referred to sexual orgies and obscene rites. Certainly several of the beliefs of the 'Carmel' (salvation coming through women, etc.) contain elements which might tend towards a form of sexual rite. Be that as it may, we have very little in the way of reliable evidence that such rites took place, though in the case of Boullan, Vintras's successor, only too much evidence is at hand to prove that such deviations were part of his doctrine. In neither Vintras nor Boullan, however, does there seem to have been conscious Satanism involved. In fact, both were convinced that one of their greatest powers and duties was the exorcism of the devil and the prevention of Satanic rites by mystical powers. Boullan's erotic 'secret doctrine' was in fact based upon a logical application of his theory of 'Unions de Vie' and the ascending ladder of perfection. It was mad and vicious, but in no way does Boullan seem to have believed he was serving the devil by these practices.

The Abbé Boullan

Joseph-Antoine Boullan was a man very different from the simple peasants and workers who made up the ranks of the ecstatics and visionaries of his day. He was a priest, and a theologian of some eminence. His doctrine, most of which he had worked out long before he examined the documents of the Vintrasian sect, was based not only upon visions and presentiments but also upon a theological exaggeration and distortion of what had originally been perfectly valid doctrines of the Church. In this it is doubly dangerous to the Catholic writer, in that it can insinuate itself more easily as a doctrine acceptable to, and in accordance with, what one already knows of the Church's beliefs.

Boullan was born in 1824 and was ordained in 1848. For two years he was a curate at Montauban, and then in 1850 he left for Rome, where he joined the *Congrégation des Missionaires du Précieux-Sang*. There he got his doctorate of theology, and in 1853 he published a translation of Maria d'Agreda's *Life of the Blessed Virgin*. From then onwards he was to pour out a succession of books and articles upon various aspects of mysticism. In these writings he tended more and more towards an attitude typical of many in the century; as M. Marcel Thomas says, in his excellent study *L'Abbé Boullan et l'Oeuvre de la Réparation*: 'L'attirance qu'il éprouvait pour les révélations privées, les prophéties, les prodiges, en un mot pour *l'extraordinaire*, bien plutôt que pour le surnaturel, ne tardera pas a l'attirer dans des pièges qu'une étude plus approfondie des grands maîtres de la véritable mystique . . . l'eût peut-être aidé à éviter.'[5]

Boullan was at this time a fervent admirer of the Miracle of La Salette which had taken place in 1846; the apocalyptic element in the message no doubt appealed to him as it had to many others, and the 'Secret' of Mélanie, which had not yet been disclosed, must have added the element of mystery which would excite him. But above all the element of reparation which was preached at La Salette seems to have impressed him and he devoted himself from now on to the diffusion of this message, particularly in the columns of a journal called *Le Rosier de Marie*.

In 1856, at La Salette, he met a young lay sister from a convent at Soissons who claimed to have been miraculously cured on the 'holy mountain' a few months previously. This girl, Adèle Chevalier, had had frequent 'revelations' ever since her cure, and she welcomed Boullan as the priest who had been foretold to her, who would help her found a new Order devoted to reparation. Soon she had been confided by her superiors to Boullan's care and was already writing, under the influence of her 'voices,' the Rule of the new Order. After various difficulties at Rome Boullan obtained permission in 1859 from the Bishop of Versailles to found a house for the Order at Sèvres. At about the same time he founded a journal called *Les Annales du Sacerdoce*.

It was at this stage that Boullan's ideas, particularly those in relation to illness and reparation, began to take the downward path which was to cause so much scandal later. Boullan saw himself as a spiritual healer, and among the healing methods which he used some of the least horrifying appear to have been the mixtures of consecrated host, urine and faecal matter which he applied to the nuns of the Order when they were ill. He also appears to have begun some of those sexual rites which were later to distinguish his adherents in Lyon; and in 1860, one morning just after Mass, he murdered a child to whom Adèle Chevalier had given birth.

Denunciations of Boullan by one of his followers made the Bishop of Versailles suspend him; but soon the accusation was retracted and he was reinstalled. When a civil court condemned Boullan and Adèle Chevalier to three years in jail for fraud, however, in 1861, the Bishop had already gained further information in the religious field and again suspended Boullan, withdrawing the sacraments from him. Boullan was thus forced to retract; as M. Thomas points out, his need for the sacraments shows us that he was far from being the anti-Catholic rebel he is sometimes depicted as. In 1869 he presented himself at his own request before the Holy Office, and while in Rome drew up the 'cahier rose' which some have described as 'the full confession of his crimes' and others as his 'justification of his beliefs and actions'. This shocking document was found by Huysmans among Boullan's possessions after the latter's death, and is now in the Reserve of the Vatican Library, to which Louis Massignon sent it in 1930.

Boullan was absolved by the Holy Office and returned to Paris. From 1870 to 1875, in a paper called *Les Annales de la Sainteté*, he put forward more fully the new and heretical ideas about reparation which he had formed in the years around 1860 and which he had already set forth in *Les Annales du Sacerdoce*. These ideas were to have quite a deal of influence on the religious thought of the end of the century. Among the readers of the *Annales* were many important clerics, and they appear also to have been part of the reading-matter taken in by several religious organisations. At this time many perfectly respectable priests seem to have accepted Boullan's theories as completely valid, and among those who were taken in by him we must count a Jesuit of some standing, Father Augustin Poulain,[6] and also Bloy's mentor, the abbé Tardif de Moidrey. Some long letters written to Boullan by Poulain in 1873, when Poulain was aged 37, will be extremely useful to us when we come to study the manner in which Boullan deformed the doctrine of vicarious suffering. Poulain speaks as pupil to master and asks for more and more details about this matter, in which he believes Boullan to have far more insight than himself. The tone is adulatory—'Que vous êtes bon de vous intéresser à moi! . . . Vous m'avez ouvert sur ce point de nouveaux horizons . . .' etc.[7]— and one receives the impression that he wishes to use Boullan's teachings as a basis for his own studies. As for Tardif de Moidrey, in a letter written in the same year he shows himself believing Boullan's claims in the field of exorcism, for he asks his help in his own case: 'Tres vénéré confrère, notre ami commun M. Gouverneur vous a parlé de moi et appelé sur moi votre bienveillance me promettant que par des moyens particuliers que la Divine Bonté a mis à la portée de votre charité, vous pourriez m'obtenir quelque lumière et quelque force. . . .'[8] Though he has a will to good, he continues, he feels that this is always more or less tied by invisible bonds. He describes the ills of his family and ascribes them to the fact that his father, when a young man, had commanded the artillery which destroyed a church in Saragossa: 'Nous sommes depuis ce temps sous une malédiction temporelle. Que faut-il faire? Pour moi je suis, je le crois, sous l'influence du démon, qui agit terriblement sur mes sens: tentations terribles contre la chasteté, et impressionabilité maladive. Impression de terreur, invincible dans les ténèbres, domination de la peur, en face de tous les dangers. . . .' Though the word 'exorcism' is not mentioned, this is no doubt what Tardif means when he refers to 'moyens particuliers'.

But despite all this the Church was being extremely watchful, and in 1875 the Archbishop of Paris, who had referred the matter to Rome, received the order to condemn Boullan, who then had to leave the Church. In this same year Boullan, now an unfrocked priest, began to correspond with Vintras and met the ageing prophet on two occasions, on one of which he received a number of the miraculous hosts which Vintras always seems to have been handing out. When Vintras died in December 1875 Boullan announced himself as his successor, and in February 1876 he went to Lyon to study the Vintrasian documents. Boullan's claim was disputed by all but three of the nineteen Vintrasian pontiffs, but he was in no way put off by this and he installed himself permanently in Lyon, surrounded by a small but fervent group of adherents.

In his examination of the Vintrasian doctrine Boullan had found several points in which it reflected the views he himself had held up till this time. This is hardly surprising, for Vintrasism reflected many of the tendencies of the more extreme religious thought of the time. All Boullan now had to do was incorporate those parts of the Vintrasian doctrine which did not coincide with his previous convictions, and this he did, performing the rites of the Vintrasian cult and announcing himself as John the Baptist, the precursor and announcer of the Third Reign. Most of his letters were now signed 'Jean-Baptiste', and he signed certain articles with the name 'Dr. Johannès', the name which Huysmans was later to take over in his novel *Là-bas*. The most important parts of Boullan's doctrines for our purpose, however, are those which he elaborated before he joined the Vintrasian cult, and which have a close connection with orthodox Christian doctrine.

Of these the two most important are (i) his conception of the doctrine of vicarious suffering and (ii) his 'secret' doctrine of the 'unions de vie'. The first, which we shall consider in the next chapter, was of immense influence not only upon Huysmans but also upon many of his contemporaries. Starting off from the orthodox conception of the matter, Boullan went wildly off in various directions which must be considered mistaken and, at times, heretical. The second also starts from orthodoxy, and it shares with the doctrine of vicarious suffering the basic conception of the communion of saints, but into it there enter various elements of the gnostic conception of man's attempt to free himself from the matter with which his spiritual being had become interwoven when it descended to this earth.[9]

What we know of Boullan's 'secret' doctrine, which was normally withheld from all but the closest circle of adepts, has come to us through the wilful deception of Boullan by a young occultist, Oswald Wirth. For a whole year Wirth wrote letters to Boullan, feigning a sincere belief in the cult, and he gradually gained more and more information about the secret doctrine. Then, at the end of 1886, he wrote to Boullan telling him how he had duped him, and laid all the documents he had got hold of before an 'initiatic tribunal' consisting of Stanislas de Guaïta and several of the other occultists who, in 1888, were to form the *Ordre Kabbalistique de la Rose ✠ Croix*. This tribunal found Boullan guilty, and in May 1887 Wirth sent Boullan a letter, dictated by Guaïta, in which he was informed of his condemnation: 'Les Initiés véritables ne sauraient souffrir plus longtemps que vous profaniez la Kabbale en vous disant Kabbaliste et en mêlant les ordures de votre imagination dévergondée aux hautes doctrines des Maîtres de la Sagesse.[10] Whether the condemnation was to death, as Boullan believed, or merely to public denunciation, as Wirth later claimed, in 1891 Stanislas de Guaïta published the full dossier in *Le Temple de Satan*, the second volume of his *Essais de Sciences Maudites*.

What were the practices which so shocked the tribunal? They appear to have been based on the concept of the ascension of the human soul from the material to the spiritual. This ascension is not always purely individual; by a contamination of this original doctrine with the Christian concepts of the communion of saints and the possibility of vicarious aid given by one member to another, the ladder of ascent becomes one of collective redemption. Each person on this ladder can thus work for his own ascension, and at the same time participate as far as possible in the ascension of others. This participation is made possible by 'Unions de Vie'. By contracting such a union with those who are above you on the scale, you can raise yourself up; by contracting such a union with those below you, you perform the same service for them.

So far this seems odd, but not damning. It is only when, in reading Boullan's letters, one begins to understand that the unions were sexual, that one sees the possibilities. Huysmans, who sided with Boullan in his battle with the Rosicrucians, and saw merely the 'open' Boullanist doctrine, believed the accusations of Guaïta to be exaggerated and untrue: 'Quant aux unions, je doute un peu qu'elles fussent matérielles. . . . Je ne vois pas tres bien la mère Thibault forniquant avec le père Misme, chez qui habitait Boullan. C'était un tas de vieillards pour qui le jeu aurait été imprudent et sans charmes.'[11] But the letters quoted by Guaïta, who on the whole strikes one as far more trustworthy a person than Boullan, give very much the other impression. The letters of the prophet return again and again to sexual images: 'C'est le Ferment de vie qui, greffé sur le principe de vie des êtres des trois règnes, leur fait monter, échelon par échelon, l'échelle ascendante de la vie. . . . Un seul n'a que des fluides. Le ferment de vie est la combinaison de deux fluides. . . .'[12] The letter of three young initiates is even clearer: 'Carmel veut dire chair élevée en Dieu, et la Lumière d'en haut vous a fait connaître comment on se célestifie ici-bas, *par l'acte même qui a été et qui est encore la cause de toutes les déchéances morales. . . .*'[13]

For Boullan the act of love, being the act of matter, was thoroughly evil in itself even within marriage; but that same act, materially performed yet transformed by spiritual intention, could be the act of regeneration. In this there is much of the delirium of a repressed man; Boullan, as we can see from descriptions of his prowess given by one of his sect,[14] must have been remarkably over-sexed and he had become a priest when still very young. The problem of sex must have obsessed him, and in the spiritualisation of what to him was an evil thing (a spiritualisation which retained the physical act itself) he must have found the escape he needed. The 'unions' were often perverted—Boullan at times went to bed with two young girls at once, incest also seems to have been tolerated, and in the 'union' with 'higher beings' from the spiritual world the unconvinced observer could merely see onanism.[15]

The foundations of this doctrine were no doubt to be found in the beliefs of Boullan long before his connection with the Vintrasian sect, if we are to go by the evidence of those earlier practices which were condemned by the Church. At the basis of it lies the conception that 'C'est par un acte d'amour coupable que la chute édénale s'est effectuée; c'est par des actes d'amour religieusement accomplis que peut et doit s'opérer la Rédemption.'[16]

From the moment of receiving the letter of 'condemnation' Boullan had begun, by every means within his power, to resist the evil spells which he believed his opponents to be laying upon him. He seems really to have believed them to be Satanists and black magicians; and in addition to his public accusations of these things, he also took the action which his belief in himself as an exorcist might warrant. Huysmans, who first came into contact with

Boullan when documenting his novel *Là-bas* in 1890, described in several letters the exorcising rites into which Boullan was flinging himself at the height of the struggle: 'Les batailles ont repris depuis ma dernière lettre, des Wagram dans le vide. . . . Boullan saute comme un chat-tigre, avec ses hosties. Il appelle saint Michel, les éternels justiciers de l'éternelle justice, puis à son autel il crie par trois fois: "Terrassez Péladan, terrassez Péladan, terrassez Péladan!"—"C'est fait," dit la Maman Thibault, qui a les mains sur le ventre.'[17]

Most people who have studied the subject have agreed that Huysmans, in placing too much faith in Boullan, received a completely false view of the struggle. And when Boullan died suddenly in January 1893 Huysmans was convinced that this was a result of black magic practised by Guaïta and his friends. Unfortunately he confided this belief to his young friend Jules Bois, to whose book *Le Satanisme et la Magie* (1895) he was later to write an important introduction. Bois, who was first and foremost a journalist, published a serious of articles in the *Gil Blas* which violently and ridiculously attacked the Rosicrucians Wirth, Péladan and Guaïta, and accused them of Boullan's death. Huysmans, in an interview with a journalist, which was published in *Le Figaro*, was imprudent enough to make the following statement: 'Il est indiscutable que de Guaïta et Péladan pratiquent quotidiennement la magie noire. Ce pauvre Boullan était en lutte perpétuelle avec les esprits méchants qu'ils n'ont cessé, pendant deux ans, de lui envoyer de Paris. Rien n'est plus imprécis que ces questions de magie; mais il est tout à fait possible que mon pauvre ami Boullan ait succombé à un envoûtement suprême.'[18] After the threat of a duel, however, Huysmans published a statement saying that he had never questioned 'le caractère de parfait galant homme de M. de Guaïta.' Bois actually fought a duel, which he later described as having been filled with sinister and supernatural influences; in this there seems to have been much imagination and little fact.

Huysmans took Julie Thibault, one of the main followers of Boullan, as his housekeeper; and she continued, as a Vintrasian priestess, to celebrate the rites of the sect in Huysmans's apartment, whither she had brought her own altar. In the summer of 1894 Huysmans, on a visit to Lyon, had an opportunity of looking through Boullan's papers, and what he saw shocked him. He realised at last how he had been misled. Nevertheless, when he later referred, on occasion, to Boullan as a 'satanique', we must realise that Huysmans often used this epithet very loosely. The eccentricity and obscenity of Boullan's beliefs were no doubt 'satanic' in the sense that, to a Catholic, the abbé may have been misled through the positive influence of the devil; but there seems little doubt that he himself saw his role as that of a bulwark against satanic influences.

As for the Rosicrucians, Guaïta was a scholarly eccentric fascinated by the occult, Wirth an impressionable youth with an interest in 'magnetic attraction' and Péladan an extrovert and an exhibitionist. None of this seems very 'satanic'; in fact Péladan, to judge from his missives to the Archbishop of Paris, appears to have considered himself as the head of a parallel and equally important religious movement, pursuing the same ends and castigating the same vices. Péladan strikes one merely as having been unintelligent and odd, Guaïta and Wirth as having been intelligent and sincere, and many of the hangers-on, such as the homosexual young poet Edouard Dubus, who died of an overdose of morphine, as having been merely the hysterical appendages which all movements such as this attract.

No, the true Satanists would not have been found among such flamboyant personages as Péladan, nor among such occultists as Guaïta, nor among such mistaken heretics as Boullan. They would be far more hidden. Huysmans's accusations against a certain priest in Bruges have been hotly denied and it seems impossible, at this date, to tell whether they were true or not. Nevertheless, in the figure of Chanoine Docre in *Là-bas*, Huysmans portrays the nature of a true Satanist, whether the information on which he based this portrait was true in the individual case or not.

Boullan, whatever his qualities, was one of the main influences in the conversion of Huysmans, who saw in him, at the time when he first knew him, 'un très intelligent et un très savant prêtre . . . un théologien consulté, un maître reconnu de la jurisprudence divine.'[19] While Huysmans deplored the fact that such a man should indulge in the hocus-pocus of Vintrasian rites, he nevertheless saw in him a priest of God and a mystic of considerable value. Many of Boullan's theological views, particularly those on vicarious suffering, were to have influence on Huysmans's thought, and considerable traces of this remain even after the author's realisation of Boullan's true nature.

The wide publicity given to these views on vicarious suffering in earlier years by Boullan's journal *Les Annales du Sacerdoce* had produced an even wider influence than that provided by personal contact; all this we shall see in Chapter Eight. Let us for the moment concentrate on the influence of those aspects of the doctrine of Vintras and Boullan which are grounded less in the tenets of orthodox Catholicism and more in various forms of occult belief.

Hello, Bloy and the Coming of the Paraclete

For the reason that Vintrasism reflects so accurately certain aspirations of the religious belief of the nineteenth century it is impossible to conclude, solely on the evidence of similarities of doctrine, that an author's work was necessarily influenced by Vintrasian doctrine. Nevertheless, such proof is not essential in any way, for we are not so much interested in material influences as in the extent to which this form of opinion appears to have permeated the religious thought of the age.[20] M. Barbeau, in his book *Un Prophète Luciférien: Léon Bloy*, traces a Vintrasian influence on Bloy through the Belgian writer Vercruysse, who was a friend of Tardif de Moidrey, whose ideas had so much influence on Bloy in the short time he knew him. Certainly several ideas of Vercruysse do seem to coincide with those of Bloy; but whether or not this distant relationship is valid the interesting thing is that these ideas were essentially those current in the period.

The expectation of the end of the world was not a belief confined to France at this time; we find it widespread in mystical circles in Russia as well, while the Mariavite heresy in Poland (which at one stage communicated with Boullan) contained many of the apocalyptic beliefs of the Vintrasians. In the writings of the early years of the Catholic Revival, Ernest Hello and Léon Bloy, above all, are convinced of the proximity of the Second Coming. In the case of Hello this is wishful thinking induced by his disgust at his own physical and mental sufferings. Writing to Bloy in the late 1870's, he says:

Il est probable que nous touchons a un événement qui sera l'Événement plutôt qu'un événement. Il faut que cet événement soit l'Avènement, ou tout est perdu. Comme c'est du Salut qu'il s'agit, il faut prier au nom de Jèsus.

La guerre qui semble approcher est probablement l'espèce

sous laquelle se présente l'Événement. Il faut que cette guerre soit autre chose que les guerres ordinaires. Il faut qu'elle soit celle que prédit l'Apocalypse. . . .[21]

Hello's preoccupation with the Last Judgement expresses itself in an odd little tale, *Le Regard du Juge* (one of the *Contes Extra-ordinaires*) and also in the short text, found among his papers, which Bloy later printed in *Le Salut par les Juifs* (1892). In both of these much of the mystery of the event resides in a 'name' which cannot be revealed; in the second, this is the 'name' of the outcast, the condemned being who stands before the Throne of Judgement: 'Il se nomme peut-être Judas, mais les Séraphins qui sont les plus grands des Anges ne pourraient pas prononcer son *nom.*' All his life Hello was perpetually searching for a 'sign' of the coming event. His impatience for such signs was one of the things which most affected Bloy in his 'years of illumination', 1878–82.

In 1877 Bloy had met the young prostitute, Anne-Marie Roulé, whom he saw it as his mission to raise up from her state of igno-miny. In the process they became lovers, and soon Anne-Marie, having been converted, began to have the most amazing religious experiences and revelations. Bloy was at first prudent with regard to these things; he feared he might be the victim of an illusion and persuaded Anne-Marie to consult a priest. But Hello, in letters written to Bloy at this time, persuaded him with some violence to take these things seriously and begged him to obtain revelations of importance from Anne-Marie. Bloy, more and more excited by all this, arrived in 1880 at a state of indescribable mystical exaltation, shared by Anne-Marie, in which 'cette fille, qui est un prodige d'ignorance et de simplicité,'[22] spoke with what Bloy believed to be the voice of the Holy Spirit. Much of what she said was completely unintelligible and, as Bloy said, 'Depuis le 19, fête de Saint Joseph, je peux dire que d'après les manières de voir ordinaires, elle est complètement folle.' Amid the intelligible part of her revelations there was much in the line of biblical exegesis which would seem to have been inspired by what she must have gathered of the ideas on this subject passed from the abbé Tardif de Moidrey to Bloy; but in the deformation of these views which she presented we can see the basis for that 'algèbre universelle' which Tardif's exegetical views were to become when extended by Bloy to the whole of human existence. Amid Anne-Marie's revela-tions, too, were premonitions of the imminent coming of the

Reign of the Holy Spirit, the Third Reign which we have already seen as being an integral part of the Vintrasian doctrine, and which is, in fact, common to many esoteric doctrines. Finally, Anne-Marie revealed to Bloy a 'secret' which he was not to reveal to others, a secret of untold weight which he kept till the end of his life, and which remained of great importance to him until the end. Innumerable suggestions have been made as to what this 'secret' in fact was, but none seems entirely convincing. We know that it dealt with the coming of the Holy Spirit, but Bloy would not reveal any details.

In 1882 Anne-Marie went entirely mad and had to be sent to an asylum. Bloy believed that in this way God had withdrawn his special favour to him, and he was extremely downcast. But in the years to come he was never to doubt the special revelations which he believed to have been afforded to him. The story of Bloy's relationship with Anne-Marie is related at length in his novel *Le Désespéré*.

What in all this is typical of the esoteric movements we have been describing? Firstly, there is the sense of a special revelation, of the Holy Spirit speaking directly to man, affording him an understanding of the *gnosis* or higher knowledge. Secondly, there is the question of a 'secret', as there had been also at La Salette. Thirdly, the medium for the revelation is a simple un-educated girl, as simple as Martin de Gaillardon, Vintras, and even the peasant children of La Salette and Lourdes. Fourthly, there is the important place taken by Woman (Eve and Mary) in Bloy's vision of the world. And, finally, there was the whole question of the Three Reigns, and the end of the world.

Bloy, partly under the influence of Hello, had already for several years looked forward to the coming end of the world. When, in 1878, Tardif de Moidrey introduced him to the whole question of La Salette and his own theories about its connection with the coming cataclysm, Bloy was only too eager to listen. Mélanie's 'secret', with its predictions of the coming of Lucifer and the Antichrist and the end of the world, was not published in full until November 1879; but details of it were known before its full publication, for Mélanie had divulged it in part long before this time. Barbeau tells us that Tardif de Moidrey's friend Vercruysse must have had knowledge of it as early as 1860, though he believed that it had announced the birth of Lucifer for 1846, whereas in fact it had said 1864. Reasoning from this, Vercruysse had taken the date for the end of the world as being 19 September 1879, believing that Lucifer, like Christ, must live for 33 years. At the end of August 1879 Tardif de Moidrey and Léon Bloy made their fateful visit to La Salette, from which Tardif was never to return, as he died there on 28 September after a sudden illness.

Bloy, on his return, began to plan the great work he was hoping to write on La Salette; but the project of bringing people to La Salette and thus to that repentance and redemption which was necessary for the regeneration of the world before the apocalypse was soon overshadowed by what, under Hello's influence and that of Anne-Marie, he saw as the imminence of that event. Among the dates which Bloy successively believed would see the Coming of the Holy Spirit, only to be disappointed each time, we must place 19 March, 28 March, 18 April, and 19 September 1880. On this last date Bloy and Anne-Marie visited La Salette in hope of the Event, but again nothing happened. Bloy continued, for the rest of his life, to believe in the imminence of the end of the world. His numerous disappointments, and his final acceptance of the 1914–18 war as the beginning of that destruction, are extremely similar to the picture Barrès draws, in *La Colline Inspirée*, of the Vintrasian prophet Léopold Baillard, who in his discredited old age, in 1870, sees in the Prussians advancing and pillaging Lorraine the fulfilment of the prophecies.

Before Anne-Marie's revelations, Bloy had regarded the coming of the end of the world in a far more orthodox manner. In a letter to Hello written on 19 April 1880 he writes, speaking of his proposed book on La Salette, 'Lorsque je l'ai entrepris, j'étais infiniment éloigné de penser à l'avènement du Saint-Esprit.'[23] He had seen the projected book as being concerned with the world as it was, i.e. the world of the Reign of Suffering, of the New Testament. His views on this matter had been ruled by the words and the tradition of the Early Fathers and had not departed from orthodoxy. But now, Bloy continues, 'mon cadre est élargi. Aujourd'hui il n'y a plus de cadre. Il a éclaté de toutes parts et le désir soudain et brûlant et dévorant du Troisième Règne s'est emparé de moi et a changé absolument mon point de vue.' It must have been Anne-Marie's revelations which brought about this lapse from orthodoxy. The theme of the Third Reign remained from then on a constant in Bloy's thought.

Luciferism

In M. Raymond Barbeau's book *Un Prophète Luciférien: Léon Bloy* an apparently plausible case is put forward to prove that Anne-Marie Roulé's 'secret' was that Lucifer himself was the Holy Spirit. M. Barbeau bases this belief on a completely coherent Luciferian doctrine which he finds underlying all Bloy's work; in his opinion Bloy is consciously deceiving most of his readers all the time. He mentions certain ideas as being 'la base de l'exégèse bloyenne, le *substratum* de sa pensée, le motif secret de son mysticisme luciférien,' but he admits that this *motif* is 'assez difficile à percer parfois.' He describes Bloy as having been very careful 'à dissimuler ses vrais sentiments, à embrouiller les pistes.'[24]

M. Barbeau's own description of this shows us how false an idea it must be. The trail is difficult to find; so can it necessarily have been intended? If it was to be entirely private to Bloy himself, what was the point of printing it? And surely everything we have seen of Bloy's impetuous character would seem to belie this picture of patient, painstaking fraud. In such an untidy thinker and writer as Bloy it is easy enough to pick out all the quotations one needs to fit almost any point of view one wishes to ascribe to the author, and people have often erred in other directions as well, and ascribed coherent *orthodox* doctrines to him which are equally far from his thought. In his perpetual reliance upon 'illumination' Bloy formed many ideas which were mutually contradictory, and much of his muddled religious thinking comes from this. Occasionally one or two of these ideas unconsciously come near to a form of Luciferism; but this is very far from the conscious Luciferian beliefs which M. Barbeau ascribes to Bloy. The trouble appears to have been that M. Barbeau's main intention was polemical. In his attempt to shock those people whom he described as 'bloyens, bloyistes, bloyaudiers ou bloyolâtres' he no doubt succeeded; but this success in no way means that he was any nearer the truth.

The concept of Lucifer, the angel of light fallen from his high seat, appealed to Bloy in the same way that the figure of the 'exile' appealed to so many people in the nineteenth century. On the purely secular level the figure of the 'exile' had been an extremely popular one among the poets of the Romantic movement, and in the religious movements of the day, such as Vintrasism, this figure had a most important symbolic importance. We see the occult significance of the exile in the poetry of Nerval, in which the

Romantic and the religious overtones meet in a gnostic, syncretist conception of the race of outcasts who, by their rebellion against the demiurge who rules the world, are the expression of truth and freedom. Later in the century many writers, e.g. Villiers, Huysmans and Bloy, were to find in Naundorff this figure of the outcast.

With Bloy the role of the outcast becomes even more profound, because for Bloy it is suffering that is the instrument of redemption. The Jews, the outcast race, have an important place in the redemption of the world, as we learn in *Le Salut par les Juifs*, and so has the Poor Man. It was only natural that at times, to Bloy, Lucifer should appear as the archetype of this form of outcast.

In Bloy's conception of history, too, everything in Creation is a part of the Trinity; in fact, both Cain and Abel must be regarded as such. At times this conception appears to be one of a symbolic parallel between everything and the Trinity; but at others everything is in fact seen as *being* a part of the Trinity itself. How, then, can Lucifer escape this identification any more than Cain can? 'Ayant tout assumé, le Sauveur de monde est, à la fois, l'Innocence même et le *Péché* même, suivant l'expression de Saint Paul.'[26] Here we see another cause for misunderstanding of Bloy's intentions on M. Barbeau's part.

Bloy's theology is a mass of contradictions and most of his opinions are thoroughly unorthodox, but there is little to prove that he was a conscious Luciferian. We cannot go into all his mystical beliefs here, but there is little doubt that they contained elements of most of the heresies of the day, and particularly of the Vintrasian sect.

While we do occasionally find in the writings of the Revival traces of that Manicheism which also appears in the poetry of Baudelaire, and while the concept of the spiritual proximity of the sinner and the saint did occasionally, through exaggeration or distortion, verge on the heretical conception of any action being valid so long as it is positive, these are merely two more examples of the tendency, at the beginning of the Revival, towards heresy founded on misunderstanding or distortion of Catholic doctrine.

The conscious, or rather self-conscious, Satanism of certain Romantic Catholics is of no great danger, because of its superficiality; a greater danger is to be found in the various forms of gnostic error towards which religious thinkers of the period only too often tended. An interest in Satanism and the occult, provided such an interest was not merely a Romantic pose, could in fact bring people to Catholicism through a gradual realisation that there *were* such things as supernatural powers; we see this effect in both Huysmans and Jules Bois. But the more dangerous form of error, a heretical belief founded on orthodox Christian doctrine, is a danger which stems *from* conversion rather than leading *to* it.

This form of error stems in part from the exaggeration of the neophyte. It was one of the dangerous directions in which the Revival might have gone; but we gradually find these elements disappearing from Catholic writings, which by the turn of the century are treading more firmly the path of orthodoxy and of that 'order' which Barrès opposes to Vintrasism in his novel *La Colline Inspirée* (1913).

Those elements which we have been describing in the Christian belief of the late nineteenth century were in fact natural if exaggerated results of a certain climate of thought within the Church. They were exaggerations of certain characteristics which we find in the works of even the most orthodox Catholic authors of the period.

Basically all this stems from an attitude to mysticism which finds expression, although at its most innocuous, in Father Poulain's *Les Grâces d'Oraison* (1901); and, to be fair to the Church of the time, even this book aroused much worry and controversy among Catholic theologians. It did reflect, however, the *popular* attitude towards mystical matters which was current in the late nineteenth century: a concentration on the external manifestations of mystical experience, and a belief in such experience as being the extraordinary grace of a few chosen ones rather than a natural extension of the life of grace.

Father Poulain's book is careful and reasonable and does not accept all mystical manifestations out of hand, though much of this carefulness, as we shall see in the next chapter, may have been due to the corrections inserted by one of Poulain's superiors. Nevertheless, in its quieter and more orthodox way Poulain's book is an example of the same outlook as had produced the fantastic collections of occurrences of supernatural revelation which were lapped up by the Catholic laity in the years preceding its appearance. Poulain himself, when younger, was to some extent in the line of thought which was fed by such works as Boullan's periodical *Les*

Annales de la Sainteté, in which innumerable examples of miracles and supernatural revelations were laid before the reader, and the *Annales du Surnaturel au XIXe siècle*, edited by Dr. Adrien Péladan (Joséphin's father), and the abbé Curicque's *Voix Prophétiques, ou Signes, Apparitions et Prédictions . . . touchant les Grands Evénements du XIXe siècle et l'approche de la fin des temps*, which went through five editions in as many years, growing considerably with each new edition.[27]

All this concentration on miracles, revelations and the extraordinary in mysticism is reflected in much of the writing of the Revival. Many of its most extraordinary and heretical exaggerations, however, such as Third-Reign millenarism, appear only in such authors as Bloy and Hello and do not further impinge on the movement, except occasionally (and unconsciously) through the direct influence of Bloy himself.

NOTES

[1] Stanislas de Guaïta, *Le Temple de Satan*, p. 504.

[2] R. Barbeau, *Un Prophète Luciférien: Léon Bloy*, Paris, 1957.

[3] Maître Maurice Garçon has expressed to me his astonishment when, on visiting a Vintrasian chapel just before the Second World War, he was shown a chest which was full of hundreds of the things. Vintrasian practices were still being observed at that time, above all in Lyon, though they were conducted in the closest secrecy. I have no proof as to their continued existence after the war, but am informed that there is almost certainly such a continuation, and that there is possibly a Vintrasian group still in London.

[4] Much of this account of the Vintrasian cult is based on M. Robert Amadou's introduction to 'Le Sacrifice provictimal de Marie', in *Tour St. Jacques*, May–June 1957.

[5] In *Tour St. Jacques*, May–June 1957.

[6] Poulain's book on prayer, *Les Grâces d'Oraison*, 1901, was to be of wide influence in the first years of this century, running to ten editions in twenty years.

[7] Le P. Aug. Poulain, S.J., to the abbé Boullan, 18 March 1873; Collection Pierre Lambert.

[8] Abbé Tardif de Moidrey to the abbé Boullan, 2 September [1873]; Collection Pierre Lambert.

[9] The 'ladder' of ascension from the material to the spiritual, which we find in this doctrine, is also very near to the Platonic conception of the ladder of ascent.

[10] Wirth, letter to Boullan, 28 May 1887; quoted in Oswald Wirth, *Stanislas de Guaïta*, Paris, 1935, p. 137.

[11] Huysmans to Adolphe Berthet (Esquirol); quoted in article by Pierre Lambert in *Bulletin de la Société Huysmans*, no. 23, 1953.

[12] Boullan to Wirth, 24 November 1886; quoted in Guaïta, *Le Temple de Satan*, p. 468.

[13] Letter from 'Nahelael, Idhelael and Anandael' to Wirth, 5 December 1886; ibid., p. 471.

[14] *Déposition de Mlle. Maria M. . . .*, 18 May 1887; quoted in *Le Temple de Satan*, p. 479.

[15] Ibid., p. 479.

[16] Guaïta, *Le Temple de Satan*, p. 451.

[17] Huysmans, letter to Berthe Courrière, 17 July 1891; quoted in Baldick, *Vie de J.-K. Huysmans*, p. 226.

[18] Op cit., p. 251.

[19] Description of Dr. Johannès in *Là-bas*.

[20] Bloy himself denied that he was a disciple of Vintras, declaring that he had never foretold an *incarnation* of the Paraclete. While this is so we must nevertheless admit that many other aspects of Bloy's thought seem to coincide with Vintrasian beliefs. Whether this is because both Vintras and Bloy were obsessed with ideas that were 'in the air' at the time, or not, one cannot say.

[21] Ernest Hello, letter to Léon Bloy (no date); printed in *Ici on assassine les grands hommes*, 1895, p. 25.

[22] Bloy, letter to Hello, 24 March 1880. On the importance of ignorance and of simplicity, see Chapter Four.

[23] Bloy to Hello, 19 April 1880; in Bollery, t. I, p. 430.

[24] Barbeau, op cit., p. 267.

[25] Ibid., p. 19.

[26] Bloy, *Le Salut par les Juifs*, 1892.

[27] In the fifth edition, 1873, the visions of Adèle Chevalier were included.

PART THREE

The Vicissitudes of a Doctrine

CHAPTER EIGHT

Vicarious Suffering

BY tracing the vicissitudes of one specific doctrine in the Catholic literature of this time we may most easily see some of the main characteristics of the period. The doctrine of vicarious suffering is the most obvious choice, for it enters in some way into almost everything written by Catholic authors between 1870 and 1914. Other aspects of Catholic thought might well, if we had space or time, deserve similar treatment; the question of the close relationship between saint and sinner, for example, or various aspects of the cult of the Virgin Mary; but it is vicarious suffering which, by its ubiquity and by the way in which it stresses the more important aspects of the thought of the Revival, has the greatest claim to study.

A Hard Religion

In the violence of their reaction against the world around them, the authors of the Revival had a natural tendency to stress those aspects of the Catholic faith which would repel the unbeliever, and even shock the tepid Christian. Barbey d'Aurevilly, in a letter to the young Léon Bloy, stresses the dangers of this state of mind: 'Monsieur Bloy, mon ami, faites votre profite de cette maxime générale. Turcaret, le parvenu, l'enrichi d'hier, est ridicule par le faste de son luxe. Il y a, en religion, des parvenus, des enrichis d'hier, qui ont le faste de leur catholicisme. Il faut prendre garde de se donner les airs de ces Turcarets-là.'[1]

Barbey's own religion was something of a showpiece, and his belief a desire to differentiate himself from those around him; but he never seems to have taken this differentiation to the lengths of creating for himself a hard and challenging religion which would rebut those who did not share his beliefs. It was for the writers of the Revival, Huysmans, Bloy, Péguy and Claudel, to turn into a reality those extreme beliefs which to Barbey had merely been literary props to sustain an atmosphere of Romantic dread.

In the case of Huysmans the horror of the outsider and the ardour of the neophyte can clearly be seen side by side. Before his conversion Huysmans was horrified at the extreme practices of those who inflicted sufferings upon themselves; in *En Route* the hero, Durtal, cries out at one point that he will never believe that the sufferings of a mystic such as Suso[2] could be to the glory of Christ. Yet Huysmans's post-conversion writings concentrate above all, and with a wealth of physical detail, on precisely this aspect of the Christian life; and it is with a certain amount of pride that Huysmans, in his letters, stresses the fact that it is this part of the Christian doctrine which is least acceptable to the average Catholic, and is usually glossed over by the clergy for that very reason:

> Au fond je sais très bien que les théories du livre [*Sainte Lydwine de Schiedam*] ne sont pas sans laisser un certain malaise aux croyants. Il est certain que cette partie du catholicisme: de l'expiation et de la souffrance, n'est guère enseignée par le clergé, de peur de faire prendre la fuite aux gens; elle est pourtant la seule vraie, celle qui découle du Calvaire; elle est la pure théologie mystique, en un mot.[3]

A similar example of the extreme change wrought by conversion is Adolphe Retté, who in a series of violent attacks upon Huysmans in the 1890's stressed what he saw as the sadism and aberration of that author's views upon suffering. In the caricature of Huysmans which he drew in 'Le Banquet', one of his *XIII Idylles Diaboliques* (1898), this was one of the main aspects of the author's work to be parodied and ridiculed; and again and again, in newspaper articles, the same criticisms are formulated:

> Et M. Huysmans, docile et suggéré, s'en fut à la Trappe. Là, c'est le triomphe du mysticisme, c'est-à-dire de cette forme spéciale du sadisme — peut-être la pire — qui consiste à faire souffrir son propre corps pour goûter d'inouïes voluptés d'âme.[4]

> Il va toujours, avec une sûreté de flair prodigieuse, jusqu'au fond de l'ordure ou jusqu'aux extrêmes limites de l'aberration.[5]

Yet when Retté himself was converted in 1906 he immediately embraced those parts of Catholic doctrine which had seemed to him the hardest to swallow, and took them to the very extremes which he had criticised. His sensation of joy and deliverance after

his first confession remind him of that author he had so despised:
'Je me souvins alors d'une page d'*En Route* où cette sensation de
délivrance est on ne peut mieux notée';[6] and we soon find him
praising as the greatest work of Huysmans that very book, *Sainte
Lydwine de Schiedam*, which had formerly seemed to him the prime
example of those tendencies he had been criticising. Indeed, we
find him taking up cudgels on that book's behalf, defending it
against attacks which cannot have been as strong as those that he
himself had launched. Writing in 1924 about Émile Baumann he
says:

> Ce qui est plus regrettable, c'est que M. Émile Baumann . . . a
> cru devoir, lui aussi, déprécier, au nom du *sens rassis*, ce chef-
> d'oeuvre de Mystique: la *Sainte Lydwine* d'Huysmans. J'ai
> peur que le pauvre garçon ne cingle, bientôt, vers les rivages
> mous de la platitude. C'est dommage car il manifestait jadis
> une certaine compréhension de la Mystique. En attendant qu'il
> vienne à résipiscence, on lui conseille de se montrer extrêmement
> modeste lorsqu'il portera des jugements sur Huysmans.[7]

Baumann's criticisms of *Sainte Lydwine* must surely have been
on the level of Huysmans's trust for the most wild of sources; they
can hardly have been based upon that author's attitude to suffering.
For Baumann's novels of the pre-war period had taken very much
the same attitude on this matter as had those of Huysmans, and in
his treatment of vicarious suffering he had dwelt just as much on
the physical aspect as had his predecessor. And, in his book on
mysticism written in the very year of Retté's attack upon him,
L'Anneau d'Or des Grands Mystiques (1924), Baumann, though he
claims in his preface that 'Je ne m'arrête pas, on le devine, aux
délices d'une mysticité sans règle, curieuse de l'anormal, de
l'indéfini, de l'inconnaissable,' nevertheless chooses those Saints
as his models whose sufferings were most extreme, and dwells
with some delight upon the details: 'Quand elle [Ste. Marguerite-
Marie] s'infligeait des peines volontaires, se faisant un oreiller avec
des tessons de pots cassés, restant cinquante jours sans boire, ou
buvant de l'eau de vaisselle, du "lessis", entaillant sa poitrine avec
un canif pour se graver sur le coeur le nom de Jésus. . . .'[8] In fact in
this book Baumann displays the same pride as had Huysmans,
contrasting the full, hard faith of the intransigent Saints he is
describing with the preparedness to compromise shown by the
bien-pensants of whom so much of the Church is made up. Speaking

of St. Marguerite-Marie he says: 'Jamais elle ne deviendra populaire comme Jeanne d'Arc. Même, sa rigueur de crucifiement, son appétit surnaturel de paraître "abjecte"; sa crainte de ne jamais assez souffrir, sa clairvoyance inouïe sur son indignité sont propres à détourner d'elle les amateurs de "vertu traitable", la multitude des demi-croyants.'[9]

In these beliefs Baumann and Retté were merely following the example of earlier writers of the Revival, reacting as a militant minority against the flood of sentimentalism and compromise which they saw in the contemporary Church. All these people believed, with Bloy, that 'une doctrine qui propose l'Amour de Dieu pour fin suprême, a surtout besoin d'être virile. . . . Il est trop facile d'émasculer les âmes en ne leur enseignant que le précepte de chérir ses frères, au mépris de tous les autres préceptes qu'on leur cacherait. On obtient, de la sorte, une religion mollasse et poisseuse, plus redoutable par ses effets que le nihilisme même.'[10]

This reaction was healthy in itself, but the extremes to which it was taken were startling. Most of these authors were converts, and seeing themselves as a minority they strengthened their resistance to outside influences rather than attempting to compromise or proselytise. All the most extreme forms of Catholic doctrine were stressed to the detriment of others, and in the process these doctrines were often made yet more extreme, up to the point of heresy. With pride these authors shocked the unprepared reader with, among other things, their excessive mariolatry, their acceptance of a doctrine of papal infallibility more extreme than that pronounced by the Council in 1870, and their stressing of the fact that God's justice had no relation whatsoever to its human counterpart. The doctrines of the close relationship between the sinner and the Saint, and of the validity of a priest however unworthy he might be, were also reiterated time and again. Miracles played a great part in the works of the time. And above all there was the concept of Christianity as a hard religion, a religion of suffering.

Humility, too, was taken to extremes, and the models became St. Benedict Labre and St. Angela of Foligno; people submitted themselves to the lowest personal abasement in order to sanctify themselves. Charles de Foucauld, in the convent he served at Nazareth, drank dish-water and ate the most disgusting of foods; Germain Nouveau's life after his conversion was very close to that of Labre, the saint he so admired. Nouveau, like Bloy, is infuriated by the way in which the law, in this modern century, prevents the man of faith from humiliating himself enough: 'La pauvreté, cette vertu du chrétien, cet état de Notre-Seigneur, cette vocation de saint Labre, sont aujourd'hui *punies de la prison* en Europe. Pauvre malheureuse Europe!'[11] 'Avec leur infâme loi de Mendicité et leur infâme loi de Vagabondage, avec laquelle ils ont atteint notre sainte religion au coeur. . . .'[12]

Suffering, above all, was seen as the lot of the true Christian. While it is undoubtedly true that suffering does play a very important part in the mystical life there is little doubt that in their enthusiasm for this aspect of the Christian life the authors of the Revival did at times weight the scales a little too far in this direction. The perpetual separation of the lovers in Claudel's dramas, the harrowing physical and mental tortures of the characters in Huysmans's gallery of Saints and in Baumann's novels, the glorification of suffering in the works of Bloy, all these things seem to overrule the other aspects of Christian thought. Only in the works of Péguy, beside Joan of Arc's dutiful acceptance of suffering, do we find a glorification of that other Christian virtue, hope.

Not that hope is lacking from the Christian concept of suffering. In fact many of the works we have just mentioned have been of extreme comfort to those who, already bowed down with suffering, can find in them an explanation and a reason for their misery. In the Christian perception of joy in suffering there is an ordering of life which is in itself balanced; it is unfortunate that in so many of the works of the Revival this perfectly valid concept should have been drowned in a frenetic search for the most extreme in human suffering. In Huysmans and several others there are disturbing overtones of sadism in this search.

Here of course is yet another reason for the overwhelming popularity, among these writers, of the miracle of La Salette. Not for them the smiling Virgin of Lourdes with her reassuring message; though they might turn to her, much of their attraction seems to have been towards that abundance of physical suffering which they saw in the 'Foules de Lourdes'. Retté, in his new-found humility, became a stretcher-bearer at Lourdes; Huysmans went there, and produced a harrowing picture of the pilgrims; other novelists occasionally used the place as a convenient setting for a miracle to spur on the plots of their novels.[13] But there seems to have been little concern for the implications of the message preached at Lourdes, the message of joy and happiness; only in the lesser, sentimental Catholic writers, the *pieusards* whom the writers of the Revival so disdained, do we find such a treatment of the miracle. Instead we find both Bloy and Péguy hoping that one day they may hear of a perfectly healthy Christian going to Lourdes to obtain the benefit of illness and suffering.

In his book on La Salette, *Celle qui pleure* (the title in itself is significant), Léon Bloy contrasts Lourdes and La Salette, and in so doing gives us many of the reasons for which he and so many other Catholic authors of the time were so much more impressed by the latter:

J'ai beau faire, je ne me représente pas la Mère du Christ douloureux dans la douce lumière de Lourdes. Cela ne m'est pas donné. Je ne sens pas d'attrait vers une Immaculée Conception couronnée de roses, blanche et bleue, dans les musiques suaves et dans les parfums. Je suis trop souillé, trop loin de l'innocence, trop voisin des boucs, trop besoigneux de pardon.

Ce qu'il me faut, c'est l'Immaculée Conception couronnée d'épines, Ma Dame de la Salette, l'Immaculée Conception *stigmatisée*, infiniment sanglante et pâle, et désolée, et terrible, parmi ses larmes et ses chaînes, dans ses sombres vêtements de 'Dominatrice des nations, faite comme une veuve, accroupie dans la solitude'; la Vierge aux Épées, telle que l'a vue tout le moyen âge; Méduse d'innocence et de douleur qui changeait en pierres de cathédrales ceux qui la regardaient pleurer.[14]

In a letter to the abbé Fontaine, Huysmans gives the same judgement on the Virgin of Lourdes: 'Ah! au fond cette Vierge, jeune, blanche, et bleue, sans enfant, sans croix, n'est pas celle que je préfère! J'aime mieux la Mère des douleurs du Moyen Age.'[15]

The conception of the Christian religion held by these writers was a heroic one, and in their own lives this heroism was at times fulfilled. Huysmans, for example, refused all pain-killing drugs when he was dying in the agonies of cancer of the mouth; he wished to suffer for others. In all the writers with whom we have been dealing there is but one dissentient voice. Poor Ernest Hello, whose life was one of physical and mental anguish, could not bear the concept of the necessity of this suffering. Time and again he begged God not to submit him to these trials, and his urgent desire for the Second Coming, in which all would be set to rights, stemmed from this personal torment. In a drawer, after his death, certain prayers were found which Bloy later printed in his article *Ici on assassine les grands homme*, a study of Hello. Parts of these prayers run thus:

O Dieu, je ne puis ni agir, ni supporter, ni attendre. . . . Je suis un prodige de faiblesse. . . . Vous savez que je suis trop faible pour vous servir dans la souffrance. Là n'est pas mon type. . . . La joie donc! La joie!

. . . Seigneur, je suis trop faible pour souffrir et pour mourir. . . .

. . . Exaucez-moi sans mérite, comme vous m'avez créé de rien. . . .[16]

Hello's attitude to the sterner side of Catholic belief was a strangely irresolute one. He translated Angela of Foligno,[17] but made of her visions something so innocuous that Huysmans, in *À Rebours*, completely underestimated that saint. In the Preface which many years later he appended to that novel, Huysmans, having by now realised how much the translation had misled him, wrote as follows:

Je n'écrirais plus surtout que les visions d'Angèle de Foligno sont sottes et fluides, c'est le contraire qui est vrai; mais je dois attester, à ma décharge, que je ne les avais lues que dans la traduction d'Ernest Hello. *Or, celui-là était possédé par la manie d'élaguer, d'édulcorer, de cendrer les mystiques, de peur d'attenter à la fallacieuse pudeur des catholiques.* Il a mis sous pressoir une oeuvre ardente, pleine de sève, et il n'en a extrait qu'un suc incolore et froid, mal réchauffé, au bain-marie, sur la pauvre veilleuse de son style.[18]

Bloy, too, mentions Hello's reluctance to say or write anything that might shock. But though in this respect Hello might seem to be far from the ideal of the authors who came so shortly after him, nevertheless there is much in his thought which appealed to them and led them to count him as one of them. He was one of the few Catholic writers of whom Bloy approved, and Huysmans, despite the adverse criticism we have just quoted, was forced to admit that in his own writings Hello was 'un manieur d'idées originales, un exégète perspicace, un analyste vraiment fort. Il était même, parmi les écrivains de son bord, le seul qui pensât.'[18] We have already seen some of the many links which join Hello to that movement which we have agreed to call the Catholic Revival.[19] It is only on the question of suffering that he appears to stand out from these other writers.

The whole question of suffering was so much in the air at the time that we even find writers like Bordeaux and Bazin gingerly approaching some of the theological implications of it, and on a very much lesser scale François Coppée in *La Bonne Souffrance* and several other sentimental writers managed to emasculate even these doctrines. The harshness of the particular approach to suffering of the writers of the Revival is vividly reflected in the work of a man closely connected with them. Georges Rouault was a close friend of Léon Bloy, and much of his approach to Christianity had been sparked off by that man of the absolute. Of that period of Rouault's art which stretches from about 1903 to 1910, Raïssa Maritain writes:

> Ses peintures noires, atroces, étonnaient et déconcertaient ses premiers amis, ses amis de l'École. Léon Bloy les lui reprochait comme une erreur. . . . Il peignait, lorsque nous le connûmes, des juges, des filles, des mégères et des clowns en des tableaux sombres et somptueux, des paysages de misère en des couleurs transparentes, et des Christs dont le visage et le corps prodigieusement déformés exprimaient le paroxysme de la Passion divine et de la cruauté humaine.[20]

Vicarious Suffering

Of all the doctrines relating to suffering which were preached at the time, that of vicarious suffering or mystical substitution was the one which most held the attention of Catholic writers. In concentrating on the vicissitudes of this doctrine we shall be able to trace many of the characteristics of the thought of the Revival.

The concept of reparation is important in the Catholic faith, resting as it does both on the doctrine of the communion of saints and on that of redemption. When God's divine majesty is offended by the words and actions of unrepentant sinners the Catholic sees it as possible for a good Christian, by means of prayer or physical and moral suffering, to restore the balance in a compensatory manner. In taking on these sufferings for the world, man is imitating and to a certain extent supplementing the sufferings of Christ on the Cross. And the most noble form of this suffering is not that which is devoted to a specific or individual end, but to the expiation of the sins of all mankind. Many saints of the Calendar (most of them women) were 'compatientes' of this type, working for the salvation of mankind in solitude and misery; and many others, unknown, must have supplemented this work.

Suffering for a specific end, however, was considered as by no means unorthodox at this time. People may take on suffering for the community in which they live, or for the salvation of those near and dear to them. They may even do so for the conversion of a particular person. A subsidiary and less important concept is that of the possibility of taking upon oneself the sufferings of those around one.

In the case of all these forms of expiation, an essential element is the free will of the sufferer. He may himself ask for suffering to be bestowed on him for a particular purpose, or he may be chosen by God to suffer for the whole of humanity. But in the latter case, even if it is God who sends the suffering to his chosen one, that person must both understand the cause of this suffering, and willingly accept it, for the sacrifice to be in any way valid. Evil came into this world through the exercise of free will; the same free will is essential to the achievement of redemption. From this there stems that conception of 'balance' which is at times added to the doctrine. God so arranges the world that the sins may be balanced by the expiatory sacrifices; but if one person, who has been chosen by God, refuses the honour which has been offered to him, the balance can always be restored in another way. A refusal is always possible; but this will in no way disturb God's pattern.

In nineteenth-century France this doctrine assumed an importance out of all proportion to the other doctrines of the Church. The possible reasons for this are many and varied. In de Maistre's works we find it explaining and compensating for many of the sufferings and horrors of the Revolution and the Empire; and certainly, at the time of the Restoration, many people felt a great need to expiate the sins of the period that had just passed. As M. Marcel Thomas points out in his excellent article *L'Abbé Boullan et l'Oeuvre de la Réparation*,[21] much stress was laid upon the blasphemy of that period and its profanation of the Sabbath, but beside these sins there were the more important questions of the whole attitude of the Revolution and Empire towards the Church, and of their wholesale taking of human life. The Chapelle de la Réparation in the Boulevard Haussmann, in which the bones of many of those killed in the Revolution were laid, is one example of the zeal for reparation shown by the nineteenth century; and the Basilica of the Sacré-Coeur, whose construction was voted for by the essentially clerical Chamber of Deputies in 1873 as a 'Basilique du Voeu National' to repair the sins of the French people, for which the 1870 defeat had been part of God's punishment, is another example of the way in which this idea of reparation on a national scale extended right through the century. There was an immense growth of pilgrimages of reparation, too, a trend which reached its utmost in popularity just after the Franco-Prussian War, when the pilgrimages to Paray-le-Monial, in honour of Marguerite-Marie Alacoque (to whom Christ, at the end of the seventeenth century, had revealed the mystery of the Sacred Heart), reached unprecedented numbers.

In the devotion to the Sacred Heart there had always been a tendency towards that sentimental approach to religion which the writers of the Revival so abhorred, and this tendency remained fairly prominent in such devotion throughout our period. Nevertheless, among those people who connected the Sacred Heart specifically with reparation, there came to be a far greater concentration on the harsher aspects of the necessity for expiation.

La Salette had been one of the main causes of the hardening of the doctrine of reparation. The sins of blasphemy and profanation of the Sabbath, which had been stressed as far back as 1816 by the angel who had appeared to the prophet Martin de Gaillardon, became here, on this mountain in Dauphiny, the grievous causes which were to bring about God's imminent punishment upon the world. God's anger, and the Virgin's grief, paint the blackest picture of doom. Mélanie herself, to whom the message had been vouchsafed, later revealed her intention of making of the mountain of La Salette 'un nouveau calvaire d'expiation, de réparation, d'immolation, de prière et de pénitence pour le salut de ma chère France et du monde entier.'[22] The missionaries of La Salette were supposed to be devoted to this purpose, and around this shrine there arose many movements of reparation, both orthodox and otherwise. In the case of Boullan the correct term is definitely 'otherwise'.

Tardif de Moidrey had devoted much of his time to organising pilgrimages of reparation; this work had been sparked off by his devotion to La Salette. Most of the Catholic writers whom we find concerning themselves with vicarious suffering are also devoted to La Salette.

In the writers of the Revival we find a perpetual preoccupation with this question. Partly this stems from the concentration on suffering; partly from the attitude towards mysticism so common in their age, where the remarkable and the extraordinary were more highly prized than the more genuine mystical experience. There is, however, one more characteristic of the age which may have helped the flourishing of this trend: in their realisation of their position as a minority, Catholics of the late nineteenth century seem to have renounced to a great degree the proselytism which is, and always will be, so great a part of Christian practice. Instead of seeking to convert those around them by a positive and physical approach they turned inwards and attempted to right society by their prayers and by their sufferings. We find people taking on suffering in order that one near to them should become converted to the Christian faith; Bloy's mother, for example, did this. We find others doing the same thing in order to convert the whole of society by mystical means. A Catholic priest, contrasting the Church's work in that age and in modern times, once described the nineteenth-century French Catholics to me as having a 'ghetto mentality'. By this he meant that this minority had decided to turn inwards rather than outwards.

Blanc de Saint-Bonnet

In the year 1849 the Catholic philosopher Antoine Blanc de Saint-Bonnet produced a volume entitled *De la Douleur*. This book, which nowadays does not appear to hold a very high place in that philosopher's works, seems nevertheless to have attracted a great deal of attention among the early writers of the Revival. Huysmans, for example, whose own writings were to devote so much space to the problem of suffering, wrote in a letter in 1898: 'Le seul livre qui vaille là-dessus est encore, malgré ses cartilages coriaces, le volume de St.-Bonnet.'[23] Bloy, in his extravagant praise of the works of Blanc de Saint-Bonnet, did not neglect this book; and Barbey d'Aurevilly, through whose advice Bloy had first been drawn to read the works of this author, describes *De la Douleur* as a book 'qui devrait être la colonne de tous ceux qui souffrent et qui ont besoin de s'appuyer sur quelque chose.'[24] Even Barrès refers to its extensively in his *Cahiers*.

Yet these authors do not seem, in fact, to have followed very closely the arguments which Blanc puts forward in his book. In each case they seem to have found there those things which they sought, but no more. Barbey saw it as a work of compassion which would console those who suffered, and he may, also, have learned here the theory of vicarious suffering of which he made use in his novel *Un Prêtre Marié*. Bloy and Huysmans appear to have found in it only the theory of vicarious suffering and to have ignored the rest; and their writings reflect a far harsher attitude towards this mystery than Barbey appears to have found in the book. None of these writers appears to have appreciated Blanc's rational approach. As in the case of his political writings, they appreciated only the result. Huysmans refers to the 'cartilages coriaces' of what is essentially a straightforward rational argument. Barbey stresses the non-rational effect the book had upon himself when, speaking of Blanc, he says: 'Grande tête et coeur plus grand encore!'[25] Bloy and Huysmans, in taking the message of vicarious suffering as the most important point of the book, have obviously read the book carelessly, skipping the argument and taking only the conclusions, for the doctrine of vicarious suffering is produced above all as a way of explaining anomalies in the rigid hierarchy of virtue which Blanc is attempting to build up. Blanc, in attempting to explain suffering, does so by a means which at the same time justifies his political opinions; when the argument appears to be breaking down, vicarious suffering is produced in order to shore it up. Blanc is the first of the writers whom we shall see using the doctrine of vicarious suffering for his own purposes, and distorting it slightly in the process.

In the *Avant-Propos* to *De la Douleur*, which he entitles *Les Temps Présents*, Blanc presents a picture of the economic and social situation of the time, and the solutions put forward by the modern age. These solutions, he feels, are false because they are based on the wrong premises: 'Il n'y a que deux lois au monde. La loi de la nature, dans laquelle les espèces supérieures mangent les espèces inférieures; la loi divine, dans laquelle les êtres supérieurs secourent les êtres plus faibles.'[26] For him, the nineteenth century has taken the first of these paths. And in their attempts to make man more happy the reformers believe that 'equality' will solve all. What man needs to realise, Blanc says, is that a change of spirit and not of worldly position is necessary. As in his other works,[27]

Blanc stresses the need for hierarchy in a Christian world. The bourgeois world is terrible because of its lack of Christian virtues; but Blanc sees the two possible revolts, Socialist and Christian, as incompatible.

Throughout this introduction we find a defence of propriety: 'La propriété . . . n'est le principe créateur et conservateur de la Société que parce qu'elle est le principe créateur et conservateur des âmes'; and of society: 'Je ne viens pas seulement vous dire que la Société est d'origine divine, mais qu'elle est l'institution divine elle-même'; and of hierarchy: 'Vous répétez que l'Évangile a proclamé l'égalite des hommes, c'est bien faux; il a proclamé l'égalité du mérite, autrement dit l'équité.' A hierarchy based on merit would produce virtues unknown to the bourgeois world as soon as Christian values became once more accepted. Work is seen as a form of *douleur* which purifies those who, through lack of merit, are lower down the scale. The higher ones show the Christian virtue of charity and the whole of society is formed on a system of paternalism. The aim is not so much to make men happy as to make them good, fulfilling their purpose in God's pattern.

The political message preached in this introduction is more subtly introduced into the main essay *De la Douleur* itself. The essay starts with a praise of grief and suffering, experience of which makes man both better and more pure. Work and the family, says Blanc, are the two important things for man: 'Or, à côté de la famille et du travail, j'ai vu le fait mystérieux de la Douleur.'[28] Happiness *is* the absolute aim, he continues, though by this he does not mean earthly good so much as spiritual happiness; and man can be raised to this spiritual happiness by means of suffering. Suffering is the natural concomitant of evil, and it exists in order to drive evil out of us: 'La douleur trempe l'être dans ses flammes pour le purifier.'[29] It is our greatest means to perfection, and in this connection Blanc praises war and the soldier's life, which brings him close to the Saints. We shall see in Chapter Eleven how common was this identification of the soldier and the Saint.

Already, in one or two comments, we find Blanc's political allegiance asserting itself; the virtue of aristocracy, for example: 'Les hommes n'ont ordinairement de valeur que de deux manières: ou ils ont beaucoup reçu de la vertu des ancêtres, ou tout acquis par la douleur.'[30]

The two most important ideas expressed in this essay are those of a spiritual hierarchy and a material hierarchy. In Blanc's mind these two things are interrelated. The 'hiérarchie mystique' consists of a series of grades ranging downwards from the 'motif du Ciel' through the 'motif de la gloire', the 'motif de l'honneur', the 'motif du juste' and the 'motif de l'intérêt' until one reaches the lowest grade, the 'motif du plaisir'. God tries to raise each man to the grade above that in which he exists, and the yeast which he uses to raise man is 'La Douleur'. Man can only be raised by love, and love is brought by suffering.

On the material level Blanc sees men as having been placed in the position they deserve:

Les hommes naissent dans les positions les plus avantageuses à leur formation. Au besoin ils savent y venir eux-mêmes. . . . La Société offre l'échelle toute faite. Ceux qui s'élèvent doivent s'élever; ceux qui redescendent doivent être de nouveau abaissés. Les âmes tombent d'elles-mêmes à leur place. Le propre poids de l'orgueil et de leur faiblesse les fait toujours toucher terre au point d'où il faut qu'elles repartent. Bien souvent la grossièreté des organes du corps vous indique la marge qui reste encore devant une âme![31]

But these patterns are to a certain extent spoiled by the fact that suffering appears to be out of all proportion to man. The extent of suffering which Blanc sees in the world is surely greater than is needed for the purposes of purification; and moreover the most holy of men can be seen to be those who suffer most. The material hierarchy seems to hold many exceptions. Faced by these facts, Blanc falls back on the doctrine of vicarious suffering. In an earlier part of the book he had already stressed the fact that suffering purified sin, but that those whose consciences were clear could console themselves by the fact that they might be expiating for others. Now, in a magnificent paean of praise for suffering, near the end of the book, he asks himself why liberty and suffering are eternal and why he finds suffering everywhere. 'Sur cette effrayante disproportion au sein de l'homme, j'émettrai une simple vue,'[32] he says, and proceeds to a description of the communion of saints and the reversibility of merits: 'C'est ainsi qu'a la lumière de l'infini, tous les hommes reparaissent les membres les uns des autres. Les mérites de chacun se répandent sur tous, dans ce mystérieux corps, par le canal de la réversibilité, véritable rétablissement de la circulation du sang de l'humanité.'[33]

This doctrine is not central to Blanc's case; nor is he sure that it is the correct answer to his doubts: 'Là n'est point toute l'idée. . . . Toujours je cherche pourquoi l'homme est sublime. . . .'[34] Nevertheless, it is this part of the book which the authors of the Catholic Revival seem most to have followed, possibly because of the emotional prose in which this doctrine is set forth, as opposed to the cold logic of much of the rest of the essay. And the very end of the book sets forth, in similarly emotional language, the heroic nature of suffering: 'Oui! je crois qu'un monde gravite dans l'espace pour toute âme qui paraît en cette vie: car le poids de la douleur qu'un coeur seul peut porter, me semble faire équilibre au poids de tout un monde. . . .'[35]

Vicarious suffering was not an important part of Blanc's doctrine, though it seems to have been regarded as such by those who followed him. It is significant therefore to note that he treats this doctrine on the whole in an orthodox manner, stressing the liberty of the sufferer: 'Ce dogme sur lequel reposent la force de ceux qui vivent et l'espoir de ceux qui meurent, ce dogme qui lie le Ciel à la terre, et la terre avec les lieux définitives de l'épreuve, repose lui-même sur la liberté.'[36] Nevertheless, Barbey d'Aurevilly was right in seeing in this book a work of consolation rather than exhortation. Blanc's main thesis is devoted to reconciling man with the social lot in which he finds himself; his study of reversibility aims at consoling those who are already suffering by convincing them that this suffering may be of some use, rather than persuading man to ask for such suffering in order to fulfil a function in the communion of saints. 'Vous qui souffrez, consolez-vous, consolez-vous!'[37]

Barbey d'Aurevilly

It is in Barbey d'Aurevilly's novel *Un Prêtre Marié* (1865) that we find the first important appearance of vicarious suffering in Catholic fiction; and this work is above all interesting to us as an example of the pre-Revival attitude to doctrine. The doctrine is not treated in its own right at all, and one is forced to conclude, after a study of the uses to which Barbey puts it, that the author is not so much convinced of the value of vicarious suffering as a religious doctrine as of the possibilities it might hold in the construction of a Romantic novel.

In this novel the whole conception of vicarious suffering is given a hysterical, disorderly treatment which at times approaches that sadism which we have seen to be one of the characteristics of 'Romantic Catholicism'. In his treatment of this theme Barbey betrays both his essential incomprehension of it and at the same time his desire to continue dealing with the same themes as in his earlier, non-Christian novels—wild, sensual love, horror, the cursed Byronian hero, the pale, suffering heroine, fatality, predictions, sorceresses, incest and all the hotch-potch of Romantic decadence.

The main plot is fairly simple; a priest, Sombreval, who has married and rejected the Church, comes back to that part of the Normandy countryside where he had lived when he was a priest, bringing with him the daughter of his marriage, Calixte. Sombreval lives up to his name; around him there is an atmosphere of fatality and malediction which is accentuated by the superstitious fear in which the local people hold him, and also by the predictions of a kind of converted sorceress, La Malgaigne, who, though she is now a Christian, retains the mysterious powers of clairvoyance which she had had before. Calixte, Sombreval's daughter, has vowed herself to the redemption of her father through her own suffering. A young nobleman, Néel de Néhou, although he was at first a prey to all the fears and scorn which the local people felt towards Sombreval, falls in love with Calixte and finds after a little while that there is much to admire and love in the strange, proud personality of Sombreval. Sombreval, who loves his daughter with a strong, fierce love and realises that his impiety is making her more and more ill (and, moreover, that the local people are accusing them of an incestuous union), pretends to have been re-converted and to wish to become once more a priest. This, we are told, aggravates his crime still more, because he is still an unbeliever; by celebrating the Mass without believing in it he is committing a form of sacrilege. After various *péripéties* the novel ends with the death of the three main characters, according to La Malgaigne's predictions.

Vicarious suffering is used here not only as a means of arousing additional horror in a Romantic melodrama, but also as the vehicle for providing two of the most popular types of Romantic character, the Byronic hero, fallen from grace, and the pale, ailing heroine. Néel's description of Calixte shows us exactly the effect which this frail beauty had upon the young Romantic paladin:

> On comprend alors quel coup de foudre lumineuse avait été dans son imagination et dans son coeur cette Calixte qui avait.

comme sa mère, la diaphanéité de certaines substances nacrées et la grâce mélancolique des eiders, et qui, de plus que sa mère, dont le front n'avait jamais cessé de porter la perle sans rayonnement du bonheur domestique et de l'amour permis, était couronnée de douleur.[38]

The lightness with which Barbey uses this doctrine for his own purposes is reflected by the lack of force which he seems to accord to it. He heightens the Romantic horror by the introduction of the sorceress La Malgaigne; yet, if we are to believe her, Sombreval's death and damnation are irrevocably determined. The tone of the book leads us to believe the sorceress's predictions, and the three main characters die, without hint of Sombreval's redemption, according to these predictions. Calixte's sufferings are offered for her father; yet the sorceress tells us that these sufferings will have no effect on her father's salvation:

Ah! cela m'a fait assez de peine, s'écria-t-elle, cela m'est un assez dur crève-coeur que de savoir qu'il n'y a plus de ressource et qu'il est perdu sans espoir! Je me suis assez débattue contre mes Voix, quand elles m'annoncèrent sa perdition, mais elles ne se sont jamais démenties et elles m'ont soumise à la fin. . . . Vère, sa fille, la Sainte de Néhou, ne gagnera le ciel que pour elle, mais le père est réservé au feu.[39]

How does this accord with Barbey's own description of Calixte's mission? 'Comme le fil d'archal le long duquel glisse la foudre, elle devait être dans la vie de Sombreval le fil conducteur de la Grâce.'[40]

When, at the end of the novel, Sombreval, far from being saved, is seen to have descended even further into his crime by his hypocrisy and blasphemy in attempting to become a priest again, we are forced to conclude that these things have been brought about not so much by evil intentions as by his fatherly love. Yet it was of this very fatherly love that Barbey had said, elsewhere, that it was the one thing which might save Sombreval:

L'abbé Hugon . . . avait mesuré le sentiment paternel de Sombreval, de ce prêtre dévoyé qui reportait sur la tête de l'enfant qui était son crime l'amour qu'il aurait dû étendre sur ses nombreux fils en Jesus-Christ.

Il avait sondé cet abîme, et s'il avait été épouvanté de sa profondeur, y pressentant cette revanche terrible d'une Providence qui punit le péché par le péché même et nous écrase le coeur sur ce que notre coeur a le plus aimé, il s'était dit aussi pourtant que cet amour, monstrueux comme tout sublime qu'on déplace, était peut-être une voie secrète — le filet tissé par les mains d'un enfant pour prendre le léviathan des mers révoltées![41]

Despite this, Sombreval's fatherly love is what makes him act in such a way as to damn himself further.

Though Barbey's treatment of the theme of vicarious suffering can thus be seen to be superficial, the odd thing is that when the doctrine is itself stated it is placed before us in a perfectly orthodox manner. Calixte sees herself as chosen by God for her task: 'Vous rappelez-vous ces pauvres brebis qu'ils marquaient l'autre jour dans le fossé des Longs-champs pour la tonte et pour la boucherie? Je ressemble à ces brebis-là, Néel. Je suis marquée pour la mort et pour le rachat de l'âme de mon père.'[42] Yet, having been chosen, Calixte has herself ratified that choice by accepting the suffering which has been laid upon her: 'Cette Souffre-douleur chrétienne adhérait à son martyre et ne désirait pas l'abréger. La pensée qu'en souffrant pour lui elle ramènerait peut-être à Dieu l'âme de son père, et qu'elle faisait, s'il échappait à l'enfer, une partie de son purgatoire, lui fermait la bouche à toute plainte et y étendait l'héroïque sourire d'une résignation presque joyeuse.'[43]

Sombreval himself underlines this exercise of his daughter's will. Why, he asks Néel, does she resist her father. Why does she try to prevent herself from loving Néel. Why does she not wish to marry anyone. Why does she not wish to recover from an illness which could be fatal. Why does she delight in these nameless sufferings which he himself cannot bear when he sees them torturing her? 'C'est qu'elle aime son Dieu plus que nous, Monsieur de Néhou! C'est qu'elle me croit un grand coupable parce que ... vous savez bien pourquoi! Vous connaissez bien ce que je suis, ce que Sombreval a été. ... C'est qu'elle veut souffrir pour son père, expier ce qu'elle croit un crime, racheter ce qu'elle appelle mon âme!'[44]

The suffering which Calixte undergoes is for a single person. We do not find here the conception of vicarious suffering for the whole of mankind. La Malgaigne at one point gives us a definition of that 'balance' so necessary to the doctrine; but the suffering in the novel itself has no such universal significance: 'Il faut bien que les bons, les innocents et les justes payent pour les pécheurs dans cette vie: car, s'ils ne payaient pas, qui donc, le jour des comptes, acquitterait la rançon des coupables devant le Seigneur?'[45]

In certain details the description of Calixte approaches that of the mystical 'compatientes,' such as the medieval Saints, or the more contemporary Anna Katharina Emmerick. Calixte is in a way stigmatised: she bears on her forehead the form of a cross, which she keeps under a kind of bandage in order to hide it from her father, to whom it might cause grief. And the detailed description of the moment of Calixte's last communion and death show her in a state of mystical transportation which restores her suffering body to its former beauty and causes her to levitate towards the host.

In the hours before her death, however, we see Barbey's sadistic imagination at its worst, as he describes in great detail the physical tortures she is enduring. And after her death, in a scene of hysteria, Néel, unable to believe that Calixte is dead, burns her feet to make sure (and thus provides her with stigmata):

— Vous rappelez-vous, — dit Néel en voyant [ses pieds] — le jour où vous disiez qu'ils étaient dignes d'avoir des stigmates? . . . Auriez-vous cru que c'était nous qui, un jour, les lui mettrions?

Et il approcha le fer rouge de ses pieds qu'il ne voyait qu'à travers ses larmes. Une fumée monta avec un bruit navrant, mais le corps de Calixte resta immobile. . . . Néel, qui y cherchait la vie avec rage et qui voulait la faire jaillir, par la douleur, des profondeurs d'un engourdissement qui pouvait la recéler encore, brûlait avec un acharnement égaré les beaux pieds insensibles que le feu rongeait, comme il aurait rongé une chair de fleur.[46]

This passage sums up much of Barbey's attitude to vicarious suffering. It becomes a vehicle for his morbid hysteria, only one vehicle among many for those Romantic and decadent traits which are common to all his works, both pre- and post-conversion. In calling this book 'un mauvais livre, livre indigne d'une librairie catholique', the Archbishop of Paris was no doubt spiritually justified. Reading it one often feels that he was at least aesthetically so.

The Abbé Boullan

In Blanc de Saint-Bonnet and Barbey d'Aurevilly we have seen two different methods of using the doctrine of vicarious suffering for one's own purposes without deforming the doctrine itself. Now we turn to a man who, centering his whole thought on the doctrine, succeeded in deforming it beyond all belief.

We have already spoken, in Chapter Seven, of that strange figure, the abbé Boullan. Most of his life and works were built around the doctrine of mystical substitution.[47] In his hands the doctrine suffered severe distortion, and to study this distortion will be interesting to us for two reasons: (i) in certain parts of his interpretation of the doctrine we shall find reflected certain misconceptions common to the age, and (ii) in the more extreme distortions which stem from his own particular religious preoccupations we shall see certain heretical interpretations of the doctrine which occasionally find their way into the work of later writers, especially Huysmans, on whom the abbé had such a powerful personal impact.

One misconception common to his time but which we find magnified in the ideas of Boullan is the tendency to see vicarious suffering in almost mechanical terms. You find someone whose sins you wish to expiate, you offer yourself for them, and an exact transference automatically takes place. Indeed on the level of the transference of suffering from one to another Boullan often seems to concern himself with the exact forms of suffering which are transferable, and the exact extent to which it is possible to change the dose. In much of this we see that concentration on the physical which is typical of the conception of mysticism held in the period. The impression one gets is that of a kind of telephone exchange in which calls are automatically put through from person to person, or rather in which a 'transpository agent' must act as intermediary. Boullan believed himself to have (or persuaded others that he had) this mystical power, which was so natural a corollary of his powers of exorcism.

It is in his views on the actual purpose and function of mystical substitution, however, that we find the more heretical part of his doctrine. This stems in part from his belief in the efficacy of the members of his *Oeuvre de la Réparation* in healing the sick. For him, the work of reparation consisted of wiping out the sins of the world; and on the other hand he believed that on the whole illness was the result of the sins of the sick man. Since illness corresponded to sin, those who were ill must either be sinners or pure souls making atonement for the sins of others. One of the functions of the *Oeuvre de la Réparation* was therefore, through the mystical powers invested in it, to heal the sick.

It was in 1860, however, that the full scope of substitution was suddenly revealed to Boullan. Adèle Chevalier had been ill and Boullan, believing this illness to be a spell cast upon her by a hostile *curé*, 'cured' her by the application of consecrated white wine. Suddenly he realised, he said, the full import of this happening: 'Alors, je compris ceci: le péché donc, comme les maladies, se transporte — et il vit — et il fait sentir ses effets dans un autre.'[48]

In a manuscript now in the collection of M. Pierre Lambert, which M. Marcel Thomas quotes in his article *L'Abbé Boullan et l'Oeuvre de la Réparation*, Boullan puts forward his new conception of the doctrine of vicarious suffering. He argues that sin, like illness, must have its own essence, and that this essence, like suffering, must therefore be transferable from person to person:

Une grande nombre de vies des saints ou saintes que Dieu a élevées à un état particulier de grâces surnaturelles sont remplies de faits où l'on raconte que ces âmes ont souffert les maladies des autres, qu'elles ont accepté les souffrances étrangères, en un mot qu'elles ont enduré des maladies qui ne leur étaient point propres et dont les autres se trouvent délivrés. . . .

Je demande dès lors pourquoi le péché ne pourrait pas aussi être transféré après acceptation de l'âme réparatrice, et où est la répugnance à cela. . . .

The expiating person can therefore not merely suffer to expiate the sins of others, but can actually take on the sins themselves and all their many characteristics. He can even take on the temptations of others:

La base de la Réparation, ce qui en est à juste titre la véritable pierre angulaire, c'est la réversibilité non pas possible, mais réelle, du péché; c'est le transfert d'une personne à une autre, sur son acceptation, des péchés étrangers dans leur être et leur espèce. . . .

Ainsi, dans la divine Réparation, le péché . . . est en nous avec ses caractères, son espèce, sa nature et toutes les formes qu'il avait dans celui qui l'a commis. L'âme réparatrice éprouve et sent le péché dans son corps, tel qu'il a été, elle constate les phases, les progrès du vice, du défaut, de la passion, en un mot elle subit toutes les crises de la loi du péché. . . .[49]

One can see to what extent this doctrine could lead to such extraordinary practices as the 'Unions de Vie'.[50] Indeed, the 'Unions de Vie' appear to have been a direct offshoot of it, for an integral part of this doctrine of reparation is that he who takes on the sins or suffering of another must be in a higher spiritual state, in a position to help the other up the ladder of perfection.

In Boullan's scheme of reparation there were three distinct degrees, which he set forth in the *Annales de la Sainteté*. The first consisted of the taking on of illness, physical suffering, and physical humiliation; the second, of taking on sin and temptation; the third, of struggles against the devil himself. The third is a logical extension of the others, for if one believes sin to be in all cases caused by the devil, and illness, temptation and sin itself to be transferable from person to person, then in taking on these sins, temptations and illnesses one is positively struggling against the devil. But in making it yet a third degree of reparation Boullan is obviously referring to direct attack on the devil such as he himself had practised by various rites of exorcism. The letter from Tardif de Moidrey to Boullan, written in September 1873, as well as letters from other correspondents, shows that Boullan was often called on for this last purpose: 'Notre ami commun Mr. Gouverneur vous a parlé de moi et appelé sur moi votre bienveillance me promettant que par des moyens particuliers que la Divine Bonté a mis à portée de votre charité, vous pourriez m'obtenir quelque lumière et quelque force . . . Pour moi je suis, je le crois, sous l'influence du démon. . . .'[51]

In a series of letters[52] written to Boullan in the year 1873 by the Jesuit Father Augustin Poulain (1836-1919) we find not only the extent to which Boullan's ideas coincided with the mystical pre-occupations of so many people of his time, but also a series of examples of the lengths to which belief in such doctrines could go. Many years later, in 1901, Poulain was to produce his work *Les Grâces d'Oraison*, which had a great success.[53] In 1873 Poulain, then 37, was already an enthusiast for the mystical life. A biographer was to speak of him in these terms: 'J'ai dit . . . ma conviction que le père Poulain fut attiré vers les études mystiques par quelques expériences personnelles. Il semble avoir été, dès sa jeunesse religieuse, un curieux de mystique, "un chercheur de plantes spirituelles rares", comme dit le père Malvy.'[54] Certainly the mystical plants he found *chez* Boullan were rare enough, and he seems to have accepted them fairly easily. Perhaps this early gullibility was reflected in his original version of *Les Grâces d'Oraison*, for Poulain's biographer admits that 'les études théologiques de l'auteur semblait avoir été insuffisantes, et la première rédaction portait des traces de cette insuffisance.'[54] When an eminent professor of theology demanded substantial changes before allowing publication Poulain at first refused. Then, however, an arbiter intervened, 'qui, en limitant les exigences du théologien à ce qui était purement doctrinal . . . les rendit plus acceptables a l'auteur, et, *en obtenant de celui-ci le sacrifice de quelques idées chères, l'insertion de quelques formules destinées à mettre en garde contre de fausses interprétations ou des applications malheureuses,* finit par amener un accord suffisant.'[55] It would be fascinating to see the original manuscript of *Les Grâces d'Oraison* to see to what extent it reflected the *naïveté* of these letters written so long before it. This very *naïveté*, particularly in the attitude to mysticism expressed in the letters, was typical of the popular approach to the subject at the time. The letters help us both to gauge some aspects of Boullan's doctrine and of its effect on those around him, and to learn something of the religious spirit of the time.

In them we learn that Poulain, as well as several people he knew at the Convent of the Visitation at Le Mans, had been very impressed by Boullan's ideas as set forth in the *Annales de la Sainteté*. Poulain was not the only one who was in personal correspondence with Boullan; we learn at one point that Poulain has been shown a letter written by Boullan to someone at the Visitation, of which the Mother Superior had crossed out several lines before showing it to him. Like so many people of this period, Poulain refers with scorn to those who do not understand 'la Mystique'.[56]

Poulain writes to Boullan as pupil to master, asking his advice and denigrating himself in face of the other's superior knowledge. The letters are concerned mainly with two things: (i) a curiosity with regard to substitution, and to other forms of the mystical life, about which Poulain is hoping to write a book, and (ii) the possibility of a substitution being effected in his own case, to cure him of the illnesses which are preventing him from writing this book. The letters are also full of remarks about other forms of mystical experience; Poulain relates a revelation afforded to a protégée of his, and discusses at some length the significance of the form of the stigmata of a certain mystic. But almost all the letters are concerned with the question of mystical substitution, from both the general and the personal viewpoint.

To start with the question of Poulain's own personal problem; in the first letter we have, that of 18 March 1873, Poulain speaks of

his illness and how impossible it is for him to work: 'Je tiens à peine
sur mes jambes et le moindre travail m'épuise.' At this time he feels
a reluctance to ask God for his own cure, even when on a pilgrimage to Lourdes, and he admits moreover that he has laid himself
open to an augmentation of his suffering by offering himself up for
the spiritual regeneration of various acquaintances. A letter from
Boullan, however, has persuaded him to take more notice of his
own health: 'Votre lettre me donne à réfléchir et me fait penser que
peut-être je ferais bien de sortir de cette indifférence sur ma santé.'

Boullan has suggested two means of cure, personal prayer and
the substitution for Poulain by another. At this stage Poulain is
very worried by this idea:

> Vous me dites qu'une sainte âme consentirait 'à m'aider'. Si
> j'examine bien le contexte, je crois deviner que ce ne serait pas
> seulement par ses prières, mais par une substitution. Si c'est cela,
> je n'aurai jamais le coeur d'y consentir. Je veux bien me sub-
> stituer aux autres, mais accepter l'inverse, serait-ce possible!
> Pauvre innocente, j'irais la faire souffrir pour un misérable
> comme moi, et pendant que je me prélasserais sans rien endurer!
> Non, il n'y a qu'un cas où je me montrerais plus accessible. Ce
> serait celui où cette personne n'aurait rien de plus à souffrir, de
> telle sorte que *ma guérison viendrait simplement de ce qu'elle change
> l'intention de ses souffrances et qu'elle les offre pour moi au lieu de le
> faire pour d'autres.*

Already in this last sentence we see traces of that automatic conception of substitution which we have been describing. This
conception comes out far more fully in a later letter, that of 11 May
1873, where Poulain, who has finally agreed to a substitution,
obviously thinks of this as being effected by an almost magical
'pouvoir transpositeur'. He himself has failed to effect the change,
he says; could Boullan, with his greater 'pouvoir transpositeur,'
possibly help him out? The passage deserves to be quoted in full:

> Vous vous souvenez que dans ma dernière lettre je vous ai
> parlé d'une personne qui un jour pourra peut-être se ranger
> près de vous. Depuis longtemps elle m'avait pressé de consentir
> à ce qu'elle se substituât à moi, et l'idée lui en était venue d'elle-
> même. Comme je vois que ma tête et mes yeux s'obstinent à ne
> pas s'améliorer, j'ai fini par dire oui. Avant de recourir à vous
> pour cette transposition, j'ai voulu essayer par mes seules prières
> et j'ai dit la messe à cette intention. Le résultat a été d'une

nullité magnifique, comme on pouvait s'y attendre. Si donc vous vouliez me prêter votre pouvoir pour ce cas-ci, vous me rendriez service.

In previous letters, not relating to his own individual case, Poulain had asked Boullan various questions of a highly technical nature about this 'pouvoir transpositeur'. In the letter of 18 March 1873, he asks two questions which again show the extraordinary belief in the automatic nature of this power:

Je veux vous demander deux renseignements au sujet de votre *pouvoir transpositeur*:

1°. Est-il plus facile de faire passer la maladie d'une personne a une autre, que de la déplacer d'organe chez un même sujet? Cela me semble être toujours de la substitution et de la transposition. . . .

2°. Dans une substitution à faire loin du principal opérateur, par exemple dans celle de la Visitation du Mans, quelle nécessité y a-t-il d'un délégué? Est-ce simplement pour glorifier les causes secondes, ou bien y a-t-il une sorte de nécessité qu'un opérateur soit présent par rapport aux personnes sur lesquelles l'action s'exerce?

And in a letter of 8 April 1873, Poulain asks some even more precise questions about the extent and limitations of the 'pouvoir transpositeur'. Can a nun, he asks, who wishes to substitute herself for another in order to alleviate her suffering, do so while still excluding from the transposition (i) interior suffering and (ii) illnesses which would prevent her from following the Rule of her Order, or which would make her a burden to others? The question seems to be this: 'Celui qui exerce le pouvoir transpositeur, peut-il renfermer à son gré la transposition dans les limites qu'il juge ainsi ne devoir pas être franchies prudemment? ou encore: le pouvoir transpositeur renferme-t-il le pouvoir de fixer des restrictions à la transposition, de lui créer, comme au fleuve, un lit qui ne l'arrête pas mais la dirige?'

In this treatment of the question of substitution we find again Boullan's idea of the ladder of perfection: the nun who is prepared to substitute for Poulain is, he believes, suitable to do so because she is 'dans un degré d'Oraison fort au-dessus du mien'.[57] She would like, however, to make one restriction on the substitution: that she should not receive it in the form of Poulain's bad eyes, because that would ruin her needlework!

Poulain follows Boullan in all those aspects of his doctrine which are exaggerations of the tendency to make of mysticism something both exceptional and concrete. The supernatural is to him ever-present: 'Peut-être que je m'abuse, mais il me semble que j'ai vu le surnaturel d'assez près pour croire sans effort à la possibilité de son action en moi.'[58] Yet in reducing the doctrine of vicarious suffering to a series of physical manifestations unfailingly carried out by the mumbo-jumbo of a human agent possessed of a superior 'pouvoir transpositeur' he is converting God's supernatural gift to man into a new form of natural phenomenon. All this is heretical enough; but we even see Poulain dabbling with Boullan's doctrine of substitution for the *sins* of others. He takes this most probably to mean the *temptations* of others, but even so this is far from orthodox Catholic doctrine: 'Pour le second degré de la réparation, j'ai une difficulté. Il consiste à supporter, pour un autre, *le poids* et *le lien* du péché. Mais je ne vois pas quel est le sens précis de ces mots figurés. Ce lien est-il la difficulté au bien, les tentations?'[59]

Poulain is sublimely unaware of the unorthodoxy of all these doctrines. He declares how much Boullan's advice is helping him in the writing of his work on the mystical life, and when questioned as to where the novelty of Boullan's treatment of mystical substitution lies, since this doctrine had always existed and 'tous les Saints ont compris qu'à l'imitation de Jésus-Christ il fallait racheter les autres par les prières et les pénitences,' replies to his questioner that 'l'idée avait surtout de nouveau l'importance qu'on lui donnait et la lumière dans laquelle on la met.'[60] He does not seem to have realised the dangerous paths he had been drawn to tread.

There is a curious atmosphere of faith healing about this whole business; a healing both of soul and body. A letter from Tardif de Moidrey[61] shows us how trusting towards Boullan people could be in these years before his condemnation, and in a letter written on 23 April 1873, we find a lady from Cherbourg, Mlle. B. de Masclary, who similarly feels herself to be attacked by the devil, writing to Boullan saying: 'Le Père Poulain que je connais depuis plusieurs années m'a parlé de vous et m'a dit que vous connaissez une sainte âme qui, par ses oeuvres satisfactoires, a le pouvoir d'apporter quelque soulagement à ceux qui sont malades *ou tentés*.'[62]

There was a great deal of charlatanry in Boullan's relations with these people and he even seems to have made a certain amount of money out of his 'powers'. In the letter just quoted Mlle. de Masclary promises to send him ten francs, and an odd little note among Boullan's papers contains the following message, addressed to Poulain's aunt: 'Mme. Poulain est chargée par son fils de dire à Monsieur Boullan de ne jamais faire allusion dans les lettres qu'il pourrait lui adresser *au Mans*, aux aumônes que le P. Poulain pourrait lui avoir faites, ou devait lui faire en échange des grâces de guérison demandées. Mille respects a Monsieur l'abbé Boullan.'[63]

The letters from Tardif de Moidrey and Mlle. de Masclary and above all the letters from Poulain have illustrated several important points in relation to Boullan's doctrine of vicarious suffering. (i) Many points of the doctrine reflect certain religious preoccupations of the time: the concentration on miracles, the belief in the positive powers of the devil, the belief in the efficacy of certain rites, the concentration on the physical side of mysticism and the reduction of it to a series of automatic responses to magical forms of invocation. (ii) Boullan's own 'open' doctrine, for these reasons, received fairly widespread belief and thus wielded great influence. (iii) The more grave aspects of the doctrine, including the transferability of sin and temptation as well as suffering, were accepted even by those whose theological training should have taught them otherwise. (iv) For these people mysticism consisted of the extraordinary and the external rather than the inner life.

Léon Bloy

In Léon Bloy's conception of man's whole existence being for the purpose of suffering, the idea of vicarious suffering holds a very important place. And while at certain stages unorthodox elements do enter into his version of the doctrine, these elements seem to have had no connection with the Boullanist heresy, but rather to have been induced by the mystical interpretation of history which Bloy had received from the teachings of Tardif de Moidrey.

In Bloy's youth his interpretation of the doctrine of vicarious suffering appears to have been orthodox in essence, though in the extremes to which he took it we see both the ardent, intransigent nature of Bloy's own belief and a reflection of the importance accorded to suffering by those of his generation. Bloy outdoes all in his devotion to suffering. In two letters, one to Georges Landry on

1 September 1871, and the other to Michel Ménard on 9 January 1877, his feelings on the subject are fully expressed.[64]

In the first of these letters he argues from a statement of Bonald's that Christ is the universal mediator between the Cause (God) and the effect (Man): as Christ is the man of sorrows, the *vir dolorum* spoken of by Isaiah, so we in our turn must become men of sorrow. 'Si notre *divinisation* spirituelle est le résultat infaillible du miracle compensateur de Dieu fait homme, la divinité du Rédempteur implique pour nous, comme conséquence invincible, l'inexorable nécessité d'être, à notre tour, des hommes et des *hommes de douleurs*.'

Suffering, Bloy claims, is our only link with the supernatural: 'il n'y a que cela de surnaturel ici-bas, la SOUFFRANCE,' everything else is human. In every Christian there exists a man of sorrows, 'et c'est celui-là qui est Dieu'. The other part of man is merely a contingent figure, a phantom of clay and blood which will eventually be dried out by the sun and dispersed by the wind. We are, says Bloy, the continuators of Christ, since we are his members, and our duty is to prolong his sacrifice on earth until it is entirely consummated. Suffering, he claims, is always supernatural if it is accepted, and always has supernatural results; every suffering is part of the Redemption and is instrumental in expiating something: 'La souffrance acceptée est toujours surnaturelle, et toujours elle a des suites surnaturelles. Toutes les fois que nous recommençons le Calvaire, nous recommençons la Rédemption; nos douleurs rachètent toujours quelqu'un ou quelque chose.' The repetition of 'toujours' in this phrase shows us the dangers which Bloy's conception of the doctrine is already reaching. True, he sees the necessity of the acceptance of suffering; but in his view of such suffering as always being efficacious in a specific way he is promoting one doctrine of the Church to a primacy over all others.

In the second letter, that written in 1877 to Ménard, the dangers appear even more clearly. True, he starts with a paean of praise to God for the respect he accords to man in leaving him free will:

Ce respect est à un tel point que jamais, depuis la loi de grâce, Il n'a parlé aux hommes avec une autorité absolue, mais au contraire, avec la timidité, la douceur et je dirai même l'obséquiosité d'un solliciteur indigent qu'aucun dégoût ne serait capable de rebuter. Par un décret très mystérieux et très inconcevable de sa volonté éternelle, Dieu semble s'être condamné jusqu'à la fin

des temps à n'exercer sur l'homme aucun droit immédiat de
maître à serviteur, ni de roi à sujet.

But soon the violence of which we have already seen hints in 1871
comes pouring out. Bloy is furious that people will not realise that
suffering is *necessary*. Those who claim that it is *useful*, he says, do
not know what they are talking about. Suffering is *necessary*, it is
the essence itself of moral life: 'Un coeur fier doit rechercher la
Douleur avec emportement, avec délire. Lorsqu'une épine le
blesse, il doit la presser avec toutes ses forces, pour ne rien perdre
de la volupté d'amour qu'elle peut lui donner en le déchirant plus
profondément.' Once again he stresses the mission of Christ as
the Man of Sorrows, and insists that by declaring us members of
Christ the Holy Spirit has clothed us with the dignity of redeemers:
'Lorsque nous refusons de souffrir, nous sommes exactement des
simoniaques et des prévaricateurs. *Nous sommes faits pour cela et
pour cela seul*. Lorsque nous versons notre sang, c'est sur le
Calvaire qu'il coule et de là sur toute la terre.'

These two letters show us that, at this stage of his life, Bloy's
view of suffering is only unorthodox through its violence and
through its exclusiveness. Suffering, Bloy tells us, is man's *only*
task in this world.

The violence of these views is reflected in the actions which Bloy
himself took in his own life with regard to vicarious suffering. We
know that his mother had offered up her health and happiness in
order that he himself should be converted; Bloy relates this matter
in a letter to Bourget written in 1877.[65] He himself, possibly moved
by the example of his mother but certainly also by his own violent
theories of suffering, offered himself up on several occasions for the
conversion of various of his friends. In a letter written to Lucile
Lalotte on 7 December 1873, he describes the extremes of suffering
to which he had been prepared to go for her brother. He had even
been prepared to offer up his mind and become an imbecile:

Ah! Je voudrais acheter sa conversion au prix du plus long et
du plus douloureux purgatoire. Avec quelle joie je souscrirais à
un tel marché! Chère âme de mon ami et cher ami de mon âme!
J'ai offert à notre cher Sauveur Crucifié, a notre douce Mère du
Sacré-Coeur, à tous les anges et à tous les Saints du Ciel le
pauvre sacrifice de mon bonheur, de mon repos, de ma santé, de
ma vie, j'ai même fait le sacrifice le plus cruel pour un vaniteux
comme moi, le sacrifice de ma pensée dont je suis si fier, j'ai

prié Dieu de faire de moi un imbécile, un objet de dégoût afin que mon bien-aimé frère Victor devînt en effet victorieux de lui-même et serviteur fidèle de N-S. J-C.[66]

It was in 1879, in the company of the abbé Tardif de Moidrey, that Bloy first visited La Salette. This place of pilgrimage, 'le Sinaï de la Pénitence, le Paradis de la Douleur,'[67] was to remain for ever afterwards the centre of his preoccupations. As Albert Béguin points out in his book *Léon Bloy, Mystique de la Douleur*, there are two great themes which run throughout the whole of Bloy's works. One is the expectation of the end of the world; the other a pre-occupation with the sufferings of the Second Person (Christ) and of the Virgin Mary. Both these themes centre on La Salette, and in both of Bloy's novels we have extensive sections dealing with this shrine, while, as well as devoting three books specifically to it—*Celle qui pleure* (1908), *Vie de Mélanie* (1912), and *Le Symbolisme de l'Apparition* (posthumous, 1925) he also makes reference to it in most of his other works.

Béguin goes on to say that all Bloy's works, whether specifically historical or not, are nevertheless the history of suffering and of expectation of the coming. And here we must realise that, by this stage of his life, suffering seems to Bloy not merely to be a supplement to the sufferings of Christ (as the doctrine of vicarious suffering would have us believe), but to be a historical symbol of the sufferings of Christ, and possibly to be *the sufferings of Christ themselves*. All history has bearing on the sufferings of Christ because all history *is* the sufferings of Christ.

Bloy had been brought to this state of mind partly because of his own personal interpretation of the exegetical theories of Tardif de Moidrey, with whom he had been in contact for a couple of years before 1879,[68] and partly because of the revelations given to him by Anne-Marie Roulé in 1880, many of which corroborated this interpretation. In Bloy's strange world everything has bearing on the Holy Trinity, and in turn, through the absence of time in this world which is a figuration of the Trinity, becomes the Trinity itself. In this plan everything that suffers is therefore a figure of Christ; this becomes more than mere symbolism and those who have, with the best will in the world, tried to explain it away as such, are mistaken in their attempt.

In a magnificent passage in *Le Salut par les Juifs* (1892) Bloy describes how the Middle Ages had understood this truth of which the modern world was ignorant: 'A force d'aimer, le Moyen Age avait compris que Jésus est toujours crucifié, toujours saignant, toujours expirant, bafoué par la populace et maudit par Dieu lui-même.'[69] The mediaeval 'compatients' are seen to have taken on the sufferings of Christ himself, and to partake of them: '—Vous êtes douloureuse et lacrymable, Notre Dame Vierge Marie, disaient-ils; à qui Vous comparer ou vous égaler? Votre contrition est comme la mer. Faites-moi pleurer avec Vous, *faites-moi porter la mort du Christ*, faites-moi le convive de sa Passion et le miroir de ses Plaies.'[70] This sharing of Christ's suffering, however, is at the same time an identification with Christ, whose suffering continues in everything that suffers:

Le fétide Judas baisait toujours son Maître au Jardin et le déplorable *fils de la Colombe*, Simon-Pierre, ne s'arrêtait plus de le renier. . . . Et cette Croix de démence, le clouement et le déclouement du Christ, ses langueurs inexprimables et les Sept Paroles qu'il prononça, la Station de la Mère et cette Mort d'entre les morts qui épouvanta le soleil pendant trois heures; tous les détails enfin de cette ribote scandaleuse de tortures dont le seul pressentiment consume les extatiques, étaient impitoyablement distincts et discernables, fixés à jamais dans le temps et dans l'espace. . . . Rien ne finissait parce que rien ne pouvait finir et que les choses finissantes renaissaient aussitôt partout. On saignait avec Jésus, on était criblé de ses plaies, on agonisait de sa soif. . . .'[71]

One must beware of ever trying to make too much of a system of Bloy's thought. He was an untidy thinker, in whose ideas on any subject one can always find plenty of contradictions. Because he believed everything to have a bearing on the Trinity, he was led into numerous equations in which those who suffer *are* Christ. Often, to a logical mind, these equations may contradict each other; for example, money is both the blood of the poor (i.e. the blood of Christ) and the Living Word of God (because, in the Bible, Bloy's exegetical studies have made it so). The Jews are at the same time the persecutors of Christ and a figure of the Trinity (because of their suffering). The very abjectness of the Jews is, to Bloy, a divine Sign of the 'permanence de l'Esprit-Saint sur ces hommes si méprisés qui doivent apparaître dans la Gloire du Consolateur, à la fin des fins.'[72]

The Jews, at times, seem to Bloy to be the expiatory sufferers *par excellence.* They are the most abject and vile of people, in his opinion; and abjectness and vileness are the necessary attributes of holy suffering. He declares his intention in writing *Le Salut par les Juifs* to be:

> Dire mon mépris pour les horribles trafiquants d'argent, pour les youtres sordides et vénéneux dont l'univers est empoisonné, mais dire, en même temps, ma vénération profonde pour la *Race* d'où la Rédemption est sortie (Salus ex Judaeis), *qui porte visiblement, comme Jésus lui-même, les péchés du Monde,* qui a raison d'attendre SON Messie, et qui ne fut conservée dans la plus parfaite ignominie que parce qu'elle est la race d'Israël, c'est-à-dire du Saint-Esprit, dont l'exode sera le prodige de l'Abjection.[73]

Beside all these adventures into a mystical world, however, Bloy occasionally gives us definitions of vicarious suffering which are perfectly orthodox. It is true that, in *Le Désespéré*, while he is explaining the mission of the Carthusian monks, which is to watch, to pray and to participate in the sufferings of Christ, we still get the impression of the whole of history being in fact the Passion of our Lord;[74] but in the same section of the book Bloy describes the mission of the *Grande Chartreuse* as being to pay 'pour tout un peuple insolvable que pressait l'aiguillon du châtiment, en accomplissement de *cette loi transcendante de l'équilibre surnaturel, qui condamne les innocents à acquitter la rançon des coupables.*'[75]

Nothing could be further, he says, from our feeble notions of equity and justice than this; and we find this theme repeated time and again in the writers of the Revival: God's justice is not to be judged by earthly standards. One day, Bloy continues, at the end of the world, we will know why so many innocent people have been made to suffer: 'Nous verrons avec quelle exactitude infiniment calculée furent réparties, en leur temps, les prospérités et les douleurs, et quelle miraculeuse équité nécessitait passagèrement les apparences de l'injustice!' We shall find this idea of the incompatibility of the human and the divine conceptions of justice recurring particularly strongly in Claudel.

In one particular Bloy forestalls Péguy; this is in his horror at the idea of an eternal hell. In *Le Désespéré* he voices this horror. He is a 'fils obéissant de l'Eglise,'[76] he says, and must therefore believe this dogma. But he declares nevertheless his solidarity with the damned. He has read all the reasonable explanations which have been given for 'la réprobation temporelle des trois quarts de l'humanité,' but still he cannot accept it fully. Bloy then proceeds to paint a picture, as does Mme. Gervaise in Péguy's *Mystère de la Charité de Jeanne d'Arc*, of Christ crying out the *Lama sabacthani* on the Cross because of his realisation of this 'rédemption inaccomplie'.

In Bloy we have found, at the basis of his religious thought, an originally orthodox conception of the doctrine of vicarious suffering which, because of his violence and exaggeration, becomes the central part of his religious belief. After the mystical crisis of the years 1878–82 this becomes bound up within that mystical pattern (or series of incomplete, mutually contradictory patterns) which was the result of Bloy's development of Tardif de Moidrey's theories.

Huysmans

In the religious writings of Huysmans the theme of vicarious suffering has a dominant place.[77] In most of his religious novels it is stressed above all other doctrines, and in *Sainte Lydwine de Schiedam* (1901) it is the cornerstone of the whole work, which is a paean of praise for suffering, the example being a medieval 'compatiente', the Blessed Lydwine (not strictly speaking a Saint, despite Huysmans's title), who devoted her life to suffering for the world around her. If, in these post-conversion writings of Huysmans, occasional elements of Boullan's doctrine are to be found, this is hardly surprising, for Boullan was almost certainly the greatest influence upon Huysmans's conversion, and it was through Boullan that Huysmans's great interest in the doctrine of vicarious suffering had been aroused.

Though, on the whole, Huysmans's treatment of this doctrine is remarkably orthodox as compared with the extremely odd views which we have seen expressed in the Poulain letters, nevertheless there are occasions when the Boullanist influence breaks through. When the abbé Gévresin first sets forth the doctrine to Durtal in *En Route* (1895), for example (and we must remember that Gévresin is in part based upon the abbé Boullan), after a perfectly orthodox opening statement in which expiatory victims are seen as suffering for the *sins* of others, he goes on to say that there is an even more arduous task, that not merely of praying or suffering for the sins of others, but of preventing or hindering them by *taking on the temptations* of others who may be too weak to withstand them. Huysmans obviously expects us to take this as the true doctrine of the Church; he almost certainly does not realise its unorthodoxy. Similarly, in *Sainte Lydwine de Schiedam*, a Boullanist influence may possibly be responsible for the extraordinary episode (based on an original source but not for that reason to be accepted as valid) in which Lydwine confesses the sins of another to a priest, and does his penance for him.

But the distinguishing characteristic of Huysmans's attitude towards vicarious suffering is the savage delight with which he seems to depict the physical sufferings involved. Even in his pre-conversion writings Huysmans had stressed ugliness and suffering, and no doubt a certain sado-masochistic element remained in the years after his conversion. This in no way invalidates the conscious intentions behind these writings, however; Huysmans was attempting to depict Catholicism as the harsh religion which he believed it to be, and to shock out of their somnolence those tepid Christians whom he saw around him. He wished to perturb those 'nombreux catholiques qui, par tiédeur de foi, par respect humain, par ignorance, relèguent de leur mieux la mystique dans les asiles d'aliénés et les miracles dans le rancart des superstitions et des légendes,'[78] and he would do so not only by his praise of the supernatural but also by his harsh depiction of suffering.

Sainte Lydwine de Schiedam is, of course, the high point of such depiction. Lydwine's sufferings are depicted in every disgusting detail and the reader is left at times with a feeling of nausea. We must not forget, however, that Huysmans had, though in lesser measure, dwelt upon this physical aspect of suffering and even self-inflicted torture in previous religious works, and that as early as 1898 Adolphe Retté, in his *XIII Idylles Diaboliques*, when wishing to satirise Huysmans, had taken as one of his points of attack this very aspect of his work. It is a cruel parody, and it was later belied by Retté's own attitude towards suffering.[79] But it does point out to us Huysmans's obsession with the most sordid details of physical suffering and, by using a great many of the author's own phrases, gains a certain amount of validity. Huysmans always seems to concentrate far more on physical than on mental suffering, and his treatment of the former is often morbid in the extreme. In *Sainte Lydwine de Schiedam* and *Les Foules de Lourdes* we find the most harrowing scenes of sickness and physical decay.

This obsession with illness as the main form of suffering is to be seen nowhere more clearly than in a strange fantasy Huysmans harboured with regard to the life of Christ. Expressing this in a letter to Dom Thomasson de Gournay, he says:

Je me suis souvent demandé, en voyant les épouvantables et les longues souffrances d'horribles maladies, s'il [Christ] n'avait pas voulu, pendant son passage sur la terre, les ressentir; car enfin, si terrible que fût le supplice de la croix, aggravé par d'ignobles préludes, si douloureux que pût être le poids des péchés qu'Il assumait — combien de martyrs furent, corporellement du moins — plus torturés. . . .

Il devait vouloir boire le calice des infirmités humaines jusqu'à la lie, ne pas vouloir qu'une souffrance terrestre lui demeurât étrangère, pour mieux rédimer. Dès lors, ne peut-on croire qu'il a enduré tous nos maux — pendant les 30 ans de sa vie cachée — car après, les maladies eussent mis un obstacle à sa mission.[80]

Immediately after stating this, however, Huysmans is stopped short by a thought which can be seen to stem from Boullan's teaching. Surely illness is a consequence of sin, he says, and Christ cannot have sinned. He is left in confusion: 'Je sais bien que, d'autre part, la maladie est une conséquence du péché — et que Lui n'avait pris que l'aspect peccamineux de notre ressemblance, que par conséquent il n'avait pas de raison d'assumer nos maladies —sinon comme nos fautes—en apparence.—Ah! ce n'est pas clair!'[80]

From this we can see that the whole Boullanist conception of the transference of *sin* from one to another is still part of Huysmans's belief. Illness is so bound up with sin that a pure soul, suffering to expiate the sins of another, *must* take on those sins and not merely the suffering. Even Christ, in this interpretation, must himself *take on* sin, and not merely expiate it, if he takes on illness. (In this pattern the sufferings on the Cross appear to be considered as being purely sufferings for the sins of others, and not a taking-on of the sins themselves—Ah! ce n'est pas clair!)

Like many other Catholics of his time, Huysmans had been enormously impressed by the sufferings of such recent 'compatientes' as Anna Katharina Emmerick (1774–1824), Louise Lateau (d. 1883) and Marie du Bourg (d. 1862). It was Anna Katharina Emmerick above all who struck them. Not only were her visions recorded in the fullest manner by the pen of Clemens

Brentano, but also, in her life of freely-accepted illness and suffering, men of the nineteenth and twentieth centuries have seen the modern reflection of those medieval 'compatientes' whose sufferings were offered to redeem the world. For Huysmans as for Massignon she had a special place in the mystery of redemption; and Huysmans, who saw in her 'la plus grande voyante des temps modernes, [celle des] réparatrices qui, avec Marie Bagnési, se rapproche le plus de Lydwine . . . l'héritière (de Lydwine) à travers des âges,' would rejoice in the cult still devoted to her by many religious bodies, including the *Amis d'Éphèse et d'Anne Catherine Emmerick*, and in the efforts that have been made for her canonisation. In Claudel, Baumann and many other writers of this period we find a consuming interest in this stigmatised Augustinian nun whose influence continues so strongly into the present day.

Huysmans might well have chosen Anna Katharina Emmerick as his model for hagiography if she had not lived so close to his own time. Instead, he chose Lydwine, the most perfect example of those medieval sufferers of whom Anna Katharina was a successor. Yet the message preached by this book is by no means a distant one. Above all, Huysmans feels, it has relevance to his own day, which he sees as being in great need of such vicarious suffering. In the passive sufferings of the 'compatientes', and in the prayers and sufferings of the monks and nuns, hidden in their cloisters, he sees the only counterblast to 'les abominations démoniaques de notre époque,'[81] of which, towards the end of the book, he paints a succinct but damning picture.

Huysmans's tendency to see the devil and his works in every event, even the most trivial, is possibly yet another trace of the strong influence which Boullan had once wielded over him. He believed that positive attacks were being made upon him at various times, such as just after his conversion, for example, when, dreaming violently sexual dreams, he believed himself to have been attacked by a diabolic succubus. For him the devil was an ever-present danger, and in a letter written to Leclaire in 1904 we see Huysmans linking what he believed to be the incredibly satanic epoch in which he was living to the fact that the monasteries, either through their unworthiness (which he discusses in many other places) or through their forced departure from France, were no longer capable of efficiently performing that work of substitution which was to keep the devil in check: 'La vie coule plus que médiocre, atterrée cependant par des assauts diaboliques extra-ordinaires, dès que la nuit vient. Et l'étrange, c'est qu'un tas de pratiquants sont dans le même cas. Il est évident que les cloîtres ne faisant plus leur métier, il répartit les épreuves sur les laïques; je ne crois pas qu'à aucune époque, le démon ait été ainsi déchaîné . . .'[82]

Apart from the Boullanist tendencies we have noted, and a certain amount of credulity with regard to all the miracles ascribed to Lydwine, Huysmans holds a fairly orthodox view of vicarious suffering:

(i) He stresses the most important form of it as being a suffering for the world in which one lives, rather than for individuals. Forty pages of the beginning of *Sainte Lydwine de Schiedam* are devoted to a picture of the atrocious state of Europe in Lydwine's time, and then we are told that 'cette existence d'expiation, elle serait in-compréhensible si l'on n'en avait tout d'abord indiqué les causes et montré le nombre et la nature des offenses dont la réparation fut, en quelque sorte, ici-bas, sa raison d'être.'[83] True, Huysmans follows his sources in every minor legend about Lydwine, regard-less of the value of the sources, and amid this swarm of miracles (which must make her, if they were true, the most authenticated Saint in Christendom) there are many cases of substitution for individuals: 'Ils [the sources] nous apprennent qu'elle ne se contenta même pas de se substituer, pour en subir le châtiment, aux crimes de l'univers et à ceux de sa propre ville; elle consentit encore à prendre à son compte les péchés des gens qu'elle connais-sait, et les maladies corporelles, qu'ils ne pouvaient supporter. . . . Elle fut, en un mot, une victime générale et spéciale.'[84] Neverthe-less, the book makes it clear to us that her main role was that of a sacrifice for the sins of the whole world.

(ii) He stresses in *Sainte Lydwine de Schiedam* the liberty of the sufferer to accept or reject her mission. Lydwine is chosen by God, but her acceptance of this suffering is necessary if it is to be in any way valid. At first she did not understand the purpose of this suffering and for four years she remained in a state of bitterness at her fate. But after a priest had explained to her at length the doctrine of mystical substitution, 'les yeux de Lydwine se dessil-laient; elle commençait à comprendre les causes de ses incroyables maladies et elle se soumettait, elle agréait d'avance cette mission que le Rédempteur l'appelait à remplir.'[85]

Occasionally, in letters and other works, Huysmans appears to forget this basic necessity for free will in the sacrifice, but the fact remains that in this work it is stressed time and again: 'Elle se fut, *de son plein gré*, offerte pour être la brebis émissaire des péchés du monde.'[86] 'Pour que cette régle [that of the balance of good and evil] s'observe, il faut, en effect, que Jésus fasse appel au concours de l'homme et que celui-ci *ne se refuse pas à le prêter*.'[87]

(iii) He sees the whole question as being intimately bound up with the communion of saints; and at the head of this communion, the Saints of the Church are equally bound in a common purpose. After the description of Europe at the beginning of *Sainte Lydwine de Schiedam* Huysmans says: 'Et ce fut alors que l'Église était sapée par les hérésies, écartelée par de dangereux papes, alors que la chrétienté semblait perdue, que Dieu suscita des Saintes pour enrayer la marche en avant du Malin et sauver le Saint-Siège.'[88] Lydwine is seen as being one of an army, all working towards the same end. Some of this army are known, some unknown. But spiritually they stretch out their hands to each other across time and space.

(iv) The theory of a necessary balance between evil and expiatory suffering is put forward to us time and again in Huysmans's public and private writings. He states the basic problem of the conflict between this conception of a balance and the conception of free will in *Sainte Lydwine de Schiedam*: 'Cette loi d'un équilibre à garder entre le Bien et le Mal, elle est singulièrement mystérieuse, quand on y songe; car, en l'établissant, le Tout-Puissant paraît avoir voulu fixer lui-même des bornes et mettre des freins à sa Toute-Puissance.'[89] In order for this balance to be effective God must call on man to help him and man must not refuse. God is infinitely respectful of man's liberty, yet God is never deceived by man, because, says Huysmans, he has always, down the ages, found Saints who will consent to pay the ransom for sin. The Saints are thus seen as exercising free will but as being by their very nature (which is why God chooses them) the kind of people who will take the right path. There is more need of such people at certain times than at others, because at these times the weight of sin on the one side of the scales is at its greatest. The age of Lydwine was such a time: 'Jamais, en effet, l'équilibre du monde ne fut plus près de se rompre.'[90] Huysmans's own epoch was, in his eyes, just such another. And to make matters worse, Huysmans sees the work of the monasteries and the saints as being insufficient in his own time to stem the tide of sin. Further sacrifices are needed. Unlike Bloy, who saw in the catastrophe of the fire of the Bazar de la Charité a punishment upon the rich and upon those with a false sense of charity,[91] Huysmans saw in it a sacrifice of pure souls for the sake of sinning humanity:

Ce jour-là, ce sont, en effet, les femmes vraiment pieuses, les femmes venues non pour arborer les toilettes et s'exhiber, mais pour aider à soulager des infortunes et à faire du bien, des femmes qui avaient toutes ou presque toutes entendu la messe, ce matin-là, et communié, qui ont été brûlées vives. Les autres s'en sont tirées. Il semble donc qu'il y ait eu une volonté du Ciel de choisir, dans cette mêlée, les meilleures, les plus saintes des visiteuses, pour les obliger à expier, dans les flammes, la plénitude sans regrets de nos péchés.[92]

Nobody, even while admitting the faults of Huysmans's conception of vicarious suffering, can deny the sincerity with which he held his views. And when he found that he himself was suffering from cancer of the mouth, he saw this as part of the Divine Will, that he should help to expiate the sins of what he saw as one of the most appalling epochs in the world's history. His acceptance of this duty led him to deny himself the use of morphine even in his worst agonies. 'Je suis peut-être le total d'une addition. Qui sait, si je n'expie pas pour d'autres.'[93] For some time before this he had seen his mission ('A l'heure actuelle, on ne peut trop se plaindre car l'on sent bien qu'il faut réparer pour soi et pour les autres')[94] but he had been uncertain of his suitability as a suffering agent:

Au fond, on n'a pas écrit sur la douleur, comme je l'ai fait, sans écopper. *Ste-Lydwine, Lourdes,* je les paie. — Sapristi! je ne me sentais pourtant pas une vocation pour cette voie de Douleurs dans laquelle on me mène. Je doute que j'y prenne jamais goût, ce qui prouve que je n'ai l'étoffe d'un Saint! Je voudrais bien que le Ciel en fût si persuadé qu'il me lâche là-dessus.[95]

In a letter written eleven days later to Myriam Harry, while repeating in much the same words most of this statement, he nevertheless replaced the words 'Je doute que j'y prenne jamais goût' with 'Mais très certainement, à la longue, je m'y ferai. . . .',[96] and a month later he was saying, 'Évidemment rien ne me sera épargné. C'est une voie à accepter.'[97] Huysmans's progress had followed that which he had ascribed to Lydwine; he had been brought to that final acceptance which would make his sufferings valid in maintaining the equilibrium of the world. From now on until his death three months later on 12 May 1907 we see Huysmans serenely accepting the most hideous of sufferings, until, near the end, he said: 'J'ai confiance. La Vierge va venir me prendre. Je ne désire pas guérir.'[98]

Huysmans is often thought of as being one of the most violent people of the Revival. Yet, as in the question of a monastic vocation (where we shall see him being far more humanly reasonable than, for example, Claudel), he is in the matter of vicarious suffering far more aware of man's limitations and God's mercy than is Bloy. Bloy saw suffering as the lot and the duty of every Christian; Huysmans saw it as the vocation of exceptional souls, who by their sanctity might set the world to rights. In *Sainte Lydwine de Schiedam* he states quite clearly that God does not inflict extreme suffering upon those who will be unable to stand it:

Il ne cherche pas parmi ceux qu'il n'a point nanti d'âmes bien robustes les poids destinés à rétablir l'équilibre de la balance dont le plateau des fautes descend si bas. . . . De même que personne n'est tenté au-dessus de ses forces, de même personne n'est chargé de douleurs qu'il ne puisse, d'une façon ou d'une autre, tolérer. Il les dose aux moyens de résistance de chacun.[99]

His letters written at the beginning of his own illness show his belief that he was in one of these lesser classes. Both this and his gradual realisation that he was not show a different conception of heroism from Bloy's wild violence. He stresses the harshness of God towards those he loves most but he does not claim that we are all called to this form of heroism. It is reserved for the saints.

In his stressing of vicarious suffering above all other doctrines Huysmans is, of course, guilty of that tendency to false emphasis typical of this age of neophytes; but there is no denying that, as well as stressing the harsher aspects of Christianity by his concentration on the details of, and the necessity for, the most extreme forms of suffering, and referring with scorn to those average Catholics who will be shocked by this, he also saw *Sainte Lydwine de Schiedam* as a work of consolation for those exceptional beings who have been chosen by God for the most extreme sufferings and may not yet have realised the magnificent work to which they have been called:

Ceux-là sont, pour la plupart, des victimes de choix; mais

combien, parmi eux, savent qu'ils réalisent l'oeuvre admirable de la réparation et pour eux-mêmes et pour les autres? cependant, pour que cette oeuvre soit véritablement satisfactoire, il sied de l'accepter avec résignation et de la présenter humblement au Seigneur.... La vérité est que Jésus commence par faire souffrir et qu'il s'explique apres. L'important est donc de se soumettre d'abord, quitte à réclamer ensuite.[100]

Sainte Lydwine de Schiedam has made as many converts as *En Route*, and in it the suffering have found consolation beyond measure. It is unfortunate that this work, the central statement of Huysmans's beliefs, should be inferior aesthetically to so many of his other books, mainly because of its overriding preoccupation with the message it is preaching and because he felt it necessary to include every fact from every source on the life of Lydwine, thus creating something of an inchoate mass instead of a clear spiritual biography.

Vicarious Suffering in some other Novelists

By the turn of the century the theme of vicarious suffering had invaded the literature of the Revival with a vengeance. Wherever one looks in the Catholic novels of the period one finds it recurring, usually as a minor detail of the action, but at times as the backbone of the plot. In Adolphe Retté's novel *Le Règne de la Bête* (1908), for example, it appears as a minor detail of the plot but nevertheless is shown as being accepted as an unquestioned part of Christian doctrine.

Charles Mandrillat, a young anarchist, is prayed for by his former colleague Chériat, now converted. Chériat is on the point of death and wishes to prevent an anarchist outrage: 'Mon Dieu, prenez-moi en rançon pour l'âme de cet infortuné; ne permettez pas que cette chose affreuse s'accomplisse.' And, sure enough, the deed is not permitted. Charles, instead of blowing up Notre-Dame, is blown up himself: 'Ainsi, *par un évident miracle de la Justice divine* le meurtre s'était retourné contre celui qui appelait le meurtre sur autrui.'[101]

We are left, however, in something of a quandary as to the meaning of the event. True, Charles has been prevented from committing the murder, and lives have been saved; but at the moment of Charles's death he was actually entering the cathedral with the intention of committing the act. Was Chériat's sacrifice aimed at stopping the event or at saving Charles's soul? These two things are shown as not being exactly the same. Admittedly, when he had been wavering a few minutes before, a supernatural force did indeed seem to have been trying to turn his will to good: 'A ce moment, une étrange faiblesse fit retomber, désarmé, le bras de l'homicide. Il y eut comme un mur d'airain qui se dressait entre lui et l'autel. Il recula, balbutiant: Je ne peux pas! . . . Je ne peux pas! . . . Ces pauvres femmes, cet enfant, ce vieillard en prière. Oh!, non, c'est trop horrible. Je ne peux pas!' But after this sense of shame has driven Charles out of the cathedral he hardens his heart once more, and it is on his return into the building that he is killed, in a state of mortal sin, while attempting a murder.

All one can say of this is that here, as in so many other matters, Retté is the perfect example of certain tendencies and dangers in the literature of the Revival. Many authors used the doctrine of vicarious suffering liberally; few with much clarity. People are perpetually offering themselves in the novels of the period, but the reader is often not completely certain as to what form the offering takes, nor as to what result it achieves or is even aiming at. Much of the substitution is on a personal level, for a specific person or a specific result, but there is also as a perpetual background the need to suffer for France because of the appalling state to which it has been reduced. For example, at the end of *Le Règne de la Bête*, the story of which is meant as one example of the general decadence of France, one of the characters makes the following promise to God: 'O mon Dieu, si pour sauver notre France qui se détourne de ta Face, il est besoin de victimes expiatoires, nous voici prêts à souffrir pour que ton Nom soit sanctifié, pour que ton règne arrive.'[102]

Similarly, in a novel published on the eve of the war in 1914, André Lafon presents us with the concept of the redemption of society by a community of expiation. In this novel, *La Maison sur la Rive*, much of this message is hidden beneath what seems to be the rather over-sentimental treatment of the story. Yet the young girl who confides to her diary that she has decided to give up her love and marry a man she does not love is doing so for the sake of her community. Her love may appear to have been adolescent and ephemeral, but her sacrifice is given meaning both by her exclamation, at the opening of the novel, that she would offer herself up willingly to anything Heaven might ask in order to save her town and her religion, and also by the figure in the background of a holy sufferer, Mathilde Cazade, whose sufferings are seen as expiating the sins of her age.

When Mathilde is dying, the young girl is appalled by the way in which the strength of the people is being withdrawn from them. Her mother replies, however, that Mathilde will help them from on high, but that it is also necessary for them to make a greater effort: 'Dieu nous voit . . . c'est à nous, si elle nous quitte, à prier un peu plus et s'il le faut à souffrir aprés elle, puisque rien ne saurait se fonder d'un peu haut et de durable que dans le sacrifice de nous-mêmes, ici-bas.'[103]

At the end of the novel we are left with a picture of the combined effort of the Saints, as the heroine calls on them all as her allies in her struggle to maintain the town against the forces of evil:

> Peut-être aussi ai-je à prier sur cette ville menacée d'où le seul effort de quelques âmes repousse encore un ténébreux ennemi; à la garder, à la défendre en union avec les saintes qui veillent sur elle: saintes encore souffrantes de la terre; nos soeurs de l'hôpital, Mathilde Cazade, Mademoiselle Franchereau, ma mère; les saintes triomphantes d'en haut que j'appelle a notre aide. . . .[104]

And so she goes on, enumerating all the saints for whose special help she prays. In this novel the question of vicarious suffering is central, but the treatment of it is sentimental. It recalls to some extent François Coppée's graceful treatment of suffering and it reminds us at every turn of Lafon's predilection for the writings of Eugénie de Guérin.

Vicarious suffering, whether used as the main theme of a book or as a minor aspect of it, suffers from two main faults in the writings of the minor post-Huysmans novelists. Either it is over-sentimentally treated, as in Lafon or in Bordeaux's *La Maison Morte*, or else it is inserted into novels with little real understanding and as a necessary appendage of that harsh doctrine which the Revival writers saw the Christian religion as being, as in Retté. The minor Catholic writing of this age is no better than in any other age; it does nothing but exaggerate the faults inherent in the better writing of the time, or in that of a previous era. At times, however, it does show us more clearly the tendencies both of the thought and of the better writing of the age. The vast popularity of the theme of vicarious suffering in the post-Huysmans era not only reflects the popularity of the theme for major writers, such as Bloy, Péguy, Claudel and even Bourget; it also reflects the preoccupation of the Catholic public at large with this problem.

Émile Baumann

Among the post-Huysmans novelists, however, there is one who, though he is little known nowadays, was at the time regarded as one of the greatest Catholic novelists of France; and in the works of this man, Émile Baumann, the doctrine of vicarious suffering takes a predominant place. To most of us his treatment of the doctrine will appear to be extreme, his creation of a plot incompetent, and his style undistinguished. But it is his very weakness as an author, on the one hand, and his public acclaim on the other, which help explain to us better than anything could the extent to which his *ideas* were popular with the Catholic literary public of his day.

Though he was born in 1868, Baumann did not produce his first novel, *L'Immolé*, until 1908; it was written in the years 1904–6. He was a fervent admirer of Léon Bloy, from whom he had learned of the cult of La Salette and derived an admiration of the writings of Barbey d'Aurevilly. Yet some elements of his treatment of vicarious suffering seem to stem from Huysmans, an author for whom he more often expressed dislike than admiration. This reluctance to accept Huysmans was typical of many Catholics in this pre-1914–18 war era, who saw in him the dilettante of his pre-conversion years, the 'aesthetic Catholic', and a man who had come to Catholicism by the most unusual and shady of paths. Some of the falsity of this picture we have already seen,[105] but nevertheless it was a very common misconception of the time.

No doubt Baumann was sincere when he said in his book *Les Douze Collines* (1929), '*L'Immolé* vint après les livres de Huysmans, *qui n'eut sur moi aucune action*, et ceux de Léon Bloy qui en eurent davantage (je n'avais lu de lui que *La Femme Pauvre*).' No doubt he was equally sincere when in his *Mémoires* (1943) he described the title of *Les Foules de Lourdes* as being antipathetic to him. But in his concentration on the physical aspect of the suffering of his hero's mother he is certainly in the line of Huysmans. The impulse need not have come from Huysmans himself; there is certainly enough in Barbey d'Aurevilly's *Un Prêtre Marié* to affect this later author; but the fact remains that, consciously or unconsciously, Baumann in this aspect of his work is very close to certain tendencies of Huysmans.

Throughout Baumann's long series of novels the theme of vicarious suffering recurs time and time again, and it is interesting to note in this connection that even in his work of hagiology, *L'Anneau d'Or des Grands Mystiques*, he has an obvious predilection for Saints who pursue this line of action, and particularly for Anna Katharina Emmerick.

In the three novels written before the 1914–18 war we shall see Baumann's literary characteristics very clearly set forth. The novels are *L'Immolé* (1908) *La Fosse aux Lions* (1911) and *Le Baptême de Pauline Ardel* (1914).

L'Immolé is about a young man, Daniel Rovère, who offers up his whole life as a sacrifice. His father, an employee in a Lyon bank, commits suicide, and Daniel, after recovering his body from the Rhône, is horrified to realise that his father may be in eternal hell. However, a priest, while confirming the doctrine of eternal hell, nevertheless holds out the consolation that at the last minute he may have repented and may now be in Purgatory. In the chapel for the souls in Purgatory Daniel offers himself to God: 'O Jésus, que je sois un expiateur, un immolé, et que rien de mon expiation ne se perde hors de vous, mais que chaque parcelle de ma vie soit un parcelle de votre vie, de votre Rédemption!'[106] The novel is the history of this immolation, *via* humiliations and sufferings, until, near the end, Daniel is defending a church against a band of anti-clerical workers and is pinioned to the door by a knife which has been thrown at him: 'Il restait évanoui, la tête pendante, son bras crucifié, semblable au *Christ* de Murillo.'[107] He is saved but is nevertheless extremely ill from the experience, and will remain so throughout his life; he knows, however, that there is a purpose behind all this: 'Il trouvait un réconfort à savoir que, pendant des années peut-être, son impotence, son inutilité de malade seraient une offrande satisfactoire pour des égarements et des blasphèmes inexpiés.'[108]

Throughout the novel, behind the main theme of Daniel's immolation, there is also that of his mother, dying of a phthisical hip. Baumann describes her sufferings in detail, even to the smell, and makes her declare herself to be suffering for the sins of the family, not only those of Daniel's father who had embezzled money for the young girl with whom he was having an affair, but also those of the previous generations, all of whom were evil in some way. Speaking to her son, she says:

Quand on est d'un sang comme le nôtre, il faut choisir: être un damné ou être un saint. Si ma soeur Germaine est entrée au cloître, chez les Bernardines, c'est qu'elle avait vu à la maison des choses terribles. ... Elle expie dans la joie; moi, j'expie dans la désolation; et quand même nous aurions la force de tout prendre, elle et moi, il t'en restera toujours un part. ... Ne t'en plains pas, il n'y a rien de meilleur que la volonté de souffrir en Dieu.[109]

To add to the agony, Baumann shows Mme. Rovère seeking for healing through a miracle. At the first attempt she is disappointed; at the second, after application of water brought specially from Lourdes, she is cured. But horror! a short while after this she again goes down with the same complaint. These agonising ups and downs, so long-drawn-out, are there merely to show us the great heroism of Mme. Rovère. She declares that she will go to the grotto of Lourdes to thank the Virgin for giving her back her suffering, a greater gift than the original cure: 'Tu pensais, mon enfant, qu'il vaut mieux agir que souffrir. Eh bien! non, vois-tu? Pour moi, il n'y a rien de meilleur que de m'immoler. Je porte en moi les douleurs et les péchés de trop d'âmes, je souffrirai bien peu pour les expier.'[110]

The theme of vicarious suffering thus fills the book; though one sometimes wonders, in the case of the hero, whether he is suffering for the sake of his father, for the sins of his family, or for the world as a whole. Certainly by the end of the book he appears to be a far more universal figure of suffering than before. At the very end we have a puzzling Aurevillian touch; Daniel is seen as an outcast, living outside the light yet awaiting its coming. Speaking to a girl whom, because of his mission, he cannot marry, he says: 'Les êtres tel que moi n'apparaissent qu'à la fin ou à l'approche des cataclysmes; j'aurais dû naître au temps des chevaliers errants; une espèce de nuit marche avec mon ombre, une nuit qui est l'attente de la Lumière; mais vous, Brigitte, vous êtes dans la Lumière; Dieu est en vous bien plus qu'en moi.'[111] This is far from the concept of the vicarious sufferer as the chosen of God; it harks back to the Romantic concept of the outcast. And in much of the rest of the novel we find traits worthy of Barbey d'Aurevilly, such as the family fate hanging over the characters, the sensuality of Daniel, his added delight in the act of love and in the loved one because of the sin he knows himself to be committing (and the risk to his eternal life), and his sudden, awful realisation that he has been sleeping with his father's mistress, the girl who had caused his father's death. Throughout the book, even after Daniel's vow, the main theme is entangled with sensual elements of this sort.

In *L'Immolé*, however, Baumann's intention is initially religious, though this is on the whole foiled by elements which distort and destroy the theme. In Barbey, of course, the basic intention was Romantic. Though Baumann sees the concept of vicarious suffering as important he does not seem to realise certain contradictions in his portrayal of it, nor does he fail to exaggerate those external elements of the doctrine which are the least important.

In *La Fosse aux Lions* (1911) the Aurevillian element becomes even stronger. The action takes place in the countryside of Bas-Poitou, in a society of landlords and tenants, tradition and the land, in which the author expresses many political sentiments worthy of Barbey.[112] The main theme of the novel is complicated by Romantic elements. For example, a young girl, thought of by the local people as a witch, calls down on the main characters a fearful curse—'Vous vous marierez . . . peut-être; mais rappelez-vous bien qu'il arrivera malheur à votre premier-né'[113]—and eventually goes mad. Madness plays a great part in the plot, and the close proximity of a lunatic asylum leads to a perpetual sense of impending doom, which is added to by various sinister presages and presentiments littered around the book. At times one feels oneself to be back in the countryside around Sombreval's Château du Quesnay in Barbey d'Aurevilly's *Un Prêtre Marié*.

From the very opening of the novel we learn of the doom which lies over the characters, and the reason for it. Young Philippe de Bradieu, on his way to see his father on his country estate, recalls his dead mother's immolation of herself *and her children* for the expiation of innumerable sins. The passage is important, as it shows us much that is false in Baumann's conception of the doctrine:

> Philippe se souvenait de confidences presque terribles: le soir d'un Vendredi saint, se représentant les désastres infinis de l'Église, l'Amour et la Justice bafoués par une France impénitente, n'avait-elle pas voué en réparation sa propre vie, celle même de ses enfants? Sa fille Claire était une première victime

acceptée, exultante d'ailleurs et parfaite. Quant à elle, le Maître venait de la prendre à la façon d'un voleur; elle n'aurait pu implorer de Lui une mort plus expiatoire, et la plus indigne des mécréantes ne pouvait guère être plus durement traitée, puisqu'elle était partie sans Viatique, sans entendre la voix du prêtre qui lui fit des Onctions. Philippe sentait obscurement se prolonger sur lui-même et sur les siens une prédestination d'holocaustes non encore accomplis. Il ne les repoussait point, soumis devant l'inconnu des Béatitudes sanglantes.[114]

In offering up her children as well as herself Madame de Bradieu is surely exceeding any power of immolation which a human being may possess. It seems an Old Testament conception, that of offering up one's family for a purpose, and it seems to lack that idea of personal free will which is essential to Christian belief. Admittedly both daughter and son are seen as accepting, or at least not repulsing, this fate which is thrust upon them; but nevertheless the fate is described as 'prédestination.' Once again, as in *L'Immolé*, we have a hero preordained to suffering; but in this case it is not initially given to him of his own choice, nor even, it would seem, of God's, but of that of another human being. Another odd feature of this passage is the conception of the mother's death without extreme unction as being a supreme fulfilment of her vocation of suffering. There is no need to point out the theological oddity of this idea.

Philippe, on his arrival in Bas-Poitou, finds his father a half-crazed alcoholic living with a chambermaid called Diane (the witch mentioned above). After she has gone mad and been taken off to the madhouse Philippe marries Alix, the daughter of a local nobleman. She too has a *penchant* for suffering; on the day of their wedding, hearing from a priest of the heroic early days of the Church, she prays for such days to return, and just before she bears Philippe's child, when he chides her for her sadness, she says: 'Je n'ai pas assez souffert, vous non plus; il me semble que notre tour approche. . . .'[115] At her *accouchement* she is calmed by reading a passage from the Maccabees dealing with torture, and a little later we find her reading *La douloureuse Passion de Notre-Seigneur*, by Anna Katharina Emmerick. Her family, too, seems to devote itself to vicarious suffering. Her brother Élisée, who has decided to go out to the desert as a White Father, offers his sacrifice for others: 'Élisée fixait le Christ saignant au dessus du pauvre tabernacle; il le savait, l'holocauste de sa jeunesse se tournerait mystiquement en pluie d'abondance sur Philippe et sur les siens, sur la Vendée dont, malgré tout, il n'était point dépris, sur la chrétienté douloureuse et les frères inconnus que, plus tard, il baptiserait.'[116]

In this complicated mass of vicarious offerings, in which we even find Daniel Rovère, the hero of *L'Immolé*, dying of tuberculosis at a monastery in Tarragona, the fate lying over Philippe and his wife seems nevertheless to stem from less reputable sources. There is the curse called down on them by Diane; there is the heredity of the Bradieu family, which is stressed time and again as being cursed (Philippe's father, before going mad, even claims to be descended from Gilles de Rais); there are the presentiments which Alix has about returning to Philippe's family castle, which she believes will bring bad luck to them; and there are innumerable signs of bad luck, from the call of a bird to the signs of the Devil which a priest sees in the vicinity. All these things naturally lead us to expect a tragedy; and, sure enough, Philippe's father in a fit of madness kills Philippe's child. They are left desolate: 'Mais elle [Alix] et Philippe comprenaient trop qu'une loi d'holocauste justifiait toute leur souffrance: Philippe ressongea au voeu de sa mère, le soir d'un Vendredi-Saint. . . .'[117]

Much of the rest of the book, after the Count's commitment to the lunatic asylum, is devoted to Philippe's battle to defend the ancient values of the Vendée against the new political ideas. This part seems to have very little bearing upon the rest of the plot, and one is left with the conviction that it is added for no other purpose than as a vehicle for political opinions; though it does show us what both Mme. de Bradieu and Élisée, by their oblations, had been wishing to do. Philippe attempts to defend the France of tradition by political action rather than by passive suffering.

This book is even more of a hotchpotch than *L'Immolé*. Vicarious suffering is brought in at almost any opportunity and used to produce an atmosphere of doom; other, non-Christian elements often seem to take the upper hand; the book seems to have no shape whatsoever and the style has little to recommend it. Even the doctrine of vicarious suffering itself is misunderstood and mistreated. In Baumann's next novel, *Le Baptême de Pauline Ardel*, where a young man offers himself up for the conversion of the young girl he loves, some of these faults are less obvious. But in Baumann's work as a whole, despite his obviously sincere Catholic belief, we see something of a throwback to the faults of Barbey d'Aurevilly on the one hand, and a distortion of various aspects of the doctrine of vicarious suffering on the other. Baumann's popularity seems to have rested solely on the extent to which his preoccupation with vicarious suffering reflected the interests of the Catholics of his day.

Paul Claudel

In the works of Claudel suffering plays an extremely important role. While this role has been stressed by many critics, none of them seem to have pointed out the various metamorphoses which Claudel's view of suffering underwent. It is this failure by both modern critics and modern audiences to appreciate the moving principles behind Claudel's beliefs on this subject which has caused many misunderstandings with regard to Claudel's plays, none being more striking than the incomprehension accorded to the central scenes of *L'Otage* (1909), in which the harsh message appears shocking even to the minds of modern Catholic audiences, who therefore attempt to interpret it in a manner more in accordance with what they see as the humane beliefs of Christianity.

What one must never forget, however, in dealing with the authors of the Revival (and people only too often fail to class Claudel with his contemporaries) is the conception of God's justice and God's values being superhuman rather than humane. God's justice and mercy may thus often appear to be injustice; but God's pattern, when understood, explains all.

In the first years of the twentieth century a great change came over Claudel's work. Much of this was almost certainly due to the harrowing experiences he went through in the years at the turn of the century: his belief in his monastic vocation and his desire to give up his literary work in order to follow it; the refusal of this vocation in 1900 and Claudel's subsequent sense of having been rejected utterly, cast out from the sight of God; in the midst of this sense of desolation, the sudden love affair he had with a married woman, as depicted in *Partage de Midi* (1905), an adultery which lasted for a few years and produced a child; and finally his sense of utter guilt with regard to this adultery, a guilt which was never to leave him, just as the memory of the woman concerned never left him. These experiences left their mark on Claudel, and from then onwards his characters, though they have symbolic purposes, do not remain as pure symbols[118] but take on a life of their own. It is from now on, too, that we find the concept of the necessary separation of lovers, that essential doctrine of Claudel's later plays, set forth with all the philosophical support Claudel feels necessary. Similarly, from now on we find that idea of order which Claudel had sought in a monastery, portrayed in the concept of order in marriage, a marriage without love, a discipline.

All this we shall discuss in Chapter Twelve. What is important for the moment is to realise that beside these changes in Claudel's writing there is another change, far more important, and that is a change in Claudel's approach to suffering. This appears to have been occasioned by his sudden appreciation of the doctrine of vicarious suffering.

I have written elsewhere[119] of the great changes which took place in Claudel's play *La Jeune Fille Violaine* between its second version in 1898 and its third version, which appeared under the title *L'Annonce faite à Marie* in 1910. Most of these changes, in my opinion, could be traced to Claudel's reading of Huysmans's *Sainte Lydwine de Schiedam* (1901), from which he had learned in full the doctrine of vicarious suffering. There is no need to go into the details here, but very close relationships between the two texts seem to make this influence clear.[120] But whether one wishes to make this connection between the two books or not, there is no denying the fact that vicarious suffering plays a great part in *L'Annonce faite à Marie* for the first time in a work by Claudel, with the exception of *L'Otage* (1909). *Sainte Lydwine de Schiedam* may not have been the only influence at work; as we have seen, vicarious suffering was a constant theme in the novels written in the first years of the twentieth century, and Claudel was a voracious reader. We know that he read Baumann's *L'Immolé*, for example, which he described as 'ce livre que j'ai tant aimé.'[121] If we take, with this, his advice to his son Pierre to read *Sainte Lydwine de Schiedam*, which he described, despite his usual dislike for Huysmans's work, as 'an important book,'[122] we see that in this period not only did his reading include important works on vicarious suffering, but he also appreciated them a great deal.

If we examine more closely the changes wrought in *L'Annonce faite à Marie* we shall not only see at its clearest this insurgence of vicarious suffering; we shall also be able to explain by this means much of the message of the play *L'Otage*, which appeared in the year 1909, a year before *L'Annonce*.

We must not think that Claudel was entirely ignorant of this doctrine in the years before this. He had certainly, before this date, been impressed by the figure of Anna Katharina Emmerick, whose visions of the life of Christ we know him to have read some time in the years 1886–90; but while he was without doubt impressed by her as a figure of sacrifice (and the theme of sacrifice is constant in Claudel's works from the very first) he does not seem to have received the message of the doctrine of vicarious suffering from her in these years before the turn of the century. We find in the plays he wrote in this period plentiful examples of suffering and sacrifice: at the end of the symbolic drama *Tête d'Or* (1889) the Princess is crucified on a tree; at the end of the second version of *La Ville* (1897) Ivors stresses the need for sacrifice in the Christian life and the futility of the search for earthly happiness; in *L'Échange* (1894) Marthe, Louis Laine's long-suffering wife, declares that all she expects is grief, and that this is her vocation. Suffering is seen, as in so many Catholic authors of this period, as the lot of the Christian; but we get no glimpse of the idea of one person suffering *for the sins of others*. Occasionally, as in *La Jeune Fille Violaine*, we see someone suffering both because she has a vocation for suffering and for the sake of the *happiness* of another; but substitution for the sins of others is to be found in only one place, and there it is not vicarious suffering in the ordinary sense of the term.

This one example is the play *Le Repos du Septième Jour* (1896), in which a Chinese Emperor, whose people are being destroyed by the shades of the dead wandering on the face of the earth, himself goes down to hell to find the cause of this invasion and save his people. The play expounds two important themes: (i) the fear of, and the meaning of, death, and (ii) the nature of evil. But the Emperor himself, in his sacrifice for his people, might seem to be performing a form of vicarious suffering. Speaking to a necromancer, he cries:

> Révèle la cause, prononce
> Le remède; quel fut notre péché? Que tout le peuple ne soit
> pas puni!
> Mais il est juste, s'il le faut, que moi, L'Empereur, j'expie et
> je meure.[123]

Again, before he goes down to hell, the Emperor says:

Que ce peuple ne périsse point! Et s'il faut que quelqu'un meure,
Comme celui qui se présente au Juge à la place du fils de la
veuve, me voici![124]

But gradually, during the course of the play, we realise that this
is not vicarious suffering in the manner to which we have become
accustomed in the literature of the period, i.e. the suffering of one
of God's creatures to expiate the sins of the others: it is a symbolic
portrayal of Christ's original sacrifice for man, with the Emperor
being a symbolic portrayal of Christ suffering for *his people*. The
similarity with the doctrine of vicarious suffering is natural, for
this doctrine was based upon Christ's original sacrifice, i.e. man was
seen as continuing this sacrifice. Yet nowhere in this play is the
idea of such a continuation of the sacrifice conveyed. Instead the
problems of death and evil are seen as being solved by Christ's
suffering, by his descent into hell, and by his Resurrection. The
Emperor returns from hell with his imperial sceptre transformed
into a Cross, and with the full explanation of 'le mal' (which can
here mean both evil and suffering) and of death. The Cross itself
is the explanation, bringing with it the realisation that true joy
lies in suffering and that true revelation lies beyond the grave.
'Moi-même je suis un signe,'[125] says the Emperor, and reveals his
face, which is now that of a leper, i.e. the living dead.

In this play, with the aid of all the biblical symbolism at his
disposal, Claudel was attempting to solve the great problems of
death and evil by reference to the mission and the message of
Christ. Of *human* suffering we learn, as in his other plays, that it is
essential to God's plan; but we do not find the universal lesson of
substitution and equilibrium which is preached in the later plays,
L'Otage and *L'Annonce faite à Marie*.

In *La Jeune Fille Violaine*, in both the 1892 and the 1898 versions, Violaine renounces her claims to the love of her fiancé
Jacquin Uri (Jacques Hury in the second version), partly because
she realises her sister is in love with him and desires the inheritance, and partly because of her realisation of the efficacy of suffering and the necessity not to be too happy in this world. She refuses
to marry Jacques, and when he accuses her of infidelity with
another, answers nothing. She gives away her inheritance to her
sister (Bibiane in the first version, Mara in the second) and is
driven out of the house by her. Mara, in the process, throws ashes
in her eyes, which later cause her to go blind.

Violaine's motives evidently have nothing to do with the idea of vicarious suffering. She sees suffering as a necessity for the Christian and as being efficacious in salvation, but no more. In a scene with Pierre de Craon at the beginning of the second version, she is taught by him the necessity of not being too happy in this world:

Jeune être heureux [he says], vous ne savez ce que c'est que souffrir,

Et cela qu'on appelle, Violaine, la misère.

La lutte, la désolation, la honte. . . .[126]

Vous êtes l'image de ce bonheur que je ne veux pas avoir; vous représentez à la fois

Ce que je donne et cela pourquoi je le donne.[127]

Violaine at first still revels in her happiness and stresses it to Pierre:

Mais pourquoi le cacher? Il est vrai que je suis heureuse.

Dans la joie, ô Pierre de Craon, je m'endors, et je me réveille, et je me rendors dans la joie. Que je sois pleine de plus de joie,

A fin d'en apporter à celui que j'aime davantage![128]

Soon, however, Pierre reveals to her the nature of sacrifice and she comes to accept this:

PIERRE DE CRAON Le don, a l'imitation de la générosité de notre Dieu,

Aux autres, afin qu'il n'y ait rien de mort en nous, de soi.

Celui qui donne, pour qu'il puisse donner, il est juste qu'il reçoive;

Et qui se sacrifie, Violaine, il se consacre.

VIOLAINE Maintenant vous m'avez dit tout et je sais tout.[129]

Suffering is thus seen as a necessary sacrifice; but when later in the play Violaine explains this sacrifice of hers she does so only in relation to her pity for Mara. She has suffered for Mara's earthly happiness and for her own spiritual good rather than as an expiation for the sins of others:

J'ai su que ma soeur vous aimait. Et, sachant ce que c'est que l'amour,

J'ai eu compassion d'elle.[130]

How different the whole conception is in *L'Annonce faite à Marie*! Here Violaine's sacrifice is seen as a substitution for the sins of the whole world. Claudel moves the action of the play back from the present day to the beginning of the fifteenth century and, like Huysmans in *Sainte Lydwine de Schiedam*, sets the scene for his expiatory sufferer by painting the terrible state of France and the world at the time, with many of the same details as Huysmans gives:

> Mais tu vois au moins que tout est ému et dérangé de sa place, et chacun recherche éperdument où elle est.
>
> Et ces fumées que l'on voit parfois au loin, ce n'est pas de la vaine paille qui brûle.
>
> Et ces grandes bandes de pauvres qui nous arrivent de tous les côtés.
>
> Il n'y a plus de Roi sur la France, selon qu'il a été prédit par le Prophète. . . .
>
> A la place du Roi nous avons deux enfants
>
> L'un, l'Anglais, dans son île
>
> Et l'autre, si petit qu'on ne le voit plus, entre les roseaux de la Loire.
>
> A la place du Pape, nous en avons trois et à la place de Rome, je ne sais quel concile en Suisse. . . .[131]

These words are spoken by Violaine's father, Anne Vercors, though Violaine herself also refers to the state of the world in the first scene of the play.[132] It is interesting that in this version of the play Violaine's speech on the necessity of not being too happy is transferred to her father, who takes this as his reason for going on a pilgrimage to the Holy Land. In the 1898 version he had merely departed by train to America to look after the children of a brother who had died. The rejection of happiness is certainly seen to be important ('Je suis las d'être heureux,'[133] sighs Anne Vercors), but Violaine's mission is seen as having an additional and more pertinent reason—vicarious suffering for the sins of the world. Violaine, in this play, ends up as a leper, and in Act III when Mara visits her she explains her mission fully, including even the demarcation which Huysmans made between the 'rôle plus expansif, plus bruyant'[134] of the male Saints, and the more passive vocation of women:

> Le mâle est prêtre, mais il n'est pas défendu à la femme d'être victime.
>
> *Dieu est avare et ne permet qu'aucune créature soit allumée,*
>
> *Sans qu'un peu d'impureté s'y consume,*
>
> *La sienne ou celle qui l'entoure*, comme la braise de l'encensoir qu'on attise!

Et certes le malheur de ce temps est grand.

Ils n'ont point de père. Ils regardent et ne savent plus où est le Roi et le Pape.

C'est pourquoi voici mon corps en travail à la place de la chrétienté qui se dissout.[135]

At the end of the play Anne Vercors, who has returned from his pilgrimage, sees what has happened and understands it. His daughter, Violaine, he realises, has seen the same problem as himself and has found the right solution to it:

Voici que je me suis scandalisé comme un Juif parce que la face de l'Église est obscurcie et parce qu'elle marche en chancelant son chemin dans l'abandon de tous les hommes.

Et j'ai voulu de nouveau me serrer contre le tombeau vide, mettre ma main dans le trou de la croix.

Mais ma petite fille Violaine a été plus sage.

Est-ce que le but de la vie est de vivre? est-ce que les pieds des enfants de Dieu seront attachés à cette terre miserable?

Il n'est pas de vivre, mais de mourir, et non point de charpenter la croix mais d'y monter, et de donner ce que nous avons en riant![136]

He sees his wife dead, his daughter dead, and Joan of Arc's ashes thrown to the winds; but he realises that these sacrifices have been worthwhile, for it is their effort in common which has made it possible that 'le Roi et le Pontife de nouveau sont rendus à France et à l'Univers, le schisme prend fin.'[137]

The continual references to Joan of Arc in this play and the great scene in Act III where we are shown all the preparations for her journey to Reims to crown the Dauphin show us to what extent Claudel saw the saving of France and the world as being a communal effort. Joan with her active material contribution and Violaine with hers which is passive and mystical are both pursuing the same end. The miracle by which Violaine resuscitates Mara's dead child takes place at the moment not only of the Incarnation, on Christmas morning, but also of the Coronation in Reims.

Anne Vercors has something of this same conception of the communion of saints when, in Act I, he denies his wife's declaration that he will be alone in his pilgrimage. 'C'est une grand peuple qui se réjouit et qui part avec moi!'[138] he says, adding that a Christian communicates with all his brothers and is never alone.

This is the play in which Claudel puts forward most clearly the

doctrine of vicarious suffering, and he puts it forward in an orthodox manner, free of all the distortions which we have seen in some
other authors. He sees it in its most noble form, that of suffering
for the sins of the whole world, not merely for the sins of other
individuals.

In later plays the doctrine is not stated so clearly but we always
find it in the background, accounting for the suffering which is
inflicted on Claudel's chosen victims; and in two characteristics
above all in Claudel's later thought we find distinct traces of the
strong influence which the doctrine had upon him. These two
characteristics are (i) the belief in the necessity of free will on the
part of the victim and (ii) the ensuing belief in an equilibrium which
God has created for this world, an equilibrium which will not be
disturbed by one person's refusal to answer the call; another way
of restoring it will always be found, and anyway God, in his infinite
wisdom, usually chooses as his victims people who he knows will
of their free will accept their task.

In the plays Claudel wrote before this time, the question of free
will does not seem to have entered into the matter; people have no
choice. The fatalism of Marthe, in *L'Échange*, is typical of this
attitude. The only character who takes suffering upon himself is
the Emperor in *Le Repos du Septième Jour*, who, as we have seen,
is a figure of Christ. The human victims behave like Violaine in
La Jeune Fille Violaine. In the version of 1898 she exclaims at one
point:

> Ce n'est pas nous qui choisissons, c'est nous qui sommes
> choisis.
> Au-dessous de la raison, au-dessous de la conscience, au-
> dessous du sens,
> Au-dessous de l'instinct, et de toute la part allumée de nous-
> memes.[139]

Mara quietly replies: 'Je comprends ce que tu veux dire et que tu
n'es point libre de faire toute chose à ton gré.'[140]

But in *L'Annonce faite à Marie*, with its full doctrine of vicarious
suffering, the question of free will becomes very important. In the
last act Violaine, explaining to Jacques Hury the reasons for her
sacrifice, says:

> Il est trop dur de souffrir et de ne savoir à quoi bon.
> Mais ce que d'autres ne savent pas, je l'ai appris et je veux
> que tu le saches avec moi. . . .

Tout ce qui doit périr, c'est cela qui est malade, et tout ce qui ne doit pas périr, c'est cela qui souffre.

Heureux celui qui souffre et qui sait à quoi bon! Maintenant ma tâche est finie.[141]

Like Huysmans's Lydwine, Violaine comes gradually to understand her suffering. In one way she has been chosen, but her acceptance was also needed. And in another way she has brought suffering on herself by the kiss she gave to the leper Pierre de Craon, a kiss of compassion. In Act III she stresses the voluntary nature of her suffering:

Puissant est la souffrance quand elle est aussi volontaire que le péché!

Tu m'as vue baiser ce lépreux, Mara? Ah, la coupe de la douleur est profonde,

Et qui y met une fois la lèvre ne l'en retire plus à son gré![142]

The free will of suffering is here connected in the most orthodox way possible with the free will of sin, which causes this suffering in the world. And the kissing of the leper, a voluntary act, which replaces the blinding of Violaine by ashes, an act of Mara's which forced suffering on Violaine, is stressed yet again by Anne Vercors at the end of the play (in the *Variante pour la scène* of Act IV): 'Toute la grande douleur du monde autour d'elle, et l'Église coupée en deux, et la France pour qui Jeanne a été brûlée vive, elle l'a vue! Et c'est pourquoi elle a baisé ce lépreux, sur la bouche, *sachant ce qu'elle faisait.*'[143]

The kissing of the leper is an act of compassion and an act of free will; Violaine's leprosy is brought on her through her own action, though she does not fully understand, at this stage, the effect her action is to have. She accepts, later, the full implications of the suffering of which this spontaneous act of compassion has shown her to be worthy. (It is interesting to note that two of the miracles ascribed to Violaine, i.e. the curing of illness by taking it on herself and the miraculous milk produced at her breast in Act III, are both miracles ascribed to Lydwine,[144] for whom the latter occurred on Christmas Eve as well.) In *La Jeune Fille Violaine* it is stressed that it is Mara who, as the instrument of God, has inflicted this suffering on Violaine:

Tout arrive par la secrète volonté de Dieu. . . .

Mara, tu as coupé le lien qui me tenait, et je ne repose plus que dans la main de Dieu même.[145]

Et alors il arriva que je devins aveugle, *sans qu'il y eût de ma faute.*[146]

It is in *L'Otage* (1909), in the very scene which causes so many people to throw up their hands in horror, that we find the most perfect expression of that equilibrium which, while seemingly at variance with the concept of free will, is in fact perfectly in accord with it. The play takes place during the reign of Napoleon I. Sygne de Coûfontaine, who, in her pride of family, has quietly and stubbornly built up again the family possessions after the Revolution, has been visited by her cousin Georges, an ardent Royalist, and has seen that it is through marriage with him (for his wife and children have been killed) that the heritage will remain in the family. She also in fact loves him. With him, however, Georges has brought an old man who is soon discovered to be the Pope, whom Georges is attempting to save from Napoleon. Turelure, the local prefect and a former valet of the family, who is seen as the man of the future, the schemer who will fit in with every régime and gain honours from every ruler, knows that the Pope is there. He asks Sygne to marry him in exchange for the Pope's safety. Sygne is furious, but when the local priest, M. Badilon, hears all this he persuades her to accept. It is this scene of persuasion which is the one we must study.

Critics such as Halévy have seen in this a vile outrage against Christian morality; others, unable to believe this of Claudel, have seen in it a condemnation of the Church's message as put in the mouth of Badilon. In both cases they are wrong, because they do not realise the questions at stake. The question is *not* the safety of the Pope, and in thinking so Halévy makes a ridiculous comparison with the situation on Calvary in which, he says, Claudel would have had Mary Magdalen settle everything by a glance at Pilate or the High Priest, so that only two crosses were needed on the hill that day. No, it is a question of Sygne's salvation, not the Pope's; and if a parallel were to be made with Calvary it would be she, in a substitution of suffering, who would be taking Christ's place on the Cross. The whole matter goes far beyond the single situation of the Pope's safety; and the consequences of it stretch right through the trilogy of which this is the first part.

There are three main reasons for the decision which is demanded of Sygne: (i) the most important, Sygne is of the race of victims and she has the vocation of suffering for the world; (ii) she is a creature of earthly pride and that pride must be broken down to make of her a creature of God; and (iii) a far wider reason but in fact the *raison d'être* of the trilogy, the family pride of the Coûfontaine is a thing of the past. God has deserted the old nobility as they have deserted God: Georges thinks of the Pope purely as a hostage on the Royalist side, not being himself a believer. Sygne's marriage to Turelure will be the symbol of the mingling of the best of the old régime with the modern world in that perpetual progress and adaptation which is essential. Because the characters by this stage of Claudel's career are more alive we must not be deceived into ignoring their symbolic value: Sygne's marriage to Turelure is just as much a symbol as were Lâla's various liaisons in *La Ville*.

It is the first two of these reasons which interest us most for our present purposes. It is Sygne's vocation to suffer; it is, as Badilon says, 'Cette chose pour laquelle il apparaît que vous avez été créée et mise au monde.'[147] Yet this vocation must be freely accepted, and God is dependent on his creature:

> O mon enfant, quoi de plus faible et de plus désarmé
> Que Dieu, quand il ne peut rien sans nous?[148]

God most certainly does not demand the sacrifice; he is pleased only by the gifts which his children give him with all their heart. Justice itself does not demand the sacrifice, and if she does not give it she remains without sin and could still receive absolution from any priest:

> Et vous, que pour sauver le Père de tous les hommes selon que vous en avez reçu vocation,
> Vous renonciez à votre amour et à votre nom et à votre cause et à votre honneur en ce monde,
> Embrassant votre bourreau et l'acceptant pour époux comme le Christ s'est laissé manger par Judas,
> — La Justice ne le commande pas.[149]

She is asked to give up her love, and her family name, and the royalist cause (we have already seen how much these mean to her); but she is also asked to go even deeper, and give up her honour, which she had engaged in the promise of marriage to Georges. This was, however, an earthly promise, and her honour is an earthly honour; God's honour is on a different plane and has different standards. Yet even divine justice does not *demand* her acceptance. 'Dieu ne veut donc pas de moi un tel consentement?' asks Sygne. 'Il ne l'exige pas, je vous le dis avec fermeté,' replies

Badilon. But then he goes on to draw a comparison between Sygne's situation and that of Christ; in neither case, he says, did justice *demand* the sacrifice:

> Et de même quand le Fils de Dieu pour le salut des hommes
> S'est arraché du sein de son Père et qu'il a subi l'humiliation et la mort
> Et cette seconde mort de tous les jours qui est le péché mortel de ceux qu'il aime,
> La Justice non plus ne le contraignait pas.[150]

Badilon asks her whether, if her cousin's children still lived and it was a question of saving him and them, she would make the sacrifice. She admits that she would, for the sake of the name and the family and because Georges is 'mon père et mon sang et mon frère et mon aîné, le premier et le dernier de nous tous'.[151] God, Badilon replies gravely, is all this to her as well, before him.

And now we come to the crux of the whole question. Sygne cries out that God has no need of her to save the Pope: 'Mais il [Dieu] n'a pas besoin de moi! Le Pape a ses promesses infaillibles!'[152] Badilon replies that this is true, but that it is not a question of saving the Pope, who has these promises, but of saving the world, which does not have them. She must save the universe by her act. The Pope has never been left in peril; God has saved him every time, but this must always be through the help of a man, who acts of his own free will.

Sygne's sacrifice is thus seen as universal, as being made for the whole world. And gradually Badilon points out to her the communion of which she is a member, all of which demands her decision:

> Ah! nous ne sommes pas seuls ici! Ame pénitente, vierge, voyez ce peuple immense qui nous entoure,
> Les esprits bienheureux dans le ciel, les pécheurs sous nos pieds,
> Et les myriades humaines l'une sur l'autre, attendant votre résolution![153]

And so the struggle goes on. Sygne despairingly cries out to God that she loves him, and Badilon, speaking with the voice of Christ, taunts her that she does not know the true love which is suffering:

SYGNE Mon Dieu! Cependant Vous voyez que je Vous aime!

M. BADILON Mais non point jusqu'aux crachats, à la couronne

d'épines, à la chute sur le visage, à l'arrachement
des habits et à la croix.

SYGNE   Vous voyez mon coeur!

M. BADILON   Mais non point à travers cette grande rupture à
mon côté.[154]

Finally, Sygne gives in and Badilon rejoices that her pride has
been broken down and that nothing is left of that earthly Sygne
whom God had not made. Before he leaves her he asks for her
pardon, which she gives him.

In attempting to understand Claudel's plays one must always
bear in mind that, though in many ways and particularly with
regard to his philosophy of history he differentiates himself quite
strongly from the other writers of the Revival, there are nevertheless many elements in his work which can only fully be understood
when placed in relation to the religious attitudes of his time. Nowhere is this more clear than in the conception of divine justice
which is most clearly stated in this scene from *L'Otage*. Claudel,
like Bloy, sees divine justice as being incomprehensible to mere
man, and at times completely opposed to purely human ideas of
justice. Sygne must not only suffer; she must also dishonour herself on the human level by repudiating her agreement with Georges.
The ultimate aim is not merely the purification of Sygne from
earthly motives nor even just the saving of the world by voluntary
sacrifice (marriage to someone one does not love, that most common
of sacrifices in the plays of Claudel); it is also the encompassing of
that historical process, the mingling of the bloods which will be
continued by the injection of Jewish blood into the family in the
next generation, that process which will continue right up to the
unborn baby with whom the last lines of the last play of the
trilogy, *Le Père Humilié*, are concerned. In this trilogy and in his
other plays Claudel is in agreement with Bloy's ideas on the nature
of divine justice as expressed in *Le Désespéré*:

> Nos courtes notions d'équité répugnent a cette distribution de
> la Miséricorde par la Justice. . . . Si, comme il est écrit, les choses
> cachées nous doivent être révélées un jour, nous saurons, sans
> doute à la fin, pourquoi tant de faibles furent écrasés, brûlés et
> persécutés dans tous les siècles; nous verrons avec quelle exacti-
> tude infiniment calculée furent réparties, en leur temps, les
> prospérités et les douleurs, et quelle miraculeuse équité néces-
> sitait passagèrement les apparences de l'injustice.[155]

Charles Péguy

Like Claudel, Péguy had certain characteristics which were typical of the Revival and certain which were not. In Péguy's case one of the characteristics which he did not fully share was the delight in the harshness of the Christian religion. In his traditionalism, his non-intellectualism, the simplicity of his belief, the violence of his intransigence against 'tepid' Christians, he was typical of his generation of Catholic writers; but he showed, by his mistrust of Bloy and by his dislike of much of Claudel's outlook, that the savagery of their delight in sacrifice was not for him. Not that he denied the place of suffering in the Catholic life, nor that he could deny the harshness of certain Christian doctrines; but in his attitude towards one of these, that of the eternity of hell, we shall see much of what differentiates him from other Catholic writers of the time. In the process we will see a little of his conception of the doctrine of vicarious suffering.

For a long time before his conversion Péguy had been obsessed by the Catholic doctrine of the eternity of hell. In his essay *Toujours de la Grippe*, for example, written in 1900, he had reacted against this doctrine with all the strength of his humanitarian socialism. It is the most odious and barbarous doctrine of the Christian faith, he says, and one which can never be accepted by a humane man:

> Ce qui nous est le plus étranger en (la foi chrétienne), et . . . ce qui nous est le plus odieux, ce qui est barbare, ce à quoi nous ne consentirons jamais, ce qui a hanté les chrétiens les meilleurs, ce pour quoi les chretiens les meilleurs se sont évadés, ou silencieusement détournés . . . c'est cela : cette étrange combinaison de la vie et de la mort que nous nommons la damnation, cet étrange renforcement de la présence par l'absence et renforcement de tout par l'éternité. *Ne consentira jamais à cela tout homme qui a reçu en partage, ou qui s'est donné l'humanité.* . . . Ne consentira pas tout citoyen qui aura la simple solidarité. *Comme nous somme solidaires des damnés de la terre . . . tout a fait ainsi . . . nous sommes solidaires des damnés éternels.* . . . Nous n'admettons pas qu'il y ait des hommes qui soient repoussés du seuil d'aucune cité. . . . *L'imagination d'un exil est celle qui répugne le plus à tout socialisme. Jamais nous ne dirons oui à la supposition, à la proposition de cette mort vivante. Une éternité de mort vivante est une imagination perverse, inverse.*[156]

Péguy continually returns to this idea of the eternity of hell in his pre-conversion works. For example, in the essay *De Jean Coste* (1902), while dealing as a socialist with purely human sufferings, he draws an extended parallel with the eternal sufferings of hell; and in the *Jeanne d'Arc* of 1897, that vast drama which became known as the 'socialist' *Jeanne d'Arc*, there is a long discussion of the problem between Jeanne d'Arc herself and the nun Madame Gervaise.

We have seen that many other Catholic writers of the period had, before their conversion, had similar misgivings about some of the harder aspects of Catholic doctrine; but on their conversion these misgivings had disappeared and they had thrown themselves wholeheartedly into the most extreme views on these same subjects. In Péguy's case, on the other hand, these misgivings remained even after his conversion, and much of his religious attitude can be explained by their continued presence.

His attitude towards the problem did change, however, and bring itself into line with his Christian belief. Nowhere is this better illustrated than in *Le Mystère de la Charité de Jeanne d'Arc* (1910), which is a reworking of the first part of the original *Jeanne d'Arc*, a reworking which consisted mainly of vast accretions to the original text, which on the whole remained as it was. The changes, often minute, in the Jeanne–Madame Gervaise scene on the subject of hell are particularly revealing of Péguy's new attitude to the problem.

In the original text of 1897 Jeanne, in an ecstasy of sacrifice and solidarity with the damned, cries out that she is prepared to offer up her own body and soul in order to save the damned:

O s'il faut, pour sauver de la flamme éternelle
Les corps des morts damnés s'affolant de souffrance,
Abandonner mon corps à la flamme éternelle,
Mon Dieu, donnez mon corps à la flamme éternelle;

Et s'il faut, pour sauver de l'Absence éternelle
Les âmes des damnés s'affolant de l'Absence,
Abandonner mon âme à l'Absence éternelle,
Que mon âme s'en aille en l'Absence éternelle.[157]

Madame Gervaise is horrified at this heretical conception of vicarious suffering. 'Taisez-vous, ma soeur: vous avez blasphémé,' she cries, and goes on to explain that while God in his infinite mercy has allowed *human* suffering to help save souls which are in danger, he would never allow us to damn our souls to *eternal* suffering in order to save souls. Even Christ himself could not do so, because he knew that even *his* eternal suffering could never be of use in saving souls.

Jeanne, appreciating this lesson, nevertheless launches into another speech in which she declares herself prepared to offer herself up to *human* suffering for the sake of the souls in hell:

S'il faut, pour tirer saufs de la flamme éternelle
Les corps des morts damnés s'affolant de souffrance,
Laisser longtemps mon corps à la souffrance humaine
Mon Dieu, gardez mon corps à la souffrance humaine;

Et s'il faut, pour sauver de l'Absence éternelle
Les âmes des damnés s'affolant de l'Absence,
Laisser longtemps mon âme à la souffrance humaine,
Qu'elle reste vivante en la souffrance humaine.[158]

Yet again Madame Gervaise interrupts her with the words 'Taisez-vous, ma soeur, vous avez blasphémé,' and explains that it is impossible to save those who are damned; even Christ found himself unable to do this, which was why, on the Cross, he had cried out with a 'clameur qui sonna faux comme un divin blasphème'.[159] Suffering can only be offered for souls that are in danger of damnation; once these souls have been condemned, they are lost beyond recall.

Madame Gervaise goes on to explain the doctrine of vicarious suffering, and particularly the necessity of God's acceptance of the sacrifice and of God's decision as to what use it is to be put to: 'Heureuses quand le bon Dieu, dans sa miséricorde infinie, veut bien accepter nos oeuvres, nos prières et nos souffrances pour en sauver une âme. Trop heureuses quand sa faveur infinie veut bien choisir cette âme parmi celles que nous avons aimés. . . .' It is strange to hear this from the mouth of a non-Catholic when in the mouths of so many Catholics and particularly in that of a theologian such as Father Poulain we have heard so much certainty of the automatic transference of sins and sufferings at the choice of the human agents.

Madame Gervaise, then, is the voice of Catholic orthodoxy, and Jeanne that of uncertain humanity; and superficially the argument appears to remain the same in the version of 1910. The same words are kept, on the whole, and the vast additions (the discussion, instead of being six pages long, now takes one hundred) are in the form of expansions (the main one being the long description of the Passion which illustrates the moment of the despair on the Cross) rather than changes. The few small changes which can be noticed, however, point to a definite shift of emphasis. In the 1897 version Péguy not only sympathises with Jeanne; he sees her revolt as valid. In the 1910 version Madame Gervaise puts forward the same views but this time it is accepted that Jeanne must conform to them.

This complete change of emphasis is shown especially by the one part of the original play which is cut out. Such cuttings are rare in the changing of the text, and its unusual nature is heightened by the fact that it is the last speech of the scene, and that it expressed the outcome of the argument.

Madame Gervaise has gone out, and the last words exchanged between the women are those which close the scene in the 1910 version. But Jeanne, instead of the single line 'Orléans, qui êtes au pays de Loire' which we find in 1910, continues for over a page to muse on what she has heard. Gervaise and Hauviette are right, she says:

O mon Dieu je sais bien que Madame Gervaise
A raison; je sais bien qu'Hauviette a raison . . .[160]

God himself she knows is right in all he does:

Et vous avez raison quand vous sauvez une âme
Et vous avez raison quand vous la condamnez . . .
Vous avez pour le mieux fait la souffrance infâme,
Éternelle à manger les douloureux damnés,
Et fait la vie humaine et la vie éternelle,
Et fait la mort humaine et la mort éternelle,
Et vous avez raison dans la vie et la mort,
Sur la terre à jamais et dans l'éternité.

Yet the very tone in which she has been saying all this leads us to expect a 'but'; and, sure enough, the 'but' comes with a vengeance. Despite her knowledge that all this is right, she says, the knowledge that at every moment people are damning themselves prevents her from praying; she is revolted by the thought:

Pourtant, mon Dieu, quand je pense qu'il y a des âmes qui se damnent; quand je pense qu'il y avait des âmes qui n'étaient pas encore damnées au moment ou j'ai commencé à vous dire cette prière et qui sont damnées a présent pour la mort éternelle; quand je pense qu'a présent que je vous parle toutes mes paroles vous trouvent occupé à damner des âmes, pardonnez-moi, mon Dieu, si je dis un blasphème: quand je pense à cela, je ne peux plus prier. Les paroles de la prière me paraissent ensanglantées du sang maudit, et mon âme s'affole à penser aux damnés; à penser aux damnés mon âme se révolte.

The suppression of this passage in the second version points to the fact that we should accept Jeanne's submission on the matter of hell, for the scene now ends on a note of acceptance. [160A] As for the many additions which have been made to the text, most of these are a mere expansion of the original, except for two new elements, both of them of some importance.

The first of these is an extended argument between Madame Gervaise and Jeanne on the question of the abandonment of Christ by his disciples, with Jeanne stolidly maintaining that the people of her day and of her country would not have abandoned him. This argument has little to do with the question of eternal hell, but is concerned rather with the question of whether positive action should be taken by Jeanne to set the world to rights. The argument is vivid, with Madame Gervaise piling up arguments and Jeanne stolidly and simply repeating the same phrases over and over again with impressive certainty. If Péguy had wished to show Jeanne reacting strongly against the concept of an eternal hell, as he had in the 1897 version, he would surely have made her argue in this manner on that subject as well.

The second added element is that of an expansion of the idea of vicarious suffering to make of it an argument in favour of Jeanne's mission. As in the 1897 version, Madame Gervaise stresses to Jeanne that man must suffer to his utmost—'et jusqu'à la souffrance extrême sans nous tuer jamais'[161]—to prevent both himself and others from being damned. But when Madame Gervaise, speaking of God's mercy, says, 'Une âme, une seule âme est d'un prix infini', Jeanne takes this up immediately, asking again and again: 'Que sera-ce le prix d'une infinité d'âmes?'[162] And when Madame Gervaise, as in the first version, says that one can *never* be sure that a living soul is damned, and that we can never be sure that our prayers and sufferings are in vain for the purpose of saving them, it is then that Jeanne exclaims: 'Et quand nous voyons, quand vous voyez que la chrétienté même, que la chrétienté tout entière s'enfonce graduellement et délibérément, s'enfonce régulièrement dans la perdition.'

Thus Jeanne's eventual mission is seen as being taken on for the whole of Christianity, and for the salvation of souls. Just as Huysmans and Claudel had seen Jeanne d'Arc's mission as being a parallel to that of Lydwine and of Violaine, so Péguy sees her as substituting herself in the same manner for the sins of others. Yet Péguy, in his stressing of the active nature of her mission, shows less inclination towards the inward-looking mentality which was one of the attributes of Catholic action in his age.

So Péguy, like the other authors of the Catholic Revival, takes vicarious suffering as a central point of his belief. In doing so he has, however, approached it from a very different angle from his contemporaries. He does not approach it from the angle of the sufferer, but from that of the recipient. It is compassion for the souls of the damned which makes him resolve to save people from this fate before it is too late; he is not moved by that frenetic search for suffering which marks so many other of his Catholic contemporaries. His belief is as heroic as theirs, if not more so; he is concerned not with his own salvation but with that of others.

To suggest, however, that he refused to take the sacraments of the Church (as he did until his death) because of his 'solidarity with the damned' is ridiculous. Of all the various reasons put forward for this strange decision, this is the least likely. For, as we have seen, this 'solidarity' is a product of his socialist period, when he found it impossible to accept the Catholic doctrine of eternal hell. After his conversion he bows to this doctrine as to other decisions of the Church as being right. He does not glory in it as Baumann appears to do in his novel *L'Immolé*; he takes it quietly and without enthusiasm. But unlike Bloy, who wrote on this matter, 'Fils obéissant de l'Église, je suis, néanmoins, en communion d'impatience avec tous les révoltés, tous les déçus, tous les inexaucés, tous les damnés de ce monde,'[163] Péguy was a true 'fils obéissant de l'Église' who, once he had accepted the doctrine, kept to it. He accepted that no action in this world could save the eternally damned, so he confined his efforts for those *in danger* of such damnation; and no amount of 'solidarity with the damned' could have made him forfeit his eternal salvation to put himself in the same situation as them, whatever M. Marcel Péguy[164] and Mr. Graham Greene[165] may suggest to the contrary. No, the situation is far more likely to have been caused by family reasons; Péguy's wife refused to be married by the Church, the children were unbaptised and Péguy could not continue to live with them and look after them *and* partake of the sacraments.

Péguy accepts the doctrine of eternal hell; but in the later 'mysteries', the *Mystère du Porche de la Deuxième Vertu* (1911) and the *Mystère des Saints Innocents* (1912), we find a heartening message of hope, the greatest of the virtues, and of God's infinite mercy to those who trust in him.

Conclusion

In the vicissitudes of the doctrine of vicarious suffering we have seen much that illuminates the period with which we are dealing. We have seen the use of it for political ends by Blanc de Saint-Bonnet, for literary ends by Barbey d'Aurevilly. Among those who have used it for its own sake we have found rank heresy on the part of the abbé Boullan, which is reflected in many people of his time; an over-automatic belief in its possibilities on the part of many, including Father Poulain and several authors; and an over-violent desire for suffering on the part of Bloy. For many writers this became the most important part of their Catholic belief, particularly for Huysmans; and after the turn of the century the whole of Catholic literature became filled with examples of this doctrine. In Claudel and in Péguy we see it returned to its original orthodoxy as a doctrine, though these two writers are extremely different in their thought. Claudel's is a heroic but savage view of the necessity for suffering in this world; Péguy's is equally heroic, but illuminated by a compassion which reveals vicarious suffering as the most humane of doctrines.

This doctrine was not merely to be found in the literary works of the time; it was also to be found throughout the Catholic belief of the time, as a central element. Massis's claim that Psichari had died on the Western Front in order to expiate the sins of his grandfather Renan was accepted by most Catholics of the time, and it is quite possible that this was his intention, despite the denials by members of the Psichari family. For in the minds of many Catholic soldiers as they went off to the front must have been a prayer that they might be offering themselves up for a purpose.

NOTES

[1] Barbey d'Aurevilly, letter to Léon Bloy, 30 October 1874. Turcaret was the main character in a comedy of that name written by Lesage, which was first performed in 1709. He was depicted as an extreme example of the *nouveau riche*, typical of the money-ruled society of the time.

[2] Suso (1295–1365), a German mystic who devoted himself to suffering.

[3] Huysmans, letter to Dr. Leven, 17 August 1901; Collection Pierre Lambert.

[4] *La Plume*, 15 April 1895, pp. 173–4.

[5] Ibid., 1 April 1898, p. 193.

[6] Retté, *Du Diable à Dieu*, 1907, p. 195.

[7] Retté, *La Basse-Cour d'Apollon*, 1924, p. 232.

[8] Émile Baumann, *L'Anneau d'Or des Grands Mystiques*, 1924, p. 260.

[9] Ibid., p. 246.

[10] Bloy, *Le Désespéré*.

[11] Letter, 21 April 1892; printed in *Oeuvres Poétiques*, 1953, p. 46.

[12] Letter, 2 September 1908; ibid., p. 50.

[13] E.g. Émile Baumann's *L'Immolé* (1908).

[14] Bloy, *Celle qui Pleure*, 1907, pp. 120–1.

[15] Huysmans, letter to the abbé Daniel Fontaine, 27 July 1905; quoted in Guy Chastel, *J.-K. Huysmans et ses amis*, p. 195.

[16] Printed in Bloy, *Ici on assassine les grands hommes*, 1895.

[17] Blessed Angela of Foligno (1248–1309). This mystic's visions are contained in *The Book of Divine Consolation of Blessed Angela of Foligno*, which has been translated from the original Latin into many languages.

[18] Huysmans, *À Rebours*, Preface.

[19] See Chapter Seven and Chapter One.

[20] Raïssa Maritain, *Les Grandes Amitiés*, New York, 1944.

[21] *Tour St. Jacques*, May–June 1957. Part of my description of the doctrine of vicarious suffering is taken from this article.

[22] Quoted in Bloy, *Celle qui Pleure*, p. 87.

[23] Huysmans, Letter to Dom Thomasson de Gournay, 3 January 1898; copy in the Collection of Pierre Lambert.

[24] Barbey d'Aurevilly, *Les Prophètes du Passé*, 1880, p. 203.

[25] Barbey d'Aurevilly, Letter to Léon Bloy, 14 August 1872.

[26] *De la Douleur*, p. LXXXVII.

[27] E.g. the Introduction to *L'Infaillibilité*.

[28] *De la Douleur*, p. 9.

[29] Ibid., p. 14.

[30] Ibid., p. 42.

[31] Ibid., pp. 121–2.

[32] Ibid., p. 216.

[33] Ibid., p. 218.

[34] Ibid., p. 219.

[35] Ibid., p. 239.

[36] Ibid., p. 218.

[37] Ibid., p. 51.

[38] Barbey d'Aurevilly, *Un Prêtre Marié*, I, p. 242.

[39] Ibid., I, pp. 340–1.

[40] Ibid., I, p. 228.

[41] Ibid., I, p. 229.

[42] Ibid., I, p. 221.

[43] Ibid., I, pp. 210–11.

[44] Ibid., I, p. 262.

[45] Ibid., I, pp. 180–1.

[46] Ibid., II.

[47] It is with Boullan that this term for vicarious suffering first gained the great currency it was to have in later years. For Boullan, it contained the concept of vicarious *sin* and vicarious *temptation* as well as that of vicarious suffering. It is in this larger sense, therefore, that it should be understood in this section.

[48] Quoted in Marcel Thomas, 'L'Abbé Boullan et l'Oeuvre de la Réparation', *Tour St. Jacques*, May–June 1957.

[49] Boullan, *La Divine Réparation par J. J. M. missionaire de Marie*; quoted in Marcel Thomas, op. cit.

[50] See *supra*, pp. 134–5.

[51] Abbé Tardif de Moidrey, letter to abbé Boullan, 2 September 1873; Collection Pierre Lambert. See also *supra*, p. 132.

[52] For the manuscript letters on which this section is based I am grateful to M. Pierre Lambert, in whose collection they now are.

[53] See p. 132.

[54] J.-V. Bainvel, Introduction to the tenth edition of Poulain, *Les Grâces d'Oraison*, Paris, 1922, p. xlii.

[55] Ibid., p. xi. My italics.

[56] In the mouths of such people as Poulain and Huysmans, this word appears to have the same oracular effect as 'la Logique' is said to have had in the mouth of Stendhal.

[57] Letter of 11 May 1873.

[58] Letter of 18 March 1873.

[59] Letter of 8 April 1873.

[60] Letter of 18 March 1873.

[61] See *supra*, pp. 132, 170.

[62] Collection Pierre Lambert. My italics.

[63] Collection Pierre Lambert.

[64] Both these letters are printed in Joseph Bollery, *Léon Bloy*, vol. I, pp. 147–52, 291–7.

[65] Quoted in Joseph Bollery, *Léon Bloy*, vol. I, pp. 227–30.

[66] Ibid., I, p. 173.

[67] Bloy, *La Femme Pauvre*, 1897, Part I.

[68] See Chapter Three for an examination of these theories.

[69] Bloy, *Le Salut par les Juifs*, p. 94.

[70] Ibid., p. 97.

[71] Ibid., pp. 110–13.

[72] *Le Vieux de la Montagne*, 2 January 1910.

[73] *Le Mendiant Ingrat*, 12 June 1892.

[74] *Le Désespéré*, Part II, pp. 80–1.

[75] Ibid., p. 67.

[76] Ibid., pp. 113–14.

[77] Robert Baldick, in his *Life of J.-K. Huysmans*, rightly points to the supreme importance of this doctrine in that author's work, and to the great influence of Boullan in the matter.

[78] *Sainte Lydwine de Schiedam*, 1901, p. 287.

[79] See *supra*, pp. 150–1.

[80] Huysmans, letter to Dom Thomasson de Gournay, 3 January 1898; copy in the possession of M. Pierre Lambert.

[81] *Sainte Lydwine de Schiedam*, p. 311.

[82] Huysmans, letter to Leclaire, 29 January 1904.

[83] *Sainte Lydwine de Schiedam*, p. 65.

[84] Ibid., pp. 64–5.

[85] Ibid., p. 104.

[86] Ibid., p. 112. My italics.

[87] Ibid., p. 49.

[88] Ibid., p. 44.

[89] Ibid., p. 49.

[90] Ibid., p. 49.

[91] See *supra*, p. 80.

[92] Ibid., p. 312.

[93] Reported by Caldain and quoted in Baldick, *Vie de J.-K. Huysmans*, p. 399.

[94] Huysmans to Leclaire, 14 December 1906.

[95] Huysmans to Leclaire, 25 December 1906.

[96] Huysmans to Myriam Harry, 5 January 1907; quoted in Myriam Harry, 'En mémoire de J.-K. Huysmans', *Revue de Paris*, May 1908, pp. 412–17.

[97] Huysmans to Leclaire, 2 February 1907.

[98] Reported by the abbé Daniel Fontaine and quoted in Baldick, *Vie de J.-K. Huysmans*, p. 399.

[99] Huysmans, *Sainte Lydwine de Schiedam*, p. 313.

[100] Ibid., p. 314.

[101] Retté, *Le Règne de la Bête*, 1908, p. 223.

[102] Ibid., p. 247.

[103] André Lafon, *La Maison sur la Rive*, 1914, p. 221.

[104] Ibid., p. 225.

[105] In Chapter Six.

[106] Baumann, *L'Immolé*, 1908.

[107] Ibid., p. 245.

[108] Ibid., p. 247.

[109] Ibid., p. 116.

[110] Ibid., p. 226.

[111] Ibid., p. 253.

[112] We shall see in Chapter Ten how, both in *L'Immolé* and *La Fosse aux Lions*, Baumann puts forward political and social ideas which are very much in line with other writers of the Revival.

[113] Baumann, *La Fosse aux Lions*, p. 123.

[114] Ibid., pp. 13–14.

[115] Ibid., p. 228.

[116] Ibid., p. 213.

[117] Ibid., p. 299.

[118] As did Lâla in *La Ville*, whose wandering from man to man is not depicted as being the result of any human impulse, but is used purely out of symbolic necessity.

[119] R. M. Griffiths, 'Claudel et Sainte Lydwine', in *Bulletin de la Société Huysmans*, no. 38, 1959, pp. 433–9.

[120] Miss Helen Trudgian's note on this subject in *French Studies* (1947) is most interesting; but it fails to take into account the fact that Claudel, at that stage of his life, was prepared to deny such influences as that of Huysmans with considerable vigour.

[121] See Baumann, *Les Douze Collines*, 1929, p. 56.

[122] Words of Pierre Claudel to the author in 1958; quoted in article 'Claudel et Sainte Lydwine'.

[123] Claudel, *Le Repos du Septième Jour*, Act I; Pléiade, Théâtre I, p. 804.

[124] Ibid., p. 815.

[125] Ibid., p. 845.

[126] *La Jeune Fille Violaine* (second version), Act 1; Pléiade, Théâtre I, p. 573.

[127] Ibid., p. 575.

[128] Ibid., p. 577.

[129] Ibid., p. 580.

[130] Ibid., p. 630.

[131] *L'Annonce faite à Marie*, Act I; Pléiade, Théâtre II, p. 30.

[132] Ibid., p. 18.

[133] Ibid., p. 31.

[134] Huysmans, *Sainte Lydwine de Schiedam*, p. 293.

[135] *L'Annonce faite à Marie*, Act III; Pléiade, Théâtre II, p. 75. My italics.

[136] Ibid., p. 105.

[137] Ibid., p. 104.

[138] Ibid., pp. 32–3.

[139] *La Jeune Fille Violaine* (Second Version), Act III; Pléiade, Théâtre I, p. 621.

[140] Ibid., p. 621.

[141] *L'Annonce faite à Marie*, Act IV; Pléiade, Théâtre II, p. 89.

[142] Ibid., p. 75.

[143] Ibid., p. 121. My italics.

[144] Louis Massignon wrote to me, after reading my article on this subject: 'Claudel s'est trahi en empruntant le *motif* du "lait, la nuit de Noel" (introuvable dans Ste. Gertrude, Ste. Mechthilde, Margaretha Ebner, quoi qu'il en dise à Amrouche). — C'était avouer, en fait, qu'il avait emprunté à "Lydwine" l'idée de la substitution compatiente, *thème* huysmansien.' Note from Massignon, 18 February 1960.

[145] Pléiade, Théâtre I, p. 616.

[146] Ibid., p. 618. My italics.

[147] *L'Otage*, Act II, Sc. 2; Pléiade, Théâtre II, p. 266.

[148] Ibid., p. 265.

[149] Ibid., p. 268.

[150] Ibid., p. 269.

[151] Ibid., p. 269.

[152] Ibid., p. 289.

[153] Ibid., p. 270.

[154] Ibid., p. 271.

[155] Bloy, *Le Désespéré*, Part II.

[156] Péguy, *Toujours de la Grippe*, 5 April 1900; Pléiade, Prose I, pp. 192f. My italics.

[157] Péguy, *Jeanne d'Arc*, 1897, Act II; Pléiade, Poetry, p. 36.

[158] Ibid., pp. 36f.

[159] This is very close to Bloy's statement on this subject, in *Le Désespéré*.

[160] Ibid., pp. 40f.

[160a] The passage in question *does* occur in *Le Mystère de la Vocation de Jeanne d'Arc*, which comprises in fact the passages which were cut out of the 1910 *Mystère de la Charité*, and which were published by the author's sons in 1925. The fact that this continuation *was* cut out (Peguy actually tore a page of the manuscript in two in order to effect the cut), shows clearly the author's changed intentions. Miss Servais' contention, in *Charles Péguy – The Pursuit of Salvation*, that this continuation showed Jeanne 'after a heart-rending struggle ... at last accepting the dogma of damnation,' is not borne out by the text.

[161] Péguy, *Mystère de la Charité de Jeanne d'Arc*, 1910; Pléiade, Poetry, p. 517.

[162] Ibid., pp. 519–20.

[163] Bloy, *Le Désespéré*, Part II.
[164] Marcel Péguy, *Le Destin de Charles Péguy*, Perrin, 1941.
[165] Graham Greene, *Brighton Rock*.

PART FOUR

Reaction

CHAPTER NINE

Escape from the Modern World

The Bourgeois Society

The Catholic authors of this period had the sense of being in exile. In the sphere of thought they seemed to be cast adrift on a boundless sea of rationalism, positivism and materialism, and in everyday life they saw around them a bourgeois society formed by those ideas, a society for which the ethics of the Second Empire were still operative and in which a man, an idea or a creed were all to be weighed on the scales of material gain. Disgust with this society is clearly expressed in almost all the authors of the Revival. Materialist philosophy was responsible for a reaction in many people which led to their conversion, and most of those who had so been converted would agree with Claudel's judgement as expressed in *Le Repos du Septième Jour* (1896). In this play the Emperor, visiting hell, is brought to the circle in which dwell the 'contemplators of matter'. The demon who is guiding him describes their fault and their punishment thus:

> De toutes les choses qui existent par le poids, le nombre et la mesure,
> Ils ont étudié les lois, les rapports et les propriétés,
> *Et niant qu'ils fussent distincts de la matière où ils adhéraient,*
> possesseurs de la science aride, c'est ainsi qu'ils se sont joints à la pierre.
> Ce petit trou qu'ils se sont creusé et dont leur corps est la mesure est la chose qu'ils savent;
> Et là pour l'éternité ils cuisent.[1]

The nullity of this materialist philosophy is shown by Besme's despairing realisation, in Claudel's *La Ville* (second version, 1897), of the inevitability of death, in the face of which he is forced to conclude that nothing exists, 'Rien n'est'. The destruction of the philosophy of materialism is seen as comparatively easy; but the destruction of the society formed by that philosophy is far more difficult, and the anarchist Avare, moved by bitter hatred, is

225

forced to conclude that no solution save that of force is possible.

This sense of futility in the face of an apparently all-powerful and unchangeable society moved many authors of the last decades of the nineteenth century to dabble in anarchism, so much in the air at the time.

The anarchists had originally been members of the Socialist International, but had been expelled by Marx and Engels. Their philosophy, stemming from the Russian Bakounin (d. 1876), had been one of a rejection of political action or of gradual change in the cause of destruction of the bourgeois society, on the ruins of which a new order could be founded. In France, they stood apart from the various cliques of the socialist movement, scorning equally the utopian claims of Jules Guesde and his followers, whose optimistic 'minimum programme' was unrealistic in the extreme, and the compromising mentality of such 'possibilists' as Benoit-Malon or Brousse, whose aim seemed to be 'slow and feasible change'. To the anarchist all these warring factions were equally wide of the mark in that they all conceived the ultimate end as having some relation to society as it then existed. Guesde was willing to countenance violence, but he would have used it in order to obtain control of the State, which he could then change in accordance with his socialist ideas. For the anarchist it was impossible to change the State enough, so corrupt was it. What was needed, the extremists among them felt, was a purification by fire and blood.

In France, the great years of terrorist anarchism were the late '80's and the early '90's, culminating in the series of acts of bomb-throwing terrorism performed by Ravachol in Paris in the years 1891–2. Ravachol was duly executed, and on 9 December, 1893, another anarchist, Vaillant, threw a bomb into the Chamber of Deputies; and in June 1894 President Carnot was stabbed by an Italian anarchist, Caserio. The violent police action taken as a result of all this was probably one of the main reasons why so little was heard of anarchism after this date. Another was the public reaction brought against anarchism by the dastardly crime of Émile Henry (1894), who wounded over twenty people in a bomb outrage in a café.

It can hardly be said that the literature of the time boasts many true anarchists, but certainly many authors dabbled in this revolutionary creed, some from conviction, some from a sense of

the dramatic and some from a sense of what was fashionable.
If Huysmans's interest was mainly a dilettante one, as is probably
the case, Claudel's appears to have been far more serious. The first
version of *La Ville* (1890) is not only a denunciation of the bourgeois society, the details of which at times bring one close to Zola;
it is also a work of profound anarchist influence, in which the only
answer to the hideous nature of the city appears to be its destruction. In his *Conversations dans le Loir-et-Cher* (1925), Claudel says
of his attitude at the time of writing this play, 'Personne n'a humé
avec plus de délice le bon air d'anarchie qu'on respirait en France
dans les années 90.'[2] It was in common with most of his friends,
he tells Jean Amrouche in his *Mémoires Improvisés* (1954), that he
had this sympathy for the anarchists, a sympathy which he now
admits with some confusion: 'Je trouvais dans l'anarchie un geste
presque instinctif contre ce monde congestionné, étouffant, qui
était autour de nous, et à l'égard duquel ils faisaient un geste,
presque celui du noyé qui cherche de l'air, jetant des bombes au
hasard, sans presque savoir où.'[3]

To a certain extent, Claudel's attitude at this stage might seem
purely that which he described to Henri Guillemin in 1942: 'une
espèce de rage anarchiste. Joie de m'imaginer tout cela s'écroulant,
volant en l'air, dans l'explosion et l'incendie'.[4] But already, in both
versions of *La Ville*, this destruction is depicted not merely as a
joyful act of despair but as the necessary means for a reconstruc-
tion of society on a Christian basis. This comes out far more clearly
in the second version of the play than in the first. Coeuvre, the
poet, has become a bishop; and, commending the men of the city
to God, he says:

> O Dieu, accepte ces mains sanglantes! accepte ces sacrifi-
> cateurs!
>
> Car ils ont fait une besogne qui t'est agréable, abattant la
> Bête qui était assise entre les collines, la cité d'Hénoch, le
> monstre du Rêve horrible et laborieux,
>
> L'hydre grouillante, la Ville vomisseuse de fumée! Et main-
> tenant, à la place du cri informe,
>
> Voici la révélation de la parole proférée; à la place des songes,
> La vérité, et la réalité de ce qui est.[5]

In several of these early plays of Claudel one finds this theme of
destruction; in *L'Échange* (1894), for example, the house of the
millionaire, Thomas Pollock Nageoire, is burned down with all his

possessions inside it. In the exultation of his mistress, Lechy
Elbernon, we find again the theme of purification by fire, and in her
extension of this fire to all capitalist society we glimpse again the
anarchist conception of complete destruction:

> C'est moi qui ai mis le feu à ta maison, Thomas Pollock, et ta
> fortune s'en va avec la fumée épaisse et jaune, et voici que tu
> n'as plus rien!
>
> Hourra! Hourra!
>
> Servantes, mettez le feu à la maison afin de la nettoyer! que
> tout ce qui peut brûler brûle!
>
> Que la manufacture brûle! que la récolte brûle quand on l'a
> mise en meules! que les villes brûlent avec les banques,
>
> Et les églises, et les magasins! et que l'entrepôt mammouth.
>
> Pète comme une pipe de rhum![6]

Similarly, in the early play *Tête d'Or* (1889), the hero, in order to
bring in the new régime, had to kill the king, the symbol of the
old order.

For Claudel, in these early plays, anarchism appears to be compatible with a form of revolutionary Christianity. Supported as it
was by a reading of the Old Testament prophets, this belief seems
nevertheless gradually to have disappeared from his works, until
later the idea of change becomes transformed into that of a gradual,
historical change in which Christianity must at each stage accept,
and attempt to adapt itself to, the new situation, adapting its mode
of attack at the same time. While Claudel's political views, like
those of so many other Catholic authors, had become by this later
stage intransigently right-wing, he was nevertheless prepared to
serve dutifully in the diplomatic service of the French Republic;
and in *L'Otage*, *Le Pain Dur* and *Le Père Humilié* he depicts
historical change as a gradual process, at each stage of which the
Christian religion has a part to play.

Claudel's case is not typical of Catholic writers of his time,
either in the early acceptance of anarchist formulae or in the later
sensible acceptance of a society within which the Catholic must
work. But his case is illuminating for these very reasons. Anarchism should have been, and was, anathema to Catholic writers,
firstly because of its connection with extreme left-wing, atheist
ideas, and secondly because of the essentially unchristian nature of
the doctrine of universal destruction. Yet it expresses (and the
example of Claudel shows us this only too clearly) the same

exasperation with the bourgeois capitalist society of the late nineteenth century which the Catholics also felt. As Huysmans said:
'Au fond, si l'on n'est pas pessimiste, il n'y a qu'à être chrétien ou
anarchiste; un des trois pour peu qu'on y réfléchisse.'⁷ The
Catholics had many different reasons for feeling this hatred and
exasperation; but the violence of the feeling was the same. Nor
must it be thought that the fate of the poor was not among the
Catholics' concerns. Time and again the misery of the working
population is stressed in Catholic works of the period. But on the
whole this concern for the poor did not turn these writers so much
towards socialism as towards a traditional, paternalistic form of
society such as they believed to have existed before the terrible age
of materialism.

The essential incompatibility of anarchism and Catholicism can
be seen in Adolphe Retté's novel *Le Règne de la Bête* (1908). Retté
himself had been at one stage an anarchist, as we learn from his
books *Du Diable à Dieu: Histoire d'une Conversion* (1907) and *La
Maison en Ordre: Comment un Révolutionnaire devint Royaliste*
(1923). But his sudden conversion showed him the error of his
ways, and in *Le Règne de la Bête* there is a severe criticism of the
materialistic society of the age, in which Retté claims that anarchism, though it is a gesture against this society, is in fact a logical
product of the education which it provides. In the Preface Retté
points to individualism, that product of the French Revolution, as
the factor which has destroyed traditional religion, the family and
the taste for hierarchy and discipline. Charles Mandrillat, Retté's
hero, has no family ties whatsoever, and like many of Bourget's
heroes he is destroyed by the lack of the coherent moral code
which the Christian religion provides. Charles sees the ignoble
nature of society, so much of which is reflected in his own father,
and turns to the despairing doctrine of anarchism. We sympathise
with him in his despair, but we are made to hate the action which
he chooses; throughout the book his beliefs are opposed by the
author to those of Christianity, and in the hours before he attempts
a bomb outrage the impression he gives to those he meets is both
mysterious and 'satanic'. He has a tendency to good; this is shown
both by his hatred of nineteenth-century society and by the
hesitation which prevents him, at first, from throwing a bomb
among some people praying in Notre Dame: 'Je ne peux pas!...
Je ne peux pas!... Ces pauvres femmes, cet enfant, ce vieillard

en prière. Oh! non, c'est trop horrible. Je ne peux pas!...'[8] But eventually his ideas become stronger than his heart and he returns to the cathedral to throw the bomb. On his way in he is struck by the swing door and the bomb goes off prematurely, killing him.[9] The moral of the book, so often repeated during the story, is summed up in the last pages in the following manner: '... Ils sont des milliers à présent, dans notre pauvre pays, qui subissent une éducation analogue à celle de Charles. On ne veut plus de Dieu: on fait le vide dans les âmes. Puis l'on s'étonne que le démon s'y installe à la place de ce Dieu qu'on jette à la voirie parmi les outrages et les crachats.'[10]

So the Catholic, in his despair at the sight of the age in which he lives, is denied the desperate action of destruction; and, being a member of a minority group with little hope of any temporal power, he has little hope of this society being changed for the better. The political views of the Catholics of this period may be violent and intransigent, but this again is a defensive reaction, that of a minority threatened by powerful hostile forces. It seems impossible to change society radically enough by purely external action; even if the Catholics gained power they would be those Catholics of whom the intransigent authors of the Revival so thoroughly disapproved—the moderates, the compromisers, the men of politics, the sentimental Catholics of an age of woolly belief. So the Catholic authors tended to turn inwards, hoping to change this society by non-temporal means: by prayer, by vicarious suffering not just on behalf of individuals, but on behalf of the whole of corrupt society, and by the Christian example which they themselves might give. Parallel to this trend there was an immense nostalgia for a time when the world was different, and when society was nearer to perfection. This is expressed partly in longings for a traditional form of government, based on hierarchy and the family. It is most clearly expressed in the obsession which so many writers of the time had for the Middle Ages, not as they were, but as dreamed up by the Romantic view of history.

The Middle Ages, for them, represented the exact opposite of the nineteenth century: an age of absolute faith, that absolute faith which was also to make Islam so much of an influence on prospective converts of the late nineteenth and early twentieth centuries. It was also an age in which the Church itself was not only free from persecution but was also inwardly pure and whole, full of faith and free from any kind of taint. Before we study the cult of medievalism and the influence of Islam, we had perhaps better examine the shortcomings which the authors of the Revival found in the Church of their time.

The State of the Church

The Church was not only outnumbered and attacked on all sides; it was also, in the opinion of these authors, rotten in itself and far from the severe ideals of which their Christianity was made. Both clergy and laity were the epitome of mediocrity, whose approach to their religion was spoiled by an excessive sentimentalism and a desire to avoid the harsh realities of Christianity; they were ignorant and timid, in both spiritual and temporal matters; on the political side, many were trying to betray their Church from inside by attempts at compromise and understanding with their enemies; and the clergy particularly were inadequate, weak and sinful. Such are some of the accusations levelled by the authors of the Revival. There is much exaggeration in what they say, but the fact that they believed it at all is yet another symptom of their disenchantment with their own times.

Some of the most violent attacks came from Huysmans, Bloy and Drumont. Bloy particularly, in a vast passage of scorn and derision in Part Three of his novel *Le Désespéré* (1886), touches upon almost every aspect of the disgust we have described. Drumont, in the long indictment entitled *Le Clergé 'Fin de Siècle'* which makes up Book Four of his work *Le Testament d'Un Antisémite* (1891), touches mainly upon the more temporal drawbacks of contemporary Catholicism, but lets himself go in violently anticlerical denunciations. Huysmans, in opinions scattered throughout his novels, shows himself to be similarly wary of the clergy, but to be more concerned with religious than with political attitudes.

Bloy states the general opinion of many of these writers when he says that the opponents of the Church are far less dangerous and far less unpleasant than the appalling modern Catholics: 'Les catholiques modernes . . . sont devenus, en France, un groupe si fétide que, par comparaison, la mofette maçonnique ou anticléricale donne presque la sensation d'une paradisiaque buée de parfums.'[11] All the violence of the *'boue revolutionnaire et anticléricale'*, he says, is of little danger in comparison with the manner in which Christians are dishonouring their God. And Huysmans was to state time and time again his opinion that the persecutions of the Combes régime were a punishment from on high for an unworthy Church.

It is the mediocrity of contemporary Catholicism which creates, in their opinion, its faults. And one of the greatest examples of that mediocrity, on the religious level, is the distortion of belief effected by the influx of a weak sentimentalism. In their own attitude to Christian belief, which they held to be that of the Middle Ages, these writers saw a hard asceticism, a heroic acceptance of suffering and an intransigent intolerance of compromise. In the faith of those around them they saw a wishy-washy, well-meaning weakness, a comfortable playing-down of suffering and a perpetual desire to avoid clashes. This sentimentalism they find reflected everywhere in Church art and architecture and in Catholic literature. In the case of Bloy, Baumann and many others, the thing that they abhor is the distortion of belief; they describe with horror the sickliness of contemporary art but they would be equally willing to criticise the artists of the Italian Renaissance for their false religious emphases. As Bloy says: 'Qu'ils eussent ou non le talent divin qu'on a si jobardement exalté sur les lyres de la rengaine, ils n'en furent pas moins les matelassiers du lit de prostitution où le paganisme fornicateur vint dépuceler la Beauté chrétienne.'[12]

Similarly Huysmans, in *La Cathédrale*, contrasts the Middle Ages and the Renaissance, to the detriment of the latter, which he describes as the death of religious art: 'Il fallut l'époque interlope, l'art fourbe et badin du paganisme, pour éteindre cette pure flamme, pour anéantir la lumineuse candeur de ce moyen âge où Dieu vécut familièrement, chez lui, dans les âmes, pour substituer à un art tout divin un art purement terrestre.'[13]

The art of their own time was, however, far below that of the Renaissance. It was summed up by the 'bondieuseries de la Place Saint-Sulpice', the *objets d'art* sold in the little religious shops in that area, which were not only aesthetically displeasing—a recurrent theme of Huysmans's pre-conversion writings, such as the novel *Les Soeurs Vatard*—but also theologically indefensible. Bloy describes the sentimental view of suffering which such shops promulgated:

Aujourd'hui, le Sauveur du monde crucifié appelle à lui tous les peuples à l'étalage des vitriers de la dévotion, entre un

Evangéliste coquebin et une Mère douloureuse trop avancée. Il se tord correctement sur de délicates croix, dans une nudité d'hortensia pâle ou de lilas crémeux, décortiqué, aux genoux et aux épaules, d'identiques plaies vineuses exécutées sur le type uniforme d'un panneau crevé. . . .[14]

He goes on to describe the sweet Virgins, the enamel, beribboned Immaculate Conceptions of Lourdes, and the whole crowd of domesticated, insipid Saints which were on sale everywhere. Similarly Émile Baumann, in his book *L'Anneau d'Or des Grands Mystiques* (1924), was to scorn 'un Sacré-Coeur bellâtre, douce-reux, à la chevelure savamment ondulée, exhibant au milieu de sa poitrine un coeur irréel, et dont la mine comme l'attitude semble vouloir faire oublier l'Homme de toutes les douleurs, *l'Ecce Homo* coiffé d'épines, le supplicié tordu sur un gibet.'[15]

This religious art infects especially the great places of pilgrimage, such as La Salette and Lourdes. As Huysmans was to say of La Salette, 'Jamais cet effroyable appétit de laideur qui déshonore maintenant l'Eglise ne s'était plus résolument affirmé que dans cet endroit.'[16] At Lourdes he is forced to the conclusion that there must be something Satanic in this dishonouring of God:

La laideur de tout ce que l'on voit, ici, finit par n'être pas naturelle, car elle est en dehors des étiages connus; l'homme seul, sans une suggestion issue des gémonies de l'au-delà, ne parviendrait pas a déshonorer Dieu de la sorte; c'est, à Lourdes, une telle pléthore de bassesse, une telle hémorragie de mauvais goût, que, forcément, l'idée d'une intervention du Très-Bas s'impose.[17]

He goes so far as to say that one is worshipping Satan when one portrays Christ or the Virgin in so ugly a way as do the creators of *bondieusarderies*, and he is almost prepared to think that the Jewish race, which is so responsible for the selling of these objects, is involuntarily pushed by a desire to betray the Messiah once more.

Much religious literature of the time reflects this torrent of sentimentalism. Bloy provides a long list of such sentimental titles and wonders whether even Sodom and Gomorrah would not appear more holy than this 'cloaque d'innocence'. The stupidity of these works, he says, corresponds to the stupidity of their titles: 'Bétise horrible, tuméfiée et blanche! C'est la lèpre neigeuse du sentimentalisme réligieux, l'éruption cutanée de l'interne purulence accumulée en une douzaine de générations putrides qui nous ont transmis leur farcin!'[18]

For both Bloy and Huysmans the type of the popular religious writer of the day was Henri Lasserre, 'un commis-voyageur dans la piété,'[18] whose book on Lourdes, *Notre-Dame de Lourdes*, was exactly the type of book to appeal to the *bien-pensants*. Huysmans even wonders whether it may not have been part of the design of God to use an 'American' type of publicity, and to choose a writer for this purpose who, because of his many faults, was bound to appeal to the Catholic public of the day: 'Pour que cette oeuvre soulevât les masses, il fallait que l'écrivain désigné pour cette besogne fût un arrangeur habile et aussi un homme qui n'eût aucun style personnel, aucune idée neuve. Il fallut un homme qui fût sans talent, en un mot.'[19]

Lasserre sums up one type of fault, but it is the writings of the clergy which, for Bloy, sum up another form of mediocrity, the ignorance and self-sufficiency of the contemporary Church. Clergy and laity are bigoted and blinded by this ignorance and drive from their midst those original minds (i.e. the authors of the Revival) who strive to see Christianity anew, in its original simplicity and strength. This ignorance was based, essentially, on the bad education the clergy received. As Huysmans says in *La Cathédrale*, 'Cet état d'infériorité, à quoi tenait-il? . . . Au système d'education, aux cours de timidité intellectuelle, aux leçons de peur qu'on leur donne dans une cave, loin de la vie ambiante et loin du jour.'[20] Their ignorance is not confined to things religious and artistic; it is above all noticeable in the world of politics and social change. Drumont describes the way in which priests write to him for advice about the social question; often they have never heard of Proudhon, Lassalle or Karl Marx.[21]

The lessons the clergy give, however, are those demanded by the laity of the day. Huysmans, though he wails at 'l'ignorance du clergé, son manque d'éducation, son inintelligence des milieux, son mépris de la mystique, son incompréhension de l'art,'[22] is nevertheless forced to admit, in the first pages of *En Route*, that any other form of priest would be ignored by the multitude. But which came first, the chicken or the egg? Whatever the answer to this, we can see in the attitude of most of the writers of the Revival the feeling that 'the purgatory of converts is to live among the Catholics'.

The clergy's ignorance is merely one among many vices attributed to it in the wave of anti-clericalism which characterises the works of the Revival. Catholic anti-clericalism is no new thing; it has been present at all stages of the Church's progress. But rarely has it been so wide-reaching and violent as in this period. Some writers, Psichari and Retté, for example, deny the faults ascribed to the clergy, and their haste to do so shows the weight of feeling which had been raised even within the Church. Almost all the Catholic writers know priests whom they value and trust, but such priests are treated as blessed exceptions to a common rule, and Péguy's mistrust of the 'curés' is not merely a hangover from his socialist days.

Priests are accused of vacillation and lack of faith, of misunderstanding of contemporary problems, of siding with the rich against the poor and with the government against the Church; and, worst of all, of sexual sin and love of money and honours. They are, at their best, apathetic, and at their worst, satanic. The authors of this period welcomed the revelation by Mélanie of the secret confided to her by the Virgin at La Salette.[23] The public statement of the Virgin, when she appeared to Mélanie and Maximin in 1846, had been a general lamentation and prediction of disaster; the reasons for divine punishment were given as being profanation of the Sabbath and blasphemy. But the Virgin also entrusted a secret to both Mélanie and Maximin, telling Mélanie that she might make hers public in 1858. A great deal of this secret, when finally divulged in 1879, was found to be a violent attack on the priests of God, who, by their bad lives, their irreverence and impiety, their love of money, honour and pleasure, had become 'des cloaques d'impureté.'

This revelation reinforced the latent anti-clericalism of the epoch and was used to support the allegations of the Catholic writers, many of which were true. A mistrust of the priests of God, such as these writers showed, can be a healthy thing; as Monseigneur Dupanloup is quoted by Drumont as saying, 'Il est bon de laisser juger les évêques. Cela est bon pour tous, cela est bon pour les évêques, bon pour l'Eglise, bon pour le pays, bon pour la dignité des moeurs et des caractères.'[24] Drumont himself states, perfectly correctly, that writing the truth about bishops does not prevent one from believing humbly and faithfully everything which the Church teaches. Those who had the privilege of the friendship of

Louis Massignon will remember the verve of his criticism of the priests of the Church, which in no way diminished the fervour of his belief or the immense impression of uprightness which he made upon the listener. 'Il n'est pas interdit,' Massignon used to say, 'de dire ce qu'on pense d'un cardinal.' And he, too, felt his wrath to be justified by Mélanie's revelations. Of Marie-Antoinette he wrote: 'Plus que Jeanne d'Arc, mourant "par" un Evêque, Marie-Antoinette "déshonorée *par*" un Cardinal, est l'annonciatrice apocalyptique de la divulgation de secret tant reprochée, soixante ans plus tard, à une voyante dauphinoise: les prêtres sont devenus des *cloaques* d'impureté.'[25]

Only too often, however, in the mouths of other writers of the pre-1914 period, allegations were formed which had no basis at all. Moreover, in the case of Drumont, for example, these allegations were based on what were basically unchristian assumptions. Of the torrent of abuse which Drumont pours upon the contemporary Church in his *Le Clergé 'Fin de Siècle'*, many of the general statements appear to be justified, if one considers the Revival's conception of the action required of the Church, but many of the individual accusations appear to be hysterical and unreliable, particularly when one places them in relation to what one knows of those who are being attacked. Drumont even took disagreement with and disavowal of his own opinions by the clergy to be signs of cowardice or dishonesty.

Drumont's two main reasons for attacking the clergy are, however, in harmony with those of most of the other writers of the Revival. The first is the lack of opposition they show to anti-Catholic forces, and their capacity for compromise; the second is their attitude towards the poor.

The first of these opinions is completely in accord with the violence of Revival feelings, in which any attempt at compromise is seen as betrayal. Huysmans refers to Catholics faced by the law on the Congregations in 1901 as an 'amas de sottise et de lâcheté';[26] and Drumont's description of the frivolity of the Catholic laity and the cowardice of the clergy in the face of the persecutions of ten years earlier fits in with the same picture. For Drumont, the example of Germany showed Bismarck being forced to back down in his *Kulturkampf* because of brave opposition by the Churches. But he can see no such opposition being possible in France, because of what he presumes to be the cowardice, and love of money and honour, of the prelates. In this world of 1891, fourteen years before the separation of Church and State, he sees all the benefits which could accrue from such a law; for the bishops of his time, nominees of the government, seem to him to be chosen because they are men who will obviously make no trouble. He sees the ordinary clergy as being much more acceptable than the bishops and much more intransigent in their ideas, and he gives many examples of the way in which the lower clergy and Catholic writers are penalised by the bishops of the very Church which they are supporting.

Péguy, in his essay *De la Situation Faite au Parti Intellectuel dans le Monde Moderne* (1906) refers to the Church's policies as 'la politique de Néarque', the attitude of the character in Corneille's play *Polyeucte* who stands for moderation and compromise and who is contrasted with the blinding faith of the hero, Polyeucte. In its fear of treading the heroic path, Péguy declares, the modern Church is treating the path of Néarque and pursuing a policy of appeasement:

> Une politique d'effacement du scandale et qu'il soit bien entendu que c'est une affaire arrangée, et que l'on n'en parlera plus, une politique de mutuel honneur et de modestie et de silence. . . . De sorte que l'on pourrait plutôt lui reprocher de manquer de dignité, que de bonté . . . de manquer d'un certain sens et de la revendication de sa propre grandeur.[27]

For most, the Church has brought its fate on its head through weakness; for some, it has done it by mixing itself too freely in politics. But both these opposed views come to the conclusion that much of the situation is the Church's own fault.

Amidst the torrent of abuse which he pours on the clergy in his book on La Salette, *Celle qui pleure* (1908), Léon Bloy quotes a formula originally stated by the philosopher Blanc de Saint-Bonnet: 'Le clergé saint fait le peuple vertueux, le clergé vertueux fait le peuple honnête, le clergé honnête fait le peuple impie.' When he had quoted the same formula in his indictment of the Church in *Le Désespéré* (1886), his target had mainly been the tepidity of Catholic belief and its distortion by the influence of sentimentalism; and he was prepared to feel that one had reached the last stage of Blanc's formula: an honest but mediocre clergy. In *Celle qui pleure*, however, he sees the formula as already outdated; for him, the clergy are now the scum of the earth, and nothing shows this so much as what he considers to be their double-dealings in attempting to hush up the message of La Salette.

The clergy were attacked on almost every point by these authors; but the main grievance seems to have been that the clergy had sided openly with the bourgeois capitalist society of the day, the materialist society of which the Catholic writers had such horror. On a low level, this was seen in the love of money ascribed to the priests. Huysmans, writing in a letter to his friend Leclaire about what he considered to be a typical piece of Church action, says: 'Ils me font penser à la Salette. Dès qu'il y a de l'argent en jeu, l'infâmie sort comme un pus et du clergé et des cloîtres.'[28]

This acceptance of bourgeois values had also led the Church to neglect the poor. Only too often the Church had become, in Péguy's words, a 'religion pour "grandes personnes" ' in which the parishes were full of 'bourgeois éclairés'.[29] Both Bloy and Péguy, in their overriding concern for the poor, are naturally to be expected to hold such opinions. But it is somewhat surprising to see the unanimity with which their opinions are shared by the other authors of the Revival. Huysmans, for example, is convinced that it is this love of money which is keeping the poor out of the Church; speaking of the poor to Dom Besse, he says: 'Quand voient-ils le prêtre? Au moment d'un baptême, d'un mariage ou d'un enterrement, c'est-à-dire quand il faut passer à la caisse de la sacristie. Faites leur croire, après, que la religion n'est pas une affaire d'argent!'[30] Drumont sees in the desertion of the poor a reason for the Church's weakness: 'L'Eglise, en perdant le peuple, a perdu son trésor de dévouements toujours disponibles; elle s'est mise de plus en plus avec les riches.'[31]

Huysmans's last confessor was a priest of great sanctity, the abbé Daniel Fontaine, who devoted himself to a poor parish at Clichy in the north of Paris and became known as 'l'apôtre des chiffonniers'. After Huysmans's death Claudel was introduced to the abbé Fontaine by the intermediary of Louis Massignon and took him as his confessor; and in the two poems which Claudel devotes to him, *Notre-Dame Auxiliatrice* (1913) and *À la Mémoire de l'Abbé Daniel Fontaine* (1921), we see something of the same concern that the Church should devote itself to the poor.

So the Church has allied itself with bourgeois society, avoiding the poor and clinging to the rich, and accepting the values of the materialist world. Every stage of the Church hierarchy is criticised by one writer or another, and Rome itself does not escape condemnation. The methods of the Index are severally criticised, and even Pope Leo XIII is execrated by several writers for what they see as his attempts at compromise.

The state of the Church appears to most of these writers (Claudel is, on the whole, an exception) to be as appalling as the state of the world around it. In fact, the persecution of the Church by the French Government may well be God's punishment upon it; as Huysmans says, 'Je commence à croire que l'ignoble Combes est vraiment un agent de la Providence et que la persécution est nécessaire.'[32] But whether the attacks be inspired by God or Satan, the fact is that the Catholic writers found little consolation for the state of society when they looked at their own Church. Their stern faith, they felt, had nothing in common with the century they lived in. They were surrounded by a morass of filth: 'sale époque, sale saison, sales gens, sales prêtres,—sale tout.'[33]

Return to the Middle Ages

Medievalism can, at times, be merely a literary fashion. A taste for archaic phraseology, a Romantic view of the past, can produce delightful, stylised writing which is often as far from the language of the era it is imitating as from the era in which it is written. The archaisms which abound in the letters of many people living at the turn of the century are witty and amusing but far from the language of the Middle Ages, owing to the writers' desire to produce the quaint and the unusual rather than the true language of the period. It is pastiche, and often quite clever pastiche, but it is usually unconvincing by its very choice of the appealing, and at times it is unscholarly by its confounding of phrases from various stages of the development of the French language.

The authors of the Revival do not, in their works, play these linguistic games. Their medievalism is something far more profound and disturbing. But it has been useful to mention the contemporary fashion for medievalism because in its unreality it reflects the stylised view of the Middle Ages which the Catholic authors held. We have seen how history, for these men, was not so much a matter of knowledge as of intuition. And their intuition led them to vast generalisations about the Middle Ages which were as far from the truth as the pastiche of the 'mediévisants' was from the true language.

These writers tended to see in the Middle Ages all those things which they would have liked to see in their own day—a society ruled by faith, a Church ruled by orthodoxy and beliefs ruled by heroism and untainted by sentimentality. Bloy writes: 'Le Moyen Age . . . c'était une immense église comme on n'en verra plus jusqu'à ce que Dieu revienne sur terre, un lieu de prières aussi vaste que tout l'Occident et bâti sur dix siècles d'extase qui font penser aux Dix Commandements du Sabaoth.'[34] In that age, he continues, all men knelt before the Almighty, in adoration or in terror. Even blasphemers and murderers knelt before him, for there was no other possible attitude in the presence of the crucified Christ. It was a harsh age, the age of mourning for Christ, when everyone wept for mercy. It was an age when man could see his fate and his duty, when these were not hidden by the cotton-wool of a sentimental religion. Both Bloy and Huysmans saw a reflection of the heroism of this age, and of its true attitude to Christianity, in its art, which had been destroyed by the Renaissance and which had never recovered.

Huysmans, even before his conversion, had had this same impression of the hardness and confidence of medieval religion, and the softness of its modern counterpart. In his prose poem *L'Ouverture de Tannhäuser*, written in 1885 for the *Revue Wagnérienne* and later included in the 1886 edition of his *Croquis Parisiens*, he described the Pilgrims' Chorus in Wagner's opera as being 'sans effusions féminines, sans câlines prières s'efforçant d'obtenir par les hasardeuses singeries de la grâce moderne le rendez-vous réservé d'un Dieu.' The chorus rolls on 'avec cette certitude de pardon et cette conviction de rachat qui s'imposèrent aux humbles âmes du Moyen Age.'[35]

Later, in a passage in *Là-bas* about his autobiographical hero Durtal, Huysmans betrays the Romanticism of this conception of the age of absolute faith, in which everyone believed whole-heartedly in the same doctrine. Durtal has been talking with the master bell-ringer Carhaix, and his mind wanders, under the effect of this conversation, to the Middle Ages: 'Et sa rêverie subitement reculée de plusieurs siècles évoqua, parmi les lents défilés de moines au Moyen Age, la troupe agenouillée des ouailles qui répondait aux appels des angélus et buvait comme le dictame du vin consacré les gouttes flûtées de leurs sons blancs.'[36] This is a literary and artistic vision, with all the dangers which that implies; but it is very close to the conception of the Middle Ages held by Huysmans after his conversion, and by other authors of the Revival.

For them it was an age not only of abolute faith, in which even the most outrageous sinner, such as Gilles de Rais, was fully aware of the power and majesty of God, and in which his very victims, whose children he had destroyed, were prepared to pray for him in his hour of trial; in the words of Huysmans, 'en sa blanche splendeur, l'âme du Moyen Age rayonna dans cette salle.'[37] It was also an age of orthodoxy in belief, untroubled by the heresies of the modern age. (Anyone with the slightest knowledge of the Middle Ages will see the falsity of this picture.) Verlaine, rejecting the seventeenth century, cries:

Non. Il fut gallican, ce siècle, et janséniste!
C'est vers le moyen âge, énorme et délicat,
Qu'il faudrait que mon coeur en panne naviguât . . .
Et là que j'eusse part — quelconque, chez les rois
Ou bien ailleurs, n'importe, — à la chose vitale,
Et que je fusse un saint, actes bons, pensers droits,
Haute théologie et solide morale,
Guidé par la folie unique de la Croix,
Sur tes ailes de pierre, ô folle Cathédrale![38]

It was an age of Saints, and an age of suffering. And those medieval Saints who most impressed the writers of the Revival seem to have been either the militant defenders of the faith, such as St. Louis and Jeanne d'Arc, or the suffering saints, the 'compatientes', whose vicarious suffering could save the world. Huysmans's book *Sainte Lydwine de Schiedam* is merely a culmination of his overriding interest in the latter, which is expressed throughout his other Christian novels; and Bloy, Péguy, Claudel, Baumann and many others show an intense interest in these Saints, whose example fortifies them in their defensive tactics towards the corrupt society in which they live.

Unfortunately, a vicarious sufferer must have something to suffer for, and in an age of perfect faith such as the Middle Ages which these writers envisaged where could the faults be which these saints were expiating? The immense sequence of 'compatientes', and the extent of their suffering, could hardly have been directed at individual cases of sin; they *must* be expiating the crimes of the society in which they lived, and of the world as a whole.

This forced Huysmans into a view of the late Middle Ages, expressed in the opening pages of *Sainte Lydwine de Schiedam*, which is almost diametrically opposite to the other view, yet which, in its desire for absolutes, is equally false. 'L'état de l'Europe, pendant le temps que vécut Lydwine, fut effroyable,'[39] he writes in the first sentence of the book. And then, for more than thirty pages, he paints an appalling picture of the end of the fourteenth century. The flails of nature are matched by the turpitude of men, society itself is falling to pieces, and in the midst of all this the Church, torn by schism and heresy and full of unworthy priests, seems to be possessed by the devil. But it was at this moment, says Huysmans, that saints were provided who, by their prayer and their suffering, could do something to halt the flood. This picture is as wild as the other view of the Middle Ages; it seems impossible for Huysmans, or for the other writers of his age, to see things by halves, and they have no realisation that history can never be cut and dried in a simple manner.

Huysmans's picture of the fourteenth century is very close to that which he and others were painting of their own century. The society of the fourteenth century is depicted as utterly corrupt, and and in its evil it is seen to be 'crucifying the Holy Spirit'. And, to add to all this, the Church is seen as unworthy:

> Pour excéder la patience de Dieu, ceux qui lui furent consacrés s'en mêlèrent. Le schisme, soufflant en tempête, avait démâté les barques de sauvetage et les bateliers de Jésus étaient devenus de vrais démons. Il n'y a qu'à lire les sermons de Saint Vincent Ferrier, leur reprochant *leurs turpitudes*, les invectives de Sainte Catherine de Sienne les accusant d'etre *cupides* et *orgueilleux*, d'être *impurs* . . . pour se figurer le poids énorme qu'ils ajoutèrent à la balance de Justice, sur le plateau du Mal.[40]

These accusations, of heresy, of cupidity, of pride, of impurity, are the same as those levelled at the clergy of the late nineteenth century, and the reactions of the expiatory sufferers are the same as those demanded of modern Christians.

In Péguy's works, the Middle Ages play a very important part and the picture is once more one of a society ruled by faith. Saints, such as St. Louis, are matched by laymen such as Joinville who have their place in the Christian pattern, a subordinate but worthy place. Joinville, who refuses to say that he would prefer to contract leprosy than to commit mortal sin, is seen by Péguy not so much as a sinner, but as a necessary part of that mass of ordinary Christians against whom St. Louis's holiness may stand out. The mass of Christians, of *French* Christians, are seen as wholeheartedly taking part in the Crusade of God.[41] Jeanne d'Arc, too, sums up for Péguy many of the virtues of the Middle Ages in her love of action and her heroic faith.

But for Péguy these are not just the virtues of the Middle Ages; they are *the* Christian virtues, which must exist in any man for his salvation. These virtues were most clearly to be seen in the Middle Ages but there has been no change of fashion in true Christianity. It is for this that he rounds, in *Un nouveau théologien: M. Fernand Laudet*, on the idea that he, a man of the twentieth century, has tried to 'se refaire une âme du quinzième'.[42] Christianity, Péguy claims, is one, there are no different standards for different generations, and the fault of *this* generation is that it has lost the sense of Christian values which the Middle Ages had. Péguy sees himself, therefore, as being one of a minority in step, while everyone else is out of step. 'La chrétienté est une dans le temps, M. Laudet, le Christianisme est un, l'Eglise est une, la communion est une. C'est pour cela que le chrétien n'a aucunement, n'a nullement besoin d'avoir recours à un archaïsme d'âme.'[42]

All centuries, says Péguy, are centuries of faith. By this he means that true Christian faith is unchanging, however small the number of people who possess it. For the other writers of the time, too, there were examples of true Christian faith in their own period. For Bloy there was, above all, himself; and he describes Marchenoir, his autobiographical hero, as 'une espèce d'homme du Moyen Age'.[43] In the monasteries, too, Huysmans sees the faith of the Middle Ages living on (though after a personal experience of monastery life he is so disappointed by its failure to live up to his preconceived ideas of sanctity that, deciding that 'le cloître n'est beau qu'en rêve',[44] and that 'on y fait certainement moins son salut que dans le monde',[45] he turns on the monks for their mediocrity and describes them as lower than the lowest of the laity). In the simple faith of peasants Péguy, Bloy and Huysmans find an echo of the faith of the Middle Ages: Huysmans, observing a crowd of pilgrims who have walked for days to reach La Salette, is astonished to find, 'hors de la solitude absolue et hors des cloîtres . . . parmi cette population de paysans âpres et durs', examples of a simple, childlike faith,[47] and Bloy, seeing a crowd of miserable people praying together after appalling floods on the Loire, is taken back to the Middle Ages: 'Car ces hommes d'oraison, ces ignorants, ces opprimés sans murmure que méprise notre suffisance d'idiots, portaient, dans leurs coeurs et dans leurs cerveaux, la Jérusalem céleste.'[48]

Among all these authors looking back to the Middle Ages, Claudel stands out as an exception. He, too, feels himself in exile in a modern world; he, too, looks back to a better time. But though much of his heroic view of Christianity and his views on suffering can be seen to be in keeping with the medieval mystics whom he had read, and though the play in which these views on suffering are most coherently put forth, *L'Annonce Faite à Marie*, is set in the Middle Ages, that stylised Middle Ages which Huysmans portrays in *Sainte Lydwine de Schiedam*, nevertheless Claudel looks back, in much of his poetry and his theatre and certainly in his masterpiece, *Le Soulier de Satin*, to another heroic age, that of the Counter-Reformation. In that age the Church, accepting change on its own merits, had counter-attacked by adaptation of itself to its new needs, and by heroic onslaught. Claudel's militant Christianity is a reflection of this age.

The Influence of Islam

The attraction of Islam was something of far more importance and profundity than the false medievalism we have been describing. For whereas any view of the Middle Ages tended to be Romantic and imaginative and consequently something of a distortion of the truth, Islam was real and contemporary. Those people who were most influenced by it were those who had actually lived among the Muslims and had experience of their faith; and this influence was not so much an afterthought of Christian belief, a searching for what one already knew one wanted, as the cult of medievalism had been, but a shock which forced unbelievers into religious belief, when faced by an overriding faith such as they had not seen in their own country.

French colonialism in North Africa brought many men into contact with Islam, and a great many of the conversions to Catholicism which Islam produced were those of officers in the French colonial army. Charles de Foucauld, Henry de Castries and Ernest Psichari are three examples of this trend; two, Foucauld and Psichari, were brought from unbelief, and Castries was forced out of the tepid Christianity so typical of the age. The serene yet active faith of the Muslims, its completeness, bowled them over and started a process of re-evaluation which led them to a Catholic faith of equal intensity.

To their names, in this study, I would add that of Louis Massignon, another great convert of the era, in whom many of the more noble aspects of the thought of the Revival remained until his death in 1962. It was as a scholar that he came into contact with Islam; and much of his early life, lived among the Arabs, and his extensive studies of the Mohammedan religion, all brought him to a mystical and miraculous moment of conversion to the Catholic faith.

Charles de Foucauld, whose later career as a missionary in the desert and as the inspiration for the *Union des Frères et Soeurs du Sacré-Coeur* for the evangelisation of the colonies (commonly known as the *Petits Frères* and the *Petites Soeurs de Jésus*) does not need to be recalled to the reader, was born in 1858. After studying under the Jesuits in the years 1872–5 he lost his faith, as he thought, irrevocably. After studying at St.-Cyr he became a *sous-lieutenant* in the army in 1878. His life at this time was one of great disorder, and in March 1881, less than a year after his regiment's first visit to Africa, he was suspended from his post for misconduct and lack of discipline and sent back to France. Two months later, at the news of the outbreak of a revolt in the Sahara, he applied to be reinstated in the army, and then took part in the eight-month campaign which followed. Already, his friend General Laperrine tells us, the Arabs had made a great impression on him, and after the end of the revolt he applied for leave to go south and study them more closely. When the permission was not given, he resigned his commission and, after learning Arabic and Hebrew, set off in June 1883, disguised as a Moroccan Jew, to make a reconnaissance of the closed kingdom of Morocco. After great dangers he returned in May 1884, and four years later his scholarly work *Reconnaissance au Maroc* was published. Laperrine, in a study of Foucauld's conversion, states his conviction that it was this year in Morocco which broke down his scepticism, through the intimate view it gave him of the unbreakable faith both of Muslims and Jews:

> Sa vie d'un an au milieu de croyants convaincus . . . porta le dernier coup au scepticisme de Foucauld. Il admirait la force que tous les Marocains puisent dans leur foi, aussi bien ces musulmans

fanatiques que ces juifs restés inébranlablement attachés à leurs croyances, malgré des siècles de persécution; aussi à son retour en France avait-il 'soif de religion'.[49]

Whether this was the exact moment or not, certainly Islam exerted a profound influence on Foucauld, as he admits in a letter written many years later to Henry de Castries:

> Oui, vous avez raison, l'Islam a produit en moi un profond bouleversement . . . la vue de cette foi, de ces âmes vivant dans la continuelle présence de Dieu, m'a fait entrevoir quelque chose de plus grand et de plus vrai que les occupations mondaines: ad majora nati sumus. . . . Je me suis mis à étudier l'Islam, puis la Bible, et la grâce de Dieu agissant, la foi de mon enfance s'est trouvée affermie et renouvelée. . . .[50]

Phrases in the *Reconnaissance au Maroc* show Foucauld's lively interest in the Islamic faith, but naturally (for this would not come within the scope of the work) show no linking of this with Christianity. Nevertheless, on his return to France in 1886 he was already showing a desire for faith, and prayed that God might give it to him. In 1888, the year of the publication of the *Reconnaissance*, he was received into the Church. Already he felt within himself a religious vocation, and after a pilgrimage to the Holy Land he took vows as a Trappist monk in 1892. But even this did not satisfy his vocation for poverty and abjection, and he was already dreaming of the idea of a community of people who should live by the work of their hands and imitate the life of Christ at Nazareth. In 1896 he was released from his Trappist vows. He immediately swore new vows of perpetual poverty and chastity and in 1897 he left for the Holy Land, where he anonymously became a servant in the convent of Clarisses at Nazareth, living as the lowest of the low and perpetually inflicting on himself forms of mortification by humility. In 1900 he returned to France, and a year later he became a priest and obtained permission to go out to the Sahara. From them until his death in 1917, murdered by marauding Touareg, he remained in North Africa, evangelising the Arabs, and later the Touareg, by his example and his prayers.

Henry de Castries (1850–1927), Foucauld's great friend, had received the same profound impression from Islam a few years before Foucauld. Castries had never left the Christian faith, but he had allowed his faith to become that tepid sham which was shared by so many of his generation. His contact with Islam had been at first a shock of humility and hurt pride; as a young officer in the colonial cavalry he had seen his troops dismount for the communal prayer. He had felt inferior in the face of such sublime faith and his first reaction had been one of anger and shame:

> J'entendais, revenant sur un ton plus élevé, l'invocation: *Allah akber!* Dieu est plus grand! et cet attribut de la divinité prenait dans mon esprit un sens que toutes les démonstrations métaphysiques des théodicées n'avaient jamais réussi à lui donner. J'étais en proie à un malaise indicible, fait de honte et colère. Je sentais que, dans ce moment de prière, ces cavaliers arabes, si serviles tout à l'heure, avaient conscience qu'ils reprenaient sur moi leur supériorité. J'aurais voulu leur crier que, moi aussi, je croyais, que je savais adorer.[51]

This first impression, which must have occurred in the mid-seventies, was later to lead to his extensive study of Islam, the results of which were published in the book *L'Islam: Impressions et Études*. It was also to lead to a resurgence of Christian faith within himself, and in 1887 he left the army to go home to his native province and attempt to fight for religious rights in a time of dire government persecution.

Ernest Psichari, the grandson of Renan, despite the fact that he had been baptised in the Greek Orthodox rite at his grandmother's insistence, was brought up in the positivist education typical of the late nineteenth century. Born in 1883, he became very friendly with the Maritains when he was at the Lycée Henri IV, and through them met Péguy; none of these people, of course, were at that time Christians. After a disappointment in love he led a life of some disorder and excess. In 1903 he joined an infantry regiment as a regular; into this decision there entered a certain desire for order and discipline, as we see in his novel *L'Appel des Armes* (1913). He went on an expedition to the Congo under Colonel Lenfant, and, as one can see from his book *Terres de Soleil et de Sommeil* (1908), the continent of Africa was already exerting a strong pull on him. But it was his campaign in North Africa, from 1909 onwards, which brought him face to face with Islam. Already the ideal of order and discipline which he found in the army may have been bringing him towards Catholicism; already the effect of the desert in its beauty and solitude may have been inducing vague religious feelings; but it is Islam that appears to have been the catalyst. Much of Psichari's conversion is related in the posthumously published novel *Le Voyage du Centurion* (1915) and in his letters to his friends.

There are, however, already hints of it in *L'Appel des Armes*. In this early novel we find the young hero, like Henry de Castries, dumbfounded by the communal prayer of his Arab followers: 'Ah! quand, au crépuscule, les Maures se prosternent vers l'Est, comment ne pas ressentir ce grand souffle divin qui court d'une rive à l'autre du Sahara et fait dans la splendeur des solitudes une invisible présence?'[52] And like Castries the young Maurice wants to cry out that he, too, has a faith: 'C'était une folie. Mais il enviait ces gens que le doute n'a point effleurés, dont le coeur est resté pur et religieux. . . . Il aurait voulu leur crier, à ces Maures: 'Moi aussi, chers enfants, j'ai mes prières et j'ai mon Dieu!'[53] He feels that these men, at this moment, are on a higher plane than himself: 'A ce moment-là, il sentait l'âme de ses hommes plus haute que la sienne. Il souffrait de sa race devenue incapable d'adoration.'[54]

All this leads to a disgust with his own country and with its abject lack of belief. In a letter written to Péguy in 1910, Psichari refers to France's 'déchéance' and suggests that historians will have nothing to say about their epoch except that 'De 1890 à 19 . . . le commerce et l'industrie prospérèrent.'[55] He continually contrasts France and the Muslims, to the benefit of the latter. This feeling of inferiority is heightened by the effect of a remark made to him by a Muslim, an effect so strong that he repeats the remark in several of his letters, and in his novel *Le Voyage du Centurion*. He had pointed out to some Moors the futility of those who would resist the French, who were so immensely powerful; one of them had replied: 'Oui, vous autres Francais, vous avez le royaume de la terre, mais nous, les Maures, nous avons le royaume des cieux. . . .'[56] In the novel his hero, Maxence, tries vainly to quote the examples of holy monks and contemplative Saints, but realises that they too stand as a condemnation of his own lack of faith. This remark of the Moor must have had something of the effect on Psichari that Castries had felt when a Muslim had said to him, comparing French lack of religion and Muslim lack of business sense: 'Leurs affaires sont comme notre religion, leur religion comme nos affaires!'[57]

Islam had impressed Psichari, as it had Foucauld and Castries, by its simplicity and by its innate mysticism. Psichari confessed to Barrès the impression made on him by people completely cut off from the modern world he so hated, and who, even those with the most temporal occupations, all had a core of mysticism.[58] Despite all these influences upon him, which seemed to lead him to Christianity, Psichari did not at first feel himself touched by the grace truly to believe. But in early 1913 he finally entered the Church. In 1914 he was one of the first to be sent to the front, and was killed in August of that year.

Louis Massignon was born in 1883, son of the sculptor Pierre Roche, who was a friend of Huysmans. The young Massignon met Huysmans for the first time when he visited him at Ligugé in 1900. In common with Foucauld and Psichari, his life before conversion was in certain aspects wild and disorderly, and he often spoke, in later years, of his later life being an expiation for these sins of youth. Unlike Foucauld and Castries, who had been brought to make researches into the religion, language and topography of North Africa by their contact with the people, Massignon had begun his Islamic studies before he left France. When he first went abroad, to Morocco in 1904, it was to do research on the spot for a study he was making of the corporations in Fez in the sixteenth century. At one point his caravan was attacked and he was forced, revolver in hand, to take command of it himself. Betrayed by his European interpreter, he decided to learn Arabic more fully. Two years later, when his book was published, he sent it to Foucauld, whose topographical study of Morocco had been so useful to him. Foucauld replied saying he was praying both for Massignon's works and for his future life. At the time this meant little to Massignon. In this same year he went out to Cairo, to the Institute of Oriental Archaeology; and it was while he was there in 1907 that he read, by chance, the first mention of the figure who was to have so much influence on him—Al Hallaj, the Muslim mystic of the tenth century who had been crucified at Baghdad for having 'loved' God.

It was in the year 1908, after he had moved from Cairo to the less Europeanised Baghdad, that Massignon went through the mystical crisis which was to change his life completely. While in Cairo he had often disguised himself as an Arab in order to attempt to understand Islam more fully. Now, on an archaeological mission to find the ruins of Okheïdir, and in similar disguise, he was captured as a spy and condemned to death by the Turks. He once described to me the night of utter despair he passed, which was suddenly lit by the sense of the prayers of invisible witnesses being offered up for him. Among these were Charles de Foucauld, Hallaj, Huysmans, and Massignon's own mother. (It was only on his return to France that Massignon learned that his mother had, at that time, been praying for him at Lourdes, and that one of the last prayers of Huysmans had been for him.)

Freed by the good offices of his hosts, the Alussi of Baghdad, Massignon remained marked by his mystical experience. From now on he was filled with a blinding faith. He decided to devote his doctorate thesis to Hallaj, whom he believed to have been instrumental in saving him. But it was the Catholic faith to which he had been converted, despite the Muslim overtones of his belief; and throughout his life he was to retain a sense of the close relation between the two beliefs, which both worship the God of Abraham.

On his return to France in 1908, Massignon wrote a series of letters to Claudel, who was then in China, asking for advice. He wrote also, in November of that year, to Charles de Foucauld, whose letter of reply, dated 8 February 1909, expresses his joy at the good news of Massignon's return to the faith of his fathers. Massignon was already playing with the idea of being a monk, or even of following Foucauld to the desert. He asked Claudel what he thought of the idea of Benedictine oblature (which would enable him to carry on his work at the same time as being a member of the Order) but Claudel answered shortly that one could not be a 'demi-moine'. Foucauld began to see Massignon as his eventual successor in his desert community. But Massignon's confessor suggested to him, in 1912, that his call was to the new Muslim University in Cairo, to which he had been invited as a professor; and his marriage in 1914 prevented any last possibility of a life in the desert.

Massignon was perhaps the only convert of this period who was to retain his admiration and enthusiasm for Islam in its entirety. Even Castries, who shows such understanding of the Islamic faith in his book on the subject, was never involved in it as deeply as Massignon. And as for Foucauld and Psichari, they both, for different reasons, found themselves contrasting Christianity and Islam after their conversion, and deciding on the necessity of converting the Muslims to Christianity.

Foucauld, several years after the event, looked back upon his conversion and disclaimed that he had ever seen any truth in the Islamic religion: 'L'islamisme me plaisait beaucoup, avec sa simplicité, simplicité de dogme, simplicité de hiérarchie, simplicité de morale, mais je voyais clairement qu'il était sans fondement divin et que là n'était pas la verité.'[59] He stresses again and again that Islam may be seductive, but that Catholicism is true: 'L'islamisme est extrêmement séduisant: il m'a séduit à l'excès. Mais la religion catholique est vrai: c'est facile à prouver. Donc tout autre est fausse. . . . Or là où il y a erreur il y a toujours des maux. . . .'[60]

This is the argument from authority: the Church tells us the Church is right; *therefore* it is right; *therefore* Islam is wrong; *therefore* Muslims must be converted to the true faith. It is on the basis of this belief that Foucauld went to the desert. But his evangelisation would not be by the word; it would (in the true 'inward-looking' manner of the Revival) be 'l'évangélisation, non par la parole, mais par la présence du Très Saint Sacrement, l'offrande du divin Sacrifice, la prière, la pénitence, la pratique des vertus evangéliques, la charité.'[61]

For Psichari, the question is not one of truth and untruth. Rather, like Barrès, he believes in keeping to the religion of his fathers and of his country. In a letter to Madame Favre, the mother of Jacques Maritain, written in 1911, he stresses the importance of tradition in religion and sees the two religions as equal in all else but this: 'Sans doute, les deux religions sont égales, mais l'une est la nôtre, celle de nos pères, de notre race, et adaptée à notre race. L'autre n'a pour nous qu'une beauté intrinsèque, nullement utilisable.'[62] Islam has thus been useful in setting him on the path to religion, but it has helped him to the faith of his fathers. After his conversion Psichari's views are even stronger. In the last pages of *Le Voyage du Centurion* he contrasts Islam and Christianity and sees in the former servitude and discouragement and in the latter a consciousness of dignity and charity. The Muslims know the one God, he says, but they see him as an intellectual concept, where we see him as our father. (There is a certain amount of falsity in this contrast.) In a letter to Péguy, as early as 4 January 1912, Psichari had stressed that 'un mauvais chrétien est un chrétien, un bon musulman ne l'est pas', and in a letter to Monseigneur Jalabert, Bishop of Senegambia, written later in the same year, he dwelt on the necessity of converting the Muslims to Christianity.

Louis Massignon, in his admiration and understanding of the Islamic religion, sees us all as worshipping the God of Abraham. His relations with the Muslims were those of co-operation and understanding, and in his attempt to bring the two religions together he was a man well in advance of his times. The World Congress of Faiths, founded in 1934 by Sir Francis Younghusband, and its French branch, founded in 1946, and containing as members such Catholics as Etienne Gilson and Gabriel Marcel, is something which has fulfilled many of his most fervent desires.

In his study of Islamic beliefs, and particularly the 'heretical' doctrines of the *sufi* Al Hallaj, Massignon found much which supported and supplemented those beliefs which he found in his Catholic contemporaries. For Massignon the dead had as much importance as the living, and one often felt, when talking with him, that his intercessors, Charles de Foucauld, Daniel Fontaine, Huysmans, were as close to him as you were. It is to Islam, also, that he owed his conception of 'compassion'; Hallaj's doctrines reinforced his own belief in intercession and in vicarious suffering, which he had already gathered from his reading of Huysmans. And above all there is the conception of the 'vow', so central to Massignon's thought, and the idea of the duty to one's host.

It was in thanks to his friends the Alussi, who had delivered him from bondage, that Massignon had made a secret vow, in Arabic, to aid the Arab peoples. But no such vow would have been needed, so great was his sympathy with these peoples; and he shared the disgust of his friend and colleague Lawrence of Arabia when, after years of danger as agents of their respective governments, they both found these governments breaking the word they, the agents, had promised to their hosts. As they both entered Jerusalem with Allenby, Lawrence voiced his disgust to Massignon; and Massignon always believed that Lawrence had driven himself into obscurity 'de dégoût d'avoir été délégué chez les Arabes révoltés turcs que nous nous étions alliés, pour nous en servir, puis les lâcher, comme s'il était permis à un homme d'honneur de livrer ses hôtes.'[63]

For Massignon, Foucauld was similarly faithful to the conception of the guest. If a depot of arms was found at Foucauld's outpost after his murder, it could not have been because Foucauld had been breaking this rule. Foucauld had sworn never to have a firearm in his cell. It must be, Massignon thought, that Foucauld 'donnait ainsi à ses ennemis "dispense plénière de verser son sang", en immolation légale.'[64] His martyrdom, on behalf of the country in which he was living, could only have been obtained by this means.

The trouble is that Massignon attributed his own attitudes to those of his contemporaries who had any sympathy for Islam. And he could not see, in Foucauld, the many traits which were at variance with his own concepts. Massignon accepted Islam as a partner in religious thought, and was concerned, till the end of his life, with the similarities rather than the differences; Foucauld saw Islam as wrong and wished to convert it. Massignon was always concerned for the oppressed, the underdog, and in his last years made many protests about French Government action in Algeria; Foucauld was convinced of the French colonial mission and did all he could to help it.

In all this Foucauld was perfectly sincere. But the military information contained in his letters to General Laperrine is hardly an example of that 'fidelity to the host' preached by the Arabs. The *Echo de Paris* of 7 April 1920 is very near the truth when it says 'Le Père de Foucauld était là-bas notre meilleur agent de renseignements . . .', and the *Bulletin de la Société de Géographie du Maroc* adds to the picture, in 1924, when it describes Laperrine and Foucauld as having consecrated their lives to the 'rude labeur d'ajouter à la plus grande France ces immensités sans bornes.'

This is far from Islam; but it is not incompatible with a certain form of Christianity. Foucauld honestly believed, as did Psichari, in the holy mission of French colonisation, as bringing both civilisation *and* Christianity to the heathen. He was still a soldier, as was Psichari. His militant Christianity saw the conquest of these wastes, and the keeping of order within them once they had been conquered, as good, and so he co-operated with all means within his power. All the same, one is shocked at a man of God preaching such violence as he does on occasion; when, for example, he is furious that a rebel has not been shot,[65] or when he says that force must be shown at all costs.[66] And the following passage, from a letter written to General Laperrine on 31 July 1916, is surprising in its joy at the total destruction of a tribe, men, women and children (even if they were rebels): 'De l'Adrar, les nouvelles sont très bonnes. Les gens de Moussa ont tué Firhoun.

Voici dans quelles circonstances. Après avoir infligé à Firhoun un désastre terrible dans lequel la plus grande partie de son tribu, hommes, femmes et enfants ont péri. . . .'⁶⁷

Denise and Robert Barrat point out quite rightly in their book on Charles de Foucauld that identification of the cause of France with the cause of God was common among members of the Church before 1914. They also point out that Foucauld's knowledge of Islam was fragmentary and incomplete. Much the same might be said of Psichari.

Massignon, in 1913, had seen little of Foucauld, with whom he had corresponded a great deal, and had seen nothing of Psichari. When he found himself unable to follow Foucauld in his task, therefore, he invited Maritain and Massis to his house, to ask them if they would put to their friend Psichari the idea that he might take Massignon's place.⁶⁸ At this time *Le Voyage du Centurion* had not been published, and one can only imagine Massignon's relief, if he read the last fifty pages or so, that Psichari had not accepted this call.

Even more one can imagine the horror of Foucauld or of Psichari if they had been able to read Massignon's prayer to St. Joan of Arc on behalf of the Algerian Muslims, which was printed in 1956. This prayer, which castigated France and all colonial governments in the name of the Saint who had liberated France itself from oppression, shocked many people. But it is the perfect example of Massignon's capacity of detaching causes from their context, and seeing them in the light of eternity.

The reason for the impact Islam had on many people at the turn of the century was that it was a religion of pure faith, far from the tepid Catholicism of the *bien-pensants*, and even further from the godless society of the Third Republic. In most of these people it was merely a catalyst which turned them to a strong, durable faith in their own religion. But in Massignon, who went into it far more deeply, it remained a permanent part of his religious outlook.

The horror which they felt at the bourgeois society of their time did not turn Catholic authors to anarchism, nor even to socialism; but it must be realised that the basic reaction was the same, even if the methods chosen to combat the situation were very different. As the socialist leader Jean Jaurès once said:

Les uns se précipitent dans la mêlée socialiste pour en finir avec le monde ignominieux qui ne sait même plus racheter la douleur de l'exploité par la joie de l'exploiteur. Les autres, comme Huysmans, dédaigneux et meurtris, se réfugient de coeur et de pensée dans le cloître, dans la grande paix ardente du moyen âge mystique.[69]

In their despair at the state of contemporary society, therefore, and in their disgust at their own Church's attitudes, the authors of the Revival turned inwards, hoping that society might be saved by non-material means, by the spiritual effect of their sufferings and their example; and they turned backwards to a feudal concept of a society ruled by order. They turned, too, towards a romanticised vision of the Middle Ages, an era in which they saw that overriding faith, that Church-centred society which they would like to see in their own age. The attempts they made at solving the social problem were ruled by a similar Romantic attachment to things of the past.

It is this whole longing for a society ruled by faith which caused the influence of Islam, upon those who came into contact with it, to be so great. This influence was in most cases a temporary one; it bowled people over, and made them turn to faith; but the faith they turned to was Catholicism, the religion of their own country. With the exception of Louis Massignon, those who came to Catholicism in this way relinquished, as their Christian faith grew, any strong attachment which they had had to Islam.

NOTES

[1] Claudel, *Le Repos du Septième Jour*; Pléiade, Théâtre I, p. 832.

[2] Claudel, *Conversations dans le Loir-et-Cher*.

[3] Claudel, *Mémoires Improvisés*, p. 73.

[4] Quoted in Henri Guillemin, Claudel et Zola, in *Les Cahiers Naturalistes*, 1959, p. 526.

[5] Claudel, *La Ville* (second version, 1897); Pléiade, Théâtre I, p. 486.

[6] Claudel, *L'Échange* (first version, 1894); Pléiade, Théâtre I, p. 718.

[7] Huysmans, letter to Zola, March 1884.

[8] Retté, *Le Règne de la Bête*, Paris, 1908, p. 229.

[9] This is based on an actual happening in 1894, when an anarchist was 'hoist with his own petard' in the entrance of the Church of La Madeleine.

[10] Retté, *Le Règne de la Bête*, p. 244.

[11] Bloy, *Le Désespéré*, Part III, 'Le Retour.'

[12] Ibid.

[13] Huysmans, *La Cathédrale*, p. 112.

[14] Bloy, *Le Désespéré*.

[15] Baumann, *L'Anneau d'Or des Grands Mystiques*, Paris, 1924, p. 270.

[16] Huysmans, *La Cathédrale*, p. 8.

[17] Huysmans, *Les Foules de Lourdes*, Chapter 6.

[18] Bloy, *Le Désespéré*, Part III, *Le Retour*.

[19] Huysmans, *La Cathédrale*, 1898, p. 10.

[20] Ibid.

[21] Drumont, *Testament d'Un Antisémite*, 1891, p. 347.

[22] Huysmans, *En Route*, p. 186.

[23] See Appendix.

[24] Drumont, *Testament d'Un Antisémite*, p. 371.

[25] Louis Massignon, *Un Voeu et un Destin: Marie-Antoinette, Reine de France*, 1955, p. 13.

[26] Huysmans, *L'Oblat*, Chapter 10.

[27] Péguy; Pléiade, Prose I, p. 1033.

[28] Huysmans, letter to Leclaire, Paris, 28 April 1903.

[29] Péguy, *Un nouveau théologien: M. Fernand Laudet*; Pléiade, Prose II, p. 848.

[30] Quoted in Cogny, *J.-K. Huysmans à la Recherche de l'Unité*, p. 173.

[31] Drumont, *Testament d'un Antisémite*, p. 243.

[32] Huysmans, letter to Leclaire, 29 April 1904.

[33] Huysmans, letter to Madame Leclaire, 19 January 1899.

[34] Bloy, *La Femme Pauvre*, Part I, p. 131.

[35] Huysmans, *Croquis Parisiens*, second edition, 1886.

[36] Huysmans, *Là-bas*, 1891, Chapter III.

[37] Ibid., Chapter 18.

[38] Verlaine, *Sagesse*, 1880, I, 9.

[39] Huysmans, *Sainte Lydwine de Schiedam*.

[40] Ibid., p. 52.

[41] Péguy, *Le Mystère des Saints Innocents*.

[42] Péguy; Pléiade, Prose II, p. 905.

[43] Bloy, *La Femme Pauvre*, Part I.

[44] Huysmans, letter to Leclaire, 26 September 1898.

[45] Huysmans, letter to Leclaire, 14 July 1898.

[46] Huysmans, letter to Leclaire, 28 November 1903.

[47] Huysmans, *La Cathédrale*, Chapter 1.

[48] Bloy, *La Femme Pauvre*, Part I.

[49] Laperrine, 'La conversion d'un housard', in *Revue de Cavalerie*, October 1913.

[50] Foucauld, letter to Henry de Castries, 8 July 1901.

[51] Henri de Castries, *L'Islam: Impressions et Études*.

[52] Ernest Psichari, *L'Appel des Armes*, p. 289.

[53] Ibid., pp. 289 f.

[54] Ibid., p. 300.

[55] Psichari, letter to Péguy, 28 August 1910; printed in *Lettres du Centurion*.

[56] Psichari, *Le Voyage du Centurion*, p. 139. See also letter to Maurice Barrès, 15 June 1912, and letter to Mgr. Jalabert, 1912.

[57] Quoted in Jacques de Dampierre's introduction to his edition of the Foucauld–Castries letters.

[58] Psichari, letter to Barrès, 15 June 1912.

[59] Foucauld, letter to Castries, 14 August 1901.

[60] Foucauld, letter to Castries, 15 July 1901.

[61] Foucauld, letter to Castries, 23 June 1901.

[62] Psichari, letter to Mme. Favre, 2 July 1911.

[63] Louis Massignon, 'Toute une vie avec un frère parti au désert: Foucauld'; 1959; in *Parole Donnée*, 1962.

[64] Ibid.

[65] Foucauld, letter to Laperrine, 31 March 1912; Bibliothèque de l'Institut.

[66] Foucauld, letter to Laperrine, 1 June 1916; Bibliothèque de l'Institut.

[67] Letter printed in George Gorrée's selection of Foucauld's letters to Laperrine, Paris, 1954.

[68] M. Henri Massis has described to me this interview with Massignon, whom he had not met before. Massignon's immediate personal impact was, he says, tremendous (as it was on all who met him throughout his life); the three of them spent the day in prayer and silence together.

[69] *La Petite République Française*, 24 March 1895.

CHAPTER TEN

Traditionalism and the Social Question

Religion of Tradition, or Tradition of Religion?

Je ne sais pas et je refuse de savoir ce que c'est que le 'catholicisme moderne'. Je ne connais que le catholicisme éternel, celui des Apôtres et de tous les Saints, le catholicisme romain et traditionnel hors duquel il n'y a pas de salut. Assurément il est impossible d'être chrétien quand on rêve un autre catholicisme que celui-là, et j'ai le plus profond mépris pour les Judas et les fauteurs d'hérésies qui voudraient faire croire que je suis leur compagnon.[1]

This furious outburst by Léon Bloy was occasioned by a newspaper article in which he and Hello were described as the leaders of 'modern Catholicism' in France. Its violence shows the repugnance Bloy and others of his era felt for any change in what they regarded as the traditional doctrines of the Church.

This traditionalism in doctrine was matched by another traditionalist conception of the Church as the binding spirit which linked modern man to his forefathers and to the spirit of his country. These ancient values had been largely forgotten in the generation previous to this, argued many Catholic authors, and what was needed was for man to stretch out, over the head of his father, to his forefathers in whose traditional concepts of faith and patriotism lay the true path. In the formula stated by Psichari in his novel *L'Appel des Armes*, and taken up immediately by Péguy in *L'Argent Suite* (1913), the Catholics of the beginning of the century were a generation 'qui avait pris le parti de ses pères contre son père'.[2]

Throughout this period there is the same concentration on traditional values both in the spiritual and temporal fields. There is one vital question, however, similar to that with which we shall consider later in the context of order and discipline: to what extent did people embrace Christianity merely because it embodied these traditional values, and to what extent was belief in these values brought by religious faith? In the great majority of Catholic writers the two forms of belief are so closely intermingled that it would not only be difficult, but also unjust, to attempt to make a decision on this problem. All one can say is that for many their Catholic belief implied not only traditional moral values, but also a traditional concept of social life and of patriotism. It is with the first of these that the present chapter will be concerned.

It would have been unnecessary for those who were primarily concerned with traditional national and social values actually to become members of the Catholic Church. They could, like Barrès and Maurras, support it from outside, admiring in it the values they sought, but with no need to commit themselves further. No, we must take it that the average author of the Revival was not *primarily* concerned with the public utility of his faith, though, in the case of many, this utility was seen as one of the primary *consequences* of that faith. Their faith reinforced their social preoccupations, rather than *vice versa*.

To all this Barrès is the most prominent exception, though his attraction to the Catholic religion, as expressed in his *Cahiers*, is strangely moving and far from the dry, pragmatic reasonings of Maurras. Barrès was a man with a strong religious feeling, a feeling which was nevertheless vague in the extreme. He saw religion as something which linked man with 'la terre et les morts', a binding force which summed up the spirit of the nation. It was the tradition passed on by one's ancestors:

> Je ne sais pas la vérité de la religion, mais je l'aime. Le penchant de ma nature m'y incline. La religion répond à des besoins, à des idées qui sont en moi et qu'il n'appartient pas à ma raison de faire taire. Elle ne peut arrêter mon coeur s'il a reconnu sa joie, son concert.

> Voilà quelle maison je veux habiter. Il me suffit qu'elle vienne de mes ancêtres sans que je sache si elle me vient de Dieu.[3]

This sense of ancestral tradition, of Catholicism being the religion of the country, leads Barrès to a form of belief in which the ancestral gods of an earlier France—for example, the goddess Rosmertha in the novel *La Colline Inspirée*—can be seen as being closely linked with the Catholic faith which succeeds them. In the play about Joan of Arc which Barrès was intending to write in 1914 (possibly with the collaboration of Edmond Rostand), Joan was to be depicted as partly a Christian Saint, partly a prophetess of the Gauls. She was to be surrounded by pagan deities as well as Christian voices, and the whole was to be seen as a synthesis of the traditional religions, which, by their national identity, were in fact one. A note in Barrès's *Cahiers* shows us the intention: 'Bien marquer que Jeanne est la petite-fille de ces dieux et ne le sait pas. Son regard n'a jamais percé le mince regard de quelques générations qui la séparent de la foule de ses grand-mères païennes.'[4]

It was because Catholicism was the present religion of national tradition that Barrès defended it, and it was because he believed that this atmosphere was the only one in which it was possible to breathe that he threw so much weight into the balance on such questions as Catholic education and the safeguarding of the old churches of France. And his attraction to Catholicism was not purely utilitarian, as Maurras's so often seemed to be; as Barrès himself said, 'Ce qui distingue mon catholicisme de celui de Maurras c'est l'intériorité (chez moi).'[5] Certainly Barrès was continually worried by his own personal religious problems, as the frequent references to them in his *Cahiers* show. He was attracted towards a firmer belief than the vague religious feeling which permeated his thought, but was continually unable to tie himself down to a full consideration of the matter: 'Suis-je croyant? Suis-je athée? Voilà de bien grands problèmes que j'ai mal médités, que je n'ai pas jugés, tranchés, mais j'ai un mouvement de vénération et si j'avais une crise religieuse, ce qu'on appelle un mouvement de la Grâce, je voudrais qu'il fût catholique.'[6]

It is this question of 'grace' which is perhaps the solution to our problem, whether we believe in this Christian concept or not. For even those who do not believe in the concept of a supernatural 'grace' are bound to admit that, in religious experience, people do believe that they experience such a force. It is the experience of 'grace' which brought about the conversion of so many in this period; and what is important, for our purposes, is to see how long they waited on the fringes of Christianity until this 'grace' should be afforded them. Psichari and Massis, for example, were both convinced of the utility and necessity of Catholicism long before their conversion, for reasons of traditionalism and order which would seem to place them in the same position as Barrès and Maurras. This was not enough to make them Christians, but merely enough to make them sympathise with the Church. What was needed in order to convert them was true belief, as Massis later pointed out:

> Notre intelligence n'avait rien à opposer à ses dogmes, bien plus, nous étions persuadés que là seulement était la vérité. Nous savions tout cela *et pourtant nous ne croyions point*, nous demeurions indécis devant le seuil de la maison de Dieu, nous hésitions devant l'affirmation qui est la gloire de l'Eglise. Et tous deux, nous nous déclarions, cette chose dérisoire, des catholiques sans la grâce. . . .[7]

If their sole concern had been with traditional values, which could be helped by the Church, these two young authors could quite easily have remained outside the Church forever. But the 'grace' they awaited finally came to them (or, if one prefers, their belief became a religious one as well); and what is interesting is that their sense of priorities changed at the same time. Psichari was later to disavow his pre-conversion novel *L'Appel des Armes* for the stress it laid on the utility of the Church's doctrines rather than on their truth.

In those authors who professed themselves to be Christians, therefore, there is little need to doubt their word and to accuse them of making use of a religion they do not necessarily believe in, because if this were so they could quite easily, like Maurras and Barrès, or Massis and Psichari before their conversion, have remained outside the Catholic faith. Nevertheless, in many Catholic writers of this period religion is so inextricably mingled with traditional political and social ideas, that to examine these is a necessary part of the study to which this book is devoted.

The Family and the Land

The fact that their Christian belief did not permit them to give credence to the doctrine of the perfectibility of man meant that, for most Catholic authors of this period, the only possible direction was not towards that fallacious progress which obsessed the contemporary humanists, but towards the solid values of tradition. These values were above all embodied in the family life and in the family hearth.

Now, the Christian life does indeed revolve around the family, but from this basic concept the authors of the Revival drew many lessons, both social and political, which went far beyond it. In essence, though, the family was seen by them as being that link with the past (the 'forefathers' rather than the 'fathers') which could bring man back to the primitive virtues of an ideal time, unscarred by the materialist and unbelieving values of the nineteenth century. Contained in this idea is that of the importance of the land; of one's native province, and of the land itself, the livelihood of that store of tradition, the peasant.

In the novels of Bazin this close relationship between the peasant, the family, the land and the traditional virtues of Christianity is very clearly stated, above all in *La Terre qui Meurt* and *Le Blé qui Lève*. A certain amount of pessimism is expressed as to the future of the country and of these values. In the novels of Bordeaux the theme of the family takes an even more important place than in the works of Bazin, and the existence of man is seen to be linked, through his family and his native land, both to the past and to the future. In the Preface to his book *Le Pays Natal* (1900) Bordeaux clearly states this ideal:

Je voudrais que ce petit livre — rare aventure d'un déraciné qui reprend racine — inspirât à ses lecteurs le goût de restituer à nos provinces francaises (trop souvent portées à exiler leurs meilleurs enfants par le spectacle de l'envie et de la médiocrité) une beauté originale et une vigueur intellectuelle qu'elles n'ont plus guère.

Je voudrais surtout qu'il contribuât à fortifier l'esprit de famille menacée par l'anarchie révolutionnaire, — cet esprit par qui la tradition se conserve, s'épanouit et s'enrichit. Car l'homme ne tient sa grandeur et sa durée terrestres que de ses antiques origines et de ses espérances. Isolé, son oeuvre est éphémère; relié par la race au passé et à l'avenir, il a le temps pour allié.[8]

He goes on to compare man with the legend of the giant Anteus, son of Heaven and Earth, who, in his struggle against Hercules, gained new strength every time he touched the Earth, his mother. Even so, says Bordeaux, when men return to their native soil they regain the treasures of the past and faith in the future: 'Car ils y retrouvent l'esprit des ancêtres, et ils comprennent que toute oeuvre durable dépasse la vie d'un homme. . . .'[8]

Maurice Barrès's novel *Les Déracinés* (1897) had made popular not only the word of its title, but also the concept involved. Man had to keep his roots in his native province; he needed to keep contact with that tradition which alone was valid.[9] The novel shows the fate of various young men from Lorraine who are uprooted not only from their native province but also from their traditions of thought by the cosmopolitan philosophical teachings of a master at the *lycée*, Bouteiller (a character based on the real-life figure of Burdeau, a philosophy teacher who later became a deputy). When these boys come to Paris their uprooting is complete. Some survive in the new atmosphere, others do not; but the message of the book is that of the necessity for tradition, and for attachment to one's own *milieu*.

We have seen the word *déraciné* repeated by Bordeaux in 1900; it holds an important place, too, in Bourget's novel *L'Étape*, published in 1902. Here the hero, Jean Monneron, is seen not only as the son of a man who has attempted to move too quickly from one class to another, thus disturbing the equilibrium not only of society but also of his own family; he is also seen as the *déraciné* whose father has uprooted the whole family from its happy peasant existence, and from the tradition of the land. Nevertheless, Jean himself, despite the teachings which his father, a university professor, has instilled in him, unconsciously turns to the values of his forefathers. The influence of his heredity is too strong for him:

> La bonne race des cultivateurs Vivarais, dont il est issu, se révolte en lui, malgré lui, contre l'erreur paternelle. Ce fils d'un Jacobin a de continuels retours vers la vieille France. Il voudrait aimer la France nouvelle, et tout l'en écarte. Cet enfant d'un incrédule étouffe dans la négation. Il est né d'un fonctionnaire et d'un déraciné; et il ne rêve, quand il s'abandonne à ses goûts, que d'une famille établie, de moeurs locales et tradition-elles, d'un milieu terrien.[10]

Much of the thought on the question of *déracinement*, which the Catholic writers of the new century took from the works of Barrès and Bourget, was in fact, though they probably did not fully realise this, based on the theories of heredity and *milieu* which these two writers had learned from their master, Taine.

In Barrès and Bourget Taine's theories had been used to prove traditional conclusions; where Taine had chosen to view questions of heredity and *milieu* in a manner which he considered to be scientific and objective, Barrès and Bourget used them to preach the maintenance of a *status quo*; and they jumped to a great many subjective conclusions both about the nature of the *milieu's* influence, and about the dangers of sudden change of *milieu*. Taine's 'scientific' method was used unscientifically, and it was used to prove moral imperatives which were no part of the original intention. In other words, the whole question of *déracinement* was merely one more facet of the belief, general among Catholic authors, in the traditional virtues of the family and the land.

These virtues find expression not only in the novel; they are also at the basis of the writings of Péguy, both in poetry and in prose, and of the plays of Claudel.

> Tiens Combernon à ma place
> Comme je le tiens de mon père et celui-ci du sien, . . .

> . . . Recueille cette moisson que j'ai semée, comme moi-même autrefois j'ai rabattu la motte sur le sillon que mon père avait tracé. . . .[11]

In much of the Catholic poetry of the day, too, family life and the family hearth hold a central position. Louis Mercier, for example, based most of his poetic thought upon these ideas. His verse is of a banality beyond description, and successive generations of French schoolchildren have learned this to their cost, for Mercier is *par excellence* the poet who is chosen for 'récitations'; but nevertheless it must be recognised that his poetry is a clear reflection of the trend of thought we have been describing, though in a somewhat sentimentalised version. In Mercier's collection of verse entitled *Le Poème de la Maison* (1906), he writes a poem addressed to each object of the household. The poem *L'Horloge* contains many of the most typical attributes of this author:

> Elle a l'air vaguement humaine
> Avec sa face d'émail blanc,
> Et sa robe couleur de chêne
> Où bat son coeur rythmique et lent.

> Elle habite un coin solitaire
> Où l'araignée a son réduit
> Et fait son oeuvre de mystère
> Sans se hâter, le jour, la nuit . . .

> Un esprit ponctuel et diligent l'anime;
> Elle est dans la maison comme un Dieu du travail
> Et chacun obéit aux volontés qu'exprime
> Son doigt de fer rigide allongé sur l'émail . . .

> Mais les beaux jours ont fui; l'horloge n'est plus neuve,
> Pauvre et noire aujourd'hui sous sa robe de deuil;

Elle a l'air humble, hélas! d'une éternelle veuve,
Et l'on trouve à son corps des formes de cerceuil.

Despite the poorness of invention and the oversentimentality, it is clear that Mercier and others like him see the peasants, the land, the family and the hearth as being primarily responsible for the continuance of the traditional Christian virtues. What rarely appears in such poetry, though often in the novel, is the concept of family life as an essential element in the conservation of the temporal State. This idea is a prolongation of the Christian view of tradition into the political field; it is a mild beginning for more positive political ideals which we shall be seeing later.

Paul Bourget and Henri Bordeaux saw the family as being the remedy for that individualism which was destroying Christian belief, the temporal State and the individual himself. In this they, and many others, were reinforced by the writings of the reactionary philosophers Bonald, de Maistre and Blanc de Saint-Bonnet. In the social and economic field, Le Play too had laid great stress on the primary need for solid, well-constituted family life within the nation.

For Bonald, the whole State rested on the family, and the survival of the State depended on the maintenance of a united family life: 'La famille étant l'élément de l'État, et l'État le développement de la famille, et ces deux sociétés étant *semblables* dans leur constitution, tout changement sera réciproque entre elles; et tout déplacement de personnes dans l'une, entraînera un déplacement de personnes dans l'autre.'[12] It was for this reason that he so strongly opposed divorce. The family is essential to the State, and depends upon the State: 'Les raisons contre le divorce, tirées de la société publique, *sont encore plus fortes que celles qui sont prises de la société domestique.*'[13]

Temporal reasons are, for Bonald, as strong if not stronger than spiritual ones. Such opinions are reflected in many authors of the Revival, though for them the temporal and spiritual have become so intertwined that the one seems a natural corollary of the other. Henry Bordeaux, for example, in *Les Pierres du Foyer*, links the concept of the family closely with that of the fatherland, and quotes both Joseph de Maistre and Charles Maurras to support this contention:

Une patrie est une assemblée de foyers. L'idée de foyer est inséparable de l'idée de patrie. 'La patrie,' disait Joseph de

Maistre, 'est une association, sur le même sol, des vivants avec les morts et ceux qui naîtront.' Une terre, un cimetière, des ancêtres, une famille, des enfants, voilà déjâ une patrie. Et M. Charles Maurras n'en donne pas une autre définition. 'Une patrie est un syndicat de familles composé par l'histoire et le géographie.' . . . La cellule nationale, comme la cellule sociale, ce n'est pas l'individu, c'est la famille . . . La force de la famille a fait, sur notre sol, la force francaise.[14]

The value of the family is here extended to the fortunes of the State, and from this it is but a step to connecting it with other specific political forces within the State. Democracy, for example, is the perfect example of that individualism to which the family is a counterblast. In Bourget's *L'Étape* Jean Monneron's family life is seen to have been destroyed by the 'democratic' view of life in which the individual is taken as the social unit. 'C'est détruire à la fois la société et l'individu,'[15] says Bourget. Not only is democracy shown as destroying the family; the family itself is seen as the perfect symbol of that national 'order' which was one of the paramount concerns of the Catholic authors of this period. Henry Bordeaux stresses the totalitarian nature of family obedience: 'La famille n'est point faite d'une série de bonheurs individuels, et parfois il lui faut sacrifier ce bonheur individuel. . . . Peu sentimentale, elle ne s'attendrit pas sur les préférences du coeur: ce qu'elle veut, c'est qu'on la serve. . . .'[16]

The importance of the family in the Catholic thought of this time leads to other, more precise political and social corollaries, and in particular to very definite ideas upon heredity, aristocracy and hierarchy.

Hierarchy

Bonald had very closely linked his ideas of the Christian family with that of an aristocracy that was essential to the State. Blanc de Saint-Bonnet, who saw work and the family as the two mainstays of the Christian life, and of the Christian State, based upon this premiss a whole system of hierarchies, both spiritual and temporal; and Le Play, attempting to find a solution to social and economic problems solely by using an experimental and historical method, had arrived, from a completely different direction from these others, at a similar traditional solution. He saw a stable family life as one of the essential conditions for a well-organised society and, believing social reform to be not only an economic but also a moral matter,[17] and trusting in man's sense of duty, he based his whole social theory upon a return to a feudal organisation of industrial society. His remedy for the bourgeois exploitation of the proletariat was therefore not a levelling but a Christian paternalist society in which all classes would realise their duties as well as their rights. In his turning to this tradition he was, like those authors who turned to an ideal Middle Ages, idealising a past which almost certainly never existed in the form he lent to it.

'Dieu a rendu la vie accessible à toutes les âmes. L'égalité ne se fût mise qu'à la portée d'une seule,'[18] wrote Blanc de Saint-Bonnet; and in his book *De la Douleur* inequality was seen as divinely instituted, and only to be understood by the Christian. For beside the great forces of work and the family there existed another force, more mysterious but even more efficacious, which was suffering. The works of Bourget are the most perfect reflection of these ideas, and of Bonald's ideas on heredity and on the class system. In *L'Étape* Bourget's main ideas are expressed in the mouth of M. Ferrand, the Catholic professor. All doctrines, claims M. Ferrand, which are not as old as society itself are errors. For society is not a conventional creation of man's; it is a phenomenon of nature, which exists according to interior laws which we must admit and to which we must submit ourselves. Two of these laws which have been seen to be true since the beginning of the world are inequality and suffering:

Le christianisme seul interprète l'inégalité et la douleur. Il leur donne un sens de justice et d'espérance. Il hiérarchise et il console. Toute oeuvre sociale faite en dehors de lui croit semer l'amour, et elle moissonne la révolte; l'apaisement, et elle moissonne la haine. . . . Il n'y a qu'un chrétien qui puisse aider le pauvre sans l'humilier, et l'encourager sans lui mentir, tout simplement parce qu'il ne lui dit pas: Vous êtes ou serez mon *égal*, mais je suis votre *semblable*.[19]

For Bourget, and for a great many others, one of the great follies of the modern age was the cult of equality. Just as they contrasted liberty (which included the concept of obedience) with independence, so they contrasted equity with equality. Equity contains the idea of social justice based on merit (which can be transferred by heredity), where equality implies a general, artificial planing-down which these writers saw as being contrary to Christian principles. Not only this, but Bourget believed the 'dogme absurde de l'égalité'[20] to be destructive of human society and of human virtues. He describes it as 'La folie de l'égalité, meurtrière à la vie, sous toutes ses formes, principe d'abaissement universel dans les moeurs, de dégradation dans les intelligences, et, tôt ou tard, de sanglant désordre dans les actes.'[21]

The whole Monneron family is seen as being doomed to destruction because they have 'brûlé l'étape', and moved too quickly from one class into another. Bourget's whole philosophy is built around a class system; each class should remain happily in its condition and *milieu* or at least not move too quickly from one class to another. Change must be gradual, and the classes in Old France are seen as having had a full appreciation of their duties as well as their rights:

> Patiemment, sûrement, elles grandissaient, ces familles terriennes, si elles en étaient dignes, par leurs vertus. . . . Elles arrivaient à la petite bourgeoisie par en bas, avec le temps; puis, de la petite bourgeoisie, si elles continuaient à se fortifier, elles montaient à la moyenne, à la haute, à la noblesse. C'était un axiome alors que la famille, dans l'état privé, devait d'abord s'enrichir par le travail, puis que, haussée d'un degré, c'est-à-dire devenue noble, elle ne devait plus que servir l'État. Bonald a vu cela merveilleusement.[22]

The same opinion, though usually not so clearly expressed, is shared by any number of Catholic writers, from Barbey d'Aurevilly to Émile Baumann.

In many of these Catholic writers an almost mystical regard for the virtues of a hereditary aristocracy remains. Aristocracy had been seen both by Bonald and Blanc de Saint-Bonnet as a 'développement social de la famille',[23] and as containing the moral heredity of the nation. This view was continued in many works, including Bourget's *L'Émigré* and Baumann's *La Fosse aux Lions* (1911), where the relationship between the noble and his peasant is seen as the essence of the tradition of stability; the hero, Philippe de Bradieu, depicts an almost idyllic view of the traditional society:

> Il contait sa joie de se voir lié par son père et une série d'ancêtres à ce sol vendéen où se perpétue, entre les possesseurs et les tenanciers, la probité des relations antiques; selon ses forces il oeuvrerait avec les paysans, la main dans la main, les retenant ainsi fidèles au patrimoine de leurs traditions et à leur

foi; appuyés l'un sur l'autre, le noble et le laboureur affermissaient la plus vivace des stabilités terrestres.[24]

It is in regional novels such as *La Fosse aux Lions* that we find the traditional class structure, which often appears so coldly set forth in the works of Bourget, depicted with a Romantic warmth which is far closer to the simple traditionalism of the Revival, whose authors were moved not so much by reason as by faith. In a tradition which stems from Barbey d'Aurevilly, with his novels of the Norman countryside and its memories of the wars of the Chouans, these other writers take us to the traditionalist parts of the country, such as the Vendée, and show us the survival of the ancient virtues in these corners of France, untainted by those democratic principles which were threatening to destroy Christian society. Yet even here in the country society is being threatened by outside influences, and much of these novels is taken up with the struggle between the old and the new.

One of the most typical examples of this kind of nostalgic literature, written just before the 1914–18 war by a young writer, Alphonse de Chateaubriant, is *Monsieur des Lourdines* (1911), whose sub-title is the perfect description of the work: 'Histoire d'un gentilhomme campagnard.' In this book the nostalgia for things past is heightened by an awareness of the danger of change. This kind of tradition has been continued down to our own day in the form of historical novels by such writers as La Varende.

So there are two trends of anti-democratic, hierarchical feeling, both based on tradition. One trend is that of a Romantic attachment to the feudal traditions of the countryside, where Christian values remained at their strongest; it is linked with the tradition of faithful adherence to the Royalist cause. The other is a reasoned view of hierarchy as an essential element both in the Christian conception of life and in an ordered society; it sees the principles of the Revolution as having destroyed both moral values and the social system through the cult of individualism. As Adolphe Retté put it, reflecting many of the ideas of the *Action Française* on the matter; 'Grâce à l'exaltation de l'individu considéré, contre tout bon sens, comme base sociale, les éléments qui formaient la Patrie Française: *réligion traditionelle, famille solidement constituée, goût de la hiérarchie et de la discipline,* achèvent de tomber en ruines.'[25]

On the question of poverty and its related social problems the attitudes of the Catholic authors were very much influenced both by the idealistic view of a perfect paternalistic society and by a horror of the principles of equality. This in no way denies those authors' genuine desire to right the social wrongs which they saw around them.

There are, of course, exceptions to the cult of hierarchy among Catholic authors, and the greatest of these is Léon Bloy. Yet even Bloy was appalled by thoughts of democracy and of equality. It was the hierarchy of the capitalist society which he abhorred; yet in his conception of the mission of the Poor, that mission of suffering and redemption which made the Poor Man the Chosen of God, and transformed him into the Suffering Christ Himself, there was little room for a society in which the poor would not exist. For this reason Bloy was opposed to any conception of social progress; as Albert Béguin says, 'Sa révolte à lui ne s'accompagne d'aucun espoir de progrès social, d'aucun désir même d'instaurer un monde d'où la pauvreté aurait été éliminée.'[26] Like Germain Nouveau, Bloy curses a society which has tried to suppress the role of the poor and the beggar. He curses it also for its false conception of charity, which he describes as being applied in a 'Protestant' manner, destroying the dignity of the poor.

So Bloy's hatred of the social hierarchy does not imply a desire to destroy it. The rich man is necessary, as is the poor man. Vices balance virtues in God's pattern for the world. Bloy's apparently contradictory position here is a parallel to his attitude towards his own poverty; his indignation against those who are privileged in this world, and his disgust at his own poverty and misery, are balanced by a mystical conception of this poverty and misery as the highest state for which man could wish, as being the very sign of God's love. It is for this reason that Bloy claims that he himself has espoused poverty for its own sake.

As for Péguy, though he rightly claims himself to be in solidarity with the poor of whom he is one, his view of society, especially in his last years, is essentially based on traditional concepts which differ little from those of the other Catholic authors. His hatred of the bourgeois capitalist society does not lead him to look forward to an ideal future; instead he looks back to an ideal past, when men were filled with a proper respect for true values: '. . . Un respect de la famille, un respect du foyer. Et surtout un goût propre et un respect du respect même. Un respect de l'outil, et de la main, ce suprême outil. . . .'[27] In those days, people worked for the sake of working, for the sake of doing a good job properly. They had a 'piété de *l'ouvrage bien faite*', and they had a pride which never asked for anything. They would have been horrified at the idea of striking in order to shorten working hours:

> Ils eussent été bien surpris, ces ouvriers, et quel eût été, non pas même leur dégoût, leur incrédulité, comme ils auraient cru que l'on blaguait, si on leur avait dit que quelques années plus tard, dans les chantiers, les ouvriers — les compagnons — se proposeraient officiellement d'en faire le moins possible; et qu'ils considéreraient ça comme une grande victoire.[28]

In this happy time, Péguy continues, the idea of equality did not even come to mind. Life was based on a hierarchy, on a happy inequality, which was in the order of things:

> On ne peut se représenter quelle était alors la santé de cette race. Et surtout cette bonne humeur, générale, constante, ce climat de bonne humeur. Et ce bonheur, ce climat de bonheur. Evidemment on ne vivait point encore dans l'égalité. On n'y pensait même pas, à l'égalité, j'entends à une égalité sociale. Une inégalité commune, communément acceptée, une inégalité générale, un ordre, une hiérarchie qui paraissait naturelle ne faisaient qu'étager les différents niveaux d'un commun bonheur.[29]

This idyllic view of a traditional hierarchical society could be that of any number of Catholic authors of the day. Péguy has the same disgust with the materialistic society based on money as these others, and he turns, like them, to the same idealised picture of the past, when the classes realised their duties as well as their rights and when even the man who was in no way a believer was nevertheless, by his very way of life, more Christian than the most Christian of modern men. For, says Péguy, again echoing the Catholic sentiments of the era, it is the *bourgeoisie* who have changed all this, infecting all classes, even the working-class, with their vices: 'Car on ne saurait trop le redire. Tout le mal est venu de la bourgeoisie. Toute l'aberration, tout le crime. C'est la bourgeoisie capitaliste qui a infecté le peuple. Et elle l'a précisément infecté d'esprit bourgeois et capitaliste.'[30] All classes have been infected with the materialist spirit and society revolves around the worship of money. The old aristocracy has become a 'bourgeoisie d'argent'; so has the good old bourgeoisie. As for the workers, their only idea is to become bourgeois: 'C'est même ce qu'ils nomment devenir socialistes.'[31] In the old days, workers had even seemed to want to work; now all they wanted was to have shorter hours and more pay. And at the same time, despite all the talk of equality in the modern world, people were less equal than ever because of the *economic* inequality brought about by the materialist ideals of society.

Like other Catholic authors, Péguy was appalled by the fate of the poor in this materialist world, and denied that such poverty and misery could have existed in the old days:

> On vivait alors. On avait des enfants. Ils n'avaient aucunement cette impression que nous avons d'être au bagne. Ils n'avaient pas comme nous cette impression d'un étranglement économique, d'un collier de fer qui tient à la gorge et qui se serre tous les jours d'un cran. Ils n'avaient point inventé cet admirable mécanisme de la grève moderne à jet continu, qui fait toujours monter les salaires d'un tiers, et le prix de la vie d'une bonne moitié, et la misère, de la différence.[32]

For Péguy, modern socialists are merely bourgeois in disguise, who have, as bourgeois intellectuals, produced purely materialist replies to materialist problems. They have invented sabotage and the desertion of work (to say nothing of military desertion, which is even worse). They know nothing of the people, or of Old France. As Péguy says, in *Solvuntur Objecta*, it is by being of the people himself that he is entitled not to be a democrat. Instead he looks back to an ideal Christian community based on the traditions of France.

The traditions he looks back to, however, are different from those of Maurras, whose beliefs Péguy claims to be essentially un-French: 'Le dernier ouvrier de ce temps-là était un homme de l'ancienne France et aujourd'hui le plus insupportable des disciples de M. Maurras n'est pas pour un atome un homme de l'ancienne France.'[33] In this Péguy is echoed by that other Republican, Barrès, who sees the political ideals of the Royalists to be imported ideas from abroad. As we shall see in Chapter Twelve, Barrès and Péguy believed the true traditions of France to be embodied in the Republic which took over from the moribund remnants of a monarchy which had betrayed those traditions. Barrès says of the Royalists:

> Ces Francais de la fin du XVIIIe siècle étaient vraiment vidés de tout. Un certain nombre émigrèrent. Sauf leur attache-

ment au Roi, *ceux-ci étaient, comme les Jacobins, sans religion, sans attachement au passé*, etc. C'est à l'étranger qu'ils prirent leur idées, qu'ils furent Chateaubriand, Bonald, Maistre, etc. . . . Tout le romantisme et toutes les idées dont vit encore *L'Action Française* furent des idées du dehors ramenées par l'émigration.[34]

Barrès and Péguy were both able to see through the unreality of the Royalists' dreams, yet their own dreams were just as unreal. All these people, in their hatred of the modern world, turned to a world of tradition which must, in their eyes, have been perfect. In their own way they were as unrealistic as the disciples of progress; their perfect past was bound to be as impossible as any perfect future.

The Social Problem

The attitudes expressed by the Christian Péguy must show us more than anything else could do the fatuity of those writers who see in Bloy and Péguy, because of their overriding interest in the poor, a line of development in the literature of the Revival which is sharply differentiated from what they call the 'traditionalist school'.

Where such historians and literary historians fall down is in their failure to realise that a concern for the poor is not necessarily confined to socialists. Throughout this period, as we saw in the last chapter, it was the intransigently reactionary authors of the Revival who condemned the contemporary Church for its neglect of the poor. Huysmans, Bloy and Drumont are among those who, in the years before the turn of the century, campaigned most strongly for recognition of this problem by the Church, and who castigated most roundly the godless, capitalist society for allowing the existence of such misery.

In fact in the first twenty years of the Third Republic the only worthwhile attempts to help the poor, by members of the Catholic Church, had been based almost entirely upon the paternalist principles of Le Play. The *Oeuvre des Cercles Catholiques de Travail*, founded by Count Albert de Mun and the Marquis de la Tour du Pin in 1871, was the only social attempt of any note; the average middle-class Catholic, himself a product of this industrial age, was completely ignorant of the existence of a social problem. The *Oeuvre des Cercles* was based on the idealised conception of a feudal, corporate structure of society, based on the principles of social duty on the part of the upper classes; its creators believed in the possibility of a peaceful co-operation between the classes. It was never entirely successful, possibly because of its failure to arouse enthusiasm in the working class itself.

Among Catholic authors it was the intransigents who welcomed most effusively the *Oeuvre des Cercles*. Veuillot, for example, had been one of its first supporters. Apart from the authors of the Revival, the strongest support for the *Oeuvre des Cercles* came from influential Catholics from country areas, where relations between the classes still remained relatively unstrained and where the links between the aristocracy and the peasantry, reinforced by land and tradition, still retained some characteristics of that 'golden age' to which de Mun and Le Tour du Pin were attempting to redirect the decadent society produced by the Industrial Revolution. The average middle-class Catholic, on the other hand, and in particular the average Catholic deputy, was usually closely connected with various big business interests, and at any rate blithely unconscious of the iniquity of the social situation created by those interests.

When, in the years after Leo XIII's encyclical *Rerum Novarum* (1891), which dealt with the problems of the Industrial Revolution and the working class, a new form of solution was sought, based on the united principles of 'religion, science and democracy', the Catholic authors of the period (with occasional exceptions, such as Georges Fonsegrive, whose novels became the bibles of the 'democratic priests'), not only retained those conceptions which had been inherent in the teachings of Le Play and in the actions of the *Oeuvre des Cercles*; they also violently attacked what they saw as the unrealistic policies of the new democratic Catholics.

The 'democratic priests' were far removed from socialism, but their social action was based on the acceptance of democracy. At the same time their mode of operation, based as it was on separate trade unions of workers and employers rather than on the communal effort, in a single trade union, of employers and employed, seemed to point less to a Christian concept of mutual trust in a paternalistic setting than to a pessimistic outlook on the need for safeguards between the classes.

For the intransigents, of whom our Catholic authors were the main examples, such ideas were almost as dangerous as socialism.

The only way to reform society was through a trust in God to reform the soul of man, as Huysmans's character des Hermies put it in *Là-bas*:

> Évidemment . . . si l'on admet que l'ignominie de ce temps est transitoire, l'on ne peut compter pour la faire disparaître que sur l'intervention d'un Dieu, car ce n'est pas le socialisme et les autres billeversées des ouvriers ignares et haineux, qui modifieront la nature des êtres et réformeront les peuples.[35]

All attempts to reconcile religion and democracy are seen to be equally unreal, and a frontal attack is delivered on such attempts in Bourget's *L'Étape*, where the author satirises not only the 'democratic priests' and their ideas, but also the popular universities founded, as another social measure, by other, non-Catholic, intellectuals.

The abbé Chanut, the democratic priest in *L'Étape*, is described by Bourget as not only being unrealistic, in the present situation, by not realising that there is no hope of compromise with the enemy, and that he will either be made use of or rejected by both friend and foe, but also as being unrealistic in the general field, in his failure to see that the principles of democracy and equality deny the most elementary principles of freedom and tradition. Bourget speaks of the attempted reconciliation of Catholicism, science and democracy as being 'la dangereuse erreur où tombent aujourd'hui tant de prêtres excellents'. Science, he says (and we have already seen how his views on science differ from those of the majority),[36] has never had to be reconciled with Catholicism for the simple reason that, as they do not have the same object, they do not evolve on the same plane. But science and democracy are irreconcilable: 'La Science démontre que les deux lois de la vie, d'un bout à l'autre de l'univers, sont la continuitié et la sélection, et les démocrates francais répliquent par le dogme absurde de l'égalité et donnent au présent, sous sa forme la plus brutale, par la souveraineté du nombre, tous les droits sur le passé.'[37]

Bourget is here merely putting into a rational form, in his own manner, the feeling which was innate in so many Catholics, that of the irreconcilability of Catholicism and democracy. He also demonstrates the dangers to the Church not only of attempted reconciliation with the enemy but also of splitting the Church internally. And in his later novel, *Le Démon de Midi* (1914), which is primarily concerned with modernism, he reintroduces the abbé

Chanut, the liberal Catholic, to show how the different forms of anarchy were equally dangerous. As the hero of the novel, Savignan, says when he sees the abbé Chanut assisting the modernist Fauchon in the celebration of a modernist Mass: 'Le Démocrate? C'est juste. Toutes les anarchies s'attirent.'[38] Bourget's main objection to those 'popular universities' at which l'abbé Chanut, in *L'Étape*, was so ill received by the atheist workers and their teachers, was not merely his distaste for democratic teachings and his mistrust of these non-Christian attempts at social work; it was also a realisation of the unreality of these contacts between intellectuals and workers, of the indigestibility of the teaching provided, and of the attempt to instil into the working classes the prejudices of the bourgeois intellectual. Bourget saw 'l'entière inutilité de ces rapports factices entre travailleurs de l'esprit et travailleurs manuels, où ceux-là ne font que s'abaisser, sans élever ceux-ci.'[39] Above all he realised the danger of certain intellectual concepts which were being instilled in these uneducated minds: principles of Progress, of Absolute Justice, of Universal Happiness and of Equality. Looking around a 'temperance restaurant' founded by the 'Union Tolstoï', Bourget's hero Jean Monneron realises that the workers are being saved from one form of intoxication only to be affected by another:

> Il savait qu'une intoxication mentale, plus redoutable que l'autre, était prodiguée à ces cerveaux de quarts de Bacheliers, comme il l'avait dit, par les mêmes mains qui s'efforçaient de les guérir de l'alcool. Il savait que toutes ces obscures pensées étaient empoisonnées par les deux idées les plus fausses, quand on prétend y trouver la règle de la vie: La Justice absolue et le Bonheur universel. . . .[40]

For Bourget, socialism was not only to be judged by the futility of its theories; it was also to be judged by the active part taken in the movement by professional philosophers, who addressed themselves 'aux instincts les plus brutaux avec les arguments les plus abstraits'.[41]

The intransigent Catholics, then, who until 1890 had been almost the only Catholics to demand a solution to the social problem and some consideration for the poor, continued after this date to pose the same questions and to suggest the same answers, scorning the solutions both of the 'democratic Catholics' and of the socialists.[42] For them, capitalist society itself was at fault; and this concept is one of the many which seem to lie at the basis of the anti-Semitism of this period. For in the writings of Drumont, where the cause of the poor is put forward with fire and passion, the nostalgia for a better society is mingled with a hatred of those elements which have corrupted present-day France, among which a principal place is taken by the Jews, whom Drumont sees as flourishing on that capitalism which has destroyed the old values. It is interesting to note that, as Mr. Weber points out in his book *Action Française*, Drumont's anti-Semitic journal *La Libre Parole* was founded in 1892 upon the proceeds of his book *Le Secret de Fourmies*, in which he described the horrors of the killing of some strikers, men, women and children, on the orders of the authorities, which took place in 1891.

Like the other intransigents, Drumont saw that 'le résultat le plus clair de la Révolution a été de rendre plus dure la situation des petits et de fortifier au contraire la situation des grands et des riches en la délivrant de toute responsabilité morale'.[43] Property and social position require a sense of duty from their possessor.

This same hatred of modern capitalist society extends to the Catholic writers of the beginning of the twentieth century, and Péguy, Baumann and even Maurras castigate it just as roundly as Bloy, Huysmans and Drumont. They, too, show a great interest in the care of the poor; and at the same time a mistrust of democratic solutions is common to a great many Catholic authors of this period.

Baumann, in his novel *L'Immolé* (1908), depicts his hero Daniel Rovère as suffocating in the atmosphere of a party of rich industrialists in Lyon, and crying out: '— L'argent n'est pas tout!'[44] He wishes to throw his glass into the face of all these plutocrats, and he is obsessed by the thought of all the workers whose misery must have paid for the pleasure of the rich. Later in the novel we see Daniel occupying himself with an 'apostolat populaire'. But this apostolate is obviously intended to be on paternalist lines, for Baumann is appalled both by democratic and by socialist ideas. His hero's aim is more to convert the poor and thus help them to understand and to cope with their suffering, than to eradicate suffering from the world.

Baumann's ideal of social reform can be seen to coincide with that of Albert de Mun's *Association Catholique de la Jeunesse Française*, founded in 1886, whose main aim was to bring man individually back to a realisation of the rights of God and the duties of man, and thus eventually to bring society as a whole back to Christian belief, after which society would right itself of itself. Baumann's hero, Daniel, is forced to the realisation that individual proselytism is the only way:

> Toutefois, sa chimère d'évangéliser à la fois toute une usine, toute une corporation était décidément culbutée. Une méthode unique s'offrait: libérer, un à un, les hommes des mauvais servages, constituer dans un premier, puis dans un second, une conscience chrétienne, et, de proche en proche, des groupes, moins étendus que fervents, s'agglutineraient entre eux, n'ayant qu'un coeur et une foi.[45]

In Baumann's later novel, *La Fosse aux Lions* (1911), we see the full force of his traditionalist, paternalist view of society. His hero, Philippe de Bradieu, sees that in the Vendée countryside the old relationship of master and servants is honoured by both parties, both of whom have a sense of their duties:

> Cette communion d'hommage, Philippe, plus que nul autre, y porta un coeur loyal; il voyait unis à son serment ses domestiques, ses métayers, la paroisse presque unanime; peu d'actes religieux avaient exalté à ce point ses énergies aimantes; entre son fief et lui s'affermissait une inviolable alliance. . . .[46]

This perfect Christian society, so different from the war of the classes in the dechristianised industrial society which Baumann had described in *L'Immolé*, is nevertheless threatened by the influx of democratic political principles from the metropolis. The last pages of *La Fosse aux Lions* show us an electoral battle, in which Philippe de Bradieu attempts to defend the traditional principles of the Christian society of the Vendée. His electoral speech shows how religious, patriotic and social values are all linked with the traditions of the forefathers:

> Ce que nos anciens ont voulu, ce qu'ils ont cru, continuons à le vouloir et à le croire, autant qu'eux, davantage si nous pouvons. . . . Il faut des bras pour le travail, donc, à chaque foyer, des fils nombreux; il faut que, là où le père commande, on lui obéisse, que la mère soit respectée, qu'on vénère les morts, qu'on révère les prêtres et qu'on adore Dieu. Il faut de la concorde et de l'estime entre les maîtres et ceux qui leur sont liés, de l'amitié entre les paroisses, un plus large amour pour cette paroisse plus large qui a nom la France, et le plus large de

tous pour la chrétienté que la terre ne peut contenir, parce qu'elle s'appelle aussi la Communion des Saints.[47]

It was in the first years of the twentieth century that a new social movement, *Le Sillon*, came into prominence, under the leadership of a young man called Marc Sangnier. It was a movement of great enthusiasm, formed around a journal of the same name. Its aim was the rechristianisation of the masses. Its characteristics were emotional rather than intellectual. But from the very beginning it contained certain elements of thought—individualism and a belief in human progress—which were bound to be anathema to the traditional Catholics; and from about 1905 onwards the movement became far more political and in this field went even further than the 'democratic Catholics' of the *ralliement* had done. Gradually, indeed, the movement became more political than religious, and after Sangnier had, in 1907, opened the movement to all 'influences animated consciously or unconsciously by the Christian spirit', the way seemed open for a new political party based on democratic principles, whose concern for social action could include all elements, both Catholic and non-Catholic. From considering its aims to be 'vivre le catholicisme' (1903) the movement had turned to the hope of being 'un mouvement laïque qui se propose de travailler pour sa part à réaliser dans notre pays la République démocratique' (1907).[48] It was for this reason, the turning of a religious movement to political ends, that Pius X was to condemn *Le Sillon* in 1910; this was in no way a condemnation of the movement's interest in social matters. The Pope expressed his sorrow that a movement in which such high hopes had been placed had become influenced to so great an extent by the modern enemies of the Church, who had instilled in it principles contrary to those of the Church. These principles included the residence of authority in the people, the levelling-down of classes, the changing of the natural and traditional foundations of society and the cult of the perfectibility of man. All this preaching of human liberty and dignity could only lead to unbridled passions and the oppression of the weak. The *Sillon* movement was thus praised for its concern with social problems but blamed for the political turn which this concern had taken.[49] On the one hand, in its refusal of authority and its preaching of individualism and liberty, it was seen by many to be a parallel to the modernists; and on the other hand, in opening itself to all of democratic views, whatever their belief, it had shown itself to have become a political rather than a religious party, and thus, in the eyes of its opponents, deserved to have religious support removed from it. Pope Leo XIII had even had, in 1901, to check the political action of the 'democratic Catholics' of the *ralliement* by his Encyclical *Graves de Communi*, in which he re-defined 'Christian democracy', denying it any political inclination whatsoever. In the same encyclical Leo XIII had also criticised the doctrine of social equality, and had stated what good works, in the social field, were to be expected from those 'to whom their situation, their fortune, their culture, give the greatest influence in society'. Social action was thus in no way to be connected with egalitarian politics. If Leo XIII felt constrained to put in such a criticism of the comparatively harmless 'democratic priests', how could one expect Pius X, a far less progressive Pope, not to react violently against the greater dangers presented by *Le Sillon*?

Among the Catholic writers, most of the older generation were against *Le Sillon* from the very beginning. Bloy, for example, attacked it on several occasions, as he had attacked the social efforts of the *Ralliement* because of its attempt to reconcile Catholicism and democracy. Though he admitted the goodwill of its members, he nevertheless showed how mistaken he believed them to be. Paul Bourget, as might be expected, took a similar attitude. Others, like Baumann, however (who, though his first novel appeared in 1908, was nevertheless a man of the older generation, having been born in 1868), were at first taken in by the movement in its early years. As Baumann was to say: 'Je n'y voyais qu'un élan d'apostolat populaire, d'ascétisme et de charité, propre à rénover la jeunesse bourgeoise encrassée de radicalisme. L'aspect politique et doctrinal du Sillon demeurait à l'arrière plan.'[50]

He described his novel *L'Immolé*, which though published in 1908 was written in the years 1904–6, as being very much in the line of what he saw of *Le Sillon*: 'Le héros, conçu alors que j'ignorais tout du Sillon, répondait au meilleur des aspirations sillonistes, au désir naïf de rechristianiser les masses enfoncées dans l'athéisme et livrées aux plus bas instincts.'[51] But, as Baumann himself points out, his hero, Daniel Rovère, was in no way a democrat. He did not believe in a future happy social order; he looked, instead, to the social order of the past. Baumann, when he eventually saw the democratic principles inherent in the policies of *Le Sillon*, rejected the movement out of hand. He describes himself, in his *Mémoires*, arguing with a Sillonist about democracy and the war between the classes, which he regarded as the natural result of the former:

> Mais . . . c'est une fatalité de la démocratie. Je connais, par example, un religieux démocrate qui s'occupe du syndicat de l'aiguille. Par système, il prend toujours parti pour les ouvrières contre les patrons. Etre mieux payées, et travailler le moins possible, voilà le rêve! Il approuve, il excite cette belle tendance. Il ne se dit pas que la lutte des classes mène à la paralysie générale du travail. Un peuple qui ne travaille plus ou qui travaille le moins est voué à tous les désastres![52]

Baumann goes on to show the unreality of the Sillonist's hope in a future which was ignorant of the solid virtues of class co-operation to be found in country areas:

> Il négligeait, comme la plupart des théoriciens, la paysannerie, plus difficile à changer que les citadins. Il ignorait ou méconnaissait la doctrine corporative, la collaboration des ouvriers et des dirigeants, des fermiers et des propriétaires, unis dans de fermes statuts par des intérêts communs, des traditions familiales, religieuses, patriotiques.[53]

Among the younger generation, many were strongly impressed by *Le Sillon*, but even so this impression seems often to have been a fleeting one and there is little in the way of literary commentary on the movement from its own side. Several of the literary group which formed itself round the *Cahiers de L'Amitié de France* in the years just before the war, for example, of whom the abbé Maugendre has given an account in his book *La Renaissance Catholique au XXe siècle*, had been at one time or another connected with this movement. Yet the novels and the poetry of André Lafon, 'cet amant de la pureté et du silence, ce fervent du recueillement et de l'humilité',[54] show nothing of this interest, and the only work produced by a member of the group which has bearing on the Sillonist movement is François Mauriac's first novel, *L'Enfant chargé de chaînes* (1913).

In this novel Mauriac, far from praising the *Sillon* movement, expresses rather his disappointment and disgust with certain aspects of it which had forced him to turn away from it. It is portrayed as one of the steps in the spiritual progress of Jean-Paul, the autobiographical hero of the novel. Jean-Paul is depicted as an introspective, over-literary young man who attempts to get out of

himself by devotion to a cause. He is overwhelmed by the personality of Jérôme Servet (Marc Sangnier); and Mauriac stresses
throughout this part of the book the almost narcissistic pose of the
leader and his dictatorial rule of the movement, a criticism that was
levelled at Sangnier by many of his disillusioned former disciples.
Above all, Mauriac saw the social action of *Le Sillon* as being
ultimately temporary and useless.

About the only novel to support Sillonism (apart from Georges
Fonsegrive's novel *Le Fils de l'Esprit* (1905), which is part of that
earlier tradition of 'democratic Christianity' of the *ralliement* set
by his novels of the 1890's) is Jean Nesmy's *La Lumière de la
Maison* (1910), an attack on outmoded political alignments and a
plea for a Christian policy towards the poor.

If many of the younger generation were drawn to *Le Sillon*, a
great many more, supported by the *Action Française*, were against
it. This was the younger generation whom Roger Martin du Gard
was to describe in the last section of his novel *Jean Barois* (1913),
and whose aspirations were expressed in the inquiry *Les Jeunes
Gens d'Aujourd'hui* (1913), undertaken by Henri Massis and Alfred
de Tarde. They based themselves firmly on authority and tradition, and their spiritual leaders were, to a large extent, such men
as Maurras and Barrès. They were, in large majority, Catholics.

In their opposition to *Le Sillon* they had been led from an early
stage by the writings not only of Charles Maurras himself but also
of all others connected with *L'Action Française*. Maurras's book
Le Dilemme de Marc Sangnier (1906) was reflected in the writings
of all his supporters, and particularly in those of Adolphe Retté.
Maurras's beliefs in order, discipline, tradition and hierarchy
naturally led him to oppose a movement based on the concepts of
liberty and progress. And at the time of the condemnation of *Le
Sillon* in 1910 his criticisms appeared justified.

But *Le Sillon* had been condemned mainly for faults which it had
in common with the *Action Française*—namely, the tying of Catholic
belief to a specifically political movement which in fact claimed
anyone who supported its *political* views rather than its religious
ones. The condemnation of *Action Française* itself in 1926 was a
tardy redressment of the balance, though as early as 1914 Pius X
had received from the Congregation of the Index the decision that
seven of Maurras's works, and the *Revue de l'Action Française*,
should be condemned. The Pope had approved the decision but

had reserved the right to choose the moment to make it public, and the war had intervened.[55] It was left for Pius XI, in 1926, to confirm the decision and to add to it the newspaper *Action Française* in its current form, particularly on account of recent articles by Maurras and Daudet.

But the *Action Française's* opposition to *Le Sillon* must not lead us to believe that it ignored the social question. In fact, in the years before the First World War this movement attempted some quite startling link-ups with the socialists.

We have already seen, in Chapter Nine, how the Catholics shared with the socialists (and with the anarchists) a hatred of the bourgeois capitalist world in which they lived. The *Action Française*, even those parts of it which were not Catholic, participated in this hatred, which it blamed on democracy and individualism. It saw the nation divided into a class warfare which destroyed the principles of order and patriotism.

The *Action Française's* solution to these problems was, however, far from that of the socialists. As Mr. Weber points out in his book *Action Française*, the socialists might, like Maurras, proclaim that the public interest was superior to private interests, and they might be equally wary of a free society and the dangers it held of anarchy and tyranny; but nevertheless their opinions on human equality and their conviction that authority has its source in the masses could never appeal to the *Action Française*, for whom authority was only clearly established by the natural hierarchy of talent or of birth. Not only the socialist idea of democracy was bound to repel a man such as Maurras; its internationalism was the very opposite of that patriotism which was at the basis of the *Action Française*.

The social ideas of the *Action Française* were based on hierarchy and differ little from those of Catholic authors of the time. Any temporary arrangement with militant socialists, who had the same hatreds and were put in the same prisons for the same type of public action, was bound to be destroyed once the basic principles were looked at more closely. Like most Catholics, the *Action Française* looked to an order in which workers and employers co-operated in corporations organised by the *élite*. Bourgeois democracy was to be destroyed, but in its place there was to be a new hierarchy.

It is hardly surprising, therefore, that many of these attempted link-ups failed, and that eventually the main socialist to join forces with the *Action Française*, first on the short-lived journal *La Cité Française* (1910) and then on *L'Indépendance* (1911), should have been Sorel, whom Émile Baumann (another contributor to *L'Indépendance*) has described as follows:

Théoricien du Syndicalisme révolutionnaire, Sorel était devenu un réactionnaire fougueux. . . . L'auteur des *Réflexions sur la violence* avait la passion de l'autorité et l'horreur des solutions bourgeoises, des compromis, des demi-mesures, du libéralisme mensonger. Au moment où je le fréquentais, il avait publié un livre, *Les illusions du progrès*, touffu, décousu, d'où ressort le dégoût de la démocratie, 'école de servilité, de délation, de démoralisation' et de la morale laïque, de celle qu'on prêchait aux jeunes instituteurs entre 1880 et 1914.[56]

What Baumann and many others failed to realise was the close and natural connection between Sorel's social ideas and authoritarian, reactionary principles of this sort. Sorel's theories on the efficacy of violence in treating social problems reflect the same disgust with contemporary society and its futile ideals as was to be found in both Catholics and anarchists at this time, though his pessimism was such that he did not believe that society would ever be righted even by violent action of the type he advocated. The violent act itself was merely useful as providing the 'extreme moments' which sustained the class struggle and through that the health and vigour of society as a whole. Progress, humanitarianism, etc., are bourgeois myths which merely help to sustain a weak and illusory semblance of society. Sorel's proposed manifesto for *La Cité Française* had been the following: 'La revue s'adresse aux hommes raisonnables qu'incommodent l'orgueil stupide de la démocratie, la sottise humanitaire, les modes venues de l'étranger.'[57]

This was the same Sorel, 'infatigable péroreur', who had monopolised the conversations in Péguy's shop as effectively as he did those of his colleagues on *L'Indépendance*. Halévy, in his book *Péguy et les Cahiers de la Quinzaine*, describes Sorel's freely expressed scorn for the intellectuals of the Sorbonne, a scorn which became one of the central points of Péguy's own thought. A great deal of Péguy's thought, not only on social matters, may have come from this source also. Sorel continued as a regular attender in Péguy's shop until late 1912, when Péguy broke with him over a matter concerning Julien Benda and Sorel's strong anti-Semitism.

However, as Mr. Weber points out, the alliance between Maurras and Sorel was bound not to last. They were only superficially in agreement on an end to be reached, in the form of an authoritarian régime. On the details of such a future régime they were bound to disagree. Apart from this, the *Action Française* itself appeared to be losing support through its dallying with socialism and syndicalism, and so this brief honeymoon came to an end.

In all the period from 1870 to 1914, the intransigent Catholics of whom the Catholic literary Revival was on the whole made up were among those most interested in social problems and the fate of the poor; the solutions they offered were paternalistic in nature, based on tradition and hierarchy; and their mistrust of democracy and progress was in part based on the conviction that it was these principles of the Revolution which had produced the industrial society of their day, in which classes were locked in struggle rather than in collaboration, and in which the pursuit of money had led to the classes forgetting their moral duties. They looked back to a golden age of mutual trust between the classes, a state which they saw partly reflected in the paternalist society of the countryside, as yet untouched by the new principles of the industrial society.

This attitude to social problems is merely one facet of the traditionalist outlook held by the majority of Catholic authors, a traditionalism which is closely linked with the concepts of patriotism and of order, which we shall examine in the succeeding chapters.

NOTES

[1] Bloy, letter to J. Florian, 24 November 1902; printed in Bollery, III, pp. 332 f.

[2] Péguy, *L'Argent Suite*, 22 April 1913; Pléiade, Prose II, p. 1160.

[3] Barrès, *Mes Cahiers*, 1909.

[4] Ibid., 1914.

[5] Ibid., 1910.

[6] Ibid.

[7] Henri Massis, *La Vie d'Ernest Psichari*, 1916, p. 26.

[8] Henri Bordeaux, *Le Pays Natal*, 1900, Preface.

[9] As Ronald Balfour points out in his article 'The *Action Française* Movement' in *Cambridge Historical Journal*, 1930, decentralisation was a cardinal feature of the nationalist doctrine preached by Barrès and by the *Action Française*.

[10] Paul Bourget, *L'Étape*, 1902, p. 26.

[11] Claudel, *L'Annonce faite à Marie*, 1910, Act I, Sc. 3; Pléiade, Théâtre II, pp. 38 f.

[12] Bonald, *Du Divorce*, 1801, p. 413.

[13] Ibid., p. 48.

[14] Henry Bordeaux, *Les Pierres du Foyer*, pp. 14 .

[15] Bourget, *L'Étape*, p. 51.

[16] Bordeaux, *Les Pierres du Foyer*, p. 24.

[17] See Le Play, *La Réforme Sociale*.

[18] Blanc de Saint-Bonnet, *De la Douleur*, 1849, p. 197.

[19] Bourget, *L'Étape*, pp. 125 f.

[20] Ibid., p. 390.

[21] Ibid., p. 139.

[22] Ibid., pp. 397 f.

[23] Blanc de Saint-Bonnet, *L'Infaillibilité*.

[24] Baumann, *La Fosse aux Lions*, 1911, p. 98.

[25] Retté, *Le Règne de la Bête*, 1908, Preface.

[26] Albert Béguin, *La Pauvreté et l'Argent*; in *Léon Bloy, Cahiers du Rhône*, 1946.

[27] Péguy, *L'Argent*, 16 February 1913; Pléiade, Prose II, p. 1053.

[28] Ibid., p. 1052.

[29] Ibid., p. 1060.

[30] Ibid., p. 1054.

[31] Ibid., p. 1047.

[32] Ibid., p. 1060.

[33] Ibid., p. 1047.

[34] Barrès, *Mes Cahiers*, 1922.

[35] Huysmans, *Là-bas*, 1891, p. 262.

[36] pp. 26–8.

[37] Bourget, *L'Étape*, p. 390.

[38] Bourget, *Le Démon de Midi*, II, 28.

[39] Bourget, *L'Étape*, p. 78.

[40] Ibid., p. 125.

[41] Ibid., p. 159.

[42] Barrès's political programme of 'national socialism' is misleading in its title, for the 'socialism' in question is nationalist and authoritarian, based on the reactionary principles of the 'yellow' trade unions of Biétry's National Socialist Party, which were essentially paternalistic in outlook and which eventually became little more than strike-breakers.

[43] Drumont, *Testament d'un Antisémite*, 1891, p. 252.

[44] Baumann, *L'Immolé*, p. 30.

[45] Ibid., pp. 203 f.

[46] Baumann, *La Fosse aux Lions*, p. 283.

[47] Ibid., pp. 325 f.

[48] From two pamphlets quoted in Dansette, *Histoire Religieuse de la France Contemporaine*, II, pp. 422–3.

[49] This criticism could, of course, also be levelled at the *Action Française* movement.

[50] Baumann, *Mémoires*, 1943, p. 308.

[51] Ibid., p. 308.

[52] Ibid., p. 311.

[53] Ibid., p. 312.

[54] François Mauriac, *La Vie et Mort d'un Poète (André Lafon)*, p. 107.

[55] This delay in putting into effect a decision of the Congregation of the Index

may well have been caused by Pius X's known support for the *Action Française*. By 1915, when Benedict XV again considered the matter, it was impossible to act in such a way against the chief exponents of French nationalism without giving the impression that the Vatican was being unduly influenced by Germany and Austria.

[56] Baumann, *Mémoires*, 1943, pp. 332 f.
[57] Quoted in Weber, *Action Française*, p. 94.

CHAPTER ELEVEN

Patriotism

IN 1915, at the height of the war, a Catholic Archbishop concluded a series of talks with these words: 'Aussi, Messieurs, me faisant l'interprète de vos sentiments, je clôture mes entretiens sur la guerre par cette profession de foi: *Je crois en la France immortelle.*' In the book, published in the same year, which was based on these talks, the Archbishop, worried perhaps by the form in which he had expressed this sentiment, felt constrained to clarify the matter by adding a footnote which ran as follows: 'Evidemment, il s'agit ici de l'expression d'un sentiment patriotique et non pas d'un article doctrinal de notre Dogmatique confessionnelle.'[1]

The very fact that he felt the need to clarify matters in this way shows the extent to which, in France at that time, patriotic and religious principles were intermingled. This was no mere product of the war; it was a situation which, in religious circles, obtained throughout the years of the Third Republic. An examination of some of the many reasons for this state of affairs will be instructive.

Firstly, however, it must be categorically stated that Catholic reasons were only a few among many for the fervent patriotic and nationalistic movements of the Third Republic. There has always been, in the French nation, a strong Republican tradition of patriotism and, indeed, of Caesarism, of authoritarian nationalism. This tradition expressed itself fairly strongly in such movements as the *Ligue de la Patrie Française* (founded in 1898, in the midst of the feeling over the Dreyfus Case) and the *Ligue des Patriotes* (founded in 1882 as an organ of revanchism). Among the supporters of Gambetta and Boulanger had been many non-Catholics of this type, and much of the anti-revisionist attitude taken by successive governments in the Dreyfus Affair can be traced to the same cause. The National Convention of the First Republic had been extremist, authoritarian and nationalistic; Bonapartism had been a natural result of these attributes. Nationalism (as it came to be known) was as much a characteristic of a certain type of Republicanism as it was of a certain type of Catholicism. In fact, among Ferry's hopes during his educational reorganisation of 1879–82 had been the replacement of the Catholic religion by the *religion de la patrie*.

It is for the specific link between nationalism and Catholicism which we must look, however; and the existence of such a link was shown many times over by the strong and almost unanimous Catholic reactions to the various national crises in this period. The *Dreyfusards* were wrong in their over-simplification of the position by ascribing all anti-Dreyfus feeling to a plot on the part of the Church; but they were nevertheless right in their assessment of the attitude of the French Church to the Affair. Counsels such as reached French Catholics from the Pope and from the rest of the Church were ignored in the welling-up of the mixture of religious and national feeling which the Affair aroused. And as with the Affair, so with questions of national defence, and of revenge on the Germans for the defeat of 1870 and for the taking of Alsace-Lorraine.

Henri Massis and Alfred de Tarde, in their book *Les Jeunes Gens d'Aujourd'hui* (1913), point to the strongly patriotic and military tendencies of the young pre-war generation they are studying and contrast it with the 'anti-militarisme universitaire' and the eclipse of such patriotism which they saw as having taken place towards the turn of the century. In the years just after the 1870 war, they claim, the nation as a whole had been full of the noble desire for revenge; but towards the end of the century a reaction had set in, a reaction echoed in certain anti-militaristic novels and in articles such as Rémy de Gourmont's Le Joujou Patriotique, which appeared in the *Mercure de France* in 1891.

Catholic authors were, on the whole, unaffected by this decline; in fact the lack of patriotism in others led on occasions to a violent assertion of their own possession of this virtue; but the full impact of the patriotic urge in Catholic literature came after the turn of the century and the Dreyfus Affair, when the ideas of Barrès had enormous influence. The international crisis of 1905 turned this trend even more firmly in the direction of anti-Germanism.

Before the turn of the century Catholic patriotism, though it had its revanchist side, was conceived in far more general terms than that of the nation's relationship with Germany; and this more general side was to remain, even amid the stresses of the First World War. For this patriotism was not merely based on that concept of national and hereditary tradition which we have seen in the last chapter; it also found a *raison d'être* in the mystical conception of France's mission as 'first-born of the Church'.

Tradition and Mysticism

It was at the time of the Dreyfus Affair that the first true awakening of extreme nationalism took place, and its wide influence was partly due to the personalities of Barrès[2] and Maurras. Before this, extreme nationalist feeling, after the decline of the Radical *revanchisme* of the 1870's, had seemed to be personified in the enthusiastic but rather ridiculous figure of the poet Paul Déroulède, who had founded the *Ligue des Patriotes* in 1882. As Barrès had clearly seen, 'Il y a du Don Quichotte dans Déroulède.' The poor man had passed his life 'à demi bafoué, roulé regulièrement'. His attempt at a *coup d'état* in 1899 failed not only miserably, but ridiculously. Yet at the funeral of this man, in 1914, there was an immense crowd not only of supporters but also of former adversaries, who saw in him an idealism they could respect.[3]

The nationalistic enthusiasm of the pre-war years, however, was not due to the efforts of Déroulède. It was fired by the emotional intensity of Barrès, and the no less emotional lucidity of Maurras. The Dreyfus generation was overwhelmed by these men, and the next generation revered them as its masters. Barrès's enthusiasm transcended political barriers, for to him anything that was truly French was good and any régime which had allowed the French national energy to fulfil itself was to be revered. Barrès remained a Republican (seeing this as the institution proper to France), despite his dislike for parliamentary democracy; his ideal was a 'plebiscitory republic' ruled by a dictator; in his gallery of heroes were kings, Napoleon I and a Republican such as Robespierre. It was for this reason that Barrès could appreciate even his worst political enemies as part of the French spirit, and welcome the war's destruction of the divisions in the French nation, and the sight of Frenchmen of all persuasions fighting together in the 'Union Sacrée'. Maurras tied his nationalism firmly to the monarchy, and this was one of the reasons why Barrès found himself further and further from Maurras's viewpoint.

Though neither Barrès nor Maurras was in these years a Catholic, their conception of tradition and patriotism came very near to that of many Catholics; and, in fact, they both used Catholicism to support this conception. For Barrès, Catholicism was the faith of his country, and he naturally was drawn to it as one of the aspects of the national tradition which was so dear to his heart. His feeling for Catholicism was emotional and in certain respects rather vague. Maurras, on the other hand, saw Catholicism as the necessary corollary to the nationalist monarchy he desired. His attitude to Catholicism was above all rational and practical. Both these writers, however, reinforced the traditional link between the country and its national, traditional religion, and it was left to the individual in each case to decide which of these two entities was the cart and which the horse.

For Frenchmen of all kinds were attracted to the nationalist cause preached by these men, and while these numbers contained many Catholics, Catholicism was not necessarily the main force which supported them. By the pre-war years it was a whole generation of youth which was behind them; and support, from the early years, had not been a matter of creed or party. As Léon Blum was later to say of Barrès, 'Il était pour moi comme pour la plupart de mes camarades non seulement le maître, mais le guide. Nous formions autour de lui une école, presque une cour.'[4] Among Catholics men like Jammes, who saw in Barrès 'un marchand de glace artificielle', were the exception.

The role of Barrès, in the case of many Catholics, had been to awaken patriotic instincts which had always lain within them without them fully realising it. Though Barrès had been politically active since the Boulanger crisis, it was at the time of the Dreyfus Affair that many were woken to these realities. As Émile Baumann says in his *Mèmoires*:

Je devins, dans cette période là, plus que patriote, *nationaliste*. Je l'avais toujours été sans y penser beaucoup. L'assaut frénétique d'une bande internationale me révéla plus fortement quelle chose grande et magnifique il fallait sauver en défendant la France, le péril de mort qu'elle courait. Je lisais les articles fulgurants de Barrès. . . . J'adhérais à la campagne de la *Patrie Française*, je propageais des tracts. . . .[5]

No doubt part of the realisation which the Catholics now had was that of the traditional place the Catholic religion had in French society, that role which Barrès described as being like the scarlet thread running through the ropes in the British Navy, to show their origin. Every aspect of French thought and French society, he said, had this Catholic thread. Catholicism and nationalism were mutually indispensable. But the French Catholics were also aroused to a realisation of the relevance of a certain mystical conception of France which has always been present in French Catholic thought: the conception of France as the 'first-born of the Church', having a divine mission. As Baumann says:

. . . C'est alors que le nationalisme, dans un sursaut de défense, par l'organe de Barrès et de Maurras, définit vigoureusement ses raisons d'être historiques, son actuelle nécessité. Barrès l'appuyait sur la terre et les morts, *en ajoutant à la constance des générations les éléments spirituels qui avaient dominé leur volonté commune.* Maurras considérait davantage les fondements politiques du nationalisme. *La France était l'oeuvre de la Monarchie et de l'Eglise — ou plutôt de l'Eglise et de la Monarchie.* Privée de ces deux piliers, elle s'effondrait. Pour moi, *j'envisageais la mission divine de notre pays*; je ne consentais plus à supposer qu'elle était révolue, puisque, dans nos désirs, et bientôt dans nos actes, elle se continuait.[6]

Catholics thus brought to Barrèsian and Maurrasian nationalism something it had not possessed, and which reinforced natural nationalistic feeling with the fervour of religious belief.

It is very difficult to tie down the mystical conception of France. It took a different form in different people. Bloy's vision, for example, was something almost unconnected with the temporal; in Claudel and Péguy, on the other hand, the temporal defence of the Church took a very high place in France's mission.

For these writers France was the temporal champion of the Church and was divinely chosen for this mission. As Claudel was to state it in his war play *La Nuit de Noël 1914*:

. . . C'est Dieu même que nous défendons, ceux-là même qui ne savent pas son nom.

Car chaque peuple est né pour lui-même, mais la France est née pour tout l'univers afin qu'elle lui porte la joie!

Ce n'est pas son corps seulement qu'elle défend, c'est son âme qui est à tout l'univers, ce n'est pas sa vie seulement qu'elle défend, c'est la parole de Dieu à tout l'univers, qui est l'éternelle joie dans l'éternelle liberté!

Et si elle doit se taire et *si Dieu doit cesser de parler français*, elle sait que ce jour-là il vaut mieux pour elle être morte![7]

Like Péguy, Claudel saw France's mission as that of the crusader, defending Christendom and at the same time extending its domain. This mission of France had been there from the earliest days, and in the crusaders of St. Louis there was an example for the men of today. Claudel saw St. Louis's vow as extending to the whole of France, through all ages:

Tout ce qui n'est pas Dieu, ô mon Dieu, tout ce qui n'est pas Votre Eglise, ô mon Dieu, pour en venir à bout, à jamais on ne se débarrassera pas de Louis!

Ce n'est pas un seul Français, c'est toute la France avec lui pour tous les siècles à jamais qu'il accroche au flanc de la Mort seconde![8]

For Péguy Christianity and patriotism are joined both by tradition and by France's chosen mission: 'La Foi est une église, c'est une cathédrale enracinée au sol de France,'[9] but this is because God has chosen the French, above all others, for his people. He has chosen them for the liberty with which they choose to follow him:

C'est pour cela, dit Dieu, que nous aimons tant ces Français,
Et que nous les aimons entre tous uniquement
Et qu'ils seront toujours mes fils aînés.[10]

And the French deserve this choice, for they have proved their worth time and again as defenders of the faith. They alone understand the designs of God and they alone put them into effect. Péguy depicts God as praising them for these qualities:

Or dans cet ordre, et dans ce secret, et dans ce mystère
Nos Français sont avancés entre tous . . .
Peuple soldat, dit Dieu, rien ne vaut le Français dans la bataille.
(Et ainsi rien ne vaut le Français dans la croisade) . . .
C'est embêtant, dit Dieu. Quand il n'y aura plus ces Français,
Il y a des choses que je fais, il n'y aura plus personne pour les comprendre . . .
Or ces Français, comme ils sont, ce sont mes meilleurs serviteurs.
Ils ont été, ils seront toujours mes meilleurs soldats dans la croisade.
Or il y a toujours la croisade.
Enfin ils me plaisent. . . .[11]

Péguy, throughout his works, is lost in a love of his country, a love which mingles continually, after his conversion, with the love of God. Like Joan of Arc, in his poem *Ève*, he is 'perdu en deux amours, l'amour de son pays parmi l'amour de Dieu.'[12] The two loves are 'within' each other; they are almost impossible to disentangle. Those long sequences of praise addressed to Paris ('Pour nous Français ville de France la plus française, la plus profondément, la plus authentiquement, la plus traditionellement française') and to the countryside of France ('ce monument unique au monde') which we find in an early essay, *De la Situation Faite au Parti Intellectuel devant les Accidents de la Gloire Temporelle*, or in *Notre Patrie*, show already the conception of France as a nation chosen from among many, with a kind of temporal consecration. The Plain of Beauce becomes, later, the setting for more religious considerations, but the same sense of France's mission and France's superiority comes across in all Péguy's writings, and the religious mission appears to come to him as a natural consequence of the temporal. Péguy's move to Christianity had been a gradual and logical one; few of his ideas needed changing in the process, for they rested on a traditionalism which was the basis both for his patriotism and his Catholicism.[13]

France's mission as first-born of the Church was proclaimed by many Catholic authors, and the pre-eminence of France in the missionary efforts of this period and the years just before it no doubt strengthened this conviction. It has been calculated that around the year 1875 out of a total of 6,100 Catholic missionaries, 4,500 were French. This vast contribution to missionary activity can be explained by many different things, including the coincidence of French colonialism and the Church's struggles within France itself, but the strength of the French missionary effort in turn lent even more credence to that belief in France's colonial mission which we have seen as a factor in the Third Republic. Foucauld, Psichari, Castries and Lyautey saw it as France's mission to bring Christianity and French civilisation to the heathen; they, too, were crusaders in the French tradition. In that intermingling of the temporal and spiritual which was central to Catholic military thought, they saw the problems of colonialism in a simple and confident light.[13a]

Foucauld expresses something of this attitude in a letter written in 1915, in which he hopes that God will soon grant victory to the French, a victory which will place Europe, the world and civilisation 'à l'abri de la convoitise et de la barbarie allemandes'. Such a victory would, he hopes, produce a peace in which France would soar once more, a peace which would open a new era for France's colonies. 'La paix et la sécurité extérieures porteront son activité vers cette belle partie d'elle-même qu'est son empire colonial, et surtout son empire africain.'[14]

It was in this same sense of mission, of crusade, that many Catholics went off to fight against Germany. They were moved not only by the patriotic desire for revenge against the country which had inflicted such humiliation on France in 1870, nor merely by the desire to expiate, by their sacrifice, the sins of their own nation; they were defending Christendom, and their nation, however low it had descended morally, was still the firstborn of the Church. This exaltation comes through to us from the pages of Psichari, and even more so from his letters; and in the words of Ernest Le Gallic, the young soldier in Bourget's *Le Sens de la Mort* (who was himself based on the figure of Ernest Psichari), the beliefs of the young Catholic soldiers of the day are expressed:

Nous les aurons, mon cousin. Entendez-vous, j'en suis sûr. Voulez-vous que je vous dise pourquoi? Ce ne sont pas vos idées, mais je vois ça si nettement que je ne peux pas m'en taire. Vaincue, la France périrait, et elle ne doit pas périr, parce qu'elle reste le grand pays catholique. Mais oui, malgré son gouvernement, ses électeurs, ses codes, ses journaux, malgré tout. . . . Vous qui ne croyez qu'à l'expérience, ne fermez pas les yeux à cette expérience-ci, je vous le demande. Nous allons vaincre, parce que Dieu va être avec nous.[15]

France might appear to be in a terrible state; Psichari's own novels had diagnosed the ills of the nation. But the mission still remained, and in times of heroism France became once more the chosen nation of God. In Claudel's *La Nuit de Noël 1914* a priest asks in wonder: 'Quoi! est-ce là ce pays de Voltaire et de Renan?' And he is answered by a child who tells him that it sees Renan's grandson (Ernest Psichari). What is he doing? the priest asks:

L'ENFANT   Il est par terre, les bras en croix, avec le coeur arraché, et sa figure est comme celle d'un ange! Il a le signe sur lui du troupeau de saint Dominique.

M. LE CURÉ   Tu vois son corps. Mais son âme, dis-nous, où est-elle?

L'ENFANT   Saint Dominique l'enveloppe dans son grand manteau avec les autres tondus.

M. LE CURÉ   Et qui vois-tu encore?

L'ENFANT   Je vois un mourant à qui on apporte Jésus-Christ

et qui essaye de faire le salut militaire! Je vois les
deux fils du général de Castelnau. Je vois Charles
Péguy qui tombe la face contre terre![16]

The figures of Péguy and Psichari, who both died at the very
beginning of the war, became the symbols of Catholic heroism in
that war, and of the natural regeneration the war had brought.
Books such as Bourget's *Le Sens de la Mort*, articles such as Barrès's
famous account of the death of Péguy, *Un Poète Français Mort au
Champ d'Honneur*, inspired the heroism of innumerable soldiers,
both Catholic and otherwise. To the priest who, in Claudel's play,
asks the question, 'Quoi! c'est là cette France impie?' the children
reply, 'c'est la France au sang pur telle qu'elle fut toujours.'[17]

In the thought of Léon Bloy, France's mission, like every other
concept with which he had to deal, became far more divorced from
reality and far more mystically significant.[18] Bloy was, like so many
of his generation, extremely patriotic; and in the world of illumination in which he eventually came to move, the figure of France came
to play a very important part. The present deplorable state of
France, which other writers saw as something passing, which
could not destroy the country's holy mission, was perceived
by Bloy to be an essential part of that mission. In his pattern for the
world, in which the outcast was the man of God, Bloy saw France
as being the modern inheritor of the ignominy of Israel, that
ignominy which made Israel indispensable to the fulfilment of
God's word. 'La fille aînée de l'Eglise . . . devenue maintenant la
Gueuse du monde' is a counterpart to all the ideas of Bloy upon the
pre-eminence of the Chosen one 'thrown from his high seat'. It is
for this reason that, amid the symbols of which Bloy's biblical
exegetical system was made up, the word 'lily' came at all times to
signify France, and the 'cry of the cock' to signify France's mystical
part in the preparation for the coming of the Paraclete.

France is the terrestrial kingdom of Christ and her history is a
prodigious continuation of the New Testament. She is, moreover,
the kingdom of the Virgin, as can be seen from the Virgin's many
apparitions in the country, at La Salette, Lourdes, etc. In Bloy's
thought all these mysteries are linked with others, such as the
mystical significance of Naundorff (the pretended Louis XVII),
another outcast. They all point to eternal truths about the Trinity,
for nothing in history fails to have bearing on this. France's
mission is spiritual, not temporal, but in Bloy's thought even the

temporal always has spiritual significance. France's temporal ignominy is thus a sign of her spiritual mission, and the war, which Bloy saw as the beginning of the Event, is the time when France's mission is to be fulfilled. Bloy conceived of France as being *necessary* to God. His vision of the nature of France's mission may have had some influence on those most devoted to him, such as Émile Baumann; but on the whole those Catholics who believed in France's divine mission and saw her as the chosen of God were far more vague about the nature of this mission and saw it as something far more straightforward.

The German Question, and Anti-pacifism

In every section of the French nation there had been a great many people who, in the immediate aftermath of the Franco-Prussian War, smarted under the ignominy of the defeat and longed for revenge and the recapture of the lost provinces of Alsace-Lorraine. Revanchism, as the political movement based upon these feelings was called, was a force to be reckoned with, and much of General Boulanger's popularity, which led to the crisis of 1889, was based on the French public's mistaken belief that his actions in relation to the Schnaebele Affair (1887) had led to the German government backing down. Partly on the basis of this, but also because of his generally belligerent public statements on the German question, Boulanger was considered by many people as the personification of that 'revanche' which they were seeking. But Boulanger failed to achieve power, mainly through his own weakness; and it was probably lucky for France, and even for the revanchists, that he did. For Boulanger was militarily unintelligent, and any campaign waged with him in command would probably have been disastrous.

After the Boulanger crisis revanchism seems for a while to have taken a back seat, though it lived on in the fiery speeches of Paul Déroulède and the other members of the *Ligue des Patriotes* and influenced large sections of the French public. The Dreyfus Affair, just before the turn of the century, while it revived nationalist sentiments, was also by its very nature concerned with those elements within the nation which opposed them. Revanchism, though ever-present, had to take second place. It was in the years after the turn of the century that revanchism began again to fill the centre of the stage, and in these years the world of literature began to play a great part in its support, and Catholic literature above all.

Novels such as René Bazin's *Les Oberlé* (1901) and Barrès's *Au Service de l'Allemagne* (1905) and *Colette Baudoche* (1909) stressed the insufferable situation of those former Frenchmen who lived in the lost provinces. These novels appealed above all to the emotions of the reader. *Les Oberlé* presents us with various cases of conscience within a typical Alsatian family. In Barrès's *Au Service de l'Allemagne* the tribulations of a young Alsatian forced to serve in the German army or to flee to France are depicted at length. In *Colette Baudoche* a young girl of Metz refuses to marry a Prussian. These novels contrasted the nobility of those who remained conscious of their duty as Frenchmen with the degeneracy of those who were prepared to become the Germans they officially were (the young soldier in *Au Service de l'Allemagne* remains proudly French); and they brought before the French public vividly and emotionally the plight of those brothers they had deserted. This lesson is repeated again and again in other works. Alphonse Daudet's short story *La Dernière Classe*,[19] a description of the last days in free Alsace-Lorraine, is the text which the children are reading in the schoolroom at the beginning of Jean Nesmy's novel *Les Égarés* (1906); and later in Nesmy's novel the old schoolmaster, M. Castagne, gives a lesson on patriotism which ends with him asking the following questions of the children, and eliciting the following replies:

— Qu'est-ce que la Patrie?
— Notre mère.
— Et l'Alsace?
— Une soeur, qui nous a perdus. Elle est en deuil, là-haut, parce qu'elle est orpheline. [On maps of the time, the lost provinces were printed in black.]

Such lessons were taught by monarchists and republicans alike, by Catholics and by anti-clericals. But a great deal of such teaching found its way into Catholic literature.

The violence of much of it is to be explained by the tepidity of many other Frenchmen with regard to the problem. As Barrès said in *Au Service de l'Allemagne*, many Frenchmen did not seem to have any idea of the 'conditions morales' in which the inhabitants of the lost provinces were living; and Péguy, in his essay *L'Argent Suite* (1913), castigated the *Ligue des Droits de l'Homme* for having declared that there was no Alsace-Lorraine question. Barrès claimed that such liberals only get worked up about oppression which is far from home, and which is more dramatic: 'Si les Alsaciens-Lorrains enduraient les brutalités qui dégradent l'Irlande, comme ils vous intéresseraient! Leur misère vous emplirait d'émotion.'[20]

Péguy, resting his case on the rights of self-determination ('dans le système des Droits de l'Homme'), claims that the Alsace-Lorraine question is one of the most perfect examples of this. Why, then, does the *Ligue des Droits de l'Homme* deny its existence? It is because they are afraid of Germany, says Péguy. They are prepared to talk at great length about oppression in other people's colonies, but they dare not speak of Alsace-Lorraine:

> Si c'est un système de la peur, mon Dieu je veux bien, mais qu'on le dise. Qu'on dise: Il n'y a pas de question d'Alsace-Lorraine parce que nous avons peur de l'Allemagne, de la force allemande. Et il y a une question des nègres de l'Angola parce que nous n'avons pas peur de la force portugaise.[21]

Péguy's feelings on Alsace-Lorraine are above all a hatred, not of the Germans who took the provinces, but of the Frenchmen who gave them up instead of going on fighting to the last man:

> Le fond de ma pensée, sur la question d'Alsace-Lorraine, c'est que je n'en veux pas aux Prussiens de les avoir pris. J'en veux à ces misérables français qui les ont lâchés. Les Prussiens n'étaient que des soldats, des vainqueurs et des conquérants. . . . Mais je méprise et je hais, mais j'en veux à ces misérables Français qui pour avoir la paix ont vendu deux provinces et ensuite sont allés pleurer à l'Assemblée de Bordeaux . . . au lieu de continuer la guerre.[22]

It is every Frenchman's duty to go on fighting, and never to give in, says Péguy. He is for the policy of the National Convention (of 1793) against that of the Bordeaux Assembly of 1871. He is for the Commune, against peace and against capitulation.

Péguy admittedly hates those who capitulated more than he hates the Germans. But his hatred of Germany is, like that held by many of his contemporaries, extremely strong, and not only tied to the Alsace-Lorraine question; nor is it merely tied to the consciousness of the new German danger, which first became obvious in the 1905 Tangier crisis (which caused Péguy to write the violently nationalistic essay *Notre Patrie*) and which was stressed by the succeeding international crises of 1908 and 1911. The danger of German imperialism became obvious to Péguy and his contemporaries, but anti-German feeling went deeper than this for them, and particularly for the Catholics. For Germany stood, in their eyes, not only for the most dangerous form of Christianity, Protestantism, but also for a tradition of scientific thought which was basically anti-Christian. Germany was dangerous both temporally and spiritually.

The hatred of German Protestantism is expressed most forcibly by Claudel, both in his play *La Nuit de Noël 1914* and in his war poems. The most dangerous element, however, is seen by most Catholics as being that form of German scientific thought which had had so much influence over Frenchmen such as Renan. Ernest Hello had seen this as long ago as 1858, when he had published his book *M. Renan, l'Allemagne et l'Athéisme au XIXe siècle*, and men such as Péguy saw in the progressive Germanification of French thought a danger greater than all temporal ones. The Sorbonne itself had become obsessed by German historical method, and by German forms of thought; as Massis and de Tarde were to say, 'C'est l'imitation de l'Allemagne qui nous a obsédés,'[23] and all those aspects of the French universities which were most virulently criticised by Péguy, Sorel and Massis were based upon German models.

So the German influence was ruining French education by its concentration on scientific method unimaginatively used; and German science and philosophy had been the basis for French atheism. Monseigneur Pons's book *La Guerre et l'Âme Française*, which reflects much of contemporary French Catholic thought on this matter, contains a chapter entitled 'De la "culture" allemande, ou un assaut d'avant-guerre contre l'âme française'. He sees German culture as being essentially anti-Catholic and anti-French, and traces the effects of Marx, Nietzsche, Kant, Lassalle, Haeckel, Strauss, etc., on French thinkers and upon modernists such as Loisy. And the French have followed these false masters! 'Cette propagande de la "culture" allemande est un manoeuvre du Pangermanisme.'[24] Mgr. Pons goes on to describe what would be the satisfaction of a dying German soldier if he realised that the Frenchman who had killed him had in his kit-bag a book by Haeckel.

Such ideas may seem extreme, but they were shared by many, to greater or lesser extent, in the years before the First World War. And at the same time as seeing these spiritual dangers many, such as the *Action Française* historian Bainville, saw in Germany a temporal danger which would never be finished until Germany itself was disunited. Maurras blamed Napoleon for having created the new kingdom of Germany from which German unity had then been so easily created. A united Germany, these men felt, was a perpetual danger not only to France, but to the world. The Kaiser's belligerent policies were merely one more example of this. A united Germany would always take the same attitude, under whatever leader and whatever the form of government.

It was in consciousness of this danger, and in a conviction of the necessity for France of military 'gloire' and honour, that so many writers of this period violently attacked the growing pacifist movement in university circles and in the Socialist movement. Not only were the pacifists seen as betraying their country to an enemy who would do nothing but take advantage of this weakness; they were also seen, by Catholics, to be denying the temporal mission of the French army.

Nesmy's violent attacks on those who 'sous le manteau du pacifisme, et sous le couvert généreux de ce mensonge, poursuivaient la désorganisation morale de la France',[25] are matched by the anti-pacifist tactics of the *Action Française*, of Barrès, and above all of Péguy. These tactics were turned against such international socialists as Jaurès and Hervé, and against those elements in the Sorbonne and the École Normale who opposed 'le service de trois ans', a form of national service which was deemed necessary for the safety of France.

Barrès's fulminations in the Chamber were based on a realisation of necessity and had no sense of personal hatred. Jaurès's opinions were mistaken, but Jaurès was a good man; and if Barrès had not been firmly convinced of the need for 'le service de trois ans' he would have been very much against it, because of the *déracinement* it would mean for the young men concerned: 'Il faut que je souhaite cette loi de trois ans qui va encore augmenter le déracinement, il faut que ja la souhaite, parce que sans cette loi détestable nous disparaîtrions.'[26]

Barrès sees, as clearly as does Péguy, that Jaurès is in fact preaching not international pacifism, but Pan-Germanism; the German workers will never take the same pacifist attitude as the French workers might. But Barrès sees in this a miscalculation on Jaurès's part, rather than a conscious policy: 'Il veut la paix, et il se trouve, que c'est la paix allemande, l'acceptation du pangermanisme, car les Allemands ne veulent pas seulement garder l'Alsace-Lorraine, ils veulent s'assurer pour des besoins commerciaux; pour assurer la vie de leur immense population, ils veulent la domination du monde.'[27] The whole question is one of great danger, in Barrès's eyes; this is no time for lofty, unrealistic principles such as those of Jaurès: 'Nous n'avons pas le temps d'écouter ceux qui nous vantent un état d'esprit supérieur au patriotisme quand nous sommes volés et à demi assassinés par un patriotisme étranger qui ne rêve que de nous achever.'[28]

The attacks on Jaurès made by the *Action Française* and Péguy were violent and often unjust. Péguy's accusations of treachery, of Jaurès being a German spy, may well have been just as responsible as the *Action Française* and many other writers for the state of mind of Jaurès's assassin, Villain, who a few days after the event, in 1914, wrote to his brother: 'Ainsi donc, j'ai abattu le porte-étendard, l'archi-traître de la Loi des Trois Ans, la bouche de fournaise avalant tout appel en provenance de l'Alsace-Lorraine. Je l'ai châtié, et mon acte est le symbole d'un jour nouveau.'[29] The famous authoress Gyp, after Jaurès's murder, declared that any patriot would have done the same.

Péguy's attitude to pacifism can best be studied with reference to his relations with Hervé, a schoolmaster who had been sacked in 1901 for a violently anti-military and anti-patriotic article, and who then became a journalist of strong anti-military tendencies. Péguy, though he was worried about the problem of personal liberty which was raised by the Hervé Affair, nevertheless, even at this socialist stage of his career, was violently opposed to such ideas. In an article called *Compte Rendu de Congrès* (1901) he stressed his opposition to this form of internationalism, which he contrasted with the true internationalism which is based on patriotism. He described the way in which, in his childhood, he had been thrilled by the military battles of France, and added:

> Je n'en rougis pas, je ne rougis pas, je ne rougirai jamais du petit garçon que je fus, que j'étais né, que l'école primaire me fit, et il vaut mieux avoir passé de ce nationalisme sincère au véritable internationalisme, il vaut mieux avoir élargi un nationalisme honnête initial en véritable internationalisme,

que de chercher dans un faux internationalisme un prétexte à
n'exercer pas certains devoirs.[30]

It was the international crisis of 1905, however, which in arousing Péguy's patriotic feelings to a higher pitch strengthened his
opposition to 'Hervéism'. The cahier *Pour la Rentrée* originally
contained a violent attack on Hervé. This was cut out before
publication, leaving nevertheless a very pointed reference to
France's parlous state in face of Germany because of its own
internal canker: 'ce vieux et ce premier peuple trouvant en lui-
même les manifestations nouvelles de la trahison la plus authentique.'[31] A few weeks later, in *Notre Patrie*, Péguy stressed once
more France's danger and rounded on the pacifists who added to this
danger. They were afraid of not being 'advanced' enough, he said.

Le peuple veut insulter, injurier l'armée, parce que cela
aujourd'hui se porte très bien; cela fait extrêmement bien dans
les meetings et toutes autres glorieuses oraisons publiques. Cela
est devenu indispensable dans toutes les manifestations et opéra-
tions politiques. Autrement, vous n'avez pas l'air assez avancé.

On ne saura jamais tout ce que la peur de ne pas paraître
assez avancé aura fait commettre de lâchetés à nos Francais.[32]

Yet this people was still as fond of war as before, underneath all
this. Like Hugo, they were hiding their true feelings under a
'hypocrisie pacifiste'. In magnificent pages Péguy describes in this
essay the poetry of Hugo, and shows how, when he saw the apparent victory of pacifism, Hugo made himself the high priest of it.
Yet 'il n'y a pas un poème de paix réussi dans tout l'oeuvre de
Victor Hugo';[33] the only successful poetry is his war poetry with
its military rhythms and its song of 'gloire' and heroism. Carried
away by this, Péguy himself, in his prose, strikes a similar martial
rhythm, pounding at the reader:

Impérieux Hugo; non pas des vers qui chantent dans la
mémoire, mais des vers qui impérieusement, impérialement
sonnent, battent, retentissent, martelés, scandés, d'un tel rythme
et d'un tel tambour qu'ils commandent le pas dont on marche,
qu'ils entrent dans les jarrets, et qu'une fois qu'ils sont entrés
dans la mémoire, lus une fois, entendus une fois, non seulement
ils ne sortiront plus de la mémoire, jamais, mais que le moment
venu, ils chasseront, brutes impériales, insoutenables régiments,
tous les autres vers de tous les autres poètes, et vous forceront à
marcher au pas, du même pas, de leur pas.[34]

Péguy's militarism was emotional and his reactions to pacifism became equally emotional as time went on. In *Notre Jeunesse* (1910), discussing the Dreyfus Affair after the event, he deplored the fact that Jaurès, 'par une suspecte, par une lâche complaisance à tout le hervéisme, et à Hervé lui-même', had made it clear that it was necessary to deny, betray and destroy France, and had thus created the political illusion that the Dreyfusist movement was anti-French. Because of such pacifist support, they had got a bad name; Dreyfusists of the good (i.e. Péguy's) type had been speaking the same language as the anti-Dreyfusists:

> Nous parlions sur le même plan. Nous parlions exactement le même langage patriotique. . . . Nous avions les mêmes pré-misses, le même postulat patriotique. Qu'en fait eux ou nous fussions les meilleurs patriotes, c'était précisément l'objet du débat, mais que ce fût l'objet de débat, c'est précisément ce qui prouve que les uns et les autres nous étions patriotes.[35]

But by taking on Hervéism, various supporters of Dreyfus had ruined the Dreyfus cause by making the issue useless. If, says Péguy, such Hervéists believed in the *necessity* of being a traitor to one's country, why should they wish to defend someone against this charge? The adherence of such people to the Dreyfus cause had caused the adversaries, rightly, to call it *le parti de l'étranger*. The founders of the party had been patriots, but '. . . On reporte sur nous fondateurs la trahison de Hervé profiteur. . . . On reporte sur nous fondateurs la trahison de Hervé parasite.'[36]

At this stage Péguy's virulence against Hervé is extreme; so what is our surprise when we find him, three years later, pushing all the extreme blame on to Jaurès, who up till now had shared it with Hervé, and playing down Hervé's dastardliness! At first the reader cannot believe his eyes, when in *L'Argent Suite* this trans-formation takes place: 'Jaurès est un malhonnête homme. Hervé est un honnête homme (et tout ce qu'on voudra, un fanatique, un frénétique, mais un honnête homme), qui a fait souvent des sottises, qui peut-être peut commettre des crimes, mais que je crois incapable d'une malhonnêteté.'[37]

What has happened? Gradually, as the essay continues, clues begin to emerge. Hervé is described as being a realist, who sees things as they are and is prepared to change seemingly unyielding principles accordingly:

> Hervé est le seul de toute la bande qui regarde un peu ce qui

passe réellement, aujourd'hui, au lieu de répéter machinalement
ce qui se dit dans les meetings; ce qui s'est toujours dit.... Hervé
est le seul de toute la bande qui ait quelquefois le courage de dire
des choses qu'on n'attend pas. C'est un des hommes du monde
qui pense le plus de travers. Mais il est le seul de la bande qui
pense lui-même, qui regarde ce qui se passe, et qui dise ce
qu'il pense, et qui ait ce courage, et qui dise ce qui se passe.[38]

Compared with this man, people like Herr and Lavisse, whom
Péguy sees as corrupting, from the École Normale and the Sorbonne, the whole political life of the country, are the lowest of the
low. They have helped to convert Dreyfusism into Combism and
Jaurèsism; socialism into Jaurèsism, the disorganisation of work
and the rousing of bourgeois instincts in the working class; and
internationalism into Pan-Germanism, 'un total asservissement à
la politique allemande, au capitalisme allemand, à l'impérialisme
allemand, au militarisme allemand, au colonialisme allemand'.[39]

How does Hervé escape this condemnation? Finally, the reason is
disclosed, as Péguy quotes at length an article by Hervé in which,
while steadily reaffirming his pacifist views, he blames the international situation on the Germans, whose crime of 1871 is only
exacerbated by their refusal to admit the existence of an Alsace-
Lorraine question. Hervé rounds on his own party for ignoring
this question: 'L'abcès purulent qui empoisonne l'Europe . . .
c'est l'Alsace-Lorraine. La plupart des socialistes de France et
d'Allemagne s'obstinent à ne pas le voir: ou, s'ils le voient, à ne
pas le dire.'[40] He insists that he is as anti-revanchist and anti-
nationalist as ever, but that he perceives internationalism to be
useless when the Germans will not play the game. The Alsace-
Lorraine question must be solved first.

This is the reason for Péguy's *volte-face* in relation to Hervé.
In place of him he puts Jaurés, who now becomes the only
'traitor': 'Pour Jaurès l'explication est extrêmement simple. Il
est pangermaniste. (Il faudrait l'en féliciter, s'il était né allemand.) Il est un agent du parti allemand. Il travaille pour la plus
grande Allemagne.'[41]

The emotional nature of Péguy's patriotism made him choose
persons, rather than their ideas, to attack, and ascribe to those
persons all the worst possible reasons for action. His hatreds were
simple and violent, and they could be revoked simply, as in the
case of the 'traitor' Hervé.

Like so many of his contemporaries, Péguy saw pacifism both as a temporal danger in the international situation and as a spiritual danger, a sign of an inner decay in the nation. In words addressed to Ernest Psichari in *Victor-Marie, Comte Hugo* (1910) he stressed that, for him, peace was only achievable by force:

> Pacificateur, qui faites la paix à coups de sabre, la seule qui tienne, la seule qui dure, la seule enfin qui soit digne . . . vous qui maintenez la paix par la force; vous qui imposez la paix par la guerre . . . et qui savez que nulle paix n'est solide, n'est digne qu'imposée; que gardée par la guerre; l'arme au pied; vous qui faites la paix par les armes, imposée, maintenue par la force des armes. . . .[42]

The Foreigner within the Nation: the Jews

In the excessive patriotism of many writers of this period there was also a mistrust of foreign elements within the nation. In the case of Maurras and many others this was directed against all 'métèques' or foreigners, not merely the Jews; but the most virulent attacks were directed against the nation of Israel.

There are many possible causes of anti-Semitism. Among these the main ones have always been: (i) the early belief of many Christians that the Jews were the principle of evil, on whom the murder of Christ must be avenged; (ii) the hatred of capitalism, which for many was represented by the figure of the Jewish financier; (iii) the nationalistic mistrust so strong in the nineteenth century, of the stranger within one's shores; (iv) an almost instinctive hatred, perhaps based on all three of these previous reasons, perhaps based on none, an unthinking following of the herd.

In the nineteenth century the first of these was perhaps the weakest; one finds, in fact, little recurrence of it even in religious writers. The other causes, however, became particularly strong towards the end of the century. Anti-Semitism was by no means a particularly Catholic thing, nor even necessarily a thing of the Right; it transcended political parties and religious beliefs. Before studying its effects specifically on Catholic authors, we should perhaps examine the progress of anti-Semitism in the period, and some of the reasons for the violence of its growth at the turn of the century.

As Mr. Guy Chapman points out in his book *The Third Republic of France: The First Phase 1872–1894*, the Jews in France, before

Patriotism

the 1880's, had been a small and fairly happy section of the French
population. Many had been Sephardic; and most of the Askenazim
had been in Alsace, and remained there, on the whole, after the
annexation to Germany. There had always been a certain amount of
anti-Semitism in Alsace, but very little in the rest of France. In the
1880's there came an influx of Jews from Russia and Poland, flee-
ing from persecution, and the picture changed as these foreign-
looking and foreign-sounding people came and added themselves
to a community which had seemed French in all but name.

So the stage was set by a mistrust of foreign elements; but in the
writings of Drumont, which were to have incalculable effect, there
was added to this the concept of the Jew as being responsible for
the capitalist society which had been destroying all the old values
and creating so much misery amongst the poor. *La France Juive*,
Drumont's famous manifesto (of 1,200 pages!), appeared in 1886.
It was to be followed by *La France Juive devant l'Opinion* (1886),
La Fin d'un Monde (1889), *La Dernière Bataille* (1890), *Le Testament d'un Antisémite* (1891) and several other works. In 1889 Drumont founded the *Ligue Antisémite*, which became a political force
of some power, and in 1892 he founded *La Libre Parole*, a newspaper
which was to pursue the same ends with unremitting virulence.

Drumont was continually incensed by the accusation, which was
so often flung at him, that he was an attacker of the Jewish religion: '. . . Il n'y a pas, dans les douze cents pages de *La France
Juive*, un outrage à un rabbin, une raillerie même inoffensive
contre les croyances dont je ne parle qu'avec infiniment de circon-
spection.' He describes, with grim humour, the form of 'dialogue
de sourds' which continually took place between him and his
detractors:

— Comment se fait-il qu'en quelques années la fortune presque entière de la France se soit centralisée entre quelques mains
juives?
— Quoi! malheureux! vous voudriez au nom des préjugés d'un
autre âge, nous empêcher d'adorer le Dieu de Jacob, de célébrer
yom-Kippour et Peçah?
— Vous vous êtes abattus comme une pluie de sauterelles sur
cet infortuné pays. Vous l'avez miné, saigné, réduit à la misère,
vous avez organisé la plus effroyable exploitation financière que
jamais le monde ait contemplé.
— C'est la fête de Soucouth qui vous gêne? Soucouth, la poét-

307

ique fête des feuillages! . . . Allons donc, soyez de votre temps, laissez à chacun la liberté de conscience!

Drumont saw the Jews as having destroyed old French values not only by their capitalism, but also by their foreignness to these values. He saw the Jews as being the centre of all the political changes which had taken place, and of the persecution of the Church. He saw his own position as being that of a defender of the Church, and years later, at the time of his decline, he felt, as Barrès put it, that 'Dieu lui-même s'est mal conduit envers lui.'[43] In fact Drumont himself said, as he began to lose his sight: 'Comprenez-vous que Dieu me fasse cela, à moi Drumont, après tout ce que j'ai fait pour lui!'[44]

For Barrès the question was far more one of race. His whole concept of France rested on 'la terre et les morts', man's relation to his forefathers, and these foreigners seemed to him to destroy the national unity. At times of stress, such as the Dreyfus Affair, his hatred of the Jews became violent, but on the whole his attitude was based on reason. He saw the Jews as destroying, both consciously and unconsciously, the traditional values of his country.

The menace of the Jews lay, for many people, not so much in such general issues as capitalism and foreign traditions as in individual cases of extortion or crooked dealing. It was Drumont's paper *La Libre Parole* which had first brought to light the Panama scandal, in 1892; the main villains of this piece had been the Baron Jacques de Reinach, Cornelius Herz, and Arton, all three of them Jews, and all of the type of shady financier whom Drumont had been castigating. It was incidents such as this, and the use made of them, which led to the general feeling, so obvious in the first stages of the Dreyfus Case, that a Jew was not to be trusted.

It was the Dreyfus Case which brought anti-Semitic feeling to its highest point, though this was not so evident in the earlier stages of the case. Gradually, under the influence of newspapers like *La Libre Parole* (in which young Léon Daudet, whose father, Alphonse, was a friend of Drumont, was already writing articles), the public became convinced not only of the Jewish accused's guilt, but also of the whole Affair as a monstrous plot geared by the Jews to destroy the army and the Church, those mainstays of traditional France. The cartoons of Forain and Caran d'Ache in the newspaper *Psst!* show the virulence of such feelings at the time.

Hatred of the Jews was made up as much of fear as of anything else; fear of the capitalist society, fear of foreigners, fear of the power of freemasons and Jews in the government, and of their force on the Republican side. And in the newspaper *Action Fran-çaise*, which took on much of the anti-Semitism of *La Libre Parole* and took its place in French journalism after Drumont handed over control of his paper in 1911, we find a mixture of all these fears, and added to them a fear of the Jew (so often bearing a Teutonic name) as a German spy within the nation.

In this paper Léon Daudet continued the tradition of Drumont, seeing in the Jew the plutocratic enemy who was destroying France, its government, its social system, its national traditions and its religion. Maurras, on the other hand, was more in the tradition of Barrès, in this period before the First World War; his anti-Semitism was incidental to his nationalism. He believed France's unity to be in danger of destruction through individualism and multiplicity of belief; he saw the only solution to this to be a reversion to traditional national values; and he saw all exceptions to these values as dangerous to the country. The Jews, like the other 'métèques', based their lives on other values and traditions and formed states within a state. Only by a restoration of the purity of the French race could France be saved.

Throughout this whole period anti-Semitism attracted men of all beliefs; it is fallacious to connect it with Catholicism or even with the Right alone. Many Catholic authors admittedly followed what had become the prejudices of the time, unthinkingly and mechanically. But others, and among them some of the greatest Catholic writers, thought deeply about the subject before making any kind of decision.

Many of those in whose work anti-Semitism appears as an incidental, hardly noticeable if one were not looking for it, are those who have little interest in or knowledge of politics, and who have taken their political ideas ready-made, and taken on the prejudices of their time. This is the case with many minor writers, particularly at the time of the Dreyfus Affair, when the legend of the 'Jewish plot' was in the air, a legend which we have seen Huysmans believing. Huysmans himself was very much aloof from politics and his anti-Semitism was of the irrational sort which has no need for theories or ideas. It reflects the reactions of many in this era. Take, for example, his immediate reaction when he discovered that his book *Sainte Lydwine de Schiedam* might be translated into

Dutch by a Jew; writing to Leclaire, he says, '. . . La pauvre *Lydwine*! . . . — je viens d'interdire sa traduction en Hollande! ! ! — imaginez que par Poelkekke j'ai appris qu'un traducteur qui s'était offert était un juif! ! !'[45] Some of Huysmans's anti-Semitism may, however, have come from the conception of the Jews as those who had betrayed Christ.

Bloy, Péguy and Claudel are three Catholic authors who spoke out strongly in favour of the Jews, each of them for different reasons.

Léon Bloy, in *Le Salut par les Juifs* (1892), proclaims his conception of the mission of the Jewish nation, of its place in the divine scheme. As with all Bloy's ideas, this is a mystical conception of some complexity in which the Jews are marked by their very misery and abjection as a chosen race. Misery and abjection are, for Bloy, signs of grace in whomever he perceives them, but Israel's mission is seen even more clearly as that of the necessary liberators of Christ for his physical reign on earth; Israel is essential to the coming of the Last Judgement. Salvation can only come 'through the Jews', who are mysteriously identified with the Paraclete. Their conversion will release Christ from the Cross: 'L'abjection même de cette Race est un Signe divin, le signe très manifeste de la permanence de l'Esprit-Saint sur ces hommes si méprisés qui doivent apparaître dans la Gloire du Consolateur, à la fin des fins.'[46]

There is no point here in going into the details of this conception. Enough to say that Bloy's view of the Jews is governed by a mystical idea which enables him on the one hand to see them as having a unique spiritual mission, and on the other hand to despise them, temporally, for that very abjection which is necessary to them. If he did not find them vile they would not have the true sign of their mission. 'Ils son *forcés* par Dieu, invinciblement et surnaturellement forcés, d'accomplir les abominables cochonneries dont ils ont besoin pour accréditer leur déshonneur *d'instruments de la Rédemption*.'[47] Physically and morally, Bloy sees each individual Jew as the vilest creature on earth: 'Au point de vue moral et physique, le Youtre moderne paraît être le confluent de toutes les hideurs du monde.'[48] And Bloy sees the former view of the Church as having been the correct one. In *Le Salut par les Juifs* he declares that he sees no reason to change the following passage, which he had written a few years before:

Le Moyen Age . . . avait le bon sens de les cantonner dans des chenils réservés et de leur imposer une défroque spéciale qui permît à chacun de les éviter. Quand on avait absolument affaire à ces puants, on s'en cachait comme d'une infamie et on se purifiait ensuite comme on pouvait. La honte et le péril de leur contact était l'antidote chrétien de leur pestilence, puisque Dieu tenait à la perpétuité d'une telle vermine.

Aujourd'hui que le christianisme a l'air de râler sous le talon de ses propres croyants et que l'Eglise a perdu tout crédit, on s'indigne bêtement de voir en eux les maîtres du monde, et les contradicteurs enragés de la Tradition apostolique sont les premiers à s'en étonner. On prohibe le désinfectant et on se plaint d'avoir des punaises. Telle est l'idiotie caractéristique des temps modernes.[49]

Thus when Bloy claims that he is going to write about Israel 'from the highest point of view' he is speaking the truth, but not in the way that some Jews (e.g. Bernard-Lazare) have since presumed. The book is in favour of Israel in the mystical sense, yet it sees Israel, in the temporal sense, as something to be hated. Bloy attacks Drumont for the 'low' way in which he has treated the Jewish question by speaking only of money, but he does *not* criticise him for his anti-Semitism:

Certes, je déteste les Juifs autant qu'il est possible, mais pour des raisons plus hautes que leurs ignobles écus. Le fait de la richesse publique entre leurs mains est, à mes yeux, un profond *mystère* qui intéresse à la métaphysique la plus transcendante et c'est ce que Drumont, avide seulement de scandales et de droits d'auteur, est incapable de comprendre.[50]

The Jews are chosen, and are to be honoured in one sense, but in another they are to be despised: 'Plus que jamais il est clair pour moi que la société chrétienne est empuantie d'une bien dégoûtante engeance et c'est terrible de savoir qu'elle est *perpétuelle* par la volonté de Dieu.[51] The mystical state of the Jewish race is directly linked with their vileness, in Bloy's mind.

Émile Baumann, who was greatly impressed by Bloy, shared to some extent his master's views on the Jewish question, and his idea of the divine mission, taken from Bloy, is fairly clearly stated in his *Mémoires*:

Je n'étais pas antisémite. Si la canaillerie, la rapacité féroce, la perversion intellectuelle de maint juif me dégoûtait d'eux, le mystère d'Israël, humilié à travers les siècles et dominateur, me prouvait la vocation unique de ce peuple irréductible, dont la conversion tardive signifiera la fin des temps.[52]

Charles Péguy was perhaps the most pro-Jewish Gentile writer of his age, and if he saw the Jewish race's mystical destiny, he saw it in a very different light from Léon Bloy. He perceived the Jews' traditional mission, but did not move off into the eschatological intricacies of Bloy; and he saw the French race, as well as being inheritors of the Greeks and Romans and of the Christian tradition, as being closely tied to the Jewish tradition as well. The French are the inheritors of the Jews, says Péguy, in that they have learned from them the infinite price of the temporal, terrestrial survival of a race, especially if that race is 'une race comme cette race la seule visiblement élue de toutes les races modernes, la race française.'[53]

Péguy's admiration for the Jews is above all personified in his great friend Bernard-Lazare, who had done so much to bring the Dreyfus Case to light. Péguy was continually defending the Jews against the calumnies perpetrated by men such as Drumont, against 'L'affirmation sans preuves, qui a si bien réussi à M. Edouard Drumont. . . . Il est beaucoup plus facile de répéter une condamnation que de motiver une accusation, et . . . cela réussit beaucoup mieux. . . . Les calomnies les plus grossières sont celles qui trouvent le plus large crédit.'[54] In relation to the Dreyfus Affair, Péguy states in *Notre Jeunesse* (1910) how ridiculous the idea of a 'Jewish plot' is. Anyone who really knew the Jews would realise that they never arouse tumults but continually seek peace. The Jews themselves had at first been among the strongest resisters of revisionism, for fear of what the Affair might bring. But a prophet had arisen, in the shape of Bernard-Lazare, and many of them had then seen the fatality of their role. But of all the resistances Bernard-Lazare had had to face, the Jewish resistances had been the strongest; and those who, later, pardoned him the least were the Jews. It was the Jews who suffered from the Dreyfus Case, says Péguy, and they suffered not only from the Affair itself, but from the betrayal of the cause which had been effected by a small group of political Dreyfusists, such as Jaurès and Hervé, none of whom was Jewish.

The true division in France, says Péguy, is between the rich and the poor, not between the Jews and the Gentiles. And the anti-

Semites, though they talk a lot about Jews, *do not really know any-thing about them*. Rich anti-Semites may know rich Jews; capitalist anti-Semites capitalist Jews; bourgeois anti-Semites bourgeois Jews; society anti-Semites society Jews; but nobody, except a poor man like Péguy, seems to know the poor and miserable Jews. It is a ridiculous thing to think that all Jews are rich. It is equally ridiculous to pretend that they are responsible for the modern world as it is, because it is they who suffer most from it: 'Tout le monde est malheureux dans le monde moderne. Les Juifs sont plus malheureux que les autres.'[55] It is even more ridiculous to criticise the mutual help provided by the close-knit Jewish society, because 'Le mutuel appui qu'ils se prêtent est amplement com-pensé, plus que compensé par cette effrayante, par cette croissante poussée de l'antisémitisme qu'ils reçoivent tout ensemble.'[56]

It is very difficult to be a Jew, because if the rich do not support the poor, people say, 'C'est pas étonnant, ils sont Juifs'; and if they do help others, people say, 'C'est pas étonnant, ils sont Juifs. Ils se soutiennent entre eux.' Similarly, if they do not listen to the cries of their persecuted brothers in other lands, people say, 'C'est des mauvais Juifs'; and if they do, people say, 'Ils nous trahissent. C'est des mauvais Francais.'[57]

A good exercise, says Péguy, is for any of us, if someone does us a bad turn, to say to ourselves: What would we have said about him if he had been a Jew? It is extremely striking, he continues, that none of France's greatest internal enemies are Jews: '. . . Il est remarquable que parmi les protagonistes de nos hontes nationales il n'y a aucun Juif. Qu'est-ce que l'on dirait si Jaurès était Juif. Qu'est-ce que l'on dirait, surtout, si Hervé était Juif?'[58] The anti-Semites cannot realise how false the picture they paint of the Jews is, says Péguy:

> Depuis vingt ans je les ai éprouvés, nous nous sommes éprouvés mutuellement. Je les ai trouvés toujours solides au poste, autant que personne, affectueux, solides, d'une tendresse propre, autant que personne, d'un attachement, d'un dévoue-ment, d'une piété inébranlable, d'une fidélité, à toute épréuve, d'une amitié réellement mystique, d'un attachement, d'une fidélité inébranlable à la mystique de l'amitié.[59]

Péguy's enthusiastic defence of the Jews is clear and straight-forward; he plants himself firmly on one side of the fence in the battle. Claudel, on the other hand, is not so much concerned with temporal controversy as with the concept of the Jews as one force among many in the changing world with which the characters in his trilogy must come to grips. Speaking of the second play of the trilogy, *Le Pain Dur*, Claudel makes this position clear:

> Dans ce drame, qui a comme partie de son sujet la Rupture des Barriéres et la Rencontre des Races, les Juifs ne pouvaient pas ne pas figurer. C'est à eux peut-être que ce congé de leur antique assujettissement rituel et juridique, leur relèvement de leur poste de témoins, posait la question la plus grave.[60]

No study of the Jewish question is intended in this play, or in its sequel *Le Père Humilié*, says Claudel: 'Le fait juif est trop important au regard de Dieu, pour qu'il soit possible d'en traiter de cette manière épisodique.' Yet we do find, in the desire for freedom from her Jewish bonds expressed by Sichel, who marries Georges de Coûfontaine, and thus adds to the mingling of the bloods which had started with the marriage of Turelure and Sygne de Coûfontaine in *L'Otage*, a parallel to the change of which the whole trilogy is a witness. And in Pensée, Sichel's daughter in *Le Père Humilié*, and her recognition of her Jewish heredity and all it means, there is a portrayal of the eternity of Israel's fate:

> Et voici que dans mes veines le plus grand sacrifice en moi s'est réuni à la plus grande infortune, et le plus grand orgueil.
>
> Le plus grand orgueil à plus grande déchéance et à la privation de tout honneur, Le Franc dans une seule personne avec le Juif.[61]

Claudel's attitude to the Jews is a sympathetic one. He nevertheless feels constrained to explain how no offence is meant to the Jews by the characters he depicts:

> Si Ali et sa fille (Sichel) paraissent au lecteur antipathiques, — *pas plus que mes autres personnages* — je ne veux pas qu'on voie là de ma part l'indice d'aucun jugement général et sommaire. Ce sont là des figures commandées par le drame, rien de plus, et dont je n'ai été que le premier spectateur. . . . *J'ajoute que c'est parmi les Juifs que j'ai rencontré quelques-uns de mes meilleurs amis.*

NOTES

[1] Mgr. A. Pons, *La Guerre et l'Âme Française*, 1915.

[2] Who appears to have introduced the word *nationalisme* into the French language.

[3] Barrès, *Mes Cahiers*, 1914.

[4] Quoted in Jean-Marie Domenach, *Barrès par Lui-même*.

[5] Baumann, *Mémoires*, 1943, p. 171.

[6] Ibid., p. 304. My italics.

[7] Claudel, *La Nuit de Noël 1914*, 1915; Pléiade, Théâtre II, p. 581. My italics.

[8] Claudel, *La Vocation de Saint Louis*, 1942; Pléiade, Poetry, p. 770.

[9] Péguy, *Le Mystère des Saints Innocents*, 24 March 1912; Pléiade, Poetry, p. 676.

[10] Ibid., p. 714.

[11] Ibid., pp. 739 ff.

[12] Péguy, *Ève*, 28 December 1913; Pléiade, Poetry, p. 1170.

[13] Early contributions by Péguy to the *Revue Blanche* (in the years around 1898) had been anti-militaristic in tone. But long before his conversion he had turned his back on such ideas and had, in fact, built up a legend of his youthful nationalism.

[13a] In the work of Louis Bertrand there is an added reason for France's colonial mission: the concept of North Africa as the natural setting for the Latin race, of which France was now the main example.

[14] Charles de Foucauld, letter to Auguste Terrier, 5 February 1915; Bibliothèque de l'Institut, MS. 5898.

[15] Bourget, *Le Sens de la Mort*, 1915, pp. 44 f.

[16] Claudel, *La Nuit de Noël 1914*, 1915; Pléiade, Théâtre II, pp. 578 f. General de Castelnau was one of the leading French generals of the First World War. He was a devout Catholic.

[17] Ibid., p. 579.

[18] M.-J. Lory devotes several pages to this problem in Appendix I of *La Pensée religieuse de Léon Bloy*.

[19] In *Contes du Lundi*, 1873.

[20] Barrès, *Au Service de l'Allemagne*, 1905.

[21] Péguy, *L'Argent Suite*, 22 April 1913; Pléiade, Prose II, p. 1195.

[22] Ibid., p. 1183.

[23] 'Agathon', *L'Esprit de la Nouvelle Sorbonne*, 1911.

[24] Mgr. A. Pons, *La Guerre et l'Âme Française*, 1915, p. 137.

[25] Nesmy, *Les Égarés*, 1906, p. 127.

[26] Barrès, *Mes Cahiers*, 1913.

[27] Ibid., 1913.

[28] Ibid., 1914.

[29] Quoted in Weber, *Action Française*, 1962, p. 111.

[30] Péguy, *Compte Rendu de Congrès*, 1 October 1901; Pléiade, Prose I, p. 390.

[31] Péguy, *Pour la Rentrée*, 26 September 1905.

[32] Péguy, *Notre Patrie*, 17 October 1905; Pléiade, Prose I, p. 834.

[33] Ibid., p. 832.

[34] Ibid., p. 822.

[35] Péguy, *Notre Jeunesse*, 12 July 1910; Pléiade, Prose II, p. 583.

[36] Ibid., p. 621.

[37] *L'Argent Suite*, 22 April 1913; Pléiade, Prose II, p. 1192.

[38] Ibid., pp. 1201 f.

[39] Ibid., p. 1205.

[40] Ibid., p. 1226.

[41] Ibid., p. 1192.

[42] Péguy, *Victor-Marie, Comte Hugo*, 1910; Pléiade, Prose II, p. 831.

[43] Barrès, *Mes Cahiers*, 1912.

[44] Ibid., 1920.

[45] Huysmans, letter to Leclaire, 28 April 1901.

[46] Bloy, *Le Vieux de la Montagne*.

[47] Bloy, *Le Salut par les Juifs*, Chapter 10.

[48] Ibid., Chapter 4.

[49] Ibid., Chapter 4.

[50] Bloy, *Belluaires et Porchers*, 1892, 'Le Bon Conseil'.

[51] Bloy, *Le Salut par les Juifs*, Chapter 4.

[52] Baumann, *Mémoires*, p. 303.

[53] Péguy, *Louis de Gonzague*, 26 December 1905; Pléiade, Prose I, p. 938.

[54] Péguy, *Compte Rendu de Mandat*, 25 April 1901; Pléiade, Prose I, p. 357.

[55] Péguy, *Notre Jeunesse*, 12 July 1910; Pléiade, Prose II, p. 627.

[56] Ibid., p. 628.

[57] Ibid., p. 631.

[58] Ibid., p. 633.

[59] Ibid., p. 629.

[60] Claudel, comment on *Le Pain Dur*, printed in Pléiade, Théâtre II, p. 1361.

[61] Claudel, *Le Père Humilié*, 1916; Pléiade, Théâtre II, p. 538. My italics.

CHAPTER TWELVE

Order

'C'EST l'amour qui refuse à jamais de sortir de cette éternelle liberté dont je suis la captive!'[1] cries Dona Prouhèze in Claudel's play *Le Soulier de Satin,* and it is perhaps in the works of Claudel that we find most clearly expressed that conception of order based on liberty (or liberty based on order) which is common to almost all the authors of the Revival. True liberty is seen as being the acceptance of an order which comes from without; captivity is seen as being the obsessive need to seek for individual liberty at all times. Gide is seen as a captive of his need to assert his individuality; Claudel is seen as being truly free, in that he has given his acceptance, and is now submissive to a rule which he could have refused.

One of the greatest horrors for the Catholic authors of this period is individualism, whether in private morality, personal modes of belief, or even politics. The dangers of modernism in belief and of democracy in politics are seen to stem from the same source. What man needs to do is submit himself voluntarily to an order in which he can place his trust, and not take on himself individual decisions of belief and policy which produce, in the field of morals, uncertainty, in the field of belief, a heretical reliance on immanent rather than transcendental truth, and in the field of politics, disorder and confusion.

In this chapter we shall examine some of the repercussions of this belief. Firstly, we shall be dealing with that further order to which so many Catholics, after their conversion, believed they should submit themselves; a freely-taken decision to submit to a rule, whether it be in the form of a vow,[2] or of a sacrifice.

The Monastic Vocation

Few of the converts of this time did not go through a period, just after their conversion, when they wondered whether a further step in the direction of order was not demanded of them. Huysmans, Bloy, Nouveau, Claudel and Psichari are but a few of those, in the literary world, who were strongly influenced by the idea of taking the vows of one or other of the Orders of the Church. The zeal of the neophyte was, perhaps, leading them too quickly to such decisions, however, for those authors who took the plunge of actively seeking admission to a monastic order were refused by those to whom they went.

Léon Bloy is the most violent example of this trend, and in the objections of the Trappist monk who refused him are contained many of the reasons for which the Catholic authors of the day were received with such mistrust by the monastic Orders. Bloy himself describes, in a letter to Barbey d'Aurevilly, the advice he has been given:

> Vous ne possédez pas encore votre coeur et, par conséquent, vous n'êtes pas en état de le donner. Si, obéissant à un mouve-ment de générosité et d'enthousiasme, vous prenez tout à coup la résolution de rester parmi nous, il y aurait à craindre qu'au bout de trois jours, vous prissiez la fuite, fallût-il pour cela escalader les murailles de notre monastère.[3]

Bloy had seen in the monastic life above all the best opportunity for that existence of reparation to which he wished to devote him-self. He had been thinking of it for a long time. But it was the death of his father in 1877 (and Bloy's belief that he himself had not only hastened that end but deprived his father of his prayers, by staying with Anne-Marie instead of rushing to his father's bedside) which made him suddenly see the necessity of this step:

> Si mon père avait le droit de compter spécialement sur moi pendant sa vie, il a encore plus le droit d'y compter après sa mort. Ce n'est pas assez de faire dire quelques messes et quelques communions. Il faut que je me dévoue entièrement, il faut une réparation complète, un sacrifice absolu et sans réserve, c'est pour cela que je veux me faire trappiste.[4]

As he explained in a letter to Barbey d'Aurevilly, before this he had been prepared to wait for signs of a vocation; now he cannot afford even to wait to see if there are any contrary indications. His reasons for going can be seen, from this letter,[5] to be a desire both to make reparation and to escape from the appalling world around him. He wished, moreover, to give himself up to God without reserve, sacrificing completely his intellectual life: 'Le plus grand malheur qui pourrait aujourd'hui m'arriver serait d'apprendre que

Dieu ne veut absolument pas que j'embrasse la vie religieuse.'

It was no doubt a realisation of this violence, and of the fact that Bloy was passionately attached to Anne-Marie Roulé, which led the Trappists to reject him. The rejection was nevertheless humanely handled, and, as Bloy describes it, hope was held out for him:

Les résultats de ses recherches sur moi et de ses prières a été que je n'étais pas encore mûr pour la vie religieuse. Il est fort possible, m'a-t-il dit, que Dieu vous y destine, je vois en vous bien des choses qui me porteraient à le croire, mais vous êtes encore agité de trop de contradictions.[6]

It should also have been pointed out to Bloy, as it was to Germain Nouveau, that it is not essential to Christian life to go to the extreme of becoming a monk. Each man is called to a different vocation in the world, according to God's divine pattern and to his own capabilities. As Nouveau was told on the occasion of one of his later attempts to live the monastic life:

Tout le monde n'est point appelé à suivre le même voie; chacun a la sienne lui permettant d'arriver sûrement au ciel. Le saint curé d'Ars, à plusieurs reprises, a tenté de se faire religieux; toujours la Divine Providence montra que telle n'était pas sa volonté. Comme lui, quoique restant parmi les dangers et les ennuis du monde, vous pouvez devenir un grand saint et je suis convaincu que vous le deviendrez.[7]

It is the ignoring, or the denying, of human limitations which is the main fault in these people's attitude to the monastic life. Bloy, Nouveau and Claudel cannot see any but the most heroic way as being that of the Christian. Having become Christian, they feel that they must give up everything, including their literary craft. They cannot conceive of their role in the Christian world as being that of a writer, rather than that of a Saint. Huysmans, here as in other things, is the reasonable exception. He longs for the monastic life but, finding that he does not have a true vocation, and finding also an incompatibility between the monastic life and his literary work, he attempts a compromise by becoming a Benedictine oblate. The contrast between Huysmans's acceptance of his position, and Claudel's despair when not accepted for the monastic life, is great; a study of these two authors will show us clearly, in the case of Claudel, the intransigence typical of the Revival.

'Aucun converti qui ne se soit demandé avec une profonde angoisse si Dieu qui lui a commandé un premier pas ne lui en demande un second',[8] writes Claudel. He realised, as much as did Huysmans, the difficulty for an artistic sensibility of giving up all those parts of the human personality on which it was most dependent. In his *Mémoires Improvisés* Claudel described to Jean Amrouche the difficulty of the decision: 'Malgré tout, on n'arrive pas à un choix définitif de l'existence, qui consiste somme toute à refouler des parties très importantes de l'homme, surtout chez un artiste, les parties d'imagination, de sensibilité, le besoin d'affection, etc. . . .'[9] Nevertheless, Claudel decided to take the 'heroic' path of suppressing all these parts of his character: 'J'avais, en somme, plus ou moins consciemment, *à les refouler* au profit de la formation rationnelle et spirituelle que je suivais alors.'[10] He therefore went to Ligugé in September 1900 and asked to be accepted as a novice, 'ayant fait le sacrifice complet d'une poésie que je croyais inutile au service de Dieu.'[11]

The sense of constraint in Claudel's description of this process shows us that he had little feeling of vocation for the monastic life but was attempting to force it on himself. Huysmans, on the other hand, started by wondering whether he had a vocation for the life, and when a Benedictine monk, Dom Delatte, tried to persuade him that, because his reason told him that the monastic life was superior to all others and that it assured his salvation, he should therefore force his will to follow his reason and let God do the rest, Huysmans was not in the slightest bit convinced:

> Cela me semblait mettre la charrue avant les boeufs, Dieu après et non avant; c'était se jeter à l'eau et le forcer en quelque sorte a vous sauver. . . .[12]

> C'est nier la vocation, la touche divine, l'impulsion, l'attrait; c'est s'obéir sans attendre l'appel du Christ auquel on prétend infliger ses vues.[13]

Claudel would appear to have been in great danger of doing these very things of which Huysmans so disapproved. Speaking of the religious vocation, Claudel declared that it was nothing if it was not the substitution of God's will for one's own, and that if one had it, 'on coule à fond son bateau, les vaisseaux sont brûlés, si je peux dire.'[14] Claudel's own inner struggles on this matter, as expressed in the *Vers d'Exil* and in the Preface to *Partage de Midi*, show that the decision was extremely difficult. In the dangerous form of suppression which Claudel was practising, and which was so obviously recognised by the monks who refused him,[15] he was very near to those 'durs-à-cuire du Bon Dieu'[16] whom Huysmans described as inflicting their own views on Christ. In his conception of the true religious as scuttling his own ship beneath him ('Heureux qui . . . coule tout son navire sous lui et passe outre par la passion et le désir'[17]), he is perilously near to Huysmans's idea of the man without vocation throwing himself into the water in order to force God to save him. That the monks were right in refusing him is shown by his reaction to their decision: 'Il est probable que si j'avais demandé d'une manière vraiment ferme de rester à Ligugé, j'y serais resté, *mais le coeur me manquait, et ce sacrifice du don principal qui constituait sans doute ma vocation personnelle était trop grand pour mes forces.*'[18]

Huysmans, when he realised his own unsuitability for the monastic life, had become an oblate, living outside the monastery but participating in some of its ceremonies and being part of the community. Claudel, who came to Ligugé six months after Huysmans's oblature ceremony, and who was therefore there at the same time as Huysmans, was overwhelmed by his rejection as a monk, and, probably because of the violence and constraint of his original attitude, went off in the wildest despair.

Writing to Louis Massignon in 1908, in reply to a question about his opinions on the conception of oblature held by Huysmans, Claudel scornfully dismissed it as being a half-solution: 'Le principal reproche que je lui fais est celui-ci, on ne se fait pas moine à moitié. Qui se fait moine entre dans une voie de perfection dont la fin unique est l'union aux volontés de Dieu et dont la première condition est un parfait renoncement à soi-même.'[19]

Of course, Claudel is right in this conception of the monastic life, and his sentiment had been expressed to Huysmans himself many years earlier by Madame Cécile Bruyère, Abbess of Solesmes: '. . . On ne peut être religieux et surtout moine a demi. . . .'[20] But Madame Bruyère, in this letter, was warning Huysmans against the dangers of *internal* oblature, within the monastery itself, as the rest of what she had to say proves. She would have had no objection to *external* oblature, as lived outside the monastery; in fact, as the *Manuel des Oblats de Saint Benoit* tells us, the whole point of oblature is that it was instituted for those who found it impossible to take on the vows of monasticism, i.e. those who had no vocation for the monastic life:

Dieu, dans sa sagesse infinie, ne convie pas toutes les âmes au même degré de perfection. La vie monastique exigeant la pratique des conseils évangéliques, et, par conséquent, le renoncement à la volonté propre, au droit de la propriété, aux joies de la famille, *ne saurait évidemment être le partage que d'un nombre plutôt restreint d'appelés,* mais néanmoins le Seigneur, voulant la sanctification de tous les hommes, se plaît à inspirer et a entretenir, *même parmi les chrétiens vivant dans le monde, le désir d'une perfection compatible avec les obligations de la vie séculière.*[21]

Seen in this way, oblature is an order parallel to monastic life rather than a way leading to it. Few men would believe that in becoming an oblate, he would later become a monk. This would be to confound noviciate and oblature. Yet this is exactly what Claudel believed when he himself became an oblate, and it explains much of his disgust at Huysmans's concept of oblature (the correct one), which he described as being 'moitié moitié.' Deprived of this solution and unable to believe that he had been considered unworthy of what he thought of as the sole way to salvation, Claudel believed himself to be rejected by God and to be condemned aimlessly to wander in his old life:

Or je voulais tout donner

Il me faut tout reprendre. Je suis parti, il me faut revenir à la même place.

Tout a été en vain. Il n'y a rien de fait. J'avais en moi

La force d'un grand espoir! Il n'est plus. J'ai été trouvé manquant. J'ai perdu mon sens et mon propos.

Et ainsi je suis renvoyé tout nu, avec l'ancienne vie, tout sec, avec point d'autre consigne

Que l'ancienne vie à recommencer, l'ancienne vie à recommencer, ô Dieu! la vie, séparé de la vie,

Mon Dieu, sans autre attente que Vous seul qui ne voulez point de moi,

Avec un coeur atteint, avec une force faussée![22]

It was while he was in this state that he had his love affair with a married woman; and in his tardy realisation of his sin, and the horror it inspired in him, we find the cause for the renewed search for 'order' which then obsessed him. Lack of order had caused his downfall, he believed; monastic order was denied him; order must be sought in a different direction, in marriage.

Claudel and Order in Marriage[23]

Le rêve de Huysmans est celui d'un béguinage ou des gens cultivés achèvent de vivre en faisant leurs dévotions [Claudel wrote to Massignon]. Ce n'est pas une retraite pour un homme travaillé par l'idée dévorante du devoir ou attaqué dans ses profondeurs par cette chose qu'on appelle si justement la 'passion'. Il y faut un sacrement spécial qu'on appelle justement l'ordre, qui donne une forme définitive à l'homme en l'emprisonnant dans une vocation irrévocable.[24]

Filled with this 'devouring sense of duty', Claudel had attempted to 'imprison himself in an irrevocable vocation' by becoming a monk and by renouncing without recall his literary gift. When, quite rightly, he was refused by the monks of Ligugé, his whole world was shattered, for he could not conceive of his purpose in life as being any less than the most heroic. He was deprived, too, of that 'order' which be believed to be essential to man. It was while obsessed with this sense of 'not belonging' that he had the adventure which he says is described in *Partage de Midi*: 'J'avais alors 32 ans, l'âge vraiment critique, et les deux premiers actes de *Partage de Midi* ne sont qu'une relation exacte de l'aventure horrible ou je faillis laisser mon âme et ma vie, apres dix ans de vie chrétienne et de chasteté absolue.'[25]

Louis Massignon used to claim that the love affair to which this refers, far from being the greatest danger to Claudel's soul, was in fact one of the best and most useful things that could have happened to Claudel at this stage of his life, together with the refusal of his monastic 'vocation', because the two events were the only moments in his career when his spiritual pride was silenced. This may, indeed, have been true, but Claudel could never have seen it as such, nor did he when Massignon suggested the idea to him many years later. He saw only the complete destruction of the stern Christian life he had been building for himself, and when this realisation finally came to him he looked around him for a new 'order' to which he could submit himself. Without such an 'order', he felt, man was in perpetual danger: 'Je crois . . . qu'en dehors des voeux et des règles de la milice ecclésiastique combinés avec une profonde sagesse l'état de célibat est des plus dangereux, moins à cause des choses de la chair, que des grandes tentations de l'acédia qui arrivent tôt ou tard, surtout aux voyageurs.'[26]

There is one solution, therefore, for a man who has been refused the 'order' of monastic life, and that is to take on the 'order' of marriage: 'Un homme non marié ou non consacré n'a pas recu d'ordre. Il reste ouvert et imparfait. Le sacrement remplace la sainte clôture.'[27]

It is this strange concept of marriage which accounts for the situation which obtains in almost all of Claudel's plays from now on, where marriages are almost always contracted with those who are not loved, and where the lovers are eternally separated. Sygne de Coûfontaine marries Turelure, in *L'Otage* (1909); Pensée de Coûfontaine must marry Orso, the brother of the man she loves, in *Le Père Humilié* (1916); Dona Prouhèze is married first to Don Pélage, and then to Don Camille, in *Le Soulier de Satin* (1924), while she is perpetually separated from her lover, Don Rodrigue.

The Pope, in *Le Père Humilié*, when giving advice to the brothers Orian and Orso, explains the purpose of marriage. Speaking to Orian, he says:

Dans tout ce que vous dites je ne vois que la passion et les sens
   et aucun esprit de prudence et de crainte de Dieu.
Cette jeune fille vous a plu et vous ne voyez rien d'autre.
Mais le mariage n'est point le plaisir, c'est le sacrifice du plaisir,
   c'est l'étude de deux âmes qui pour toujours désormais et
   pour une fin hors d'elles-mêmes
Auront à se contenter l'une de l'autre.[28]

It is Orso who must marry Pensée, just as in *Le Soulier de Satin*, when Don Pélage dies, Prouhèze marries Don Camille. Don Pélage, in this play, stresses again the divorce between love and marriage:

Ce n'est pas l'amour qui fait le mariage mais le consentement
Ni l'enfant que je n'ai pas eu, ni le bien de la société, mais *le
   consentement en présence de Dieu dans la foi.*[29]

Marriage is a duty and an order; and the breaking of the marriage vow is seen as a heinous sin. But for this very reason marriage is seen as being an effective instrument in that separation of lovers which is essential to their salvation. Rodrigue, towards the end of the stage version of *Le Soulier de Satin*, recoils as Prouhèze lifts her hand, with its wedding-ring, towards him, and though he has crossed half the world to see her he finds that he cannot take her.

Like the medieval troubadours and the Renaissance neo-Platonists Claudel sees true love as lying outside marriage. But to this conception he adds that of the necessary suffering which will purify the souls of the lovers. Like the troubadours, he sees that this true love must be pure. Guided by his own experience in China, he sees adultery as destroying the soul and body:

> Au lieu de les illuminer, il les brûle. Au lieu de les consommer, il les consume. Au lieu de s'apporter l'un à l'autre le salut, ils s'apportent l'un à l'autre la damnation. . . . Dans le mariage il y a deux êtres qui consentent l'un à l'autre, dans l'adultère il y a deux êtres qui se condamnent l'un à l'autre.[30]

The true lover must suffer, and his suffering will not only save him and his loved one but will also bring him closer to an understanding of God. At the beginning of *Le Soulier de Satin* a dying Jesuit prays for his brother, Rodrigue, in such a way that the whole plot of the play is made clear to us:

> Apprenez-lui que Vous n'êtes pas la seul à pouvoir être absent! Liez-le par le poids de cet autre être sans lui si beau qui l'appelle à travers l'intervalle!
>
> Faites de lui un homme blessé parce qu'une fois en cette vie il a vu la figure d'un ange!
>
> Remplissez ces amants d'un tel désir qu'il implique à l'exclusion de leur présence dans le hasard journalier
>
> L'intégrité primitive et leur essence même telle que Dieu les a conçus autrefois dans un rapport inextinguible![31]

The Platonic elements in this passage are obvious; but to the Platonic conception Claudel adds, in the play itself, that idea of necessary suffering which we have seen in Chapter Eight. The suffering is not only valuable for their own salvation; it is also important for that of the world, right up to the moment when Rodrigue, at the end, ragged and in chains, is accepted by a nun to do menial tasks in a convent.

It is marriage which provides the order and the discipline which permits such heroism as the separation of the lovers' demands. Marriage has become the new frame for the heroic life which Claudel saw as being demanded of the Christian, and it has replaced that monasticism which was denied him.

The Army and the Church

In the works of many Catholic philosophers of the nineteenth century, war and the army were seen as being closely connected with the Christian life. Joseph de Maistre observed the fact that war did not degrade the soldier but on the contrary tended to make him more perfect. The nobility of the soldier, in his eyes, was capable of ennobling even the most apparently ignoble of actions. Blanc de Saint-Bonnet, following him, saw in war something divine, because by giving the opportunity for sacrifice it put the soldier on the way to perfection. Here, again, is that concentration on the necessity for sacrifice which becomes so typical of the thought of the Revival: 'La guerre est divine parce qu'ouvrant carrière au sacrifice, elle forme les âmes pour Dieu.'[32] Blanc quotes Mahomet as saying that the whole earth would be entirely corrupt if it were not for the purifying influence of war, and Euripides as describing Helen's beauty as having been the instrument whereby the gods could bring war to the earth and make that blood flow which might purify an earth which was soiled by excessive crimes. In this pagan concept there is much that is similar to the idea of substitution for the sins of others through death in war, an idea common to many Catholic authors, including Psichari and Bourget.

In this capacity for sacrifice, Blanc de Saint-Bonnet saw a relationship between the soldier and the saint, a relationship which was to be stressed for slightly different reasons by other writers. He believes the soldier to be linked to the saint by sacrifice, in which the soldier is in the line of perfection (i.e. in a lower grade) which is topped by the saint:

Il n'y a rien de bon au monde comme les saints et les vieux soldats! . . . C'est à dessein que je vois le soldat suivre la même ligne d'éducation que le saint. La civilisation a commencé par la guerre, elle finira par la Sainteté. L'une entreprend et l'autre achève l'école du sacrifice. Toutes deux firent naître en l'homme la soif sacrée de la mort.[33]

In the works of the Catholic writers of the end of the nineteenth century and the beginning of the twentieth (with the exception of Huysmans, whose own army experiences in 1870 were hardly heroic), this conception of a close link between army life and the Church remains very clear, and this connection does not rest solely, as some historical writers have suggested, upon the fact that the army and the Church were the only two careers left open, thanks to the infiltration of Masonry and Republicanism into all other professional employments, to the young Catholic and to the young aristocrat. Even if such circumstances had not been operative, the ranks of the army would still have been filled with Catholics, not only because of the religious conception of sacrifice in war, but also because of the feeling that, both in the army and in the Christian religion, there was an 'order' which linked them closely, and a similar preoccupation with the tradition and patriotism which were being neglected, Catholics felt, by Republican France.

Ernest Psichari, the young writer who was attracted both to the army and to the Church by the traditionalism and patriotism of which he saw them as the repositories, standing out against the appalling modern age which was forgetting these values, would nevertheless not have been so attracted to these bodies if he had not seen in them that 'order' he was seeking. This 'order' he sought first of all solely in the army, and it was only gradually that he came to see in the Church the further embodiment of the values he was seeking. He is but one example of many who were attracted to the Church by the 'order' for which it stood, and his case is particularly interesting because, instead of proceeding from the Catholic concept of order to an involvement in things military, as had so many of his contemporaries, his spiritual progress had been in the opposite direction. The outcome is the same: a conviction of the close relationship between the army and the Church as temporal and spiritual examples of order.

Psichari's attraction to the army was originally unconnected with Christianity. In a letter to Mme. Favre, the mother of Jacques Maritain, written in 1909, he said of the new novel he was planning (which was to become *L'Appel des Armes*, 1913):

> Le principal personnage serait l'armée, l'antique institution qui nous rattache au passé, toujours pareille et identique à elle-même, dont la beauté réside dans son immutabilité, l'armée toujours isolée, non mêlée à la nation, mais au-dessus d'elle.... Quel bon coup de pied à donner au siècle, quel soufflet aux partisans des concessions! L'armée serait plantée là, pas moderne du tout, *avec le rôle, la mission supérieure de sauvegarde qu'avait autrefois l'Eglise et que celle-ci ne peut plus avoir.*[34]

Psichari's dissatisfaction, after his conversion, with the novel *L'Appel des Armes* was partly based on the preponderant part the army played in the book, with the Church far less in evidence than in his later novel, posthumously published, *Le Voyage du Centurion* (1915). Yet in the earlier novel, despite such remarks as 'L'armée, *seule aujourd'hui*, et malgré les efforts que l'on a faits, possède une tradition',[35] we do find a sense, particularly in the latter part of the book, of the Church's condition as being parallel to that of the army. Psichari refers to the vocation of the soldier as being comparable to that of a monk, and in an important passage he compares the mysticism of the army with that of the Church. He describes M. Vincent, the hero's father, as seeing in these two bodies an alliance against those progressive ideas which he shared with so many others of his time, and as describing this alliance, in the familiar phrase, as that of 'le sabre et le goupillon'. Maurice Vincent suddenly realises that these words of his father are partly true.

In the phrase 'Ense et cruce', he muses, one can see the symbols of two dogmas, two systems; and, while these are different systems, and by no means closely allied as his father claims, they do share common mystical bases:

> . . . Et pourtant, comme les deux signes se marient bien dans le ciel illuminé de Maurice, et comme, tous les deux, il les aperçoit tout près l'un de l'autre, apparaissant tout seuls, et auréolés de surnaturels rayons!
>
> Ç'est qu'il est une marque commune a toutes les mystiques, et cette marque est la recherche d'une haute passion qui nous ravisse hors de nous-mêmes, et nous contraigne de pleurer d'amour.[36]

Admittedly, Psichari still depicts his hero as being unconvinced of the validity of Christian belief:

> Je t'accorde, si tu veux, que nos prières, a nous soldats, sont aussi vaines que celles des prêtres. Mais telles qu'elles sont, je les préfère encore aux déductions des doctrines de raison et aux prétentions des doctrines de science. Tant mieux, si c'est une folie que ces prières. Je suis ainsi, de les préférer.[37]

But he nevertheless declares, both in his letters of this time and in his book *L'Appel des Armes*, the necessity for the priest, the scholar and the soldier, who all three have a 'spiritual order' and a mysticism of their own which is essential to the country: 'Il n'y a pas de régime plus intolérant que la République, peut-être parce qu'il n'y en a pas de plus instable. Tout ce qui est d'ordre spirituel a été persécuté: le prêtre, le soldat, le savant. Et ce crime a été prémédité, voulu.'[38]

By the end of *L'Appel des Armes* the hero, under the influence of Islam, is already coming closer to the Christian religion. All the reasons which Psichari has found for accepting Christianity, whether they be order, tradition, patriotism or the example of the

Muslims, may have brought him close to conversion, but the necessary belief was lacking. Henri Massis has described both himself and Psichari as having taken all but this last step, which was for a while denied them by divine grace. In a letter to Maurras written after his own conversion Psichari expresses his belief that Maurras, convinced of the force and utility of the Church, is in the same situation that he was in until the moment of grace.

In *Le Voyage du Centurion*, the novel of Psichari's conversion, the various things which brought him to Christianity are seen as being common both to the Church and to the army. The centre is now the Church, and in his concept of the Christian 'order' achieved in the military life Psichari is entirely in line with the Catholicism of his day. This order is seen as the true liberty: 'Maxence entrevoit que le plus haut état de la conscience humaine est là, dans cet accord suprême de l'effort avec la soumission, de la liberté avec la servitude, et que cet accord ne se fait nulle part ailleurs qu'en Jésus-Christ.'[39] All individual efforts at a moral life are castigated by Psichari as being the faults of the stoics and the Huguenots, and as leading to pride, which spoils everything. In Christ, on the other hand, one aspires to the heights, while realising that one is infinitely low, 'Et cela est vrai, puisque nous sommes dans la liberté, autant que dans la servitude.' God has chosen the soldier above all other men, 'afin que la grandeur et la servitude du soldat fussent la figuration, sur la terre, de la grandeur et la servitude du chrétien.'[40]

Though Psichari looked to a further order, that of a Dominican friar, soon after his conversion, he was deterred from this by various reasons, the greatest of which was his conception of the military life as an order bestowed on him by God:

Je crois qu'Il me demande en ce moment de continuer à servir la France qu'Il aime tant, et à rester dans l'armée, qui a besoin de soldats chrétiens. Mais je ne veux pas vivre autrement que pour la gloire de notre père des Cieux, et c'est un soldat du Christ que j'ambitionne d'être, *miles Christi*.[41]

Like so many of his contemporaries, he saw the First World War as being good and necessary to the honour and greatness of France. He described it as a 'grande et magnifique aventure',[42] yet he also saw it as an occasion not only for personal perfection but also for a reparation for the sins of the nation. France is at last, he feels, acting as she should.

The Catholic of this age conceived of war as having four important purposes, all of which are expressed in Mgr. A. Pons's book *Le Guerre et l'Âme Française* (1915). These aims are (i) individual purification, by which the country itself will be made more perfect; (ii) individual sacrifice for the souls in Purgatory and for the rehabilitation of the nation; (iii) a patriotic defence of the country (as we have seen in the previous chapter), and the defeat not only of the German army but also of that German culture which had been invading France in the last century; and (iv) the defence of the Church in the person of its first-born, France.

We have already seen something of the effect which patriotism and the desire for revenge on Germany and for the recovery of Alsace-Lorraine had had upon French life (not only Catholic) before the Great War, but in the last concept, that of the defence of the Church by the army, there is more than that mere patriotism which saw France as first-born of the Church. There is also the theological concept of the necessity of both the temporal and the spiritual in the Church's life, and of the place of the army in the spreading of the Church's message. For the 'order' which the Catholic saw in the army was not merely one of personal import; the army itself had a place in the scheme of things.

Péguy sees and states this most clearly in his essay *L'Argent Suite* (1913), and it is natural that the fullest statement of it should come here, because in Péguy's writings the question of the intermingling of the temporal and spiritual takes a very important place. In this essay, however, Péguy merely expresses more clearly the feelings of many.

Everything depends on the army, and on physical power and order, he says; until such order is established nothing else can be established, whether it be law, art, or religion: 'L'armature militaire est le berceau temporel où les moeurs et les lois et les arts et la religion même et le langage et la race peuvent *ensuite, mais ensuite seulement, et alors seulement,* se coucher pour grandir.' The temporal, says Péguy, is essentially military, and even when people say it is financial they are saying this because they are thinking of money as a military force. It is this temporal military force which decided where the Latin declensions and conjugations were heard; it was this force which decided the limits of all things, temporal or spiritual: 'Le soldat mesure la quantité de terre où on parle une langue, où règnent des moeurs, un esprit, une âme, un culte, une race. Le soldat mesure la quantité de terre où une âme peut respirer.'[43]

In this pattern the quantity of temporal ground which the soldier measures, says Péguy, is the same as the spiritual ground and the intellectual ground. The Roman soldier measured the extent of Roman civilisation, but he also measured the extent of the Christian religion, in the time of the Roman Empire. The Roman soldier was *necessary* to the pattern of God, just as the Roman Empire itself became the necessary temporal counterpart to the Christian faith:

C'est l'un des plus grands mystères mystiques . . . que la nécessité de Rome dans la destination temporelle de Dieu . . . Il fallut le préfet pour qu'il y eût l'évêque. C'est certainement un des plus grands mystères du monde, et c'en est peut-être le plus grand, que cette inquiétante, que cette mystérieuse place laissée au temporel dans le mécanisme total et ainsi dans le gouvernement, dans le sort du spirituel.[44]

Péguy's belief in the spiritual mission of the soldier explains much in the argument between Jeanne d'Arc and Madame Gervaise in *Le Mystère de la Charité de Jeanne d'Arc*. It also explains his predilection for Saints such as St. Louis and crusaders such as Joinville. He sees France as continuing the spiritual–temporal mission of the Crusaders, and in *Ève* (1913) he raises the great shout of blessing on those who perform God's temporal mission:

Heureux ceux qui sont morts pour la terre charnelle,
Mais pourvu que ce fût dans une juste guerre . . .
Heureux ceux qui sont morts dans les grandes batailles,
Couchés dessus le sol a la face de Dieu . . .
Heureux ceux qui sont morts pour des cités charnelles,
Car elles sont le corps de la cité de Dieu . . .[45]

It was partly this sense of the soldier's mission which made most Catholics lend so much support to the militaristic revanchist movement which we have seen growing up after the turn of the century. It mingled with their innate patriotism and made them see France's salvation as coming from a determined temporal effort against the powers of Germany, of Protestantism and of German philosophy, all of which became associated with the German temporal power over Alsace-Lorraine. The First World War was welcomed by such men as Péguy and Psichari as a new crusade. In the works of

Claudel, Bourget and many others we also find this concept of the mission of the army.

But the army is seen by many people not only as defending France and the faith against outside influences and enlarging the reign of Christ on earth, but also as being the symbol and the keeper of that political order on which the Christian religion is founded. As Péguy does in *L'Argent Suite*, Nesmy stresses this aspect when he describes pacifists as being the typical representatives of 'la France nouvelle, lâche, frondeuse, dépravée, ennemie de l'ordre et de la discipline'.[46] This political order, as a basis for the order of Catholicism, was seen in very many different ways, and has led to many misunderstandings of the Catholic viewpoint.

Political Order

The personal order implied by Catholic belief led a great many Catholics in this period to a belief in the necessity for order on the national scale. Liberal ideology was seen by these people as a basis for disorder of all kinds, and, while not all of them went to the extreme of monarchism, a significant number did so.

Unsympathetic observers have been led to see, in this close connection between religion and politics, a conscious utilisation of the Catholic religion by people with primarily political preoccupations, but this view is essentially false. While a man like Maurras, who was not a Catholic, did make use of Catholicism in such a way, there were, among the partisans of political order, innumerable shades of religious and non-religious feeling. Just as Maurras, gathering to his flag all those who would be willing to support his cause whatever their other allegiances might be, saw in Catholicism one of the greatest props for this cause, even so a great many Catholics saw in right-wing movements such as the *Action Française* both a fulfilment of the Catholic conceptions of tradition and order and a present help in times of trouble, when the Church needed a strong protection against the violently anti-clerical preoccupations of the Third Republic. Catholic support of right-wing politics ranged between a perfectly sincere conception of such politics as being theologically sound, and a pragmatic belief in the necessity temporally to protect the Church.

In the first years of the Third Republic the Church was necessarily monarchical in outlook, and this tradition remained so strong that Leo XIII's attempts at fostering a *Ralliement* to the Republic were doomed to failure at the time. Then, after the turn of the century, the doctrines of Maurras and the *Action Française* renewed the conception that tradition and order were incarnated only in a monarchy, and many of the younger generation of Catholics were brought to monarchism in this way.

By no means all Catholic authors of this period were Royalist, but even among those who were not, a majority appear to have held the concept of the necessity for political order. The traditionalism of many, their desire for a hierarchical society based on that tradition and for a powerful society supporting a patriotic army, naturally led them either to Royalism or to some other form of totalitarian philosophy; as Bourget said, the national motto should not be 'Liberté, Egalité, Fraternité' but 'Discipline, Hiérarchie, Charité'[47]. The few who saw in a Republican government the best solution were, like Péguy, nevertheless still obsessed by the idea of order. For Péguy the First Republic had been the new Kingdom of France because it had had the force for order which the last of the kings had not had:

Louis XVI, n'étant plus roi, fut déplacé par un gouvernement plus roi. *Ce Louis XVI était bon. Ce n'est pas cela que l'on demande à un gouvernement. Ce que l'on demande a un gouvernement, c'est d'être ferme.* Ce Louis XVI était un gros, un doux, un bon, un pacifiste, un débonnaire, un humanitaire. Un philosophe. On le lui fit bien voir. Il fut déplacé par les suivants. Roi fainéant il fut déplacé par la jeune République comme les derniers Mérovingiens, devenus fainéants, furent déplacés par les jeunes Carolingiens, comme les derniers Carolingiens, devenus fainéants, furent déplacés par les jeunes Capétiens. La République fut la quatrième dynastie; forte dans sa jeunesse.[48]

Similarly Barrès, though he held out strongly for the Republic again Maurras's idea of a monarchy, saw this Republic as being ruled by one strong man. A dictator was needed, but this dictator should be created by universal suffrage.[49] Barrès was too much of a realist to deny the power of the masses. In his *Cahiers* he gives two political principles:

1. Qu'il faut gouverner d'après les gens sensés et souvent malgré la majorité. . . .

2. Qu'il n'y aurait pas moyen de faire tenir tranquille l'opposition dans une monarchie. . . .[50]

These two principles explain why, when asked to contribute to

Maurras's *Enquête sur la Monarchie,* Barrès stressed that a powerful government has to rely on the electoral system, and that order can only be maintained in this way. One has the impression that Barrès would have been enthusiastic about the Fifth Republic. Those authors who, while remaining Republicans, were nevertheless in favour of a strong nationalistic government of an authoritarian, imperialistic style, were representative as much of that Jacobin tradition which was so strong in Republican France as of the Catholic tradition of order. Catholicism was not the only politically authoritarian influence in France at this time, as the Boulanger Affair had clearly shown; it was, however, an extremely important part of the anti-democratic feeling in the country.

The vast majority of the Catholic authors of this period were violently anti-democratic. Huysmans, though he took little active interest in politics, nevertheless stood on the right wing on most of the main issues of the day; he despised democracy, which to him was 'l'adversaire le plus acharné du pauvre', and he described progress as 'l'hypocrisie qui raffine les vices'.[51] While he was not necessarily prepared to see General Boulanger as the panacea for all evils, in this he was merely showing his essential pessimism, which failed to see any solution for the ills of the materialistic society.

Léon Bloy, for the first years of his career, was strongly influenced, as were so many of his contemporaries, by the extreme right-wing philosophies of such writers as de Maistre, Bonald and Blanc de Saint-Bonnet. After his spiritual crisis of 1878–82, however, he detached himself from politics and became, like Huysmans, a man who was against everything in the materialist society. Nevertheless, he remained a partisan of order, that order which would place erring mankind under the control of a strong, superior being: 'Jusqu'à la venue de l'Esprit qui renouvellera la face de la terre, les hommes en général doivent être gouvernés avec le bâton, que ce bâton soit une trique de chef de bande ou une crosse épiscopale.[52]

Paul Bourget was one of the greatest opponents of democracy and in his works we find this opinion backed by arguments from all sources, both rational and positivist. As in his other opinions, he does not deny his debt to Taine, Renan and Comte, and he shows to what extent their rational opinions coincide with those of Bonald and de Maistre. Decrying the way in which so many people of his day speak of the difficulty of reconciling Catholicism, Science and Democracy, as though the last two terms were on one side and the first on the other, Bourget claims that the situation is completely the opposite. Both scientists and Catholics, he observes, are convinced of the absurdity of the dogma of equality and of the sovereignty of the multitude. There is a '. . . saisissante coïncidence entre les doctrines politiques issues de l'observation positive et l'enseignement traditionnel que la sagesse de nos pères avait fixé dans les fortes coutûmes d'autrefois'.[53] People appear to be blind to the fact that the coincidence of Comte and Bonald, and Taine and de Maistre, in fundamentally identical theories of government points to 'la banqueroute que l'avenir réserve aux faux dogmes de 1789 et à leurs partisans'.[54] Bourget himself is appalled by 'le mal d'anarchie dont notre pays souffre depuis 1789, et dont il menace de mourir'.[55] He sees this disease as having now spread not only through the institutions of the nation but also to the depths of people's conscious and unconscious minds.

Émile Baumann, in his *Mémoires*, declares how much the Republic was associated in his mind with images of disorder and terror. Here, like so many other Catholics of his period, he was moved by the traditional association of the Republic with the attack on religion.

It was for this reason that Leo XIII's attempt at *Ralliement* had so little success. In the world of literature, *ralliés* such as Georges Fonsegrive were an exceptional minority. The Church was traditionally right-wing in France, and the Church was also under violent attack from the Republic; this vicious circle made it natural that most Catholics should mistrust any attempt at compromise as being a betrayal of the Church into the hands of a hostile Republic.

Behind all these contingent reasons for support of the Right, however, there remains always the more philosophical reason of the Church's belief in order. Maurras, in a passage of great understanding, states the importance of that belief as seen by an outsider:

La règle extérieure n'épuise pas la notion du Catholicisme, et c'est lui qui passe infiniment cette régle. Mais où la régle cesse, l'harmonie est loin de cesser. Elle s'amplifie au contraire. Sans consister toujours en une obédience, le Catholicisme est partout un ordre. C'est à la notion la plus générale de l'ordre que cette essence correspond pour ses admirateurs du dehors.[56]

Adolphe Retté, whose sudden conversion brought him from the extreme left in politics to the extreme right, was one of the Catholics who became a member of the *Action Française*. In his declarations on this subject there is evidently a desire to outshine even his leader's extreme views. He does, however, state in an extremely clear form the two choices which a great many Catholics saw before them:

> Instabilité, incohérence, insécurité, individualisme destructeur, prédominance de la médiocrité envieuse, dissolution de la famille, tels sont les fruits de la démocratie en France, depuis cent trente ans.

> Stabilité, continuité, sécurité, autorité familiale, développement des élites, tels furent et tels seront les fruits de la Monarchie.[57]

The influence of Maurras was immense upon Catholics, because he could put so clearly and, they felt, rationally, the political views which they believed to be logical to Catholicism. Ernest Psichari, writing to Maurras in 1913, declared that the Church could not but profit from the 'grand courant d'idées saines et robustes dont L'Action Française est la source'. He describes Maurras as '. . . le seul homme de nos jours . . . le seul qui ait construit une doctrine politique vraiment cohérente, vraiment grande, le seul qui ait appris la politique non dans les parlotes et les assemblées, mais dans Aristote et dans saint Thomas. . . .'[58]

Jacques and Raïssa Maritain were brought towards the *Action Française* by Father Clérissac, one of the many priests of the time who was strongly influenced by the movement; and among others of the younger generation who were firmly attached to it well after the 1914–18 war we must count Henri Massis and Georges Bernanos.

In most of the Catholic novelists and poets of the period before 1914, even in such Republicans as Péguy, there was a hatred of and a disgust with the Republican government of the day, in which they felt none of the principles of good government to be epitomised. It had neglected tradition, it had neglected true patriotism, it had neglected order, it had persecuted the Church. It was for these reasons that there was so much opposition, among Catholic writers, to the liberal Catholics, whom they saw as attempting an impossible compromise.

From 1870 onwards, we find Catholics taking an important part in any great political event where the question of order is raised. They were among the strongest supporters of MacMahon in the troubled first years of the Republic; they were not so numerous in support of Boulanger in his attempt to seize power (possibly because of the anti-clerical nature of some of his earlier statements) but they were still a very significant number; and at the time of the Dreyfus Affair a great majority of Catholics were anti-Dreyfus. This was partly because they saw the supporters of democracy and anti-clericalism so strongly ranged on the other side, but partly, also, because the very idea of questioning the authority of the tribunal was a threat to all authority. When, later, many *anti-dreyfusards* began to see that Dreyfus might in fact be innocent, they nevertheless believed that the things at stake made it necessary that he should remain condemned. On the one hand, Authority should not publicly be shattered; on the other, the forces hostile to the Church and to the army should not be allowed to triumph. Beside this, the fate of one man was seen as having little importance. As Paul Bourget said to Maurice Paléologue: 'La Justice? Eh bien, je m'en moque, de la Justice!'[59]

Péguy, though he reacted against the contemporary Republic in his post-conversion writings, saw no reason to go to the extreme of Royalism. He regretted the close connection between religion and the politics of the Royalist Right:

> Il faut qu'il y ait une raison pour que, dans le pays de saint Louis et de Jeanne d'Arc, dans la ville de sainte Geneviève, quand on se met à parler du christianisme, tout le monde comprenne qu'il s'agit de Mac-Mahon, et quand on se prépare à parler de l'ordre chrétien pour que tout le monde comprenne qu'il s'agit du Seize-Mai.[60]

His own conservatism, he claimed, was that of the Republic, the true Republic of 1789, from which the present political régime was so far: 'Les hommes de la Révolution Francaise étaient des hommes d'ancien régime. Ils *jouaient* la Révolution Française. Mais ils *étaient* d'ancien régime.'[61] Compared with this, said Péguy, the modern Royalists are modernists; they are not men of Old France: 'Ils sont réactionnaires, mais ils sont infiniment moins conservateurs que nous. . . . On peut dire littéralement que ces partisans de l'ancien régime n'ont qu'une idée, qui est de ruiner tout ce que nous avons gardé de beau et de sain de l'ancien régime.' They call themselves *ligueurs* but they seem to forget that the *ligue* was not an institution of the monarchy, '. . . mais qu'elle en était une maladie au contraire, et l'annonce et l'amorce des temps futurs, le commencement de l'intrigue et de la foule et de la délégation et du nombre et du suffrage et d'on ne sait déjà quelle démocratie parlementaire.'[62] Péguy's Republicanism, then, was no compromise, but a Romantic vision of the Republic as repository of both tradition and order, rather than an arena of democracy. It is, in fact, very similar to the nationalist Republicanism of Barrès.

Claudel is more modern than most of his contemporaries in his realisation of the necessity of living in and adapting to a changing world. He himself had a long career in the consular service of the Republic, a thing almost unthinkable for a Catholic at that time, and in this career he was supported by his strong and lasting friendship with the Republican Freemason Philippe Berthelot. His plays give the same message of the necessity for acceptance of change, and for adaptation to new conditions in the realisation that God's pattern for the world has a significance beyond our knowledge. Though a Catholic of his age in so many ways, Claudel was ahead of his contemporaries in many others. He was a man of order and tradition, whose views were essentially right-wing, yet he was also a man who saw political reality.

Not all Catholic writers of this period dabbled with politics, yet even the poet Jammes was not completely cut off from such ideas. It is amazing, when one looks at any purely historical study of the period, to see how many Catholic writers even took a practical part in political events. Louis Bertrand, Henry Bordeaux, Henri Massis, Émile Baumann, Henri Ghéon, Jacques Maritain and many other Catholic authors became connected with *L'Action Française* to a greater or lesser extent (though more strongly after the 1914–18 war); and movements such as the *Ligue de la Patrie Française* had strong literary support. Among Catholic writers after 1900, non-participation in political ideas is exceptional.

Order within the Church

For the Catholics of this era the Church stood above all for order and authority, and in these years just after the Vatican Council this authority seemed above all, in matters both temporal and spiritual, to be vested in the person of the Pope, God's representative on earth.

The statement of papal infallibility at the Vatican Council in 1870 was, in fact, far less extreme than had been hoped for by the most violent supporters of the measure, men such as Veuillot and Blanc de Saint-Bonnet. Nevertheless, the dogma itself marked the final defeat of Gallicanism within the Church (though already by this date Gallican ideals seemed, to observers, to be more identified with Englishmen such as Ullathorne than with the majority of French Catholic thinkers), and the French Catholics, already so strongly influenced by the writings of Veuillot in *L'Univers*, were on the whole firmly involved in an extreme of ultramontanism which, by the very fact that the work of the Council on the matter of infallibility remained uncompleted and therefore uncertain, was able to apply to the question the extremes of the pre-1870 thought on the matter.

Blanc de Saint-Bonnet is a perfect example of such thought. He believed that in the Pope all power, both spiritual and temporal, should be vested.[63] In the hierarchical system on which all Blanc's thought was based, he saw civil power in the nation as resting with the King, in whom not only order was to be found, but also the legitimism afforded by divine right. Over the King, however, there was the Pope, whose power, both temporal and spiritual, was not to be usurped by his subordinates. Blanc states, in his book *L'Infaillibilité* (1861), the four 'Rights' which hold society together: Infallibility, Royalty, Heredity, and Property. Each of these had been attacked by a modern 'Error': Gallicanism, Liberalism, Republicanism and Socialism. Gallicanism erred by trying to attribute the rights of the Pope to members of the Council, and to Kings; Liberalism, by attributing the rights of Kings to assemblies and to the multitude; Republicanism, by overthrowing, in the name of so-called innate rights, those rights which man has acquired by his merit; and Socialism, by distributing capital to those who have not created it.[64] In this system, the condemnation of democracy can be seen to go hand in hand with papal infallibility, and the ordered temporal world is headed by its supreme ruler, the Pope. What happens, then, when a Pope comes who appears to advise his people to espouse democracy, and forget legitimism?

In the last years of the pontificate of Pius IX, not only the clergy but also the mass of the Catholic laity in France were overwhelmingly influenced by the policies set forward by Veuillot in

L'Univers, policies which seemed to have received their triumph in the 1870 Council and which, in their intransigence, were so close to the policy of the Pope himself. The public, then, was little prepared to receive the shock of the new policies of Pope Leo XIII, whose pontificate started in 1878. Leo was the very opposite of Pius in his moderation and readiness for change, and in that he attempted to conform himself to his age. The only way he could see to improve relations between the Holy See and the nations of Europe was to avoid his predecessor's intransigence. Above all, when he turned to France, he saw the necessity for a reconciliation between the Church and the Republic.

Though Leo attempted to be prudent about the broaching of this subject, no amount of prudence could have prevented the anger of the intransigent Catholics. Long before the open call to *Ralliement*, which began with a speech made in Algiers by Cardinal Lavigerie (at the Pope's request) in 1890 and which had its official statement in the Encyclical *Au milieu des sollicitudes* (1892), French Catholics had been reacting against the Pope's liberal policies. So much so that, as early as 1884, after seeing the reactions to his Encyclical *Nobilissima Gallorum Gens*, the Pope had been moved to say, in an open letter to Cardinal Guibert, that 'it was for the Holy Father alone to decide, in governing the Church, which policy was best adapted to the time and to the circumstance'.[65] This statement not only showed opportunism of a kind which many Catholics thought unfitting for the Church (as Veuillot had said of liberals some years before: 'Suivre le courant, c'est en quoi se résument les fameuses inventions du libéralisme'[66]); it also contained a statement of papal authority in political matters which went far beyond the official conception of infallibility, and which *should* have been pleasing to the intransigents (though worrying to liberal Catholics, even if their cause was helped by it).

Here we see the terrible position in which the intransigents found themselves. Léon Bloy, for example, declared himself as being for both spiritual and temporal theocracy:

Je suis pour la Théocratie absolue, telle qu'elle est affirmé dans la Bulle *Unam Sanctam* de Boniface VIII.

Je pense que l'Église doit tenir en main les Deux Glaives, le Spirituel et le Temporel, que *tout* lui appartient, les âmes et les corps, et qu'en dehors d'Elle il ne peut y avoir de salut ni pour les individus ni pour les sociétés.[67]

Yet when faced by the ideas of Leo XIII on social or political matters, Bloy was forced to the conclusion that as they did not coincide with his own views on these matters they must be purely the ideas of Leo XIII and in no way divinely ordered. We have seen the fury that Bloy expended on Leo XIII when the latter was on his deathbed; in accusing Leo of having helped to destroy the Church, Bloy showed that he no longer believed infallibility to extend to temporal judgements or to temporal power.[68]

The case of Leo XIII did more than anything else to destroy the intransigents' wish to extend papal infallibility to all matters, not only to *ex cathedra* statements on doctrine. For though Eugène Veuillot, who had now taken over *L'Univers* from his brother Louis, took his Ultramontanism to the extent of approving the papal policies in all their details, and though a politician like Albert de Mun might come into line, most intransigents from now on began to restrict their ultramontanism to matters spiritual. Criticism of Leo XIII's temporal policies was rife in the Catholic literature of the time.

Georges Fonsegrive was the only novelist of any note to become a *rallié*. His *Lettres d'un Curé de Campagne*, which appeared in *Le Monde* in 1893 and were published in book form in 1894, became the favourite reading of the 'democratic priests' whom Leo XIII's encyclical *Rerum Novarum* (1891), together with his policy of *Ralliement* to the Republic stated in the encyclical *Au milieu des sollicitudes* (1892), had encouraged. In 1894 Fonsegrive was sufficiently encouraged by the popularity of the *Lettres d'un Curé de Campagne* to produce a sequel, *Lettres d'un Curé de Canton*, firstly in the newly-formed *La Quinzaine* and then in book form in the following year. Though he had killed off his hero by the end of this volume, he was nevertheless constrained to produce yet another sequel, *Journal d'un Evêque*, which, after appearing in the *Revue du Clergé Francais*, was published in book form in 1897. In this book, which was set in the future, he foretold the separation of Church and State, but miscalculated by making it take place in 1921 rather than 1905.

Fonsegrive's democratic priest is a *rallié*, however, because he believes in that 'order' we have been describing. He takes his orders from Leo XIII in all matters and does not attempt to hedge, like so many of the intransigents had done. Fonsegrive realised that though the Pope's infallibility only had reference to defining doctrine or condemning dogmatic error, he nevertheless, when dealing with questions of faith, morals or Church discipline, wielded a power which it would be difficult to question. For men such as Fonsegrive temporal matters were so intermingled with spiritual ones that the old dictum of the Pope's fallibility in pronouncing on temporal matters meant nothing to them. Fonsegrive, as his later career and later works show, was prepared to sacrifice anything to the Church's authority.

So it was that, after 1907, he abandoned the more extreme of the modernist positions which he had been approaching before that date. In a book of his which appeared posthumously in 1920, *L'Évolution des Idées dans la France Contemporaine, de Taine à Péguy*, he drew a sharp distinction between those modernists who submitted to the authority of the Church and those who refused to do so. Loisy is strongly criticised for his refusal to accept Church authority on matters of biblical exegesis: 'chez lui, la science primait la foi et l'histoire primait la théologie'.[69] And in his description of Bourget's book *Le Démon de Midi* Fonsegrive shows to what extent his modernist tendencies were tempered with a regard for the Church's authority. The abbé Fauchon, the modernist priest, is seen as the cause of the disasters of the book, and the following conclusions are reached:

> L'abbé Fauchon . . . en voulant rejeter le poids de l'autorité et de la discipline dogmatique de l'Église est délesté de tout ce qui pouvait lui fournir une règle de conduite. . . . Ainsi se vérifie encore une fois par l'expérience la nocuité de tout ce qui, théorie ou pratique, va au rebours des enseignements du catholicisme.[70]

These words might have been spoken by any of our intransigent Catholic authors. They show to what extent the ideas of 'autorité', of 'discipline' and of a personal 'règle de conduite' were closely linked at the time, and how important they were. Fonsegrive accepted Leo XIII's policy of 1891 and 1892; he played with the ideas of modernism (both of the type of Loisy and of that of the 'philosophical modernists'); but he accepted Pius X's condemnation of these ideas in 1907 and withdrew his paper *La Quinzaine*, just as the Sillonists bowed to papal authority in 1910. He showed as much deference to papal authority, one might say, as the most ultramontane of intransigents.

Many intransigent Catholics were reassured by Pius X's firm

stand against the Republic. Even those few (such as Drumont) who had in the past looked forward to the separation of Church and State as a way towards greater freedom for the Church followed Pius X closely in his condemnation of this measure, because of the unilateral way in which it had been effected and because of the dangers it involved in this particular form, and above all because of their belief in the authority of the Pope. Now that a Pope had come of whose attitudes they approved, both in the spiritual and temporal field, papal authority could be invoked in both fields.

On spiritual matters Catholic authors of the Revival had always taken the greatest care to remain in obedience. Hello had always been most careful, in print, to remain within the bounds of prudence. Bloy declared himself 'fils obéissant de l'Eglise', and even those aspects of his works which appear to be heretical are almost certainly unconsciously so. Huysmans obviously did not realise certain aspects of his views culled from Boullan to be verging on heresy.

As for most of the other Catholic writers of the time, they viewed with mistrust any movement divorced from the traditional religion, based on divine transcendental authority, which was theirs. The various forms of modernism, particularly, were viewed with much distaste. And when papal condemnation of modernism took place with the decree *Lamentabili sane exitu* and the Encyclical *Pascendi* in 1907, in the pontificate of Pius X, many Catholics, as Dansette says, 'enchérissent sur les rigueurs pontificales.'[71] A similar reaction met the condemnation of *Le Sillon*, the organ of social Catholicism, in 1910.

This violent intransigence in the ways of traditional Catholicism is typical of most Catholic 'creative' writers of the time, even before the condemnations. After them the attacks became even more violent and are epitomised in Paul Bourget's *Le Démon de Midi* (1914), where the errors of modernism are compared with the stability, security and discipline of the Catholic Church.

It was this discipline and order which Barrès saw within the Catholic Church which made him, at the end of his novel *La Colline Inspirée*, waver between his enthusiasm for the spirit of the country and its tradition, and his understanding of that order which the Church can bring. The chapel says to the plain:

Ta liberté, dis tu? Mais comment ma direction pourrait-elle ne pas te satisfaire? Nous avons été préparé, toi et moi, par tes

pères. Comme toi, je les incarne. . . . Maison de ton enfance et tes parents, je suis conforme à tes tendances profondes, à celles-là même que tu ignores, et c'est ici que tu trouveras, pour chacune des circonstances de ta vie, le verbe mystérieux, élaboré pour toi quand tu n'étais pas. Viens à moi si tu veux trouver la pierre de solidité, la dalle où asseoir tes jours et inscrire ton épitaphe.[72]
Barrès concludes with an opinion that both the voice of the plain and that of the chapel must be heard, and that enthusiasm and order must mingle; but this conclusion nevertheless condemns such aberrations as that of the brothers Baillard (i.e. the Vintras heresy) in that this goes against that order which one can find in the Church. This order is shown as being essentially liberty, in that it coincides with the deepest needs and desires of national and religious tradition. In this, as in so many other aspects of Catholic order, we come back to the idea of liberty through order which is the essence of Catholic thought in this period.

The Catholics of this period were filled with what M. Julien Gracq, speaking of Claudel in his essay 'Pourquoi la littérature respire mal',[73] describes as 'le sentiment du oui'. Yet M. Gracq, in this essay, commits the error of many outside observers when he describes Claudel's acquiescence as containing no element of choice, as being '. . . un appétit formidable d'acquiescement, qui a des côtés grandioses et des côtés qui le sont moins, mais où il n'est pas question de choisir.' On the contrary, Claudel has a choice; it is in full liberty that he acquiesces. Like so many of his contemporaries, he draws a valid distinction between liberty and independence, a distinction which we find drawn a good hundred years before in the *Mémoires* of Rivarol, where that author is discussing the Declaration of the Rights of Man. Distinguishing between man in his natural state and man in his social state, Rivarol continues:

Dire que tous les hommes naissent et demeurent libres, c'est dire en effet qu'ils naissent et demeurent nus. Mais les hommes naissent nus et vivent habillés, comme ils naissent indépendans et vivent sous des lois. Les habits gênent un peu les mouvemens du corps; mais ils le protègent contre les accidens du dehors; les lois gênent les passions, mais elles défendent l'honneur, la vie et les fortunes. Ainsi, pour s'entendre, il fallait distinguer entre la liberté et l'indépendance: *la liberté*

*consiste a n'obéir qu'aux lois, mais dans cette définition le mot
obéir s'y trouve; tandis que l'indépendance consiste a vivre dans
les forêts, sans obéir aux lois, et sans reconnaître aucune sorte de
frein.*[74]

Claudel and his contemporaries went further than this and saw
that independence of this type could become the worst kind of
constraint. It was in their liberty *to obey* that true freedom lay, and
Claudel said *oui*, '. . . à Dieu, à la Création, au pape, à la société, à
la France, à Pétain, à de Gaulle, à l'argent, à la carrière bien
rentée, à la progéniture de patriarche, à la forte maison, comme il
dit, qu'il a épousée par-devant notaire,'[75] with full liberty and with
full consciousness. This whole concept of liberty within order
explains many of the characteristics, both spiritual and temporal,
of the Catholic writing of this period.

NOTES

[1] Claudel, Pléiade, Théâtre II, p. 842.

[2] 'Aucun progrès n'est possible, dans le monde, disait Gandhi, sans une prise de volonté inflexible: un voeu.' Louis Massignon, *Archaïsme et modernisme en Islam*, 1961.

[3] Bloy, letter to Barbey d'Aurevilly, 8 October 1877; printed in Bollery, *Léon Bloy*, Vol. I.

[4] Bloy, letter to Anne-Marie Roulé, 28 July 1877; ibid.

[5] Bloy, letter to Barbey d'Aurevilly, July 1877; ibid.

[6] Bloy, letter to Barbey d'Aurevilly, 8 October 1877; ibid.

[7] Frère Marie-Bernard, O.I.C., letter to Germain Nouveau, 13 January 1910; printed in Introduction to *Oeuvres Poétiques*, Paris, 1953.

[8] Claudel, letter to Louis Massignon, 19 November 1908; communicated to the author by Louis Massignon.

[9] Claudel, *Mémoires Improvisés*, pp. 120 f.

[10] Ibid., my italics.

[11] Claudel, letter to Massignon, 19 November 1908.

[12] Letter to Mme. Cécile Bruyère, Abbess of Solesmes, 3 September 1898.

[13] Huysmans, *L'Oblat*, p. 8.

[14] Claudel, *Mémoires Improvisés*, pp. 152 f.

[15] Though Claudel declared later that it was the voice of God himself which told him not to go on, letters which he wrote nearer the time make it clear that it was, in fact, the monks who refused him. See my article, Claudel et Huysmans— *Deux Oblats*, in *Bulletin de la Société Huysmans*, No. 40, 1960.

[16] Huysmans, *L'Oblat*, p. 7.

[17] Claudel, *Ste. Thérèse*; Pléiade, Poetry, p. 625.

[18] Claudel, letter to Massignon, 19 November 1908; communicated to the author by Louis Massignon.

[19] Claudel, letter to Louis Massignon, 19 November 1908.

[20] Madame Cécile Bruyère, letter to J.-K. Huysmans, 7 September 1898.

[21] *Les Oblats de Saint Benoît*, Monastère des Bénédictins de St. Louis-le-Temple, Paris, 1918; my italics.

[22] Claudel, *Partage de Midi*, 1905, Act I; Pléiade, Théâtre I, p. 1006.

[23] Some of the ideas in this section are taken from an excellent paper by M. Paul-André Lesort, which was read at the Décade Claudel at Cérisy in July 1963.

[24] Claudel, letter to Massignon, 19 November 1908.

[25] Ibid.

[26] Ibid.

[27] Ibid.

[28] *Le Père Humilié*, 1916, Act II, Sc. 2; Pléiade, Théâtre II, p. 523.

[29] *Le Soulier de Satin*, 1924, 2e Journée, Sc. 3; Pléiade, Théâtre II, p. 721. My italics.

[30] Preface (1948) to *Partage de Midi*; Pléiade, Théâtre I, p. 984.

[31] *Le Soulier de Satin*, 1ere Journée, Sc. 1; Pléiade, Théâtre II, pp. 654 f.

[32] Blanc de Saint-Bonnet, *De la Douleur*; note to p. 60, quoting de Maistre.

[33] Ibid., note to p. 47.

[34] Psichari, letter to Mme. G. Favre, 15 September 1909; in *Lettres du Centurion*, p. 41.

[35] Psichari, *L'Appel des Armes*, p. 70.

[36] Ibid., p. 168.

[37] Ibid., pp. 168 f.

[38] Psichari, letter to Henri Massis, 9 July 1911. Cf. *L'Appel des Armes*, pp. 197 ff.

[39] Psichari, *Le Voyage du Centurion*, 1915, p. 176.

[40] Ibid., pp. 177 f.

[41] Psichari, letter to Father Clérissac, 29 February 1913.

[42] Psichari, letter to his mother, 20 August 1914.

[43] Péguy, *L'Argent Suite*, 22 April 1913; Pléiade, Prose II, p. 1162. My italics.

[44] Ibid., p. 1164.

[45] Péguy, *Ève*, 28 December 1913; Pléiade, Poetry, p. 1026.

[46] Jean Nesmy, *Les Égarés*, 1906, p. 303.

[47] Bourget, *L'Étape*, 1902, p. 394.

[48] Péguy, *L'Argent Suite*, 22 April 1913; Pléiade, Prose II, p. 1190. My italics.

[49] This desire for a 'plebiscitary Republic' was a central part of the nationalist doctrine, and was, as Ronald Balfour points out in his article 'The *Action Française* Movement', a far more realistic policy than Royalism, as promulgated by Maurras.

[50] Barrès, *Mes Cahiers*, 1920.

[51] Huysmans, *Là-bas*, Chapter 20.

[52] Bloy, *Mon Journal*; quoted in M.-J. Lory, *La Pensée Religieuse de Léon Bloy*.

[53] Bourget, *L'Étape*, 1902, p. 390.

[54] Ibid., p. 391.

[55] Ibid., p. 8.

[56] Maurras, *Le Dilemme de Marc Sangnier*, Preface.

[57] Retté, *La Maison en Ordre*, 1923, p. 316.

[58] Psichari, letter to Charles Maurras, 1913; *Lettres du Centurion*, pp. 265 ff.

[59] Quoted in Weber, *Action Française*, 1962.

[60] Péguy, *L'Argent*, 16 February 1913; Pléiade, Prose II, p. 1067.

[61] Ibid., p. 1068.

[62] Ibid., p. 1069.

[63] The *Action Française* was later to accord all spiritual power to the Pope, but to retain all temporal power for the King.

[64] Blanc de Saint-Bonnet, *L'Infaillibilité*, Avant-propos.

[65] Dansette, *Histoire Religieuse de la France Contemporaine*, Vol. II, p. 66.

[66] Veuillot, *Mélanges*.

[67] Bloy, *Mon Journal*, 1897.

[68] In fact, for a man like Bloy, who saw authority as lying in revelation, the prophet's mission eventually appeared to be more important than the priest's, and true knowledge (as with the Vintrasians) to be afforded to him personally rather than to the Church of his time.

[69] George Fonsegrive, *L'Évolution des Idées dans la France Contemporaine, de Taine à Péguy*, p. 221.

[70] Ibid., p. 264.

[71] Dansette, *Histoire Religieuse de la France Contemporaine*, Vol. II, p. 462.

[72] Barrès, *La Colline Inspirée*, 1913, p. 340.

[73] Julien Gracq, *Préférences*, pp. 92 f.

[74] Rivarol, *Mémoires*.

[75] Julien Gracq, *Préférences*, p. 93.

PART FIVE

CHAPTER THIRTEEN

Conclusion

IN studying this period of Catholic literature we have naturally been led to deal with certain aspects of the thought of the period which might appear unfortunate or excessive to modern eyes. This denotes no desire to discredit Catholicism, which could never be discredited by such means; nor does it even reflect a condemnation of the authors concerned, for intentions must always be considered as well as their results. We must see the Catholic beliefs we have been studying in their relation to the progress of the Church, while seeing also the reasons for their rejection of this progress; we must try to understand the individual authors, and the stresses which forced them to violent and unreal extremes.

The average non-Catholic, unversed in the history of that religion, tends to see in it an unchanging monolith, impervious to any kind of modification of its doctrines. Nothing could be further from the truth. The Church has always existed in a healthy state of internal dissension upon many matters, and in time this dissension has often led to important doctrinal changes. These changes have always led, however, in the direction of a deeper understanding and clearer interpretation of the fundamental mysteries of the faith, none of which have been contradicted except by those who, by their very excesses, have been forced to leave the Church.

Nobody, therefore, would expect the Catholicism of the 1960's to be in every respect similar to the Catholicism of the period 1870–1914. And when we consider that, amid the steady progress of the Catholic faith which we have been describing, the Catholic literary Revival represents a turning-back to the values of previous generations, and of previous centuries, it becomes clear that, while it is of great historical curiosity for that reason, and of a certain historical importance for the lasting influence that it had on some sections of French thought, it can certainly not be taken as a means to indict the Catholic Church in general.

Indeed, as we have seen, the ideas of many of these authors were not merely outdated; they were often exaggerated to the point of heresy. In the theological field certain doctrines, such as that of vicarious suffering, became distorted out of all recognition; the glorification, by contemporary non-Catholics, of purely human knowledge produced a scornful rejection of any place for 'science' or reason in the religious life; and the fear of an individual approach to religion, coupled with this rejection of the intellect, led to that attitude towards the supernatural and the mystical life which is often to be found in the 'popular' religion of less educated Catholic areas, where it mingles only too easily with the remnants of earlier religions, but which, in its almost 'magical' emphasis on the concrete and automatic nature of mystical revelation, is far more rarely to be found in the higher reaches of Catholic thought.

In the political field similar extremes were to be found, and these extremes were even more peculiar to the Catholicism of a specific period and a specific country; though the influence of these ideas still lingers on to a certain extent in some areas of French political thought.

Extremes are bred by extremes; and much of the violence of the opinions expressed by the authors of the Revival is explained in part by the position in which they found themselves, or in which they imagined themselves to be.

Fear appears to have been one of the main driving forces which forced them to extremes of reaction: fear of those anti-Catholic forces which appeared to be trying to destroy the Church from without; fear of those trends within the Church which seemed to be attempting to tear down its bases for belief; fear of the progressive movements, both social and political, whose attempts at compromise were seen as betrayals, as forces destroying the Church's unity in the face of its rabid enemies; fear, above all, of all kinds of change, political, social and religious.

Much of this fear was unreasoning. Amid a violently changing world these traditionalists clung desperately to any straw which might link them to what seemed a more perfect past. The present seemed to them to be wholly bad; atheism, individualism and materialism had destroyed society, and the Church was under siege; even within the Church itself all was not well. Small wonder that they should react so wildly against the society they so prejudged; though their reaction only too often took the form of cutting themselves off even more firmly from this society and escaping into a world of their own. They sought a past which had never existed. They found a reflection of it in a society ruled by faith, such as Islam. But all their efforts to change their own society were as unreal as their imagined Middle Ages. Their hatred of capitalist bourgeois society and their desire to alleviate the misery of the poor turned them towards paternalist social doctrines based on an ideal and unreal past. Their hatred of the Republic, as an incarnation of anti-Catholic forces, turned them, in many cases, towards a monarchism which was already becoming politically unrealistic.

Their efforts for the advancement of their own faith were similarly affected by this fear, the fear of a minority faced by overwhelming odds. They turned inwards rather than outwards, and their attempts at proselytism were effected by personal prayer and the acceptance of individual suffering, rather than by outward attempts at persuasion. This trend was not, of course, caused only by fear; the whole tendency, which we have noted, towards an exaggeration of the material effects of the mystical life naturally led men to feel that this was the most important and effective sphere of action.

The fear of which we have been speaking was too great to have been caused purely by the Church's position as a minority. Other strong forces must have been at work. One of the greatest of these forces, in the political field, was the intolerance shown to the Catholic Church by its enemies. This intolerance was itself in part caused by fear. The Republican anti-clericals and the Catholics stood against each other in mutual fear and mistrust, much as the United States and Russia stood just after the Second World War; they over-estimated their opponents' strength, and attributed to them the most extreme of views and the most dangerous of motives, and these misconceptions were heightened by various contemporary political events, until both sides were forced into the extreme positions of which they were being accused. Intolerance was rife on both sides; catchwords, slogans and over-simplifications were as common on the Republican side as upon the Catholic. But one of the greatest causes for the Catholic retreat into extremism must be seen in liberal intolerance of a particular kind: the confident assumption of one's own right-mindedness, the refusal even to consider the opinions of the other side as being

353

anything but in extremely bad taste, the perpetual use of certain words as emotive sounds to brand everything in a certain political direction as being equivalent to the worst extremes of that tendency, the appalling ignorance of one's own intolerance. It is such liberal tendencies, coupled with so many people's need wholeheartedly to embrace a cause before fully examining its implications, which exacerbate, in our own day, certain international and national situations, and drive so many people to extremes similar to those taken by the authors of the Catholic Revival, and by so many of their readers. It is hard to say which side, in France, was more to blame at the turn of the century; but certainly they drove each other to extremes which left little in the middle. Liberal Catholicism was regarded by both sides as a hybrid, which was dangerous in that it might give in too much to the other side. The only way to succeed was to remain firm on rigid principles.

In the social sphere, socialism or anything approaching it was eschewed by most Catholic authors for widely differing reasons. Partly there was a fear of the power of the people, which still remained as a result of the popular rebellion in the first year of the 1848 Republic, which had so destroyed the confidence, in Catholic circles, in the social work of men such as Ozanam; partly there was a disbelief, based on Christian principles, in egalitarianism. A society based on order, and on a divinely-instituted hierarchy, could reasonably rest on equity, but not on equality. For all men are *not* equal. In an optimistic view of society, which saw it as being in essence perfect, but corrupted by a materialist bourgeois element, Catholic authors preached a return to a hierarchical society in which each class would realise its duties as well as its rights, in which the rich and poor, high and low, would all work harmoniously together, and in which the rights of the poor would be safeguarded not by unions which faced the employers as enemies, but by guilds in which workers and employers worked together as friends. This unreal dream was another of the escapes to the past so typical of Catholic authors of the time; living in a society where the Church had little or no power, they imagined that in a society where Christian values prevailed all would be perfect and had, indeed, been so in the past.

It was possibly the violence of political reactions, and the realisation of the need for the Church to present a united front against its enemies, which caused these writers, in the religious field, to react against any form of change or progress in Christian doctrine. Or perhaps it was merely their basic misunderstanding of the nature of the Catholic faith, thinking of it as a permanently static thing. For change, as we have seen, is in the Catholic faith, as in the Anglican, a necessary thing. The authors of the Revival reacted against the modernists, however, not only for these reasons; in some respects they were right to reject the extremes of modernism, but in so doing they were drawn to conclude, in their usual over-simplification of things, that all attempts at questioning and at progress partook of these extremes. Change within the Church is always necessary, but it must be gradual, and it must be a certain type of change. A continual reassessment of Christian doctrine is very necessary, for in every age it is, like a translation, adapted to a particular situation as to a particular language. The situation changes, and so must the statement and the emphasis of Christian doctrine; but this recasting must have a continuity with the past, and must not attempt to change the fundamental truths underlying the faith. Much of the new approach embodied in the various forms of Roman Catholic modernism was correct in this very way; but the excesses of a few, and the misunderstanding by the traditionalists of the basic intentions of the new thought, drove the reactionary elements within the Church, including the writers of the Revival, into an even more remote corner, as far from the true path of the Church's progress as were the excesses against which they were reacting. While it is the modernists and the liberal and social Catholics who have contributed most to the present political and religious outlook of the Church, they were nevertheless, at the time, small outposts amid a sea of reaction.

The First World War changed many of these attitudes. It brought, above all, Church and Republic much closer to reconciliation. Many of the more extreme political positions taken by both sides were little by little relinquished. But, while such attitudes might no longer be necessarily those of the whole Church in France, old beliefs die hard, and the influence wielded by the writers of the pre-war period remains strong in certain sections of the community, above all in the political field, but also in the religious, and indeed in the literary world.

Politically, French Catholicism in great part remained imbued, after the 1914–18 war, with the policies of Barrès and Maurras. Maurras's *Action Française* retained great influence, and its condemnation by the Pope in 1926 caused *crises de conscience* in many Catholic hearts, and schisms in many Catholic families. Added to this, the majority of French bishops, in these immediately post-war years, were *Action Française* bishops created by Pius X; so that that Pope's influence remained strong in France long after his death. The condemnation of the *Action Française* naturally caused a certain dropping-off of its Catholic support; but there is small doubt that a large portion of the Church still favoured essentially right-wing views, and that opposition to the Republic, though not so strong or so widespread in Catholic circles as before the war, was still a far from negligible force. Indeed, tradition, order and patriotism, those moving forces behind the political actions of the writers of the Revival, were in many cases the causes for certain Catholics' support of Pétain in 1940. His dictatorship preached *Travail, Famille, Patrie*, a true mingling of the sentiments of a Le Play and a Barrès; and in the order of dictatorship many saw a refuge from their new bogey, the *Front Populaire*, and ultimately communism. Yet, strangely enough, in today's support for de Gaulle we find many of these same characteristics lingering on, though in lesser quantity. De Gaulle stands, in the eyes of many, for Catholicism, for patriotism (the patriotism which does not give in, as Péguy would say) and for order, in the form of a 'plebiscitary Republic' of which Barrès would have approved. De Gaulle's own ideas, particularly those on international relations, are often tied in a completely unrealistic way to the concepts of the period in which he grew up. It was strange to notice, in a recent article on the General's foreign policy in *L'Express*, several mentions of both Péguy and Maurras.

Even outside France there are traces of such influence between the wars. Salazar's dictatorship in Portugal was essentially based on *Action Française* principles, Maurras was feted in Madrid, and Péguy was mentioned by Mussolini as one of the influences on the formation of the fascist movement in Italy.

But the Catholic literary Revival was in many ways merely a reflection of attitudes and opinions typical of a certain section of public opinion at the time. It no more instituted such opinions than it instituted Catholicism itself. Such extremes of thought, both in the political and religious field, were bound in the nature of things to occur at this particular point in time. What is remarkable, however, is the way in which the most articulate part of the

Catholic community, its cultural *élite*, took up what were essentially the *simpliste* views of a bewildered mass.

One can see, on the religious side, the reasons for the immense flowering of the more extreme forms of mystical belief which took place towards the end of the century. One can see on the political side the causes of that apparently unreasoning fear and hatred of certain sections of the community, which continued in large sections of the Catholic public right up to the Second World War.[1] Where the Revival is important, however, is in the currency it gave to such ideas, and in the effect it had on those who read its works in their youth. The ideas of the Revival, both political and religious, may have seemed outdated by the end of the First World War; but their influence lingered on in whole sections of the Catholic community, those sections who might well have shied away from purely religious writings and from political tracts, but who imbibed the same lessons even more fully, while at the same time more subtly, through their reading of novels, and also from the theatre and poetry of the Revival. A study of these influences would repay the effort; it is unfortunately not part of the scope of this book.

Another worthwhile study would be that of the later literary influence of the Catholic Revival. In one sense one could say that this was boundless; for until the Revival there was little in the way of Catholic literature which could be taken seriously, and the flourishing of Catholic writing which this century has seen is directly attributable to the trail-blazing of the Revival. We, who have become so accustomed to spiritual themes in the novel and in the theatre, both in England and in France, can hardly realise what a revolution in literary taste this new trend illustrated.

In another sense, however, the post-war Catholic literary world began to move away from the specific literary and religious characteristics of the Revival. Just as the religious climate was gradually changing, so, for example, in the novels of François Mauriac we find a growing concern with the individual problems of the individual soul, and an almost Jansenist aversion to many of the more extreme characteristics of the pre-war Catholic novel.

The Catholic Revival lived on, however, in various authors whose faces seem almost resolutely turned towards the past, rather than towards a future Catholic literature based on the Church as it is, and not as it was romantically believed to be. Not only Claudel, who continued in the same ways of thinking until his death; but also two of the great Catholic novelists of the inter-war years, Bernanos and Graham Greene.

Bernanos retained much of the cornered fury and violence of his predecessors. He associated, like them, individual names and faces with the doctrines he abhorred, and attacked his targets without mercy. In his polemical fury he can only be compared with his masters, Bloy and Drumont. Bremond and Gide were relent-lessly pursued in his works. And his ideas were, at the outset, very close to those of his predecessors. He abhorred modernism, as we can see in *L'Imposture*; he feared and hated the Republic, the liberals, the Freemasons and the Jews. *La Grande Peur des Bien-pensants*, his biography of Drumont, shows his great sympathy for his master, and many of those better qualities, e.g. anti-capitalism and concern for the poor, which he had imbibed at the same time as his anti-Semitism. Bernanos stood for traditional Christianity against modernism, for the right against liberalism, for the *Action Française* against the Republic. His change of side, at the time of the Spanish Civil War, may have reversed a great many of these opinions;[2] but he certainly retained that other characteristic of the Catholic Revival which had so filled his work: the infinite capacity for over-simplifying situations, for identifying individuals with policies, and for neglecting no means of vilifying an opponent. He had, in a certain sense, changed sides; but his opinions were essentially the same.

The religious attitudes taken in his works reflect the Revival too, and not only in the matter of the attacks on modernism. The miraculous, the mystically extraordinary, all find their place in his work; as, for example, the whole section of *Sous le Soleil de Satan* in which a dialogue with the devil, real and tangible, occurs. Dream or no, this *rencontre* is of enough importance in the novel to mean more than a hallucination.

It is in Graham Greene, however, that the literature of the Re-vival is most clearly reflected. The quotations from Bloy, the reference to Péguy at the end of *Brighton Rock*, would point to this influence even if we did not have much clearer indications in the texts themselves. Greene retains much that is typical of the religious outlook of his French predecessors; he often seems, as they did, to be stressing all those aspects of Catholic faith which are most difficult for an outsider to accept. The necessity of suffering is everywhere portrayed; the closeness of the saint and the sinner, the insufficiency of those who are unconsciously between the two, is stressed in *Brighton Rock* and in many other novels; in *The End of the Affair* much of the plot revolves around a miracle; in *The Power and the Glory* a 'whisky priest' is still, because he is a priest, a worthy vessel, and is forced, by the power which his priesthood gives him, to be worthy despite his faults. Greene's views on the mystical life often verge on the heretical, too, in a similar manner to his predecessors. His views on vicarious suffering for example: in *The Potting Shed* a priest has offered to *lose his faith* in order that his dead nephew may be restored to life, and the offering has been received; for twenty years he has lived without faith, not even realising the miracle that had occurred, or remembering the bargain he had made. Similarly, in *The Power and the Glory* the 'whisky priest' makes the following request: 'O God, give me any kind of death—without contrition, in a state of sin— only save this child.' His prayer for suffering is answered.

Greene's Catholicism is harsh and magnificent, sharply differentiated from the religion of the *bien-pensants* (and as an Englishman he is reacting against homely Anglicanism, too). It is hardly surprising that the greatest continuator of the traditions of the Catholic Revival should be in England, where Catholicism is still the religion of a minority, surrounded not so much by opposition as by deadly apathy.

Many other writers, from 1914 to our own time, have been influenced in smaller or greater measure by the Catholic literature of 1870–1914. Study of all this does not, however, come within the scope of the present work.

The lasting literary influence of the Revival points to much, in its religious characteristics, which favoured literary expression. If, in its way, Catholicism at this time revivified certain literary forms, it did so in an extremely dramatic manner precisely because it was this certain type of Catholicism. The reaction against realism in the novel was accentuated by the contemporary conception of mysticism as something both concrete and extraordinary; plots could be made to revolve around the supernatural, and the whole mechanical business of an extreme conception of vicarious suffering, of a belief in the efficacy of rites as opposed to works, and of an almost magical superstition, made the novel move from an excess of realism to a new, unreal world in which none of the old values seemed to exist. The bounds of material reality were surpassed, and in their place came a new system of values, seemingly as remote from that reality as the metaphysical systems of Hoffmann and the German Romantics, yet differing from such experiments in the sense that it was *true*, and thus perpetually intermingled with visible reality. In a sense, too, this new form of novel turned away from the detailed study of human psychology; true, a great many novels were studies of the development of a human soul, several of them being autobiographical in nature; but this study always proceeded from the influence upon the human soul of the outside effects of divine grace, and these effects were always taken for granted, though the study of them in detail (as in Huysmans's *En Route*) was at times remarkably subtle and convincing. It is far from such studies, however, to the searing documents of human psychology which we find in the novels of Mauriac, which after the war became the foremost works in a new tradition of Catholic writing.

The turning from realism, and from the psychological novel, was thus favoured by the form taken by turn-of-the-century Catholicism. Not that many of the novels so produced were successes; far from it. But the few outstanding novels produced by this movement, the impetus which they gave to Catholic writing, and the healthy reaction they provided to an over-materialistic literature show the whole venture to have been an important and essential part of the history of French literature. This is amply illustrated by the fact that, while Huysmans and Bloy are still widely read, and are even reprinted in the *Livres de Poche* series, Catholic writers who, while pursuing religious ends, remained on the whole within the previous tradition of the novel, such as Bazin, Bordeaux and even Bourget, are now largely forgotten except by literary historians and pious schoolmasters.

If the religious novel was something new, religious poetry was certainly not so. But here the specific characteristics of the Revival were to be of equally great effect, in its few great poets. Catholic poetry up to this time had on the whole been sweet, sickly, pious and sentimental. This tradition was to continue, and still does; but the rigour of the Revival, its hatred of sentimentality and of the *bien-pensants*, was eventually to find its voice in the harsh message of the later poetry of Germain Nouveau, in the clear-cut simplicity of Jammes (who, despite his subject-matter and his simplicity of style, has a rigour of thought and expression which on the whole avoids the trap of sentimentality), in the proud bombast of Claudel, and in the angular repetitions, the urgent litanies of Péguy.

And it is in the theatre that the Catholic Revival has perhaps had its greatest influence, through the genius of one man, Paul Claudel. He took the Symbolist theatre and made of it something capable of success by binding his poetic symbolism round a central, all-embracing and comprehensible theme; by the fact that this theme was Christianity he opened the way for all those who, fired by his poetic genius and dramatic imagination, have renewed the concept of Christian verse-drama; and by the fact that this theme was Catholicism, that part of the Christian faith most rich in symbol and allusion, he inspired a renewal not only of Christian drama but of Catholic poetry, so that (even though his own non-dramatic verse is on the whole inferior to that in his plays) there are few modern French Catholic poets who have entirely escaped his influence.

The Catholic Revival, then, was in its ideas very much a product of its age, though because of the fact that these ideas were expressed in the literary forms most read by a wide public, many of them have survived to greater or lesser extent in people of the generations to which it addressed itself. In the history of literature the Revival was not only important for its healthy reaction against certain current literary conceptions; it also provided certain literary works of genius, particularly those of its greatest figures, Péguy and Claudel, and has exerted a strong influence on succeeding Catholic literature.

This study has been an attempt to explore certain aspects of the thought of the Revival. Naturally it is incomplete. Certain problems have been set aside—for example, the place of morality in the Catholic novel, because, though the question rears its head in the case of certain authors such as Barbey d'Aurevilly and Émile Baumann, it is a problem far wider than the context of the Revival, and would need to be studied in relation to such authors as Mauriac and Graham Greene as well.

This has been an attempt at a dispassionate appraisal of certain attitudes peculiar to this literary movement. I have tried, as far as possible, to remain unbiased, and to express the opinions of those I have been studying without too much in the way of personal praise or criticism of their ideas, ideas which are interesting above all in the way they explain much that is difficult for the modern reader to comprehend in the literature of that time.

NOTES

[1] Though, as Vercors points out in his *L'Imprimerie de Verdun*, such hatred was by this time a kind of automatic, unreasoning reaction, which was destroyed when it came into contact with the reality, for example, of Nazi anti-Semitism.

[2] Though his reaction again fascism is essentially that of an old-fashioned man of the right against the horrors of modern-style authoritarianism, rather than a 'conversion to liberalism' such as has been attributed to him by certain writers.

APPENDIX

The Miracle of La Salette

THE following is part of the shepherdess Mélanie's own account of the message divulged to her by the Virgin at La Salette on 19 September 1846.

. . . J'aperçus . . . une très Belle Dame assise, ayant la tête dans ses mains. Cette Belle Dame s'est levée, elle a croisé médiocrement ses bras en nous regardant et nous a dit: 'Avancez, mes enfants, n'ayez pas peur, je suis ici pour vous annoncer une grande nouvelle.' Ces douces et suaves paroles me firent voler jusqu'à elle, et mon coeur aurait voulu se coller à elle pour toujours. Arrivée bien près de la Belle Dame, devant elle à sa droite, elle commence le discours, et des larmes commencent aussi à couler de ses beaux yeux:

Si mon peuple ne veut pas se soumettre, je suis forcée de laisser aller la main de mon Fils. Elle est si lourde et si pesante que je ne puis plus la retenir.

Depuis le temps que je souffre pour vous autres! Si je veux que mon Fils ne vous abandonne pas, je suis chargée de le prier sans cesse. Et pour vous autres, vous n'en faites pas cas. Vous aurez beau prier, beau faire, jamais vous ne pourrez récompenser la peine que j'ai prise pour vous autres.

Je vous ai donné six jours pour travailler, je me suis réservé le septième, et on ne veut pas me l'accorder. C'est ce qui appesantit tant le bras de mon Fils.

Ceux qui conduisent les charrettes ne savent pas parler sans y mettre le Nom de mon Fils au milieu. Ce sont les deux choses qui appesantissent tant le bras de mon Fils.

Si la récolte se gâte, ce n'est qu'à cause de vous autres. Je vous l'ai fait voir l'année passée par les pommes de terre, et vous n'en avez pas fait cas; c'est au contraire, quand vous en trouviez de gâtées, vous juriez et vous mettiez le Nom de mon Fils. Elles vont continuer à se gâter; à la Noël il n'y en aura plus.

363

Si vous avez du blé, il ne faut pas le semer.

Tout de que vous sèmerez, les bêtes le mangeront; et ce qui viendra tombera tout en poussière quand vous le battrez. Il viendra une grande famine. Avant que la famine vienne, les petits enfants au-dessous de sept ans prendront un tremblement et mourront entre les mains des personnes qui les tiendront; les autres feront pénitence par la faim. Les noix deviendront mauvaises; les raisins pourriront.

. . . Puis la Sainte Vierge me parla et me donna un secret en français. Ce secret, le voici tout entier, et tel qu'elle me l'a donné:

1. Mélanie, ce que je vais vous dire maintenant ne sera pas toujours secret; vous pourrez le publier en 1858.

2. Les prêtres, ministres de mon Fils, les prêtres, par leur mauvaise vie, par leurs irrévérences et leur impiété à célébrer les saints mystères, par l'amour de l'argent, l'amour de l'honneur et des plaisirs, les prêtres sont devenus des cloaques d'impureté. Oui, les prêtres demandent vengeance, et la vengeance est suspendue sur leurs têtes. Malheur aux prêtres et aux personnes consacrées à Dieu, lesquelles, par leurs infidélités et leur mauvaise vie, crucifient de nouveau mon Fils! Les péchés des personnes consacrées à Dieu crient vers le ciel et appellent la vengeance, et voilà que la vengeance est à leurs portes, car il ne se trouve plus personne pour implorer miséricorde et pardon pour le peuple; il n'y a plus d'âmes généreuses, il n'y a plus personne digne d'offrir la Victime sans tache à l'Eternel en faveur du monde.

3. Dieu va frapper d'une manière sans exemple.

4. Malheur aux habitants de la terre! Dieu va épuiser sa colère, et personne ne pourra se soustraire à tant de maux réunis.

5. Les chefs, les conducteurs du peuple de Dieu ont négligé la prière et la pénitence, et le démon a obscurci leurs intelligences; ils sont devenus ces étoiles errantes que le vieux diable traînera avec sa queue pour les faire périr. Dieu permettra au vieux serpent de mettre des divisions parmi les régnants, dans toutes les sociétés, dans toutes les familles; on souffrira des peines physiques et morales; Dieu abandonnera les hommes à eux-mêmes et enverra des châtiments qui se succéderont pendant plus de trente-cinq ans.

6. La Société est à la veille des fléaux les plus terribles et des plus grands événements; on doit s'attendre à être gouverné par une verge de fer et à boire le calice de la colère de Dieu.

7. Que le Vicaire de mon Fils, le Souverain Pontife Pie IX ne sorte plus de Rome après l'année 1859; mais qu'il soit ferme et géné-

reux, qu'il combatte avec les armes de la foi et de l'amour; je serai
avec lui.

8. Qu'il se méfie de Napoléon; son coeur est double, et quand il
voudra être à la fois Pape et empereur, bientôt Dieu se retirera de
lui; il est cet aigle qui, voulant toujours s'élever, tombera sur l'épée
dont il voulait se servir pour obliger les peuples à se faire élever.

9. L'Italie sera punie de son ambition en voulant secouer le joug
du Seigneur des Seigneurs; aussi elle sera livrée à la guerre; le sang
coulera de tous côtés; les églises seront fermées ou profanées; les
prêtres, les religieux seront chassés; on les fera mourir, et mourir d'une
mort cruelle. Plusieurs abandonneront la foi et le nombre des prêtres
et des religieux qui se sépareront de la vraie religion sera grand;
parmi ces personnes il se trouvera même des Evêques.

10. Que le Pape se tienne en garde contre les faiseurs de miracles,
car les temps est venu que les prodiges les plus étonnants auront lieu
sur la terre et dans les airs.

11. En l'année 1864, Lucifer avec un grand nombre de démons
seront détachés de l'enfer: ils aboliront la foi peu à peu et même dans
les personnes consacrées à Dieu; ils les aveugleront d'une telle manière,
qu'à moins d'une grâce particulière, ces personnes prendront l'esprit
de ces mauvais anges; plusieurs maisons religieuses perdront entière-
ment la foi et perdront beaucoup d'âmes.

12. Les mauvais livres abonderont sur la terre, et les esprits de
ténèbres répandront partout un relâchement universel pour tout ce qui
regarde le service de Dieu; ils auront un très grand pouvoir sur la
nature; il y aura des Eglises pour servir ces esprits. Des personnes
seront transportées d'un lieu à un autre par ces esprits mauvais, et
même des prêtres, parce qu'ils ne se seront pas conduits par le bon
esprit de l'Evangile, qui est un esprit d'humilité, de charité, et de zèle
pour la gloire de Dieu. On fera ressusciter des morts et des justes. Il y
aura en tous lieux des prodiges extraordinaires, parce que la vraie foi
s'est éteinte et que la fausse lumière éclaire le monde. Malheur aux
Princes de l'Eglise qui ne se seront occupés qu'à entasser richesses sur
richesses, qu'à sauvegarder leur autorité et à dominer avec orgueil.

13. Le Vicaire de mon Fils aura beaucoup à souffrir, parce que,
pour un temps, l'Eglise sera livrée à de grandes persécutions; ce sera
le temps des ténèbres; l'Eglise aura une crise affreuse.

14. La sainte foi de Dieu étant oubliée, chaque individu voudra se
guider par lui-meme et être supérieur à ses semblables. On abolira les
pouvoirs civils et ecclésiastiques, tout ordre et toute justice seront

foulés aux pieds; on ne verra qu'homicides, haine, jalousie, mensonge et discorde, sans amour pour la patrie ni pour la famille.

15. *Le Saint-Père souffrira beaucoup. Je serai avec lui jusqu'à la fin pour recevoir son sacrifice.*

16. *Les méchants attenteront plusieurs fois à sa vie sans pouvoir nuire à ses jours; mais ni lui, ni son successeur ne verront le triomphe de l'Eglise de Dieu.*

17. *Les gouvernants civils auront tous un même dessein, qui sera d'abolir et de faire disparaître tout principe religieux, pour faire place au matérialisme, à l'athéisme, au spiritisme et à toutes sortes de vices.*

18. *Dans l'année 1865, on verra l'abomination dans les lieux saints; dans les couvents, les fleurs de l'Eglise seront putréfiées et le démon se rendra comme le roi des coeurs. Que ceux qui sont à la tête des communautés religieuses se tiennent en garde pour les personnes qu'ils doivent recevoir, parce que le démon usera de toute sa malice pour introduire dans les ordres religieux des personnes adonnées au péché, car les désordres et l'amour des plaisirs charnels seront répandus par toute la terre.*

19. *La France, l'Italie, l'Espagne et l'Angleterre seront en guerre; le sang coulera dans les rues; le Français se battra avec le Français, l'Italien avec l'Italien; ensuite il y aura une guerre générale qui sera épouvantable. Pour un temps, Dieu ne se souviendra plus de la France ni de l'Italie, parce que l'Evangile de Jésus-Christ n'est plus connu. Les méchants déploieront toute leur malice; on se tuera, on se massacrera mutuellement jusque dans les maisons.*

20. *Au premier coup de son épée foudroyante, les montagnes et la terre entière trembleront d'épouvante, parce que les désordres et les crimes des hommes percent la voûte des cieux. Paris sera brûlé et Marseille englouti; plusieurs grandes villes seront ébranlées et englouties par des tremblements de terre: on croira que tout est perdu; on ne verra qu'homicides, on n'entendra que bruits d'armes et blasphèmes. Les justes souffriront beaucoup; leurs prières, leur pénitence et leurs larmes monteront jusqu'au Ciel, et tout le peuple de Dieu demandera pardon et miséricorde, et demandera mon aide et mon intercession. Alors Jésus-Christ, par un acte de sa grande justice et de sa miséricorde pour les justes, commandera à ses anges que tous ses ennemis soient mis à mort. Tout à coup les persécuteurs de l'Eglise de Jésus-Christ et tous les hommes adonnés au péché périront, et la terre deviendra comme un désert. Alors se fera la paix, la réconciliation de Dieu avec les hommes; Jésus-Christ sera servi, adoré et glo-*

rifié; la charité fleurira partout. Les nouveaux rois seront le bras droit de la Sainte Eglise, qui sera forte, humble, pieuse, pauvre, zélée et imitatrice des vertus de Jésus-Christ. L'Evangile sera prêché partout, et les hommes feront de grands progrès dans la foi, parce qu'il y aura unité parmi les ouvriers de Jésus-Christ, et que les hommes vivront dans la crainte de Dieu.

21. Cette paix parmi les hommes ne sera pas longue; vingt-cinq ans d'abondantes récoltes leur feront oublier que les péchés des hommes sont cause de toutes les peines qui arrivent sur la terre.

22. Un avant-coureur de l'antéchrist, avec ses troupes de plusieurs nations, combattra contre le vrai Christ, le seul Sauveur du monde; il répandra beaucoup de sang, et voudra anéantir le culte de Dieu pour se faire regarder comme un Dieu.

23. La terre sera frappée de toutes sortes de plaies (outre la peste et la famine qui seront générales); il y aura des guerres jusqu'à la dernière guerre, qui sera alors faite par les dix rois de l'antéchrist, lesquels rois auront tous un même dessein et seront les seuls qui gouverneront le monde. Avant que ceci arrive, il y aura une espèce de fausse paix dans le monde; on ne pensera qu'à se divertir; les méchants se livreront à toutes sortes de péchés; mais les enfants de la Sainte Eglise, les enfants de la foi, mes vrais imitateurs, croîtront dans l'amour de Dieu et dans les vertus qui me sont les plus chères. Heureuses les âmes humbles conduites par l'Esprit-Saint! Je combattrai avec elles jusqu'à ce qu'elles arrivent à la plénitude de l'âge.

24. La nature demande vengeance pour les hommes, et elle frémit d'épouvante dans l'attente de ce qui doit arriver à la terre souillée de crimes.

25. Tremblez, terre, et vous qui faites profession de servir Jésus-Christ et qui, au dedans, vous adorez vous-mêmes, tremblez; car Dieu va vous livrer à son ennemi, parce que les lieux saints sont dans la corruption; beaucoup de couvents ne sont plus les maisons de Dieu, mais les pâturages d'Asmodée et des siens.

26. Ce sera pendant ce temps que naîtra l'antéchrist, d'une religieuse hébraïque, d'une fausse vierge qui aura communication avec le vieux serpent, le maître de l'impureté; son père sera Ev.; en naissant, il vomira des blasphèmes, il aura des dents: en un mot, ce sera le diable incarné; il poussera des cris effrayants, il fera des prodiges, il ne se nourrira que d'impuretés. Il aura des frères qui, quoiqu'ils ne soient pas comme lui des démons incarnés, seront des enfants de mal; à douze ans, ils se feront remarquer par leurs vaillantes victoires qu'ils remporteront; bientôt ils seront chacun à la tête des armées, assistés par des légions de l'enfer.

27. Les saisons seront changées, la terre ne produira que de mauvais fruits, les astres perdront leurs mouvements réguliers, la lune ne reflétera qu'une faible lumière rougeâtre; l'eau et le feu donneront au globe de la terre des mouvements convulsifs et d'horribles tremblements de terre, qui feront engloutir des montagnes, des villes.

28. Rome perdra la foi et deviendra le siège de l'antéchrist.

29. Les démons de l'air avec l'antéchrist feront de grands prodiges sur la terre et dans les airs, et les hommes se pervertiront de plus en plus. Dieu aura soin de ses fidèles serviteurs et des hommes de bonne volonté; l'Evangile sera prêché partout, tous les peuples et toutes les nations auront connaissance de la vérité!

30. J'adresse un pressant appel à la terre; j'appelle les vrais disciples du Dieu vivant et régnant dans les cieux; j'appelle les vrais imitateurs du Christ fait homme, le seul et vrai Sauveur des hommes; j'appelle mes enfants, mes vrais dévots, ceux qui se sont donnés à moi pour que je les conduise à mon divin Fils, ceux que je porte pour ainsi dire dans mes bras, ceux qui ont vécu de mon esprit; enfin j'appelle les Apôtres des derniers temps, les fidèles disciples de Jésus-Christ qui ont vécu dans un mépris du monde et d'eux-mêmes, dans la pauvreté et dans l'humilité, dans le mépris et dans le silence, dans l'oraison et dans la mortification, dans la chasteté et dans l'union avec Dieu, dans la souffrance et inconnus du monde. Il est temps qu'ils sortent et viennent éclairer la terre. Allez et montrez-vous comme mes enfants chéris; je suis avec vous et en vous pourvu que votre foi soit la lumière qui vous éclaire dans ces jours de malheurs. Que votre zèle vous rende comme des affamés pour la gloire et l'honneur de Jésus-Christ. Combattez, enfants de lumière, vous petit nombre qui y voyez; car voici le temps des temps, la fin des fins.

31. L'Eglise sera éclipsée, le monde sera dans la consternation. Mais voilà Enoch et Elie remplis de l'Esprit de Dieu; ils prêcheront avec la force de Dieu, et les hommes de bonne volonté croiront en Dieu, et beaucoup d'âmes seront consolées; ils feront de grands progrès par la vertu du Saint-Esprit et condamneront les erreurs diaboliques de l'antéchrist.

32. Malheur aux habitants de la terre! il y aura des guerres sanglantes et des famines; des pestes et des maladies contagieuses; il y aura des pluies d'une grêle effroyable d'animaux; des tonnerres qui ébranleront des villes; des tremblements de terre qui engloutiront des pays; on entendra des voix dans les airs; les hommes se battront la tête contre les murailles; ils appelleront la mort et, d'un autre côté, la mort fera leur supplice; le sang coulera de tous côtés. Qui pourra vaincre, si Dieu ne diminue le temps de l'épreuve? Par le sang, les larmes et les prières des justes, Dieu se laissera fléchir; Enoch et Elie seront mis à mort; Rome payenne disparaîtra; le feu du ciel tombera et consumera trois villes; tout l'univers sera frappé de terreur, et beacoup se laisseront séduire parce qu'ils n'ont pas adoré le vrai Christ vivant parmi eux. Il est temps; le soleil s'obscurcit; la foi seule vivra.

33. Voici le temps; l'abîme s'ouvre. Voici le roi des rois des ténèbres. Voici la bête avec ses sujets, se disant le sauveur du monde. Il s'élèvera avec orgueil dans les airs pour aller jusqu'au ciel; il sera étouffé par le souffle de saint Michel Archange. Il tombera et la terre qui, depuis trois jours, sera en de continuelles évolutions, ouvrira son sein plein de feu; il sera plongé pour jamais avec tous les siens dans les gouffres éternels de l'enfer. Alors l'eau et le feu purifieront la terre et consumeront toutes les oeuvres de l'orgueil des hommes et tout sera renouvelé: Dieu sera servi et glorifié.

La Sainte Vierge pleurait presque tout le temps qu'Elle me parla. Ses larmes coulaient lentement une à une jusque vers ses genoux; puis, comme des étincelles de lumière, elles disparaissaient. Elles étaient brillantes et pleines d'amour.... Les larmes de notre tendre Mère, loin d'amoindrir son air de majesté, de Reine et de Maîtresse, semblaient, au contraire, l'embellir, la rendre plus aimable, plus belle, plus puissante, plus remplie d'amour, plus maternelle, plus ravissante; et j'aurais mangé ses larmes, qui faisaient sauter mon coeur de compassion et d'amour....

Select Bibliography

THIS bibliography is confined to the critical and historical works which have served in the study of this period of French literature. The works by the Catholic authors themselves are on the whole mentioned in the text or in footnotes and are not therefore listed here.

A bibliography containing all the works read while studying this period would be excessively long and of little use to either the scholar or the general reader. Let it be stressed that the works here listed are those which have been found to be of most use. Those which have been outstandingly useful are marked with an asterisk.

*AMADOU, ROBERT, 'Le Sacrifice Provictimal de Marie', *Tour St. Jacques*, May–June, 1957

ANDRIEU, JACQUES, *La Foi dans l'Oeuvre de Paul Claudel*, Paris, 1955

ARCHAMBAULT, PAUL, *George Fonsegrive*, Paris, 1932

AUTIN, ALBERT, *Le Disciple de Paul Bourget*, Paris, 1930

—*Henri Bremond*, Paris, 1946

*BALDICK, ROBERT, *The Life of J.-K. Huysmans*, Oxford, 1955

*BALFOUR, RONALD E., 'The *Action Française* Movement', *Cambridge Historical Journal*, 1930

BARBEAU, RAYMOND, *Un Prophète luciférien: Léon Bloy*, Paris, 1957

*BEAUMONT, ERNEST, *The Theme of Beatrice in the Plays of Claudel*, London, 1954

*BÉGUIN, ALBERT, *Léon Bloy: mystique de la douleur*, Paris, 1948

BÉSUS, ROGER, *Barbey d'Aurevilly*, Paris, 1958

*BOLLERY, JOSEPH, *Léon Bloy: essai de biographie*, 3 vols., Paris, 1947

BRICAUD, JOANNY, *J.-K. Huysmans et le satanisme*, Paris, 1912

—*Huysmans: occultiste et magicien*, Paris, 1913

—*L'Abbé Boullan*, Paris, 1927

BRANDRETH, H. R. T., *Huysmans*, London, 1963

*BROGAN, D. W., *The Development of Modern France 1870–1940*, London, 1940

—*The French Nation*, London, 1957

BRUNO, DE J.-M., FATHER, SUZANNE BRESARD, DR. JEAN VINCHON, 'La Confession de Boullan', *Études Carmelitaines, Satan*, 1948

*BURY, J. P. T., *France 1814–1940*, 3rd edition revised, London, 1954

BUSH, WILLIAM, *Souffrance et expiation dans la pensée de Bernanos*, Paris, 1962

BUTLER, DOM CUTHBERT, *The Vatican Council 1869–70*, London, 1930

CALVET, J., *Le Renouveau Catholique dans la littérature contemporaine*, Paris, 1927

CATTAUI, GEORGES, *Léon Bloy*, Paris, 1954

CAUWES, ABBÉ, *Ernest Hello: Vie — Oeuvre — Mission*, Tournai-Paris, 1937

CHAIX-RUY, JULES, *Donoso-Cortès*, Paris, 1956

CHALLAYE, FÉLICIEN, *Péguy socialiste*, Paris, 1954

*CHAPMAN, GUY, *The Third Republic of France: The First Phase 1872–94*, London, 1962

—*The Dreyfus Case: A Reassessment*

CHASTEL, GUY, *J.-K. Huysmans et ses amis*, Paris, 1957

CHIARI, JOSEPH, *The Poetic Drama of Paul Claudel*, London, 1954

CHRISTOFLOUR, RAYMOND, *Louis de Cardonnel: pèlerin de l'invisible*, Paris, 1939

—*Prophètes du XIXe siècle*, Paris, 1954

*COGNY, PIERRE, *J.-K. Huysmans à la recherche de l'unité*, Paris, 1953

COLLEYE, HUBERT, *La Poésie catholique de Claudel*, Liège, 1945

DAOUST, JOSEPH, *Les débuts bénédictins de J.-K. Huysmans*, Abbaye St. Wandrille, 1950

*DANSETTE, ADRIEN, *Histoire Religieuse de la France Contemporaine*, Paris, 1948

DELAPORTE, JEAN, *Connaissance de Péguy*, 2 vols., Paris, 1959

DOMENACH, J.-M., *Barrès par lui-même*, Paris, 1954

FERCHAT, JOSEPH, *Le Roman de la famille française: essai sur l'oeuvre de M. Henry Bordeaux*, Paris, 1912

FONSEGRIVE, GEORGE, *L'Évolution des Idées dans la France Contemporraine, de Taine à Péguy*, Paris, 1921

FOWLIE, WALLACE, *Paul Claudel*, London, 1957

—*Ernest Psichari: A Study in Religious Conversion*, London, 1939

FRASER, ELIZABETH M., *Le Renouveau Religieux d'après le Roman Français de 1886 à 1914*, Paris 1934.

FRICHE, ERNEST, *Études Claudeliennes*, Porrentruy, 1943

FUMET, STANISLAS, *Claudel*, Paris, 1958

—*Ernest Hello ou le drame de la lumière*, new edition, Paris, 1945

*GARÇON, MAURICE, *Vintras: hérésiarque et prophète*, Paris, 1928

GIGUET, A., *Blanc de Saint-Bonnet*, Paris, 1919

GIRAUD, VICTOR, *Maurice Barrès*, Paris, 1922

—*Paul Bourget: essai de psychologie contemporaine*, Paris, 1934

GODFRIN, J., *Barrès: mystique*, Neuchâtel, 1962

GOÏCHON, A.-M., *Ernest Psichari*, Paris, 1925

GRANGE, L., *Le Prophète de Tilly*, Paris, 1897

GUILLEMIN, HENRI, *Claudel et son art d'écrire*, Paris, 1955

*GUYON, BERNARD, *Péguy*, Paris, 1960

*HALEVY, DANIEL, *Péguy et les Cahiers de la Quinzaine*, Paris, 1943

HALTER, RAYMOND, *La Vierge Marie dans la vie et l'oeuvre de Paul Claudel*, Paris, 1958

HOROVITZ, IRVING, *Georges Sorel: Prophet without Honour*, Harvard, 1951

HUMPHREY, RICHARD, *Radicalism and the Revolt against Reason*, London, 1961

JOHANNET, RENÉ, *Joseph de Maistre*, Paris, 1932

LAMBERT, PIERRE, 'En Marge de là-bas: une cérémonie au 'Carmel de Jean-Baptiste' à Lyon', d'après J.-A. Boullan, *Bulletin Huysmans*, no. 25, 1953

LATREILLE, A., PALANQUE, J-R., DELARUELLE, E., RÉMOND, R., *Histoire du Catholicisme en France*, vol. 3, *La Période contemporaine*, Paris, 1962

LAVER, JAMES, *The First Decadent: being the strange life of J.-K. Huysmans*, London, 1954

LESORT, PAUL-ANDRÉ, *Claudel par lui-même*, Paris, 1963

LHERMITTE, JEAN, 'Huysmans et la mystique', *Tour St. Jacques*, May–June, 1957

*LORY, MARIE-JOSEPH, *La Pensée religieuse de Léon Bloy*, Bruges, 1951

—*Léon Bloy et son époque*, Paris, 1944

MADAULE, JACQUES, *Le Génie de Paul Claudel*, Paris, 1938

—*Le Drame de Paul Claudel*, Paris, 1947

—*Paul Claudel: dramaturge*, Paris, 1956

MALLET, ROBERT, *Francis Jammes: le jammisme*, Paris, 1961

—*Francis Jammes: sa vie, son oeuvre, 1868–1938*, Paris, 1961

Manuel de la littérature catholique en France de 1870 à nos jours, Paris

MASSIGNON, LOUIS, 'Notre-Dame de la Salette et la conversion de J.-K. Huysmans', *La Salette: témoignages*, Bloud et Gay, 1946

*Parole Donnée, Paris, 1963. This contains several articles of value.

MASSIS, HENRI, *Maurras et notre temps*, Paris, 1951

—*Ernest Psichari*, Paris, 1915

—*Jugements*, Paris, 1923–4

MAUGENDRE, ABBÉ, *La Renaissance Catholique dans la littérature du XXe siècle*, Paris, 1962

MAURIAC, F., *La Vie et la Mort d'un Poète, André Lafon*, Paris, 1924

MERCANTON, JACQUES, *Poésie et religion dans l'oeuvre de Maurice Barrès*, Lausanne, 1940

MÉRY, G., *La Voyante de la rue du Paradis*, Paris, 1896

MORICE, LOUIS, *Verlaine: le drame religieux*, Paris, 1946

**O'BRIEN, CONOR CRUISE, *Maria Cross*, London, 1953

**OZOUF, MONA, *L'École, l'Église et la République 1871–1914*, Paris, 1963

PIOU, JACQUES, *Le Ralliement: son histoire*, Paris, 1928

POULAT, ÉMILE, *Histoire, dogme et critique dans la crise moderniste*, Paris, 1962

**PRAZ, MARIO, *The Romantic Agony*, London, 1951

PREVOST, JEAN-LAURENT, *Le Roman Catholique a cent ans*, Paris, 1958

RÉMOND, RENÉ, *La Droite en France de 1815 à nos jours*, Paris, 1954

RICORD, J., *Louis Bertrand: l'Africain*, Paris, 1947

ROLLAND, ROMAIN, *Péguy*, 2 vols., Paris, 1945

SERRE, JOSEPH, *Ernest Hello: l'homme — le penseur — l'écrivain*, Paris, 1903

**SERVAIS, YVONNE, *Charles Péguy: The Pursuit of Salvation*, Cork, 1953

SPENCER, P. H., *Politics of Belief in Nineteenth-century France*, 1954

STEINMANN, JEAN, *Léon Bloy*, Paris, 1956

THERIVE, ANDRE, *J-K. Huysmans: son oeuvre*, Paris, 1924

**THOMAS, MARCEL, 'L'Abbé Boullan et l'Oeuvre de la Réparation', *Tour St. Jacques*, May–June, 1957

TREVOR, MERIOL, *Newman: Light in Winter*, London, 1962

**TRUC, GONZAGUE, *Histoire de la littérature catholique contemporaine*, Paris, 1961

*VIDLER, ALEC R., *The Modernist Movement in the Roman Church, its Origins and Outcome*, Cambridge, 1934

—*Prophecy and Papacy: A Study of Lammenais, the Church and the Revolution*, London, 1954

—*A Century of Social Catholicism 1820–1920*, London, 1964

VILLEFRANCHE, M., *Dix grands chrétiens*, 1892

*WEBER, EUGEN, *The Nationalist Revival in France 1904–14*, Berkeley, 1959

*—*Action Française*, Stanford, 1962

WIRTH, OSWALD, *Stanislas de Guaïta*, Paris, 1935

WOOD, J. S., *Un Aspect du mouvement traditionaliste et social dans la littérature Française contemporaine: R. Bazin, sa vie et son oeuvre*, Paris, 1934

WOODCOCK, GEORGE, *Anarchism*, Harmondsworth, 1963

YARROW, PHILIP, *La Pensée politique et religieuse de Barbey d'Aurevilly*, Geneva, 1961

Index

Index

AA*

Index

Index

Index